THE
SHAPE OF
CATHOLIC
HIGHER
EDUCATION

THE
SHAPE OF
CATHOLIC
HIGHER
EDUCATION

Edited by

*ROBERT
HASSENGER*

With a Foreword by
DAVID RIESMAN

THE UNIVERSITY OF CHICAGO PRESS

CHICAGO AND LONDON

Library of Congress Catalog Card Number: 67–15953

THE UNIVERSITY OF CHICAGO PRESS, CHICAGO & LONDON

The University of Toronto Press, Toronto 5, Canada

TO OUR STUDENTS

FOREWORD

Even for the insider, the shape of Catholic higher education in the United States is easy to oversimplify, and for the outsider (whether in the United States or elsewhere) oversimplification is almost inescapable. Most non-Americans, in fact, find it difficult to credit the incredible diversity of America: the many different ways there are of being "American"; the many different sorts of places given the designation "college"; the many different sorts of people in terms of ethnic group, social class, sophistication, self-definition, who answer to the name "Catholic." This particular outsider has been working for the past few years (with Christopher Jencks) on a study of Catholic as well as other colleges. With this in view, we have read a good deal of what has been written on the subject, visited a small number of the 300 or so institutions (but none of the seminaries), read their student newspapers and catalogues and other memorabilia, talked with faculty and ex-faculty, and sought out at professional meetings and elsewhere men like Robert Hassenger, Robert McNamara, S.J., Paul J. Reiss, and others whose work is represented in this particular volume. Had this book been available to us when we began, it would have been of the very greatest help, for nowhere else does there exist such a compendium of "hard" data, historical perspective, inside criticism, and speculation about what the future holds.

In a recent essay, David Thomas states that in Sweden social science has muted the edges of political polemic, testimony in part to the work of the great Swedish economists.[1] A macroscopic political economy may have this effect more readily than the sorts of social-psychological research represented in this volume by Hassenger's chapters on "Mary College" and on the impact of Catholic higher education, or the more theoretical sort of sociological analysis illustrated by Paul Reiss's contribution. These "newer" social sciences lack the majesty and the inclusiveness of economics. Moreover, as the political scientist Julian Foster shows in his chapter, the Catholic liberal arts colleges, perhaps especially the Jesuit ones, have in the past had what I would regard as an Ivy League superiority to these newer social sciences, preferring instead philosophy and history. Correspondingly, one cannot expect that this book or others of a similarly empirical temper (present also in forthcoming studies by Father Andrew Greeley and by James Trent, for example) will contribute to the "end of ideology" either in Catholic self-criticism or

[1] David Thomas, "Ideology — Death or Transfiguration?" *Harvard Review*, IV (Summer-Fall, 1966), 88–95.

apologetics. Yet this growing body of work seems likely not only to furnish combatants with ammunition but also to help them frame the arguments with greater relevance and to minimize defensiveness.

Even the chapters in this volume that attack vested obscurantism or insensitivity in Catholic higher education (such as Julian Foster's on Santa Clara, John Leo's on St. John's University on Long Island, Francis Kearns' on Georgetown) testify to the stir and ferment in the Catholic colleges in recent years. A dozen years ago, as I can testify from my work on the Academic Freedom Study sponsored by the Fund for the Republic, there was incomparably less.[2] The altered temper reflects both the historical situation Philip Gleason clarifyingly depicts in chapter 2 and some very contemporary developments. As the American church has become less closed and defensive, young dissenting Catholics have been less inclined to feel that they must leave it in order to feel free and independent. Regarding the church as belonging to them as much as to anyone else, and encouraged by finding allies both here and abroad, they have preferred to stay in the church to fight for their beliefs, criticizing and reforming from within rather than joining the "leakage" to the supposedly secular but often idolatrous world. When I commented on this briefly to a youngish Catholic professor who had been in the Catholic Worker Movement, saying that twenty years ago he would have left the church, he replied that it was still *his* church and he was damned if he was going to define himself out of it, although his view of its leadership, its liturgy, its complacently faithful, and its educational systems verged on the libelous. (Perhaps there is an analogy here in the declining tendency of alienated young Americans to expatriate themselves to Paris or even to Tokyo; there are fewer illusions about foreign climes and the young are perhaps more willing today to stand and fight as Americans.)

Long before Vatican II there were critical voices within American Catholicism (such as the impressive one of John Courtney Murray, S.J.) which had limited, if any, support from their orders and dioceses. Vatican II allowed some of these religious and lay critics to surface and to connect with the more cosmopolitan Catholics of the Netherlands or France or Germany. But the same process exposed these dissidents as more than mere troublemakers of no import, and in the last several years we have seen something of what might be called a Vatican backlash mounted by some of the more conservative elements in American (and curial) Catholicism. In his concluding chapter, "The Future Shape of Catholic Higher Education," Hassenger provides vignettes of some of the innovative and of the traditionalist elements in Catholic higher education, ranging from the sort of free-swinging experimentalism of Immaculate Heart College in Los Angeles and Webster College outside St. Louis to the ambivalent effort of the Vin-

[2] See Paul Lazarsfeld and Wagner Thielens, Jr., *The Academic Mind: Social Scientists in a Time of Crisis* (with a field report by David Riesman) (Glencoe, Ill.: The Free Press, 1958).

centians (also described by John Leo) to put St. John's University back into its paternalistic quiescence. He remarks on something I have also observed, namely, that some of the educational leaders now bypassed by the onrush of iconoclasm are precisely those who were among the first liberals to open a few windows in the colleges; they are like the liberals in Civil Rights who are always astonished and often sad as they are bypassed by a newer radicalism which relegates them to the enemy camp. I would add that such polarizations reflect the discovery that long-needed reforms, when at last accomplished, resolve fewer problems than had been anticipated, and uncover more intractable problems still — all of contemporary Catholicism would appear to be making this same post-Conciliar discovery, leading the radicals to desperate measures and many liberals to disillusionment.

Perhaps because of their second-class citizenship vis-a-vis priests, some of the most adventurous educational leaders have been sisters, and some, the most conservative also (to whom, with charitable anonymity Mr. Hassenger pays his respects in this same chapter). The Catholic colleges for women are so very numerous and there are so many more sisters than priests that it is perhaps understandable that both the institutions and the orders which manage them are spread out along a wider range, reflecting both the experimentalism and the traditionalism in the various communities of sisters. At the same time, the Catholic women's colleges have a greater leeway than the men's colleges and universities or the great coeducational universities because the education of daughters, piety and chastity aside, has never been taken as seriously as the education of sons. The majority of women's colleges in America are Catholic, and as with the secular ones such as Bennington and Sarah Lawrence, the best are very good indeed. And I think here not only of the socially and academically elite ones such as Manhattanville or Trinity (although these, like women's colleges in general, are not wealthy), but of those, such as Webster or Immaculate Heart, which attract neither brilliant students nor for the most part socially elite ones and yet do a great deal to help their students become self-critical and awake and not merely docile and diligent. Hassenger gives SAT scores of these two colleges, and they do not compare with those of Notre Dame or Boston College or Trinity. But in considering the impact of the colleges, it is, of course, all too common and easy to focus on the students they turn out rather than to compare in detail the finished product with the entering freshmen. It is in these latter terms of what economists would call "value added" that colleges should really be appraised. And it is in such terms that Immaculate Heart and Webster are distinguished colleges, even though they do not produce many "distinguished" graduates. The urban women's college, "Mary College," that Hassenger describes at great length in chapter 4 has a more mixed effect on its students, depending on their social class and ethnic background to begin with; thus, the middle-class Irish young women trapped there because they lack the talent or energy to go elsewhere were perhaps too enameled to be greatly influenced by their college experience, in contrast, for example, to a working-class Polish girl who, contrary to family expectations, hopes to make a career in the natural sciences.[3]

From the account of "Mary College," I had gained the sense that the ablest faculty were the young sisters who had taken their doctorates at the major secular universities and the somewhat older sisters who, in the close life of the community, had been influenced by these. In contrast, the lay faculty — as at many women's colleges — was transient and tended to move on after obtaining the Ph.D. Yet, of course, the religious, whether male or female, constitute a smaller and smaller minority of the faculty in Catholic colleges. The number of religious is probably not keeping pace with growth in population and cannot conceivably keep pace with the growth in *college* populations, let alone with the growth in such fields as the natural sciences and many of the social sciences in which the Catholic colleges have to look to laymen for staffing. The dwindling role of religious is even more obvious at those urban commuter universities founded by Catholics to provide the first steps into professional life for the Catholic lower strata of our big cities. At universities like Marquette, the University of Detroit, and Loyola or DePaul in Chicago, the law, business, and other professional schools have been largely staffed by laymen, by no means always Catholic, and have attracted as students the less-privileged urban dwellers, also not invariably Catholic. Some of the laymen in my own observation have been more "Catholic" than the religious and grateful to the latter, but increasingly there is open tension between the clerical "management" and the lay "labor force." There is also restlessness among the students, especially at the better places, for dissent, as Foster and Kearns both recognize, is a sign of life.[4]

For quite a while, some of the more radical religious have been wondering whether their orders should be in the business of running colleges and whether the colleges should not be turned over to lay administrators and trustees. As this book was going to press, this current of thought came into the open with announcements that Webster College's president, Sister Jacqueline Grennan, was resigning from the order and that the college would be turned over to a lay president and board; Notre Dame, Fordham, St. Louis University, and Holy Cross all announced the laicization of their boards of trustees in whole or in part (as Manhattan College had done at an earlier point). Similar moves are under consideration at Georgetown, Catholic University, and elsewhere. No

[3] In the course of his work at "Mary College," Hassenger developed a differentiated set of answers to the question, "What is religion?" He discriminates among a variety of Catholic religious styles including the moralistic, the apostolic, the intellectual and so on, again illustrative of the many ways of being a Catholic in America.

[4] Further empirical evidence that, on the whole, the better the college, the more critical its abler students become, is provided in Andrew M. Greeley, "Criticisms of Undergraduate Faculty by Graduates of Catholic Colleges," *Review of Religious Research*, V. (Winter, 1965), 96–106.

doubt, a certain degree of laicization will help attract funds and faculty members who fear a clerical "power elite." Yet I have detected a certain anti-authoritarian romanticism among some of the religious who put such high hopes in the laity. It is unlikely that the lay trustees will be people like Nancy Rambusch, Daniel Callahan, Michael Novak, or Michael Harrington, but rather will be the contractors, steel barons, insurance executives, public officials, mass media and public relations tycoons, many of whom still see the Catholic colleges as turning out patriotic, sports-loving, smooth but unsophisticated young men and piously protected "feminine" young women. Lay trustees of Catholic, as of other colleges, are apt to care more about the pedagogic work of the faculty than about its research, and presidential leadership may be hard put to persuade them that academic upgrading by the conventional academic routes requires placing the care and feeding of faculty above the care and feeding of undergraduates.

Correspondingly, the tremendous advances made by the best Catholic colleges in the last few years have not come about through participatory democracy either at the faculty or the student level, but through the impact of brilliant, often charismatic, and frequently tyrannical leadership.[5] (The same is true of other upwardly mobile academic institutions.) I recognize that since many lay faculty and students believe that things will be freer and better if the religious loosen their control, the effect of such loosening may indeed be a greater emancipation. But I would rather see a similar result brought about by the kind of consolidation that Hassenger describes in his appendix on "The Catholic University of Chicago." It is doubtful, however, that any such plan as his will be realized. For neither the financial pinch nor the problem of attracting faculty and students has led to any "master plan" for Catholic higher education, not even a "Jesuit plan" for the twenty-eight Jesuit colleges; the competition among these institutions both in the same territory and increasingly in the nation as a whole for Catholic and non-Catholic dollars, students and faculty is quite unmitigated. As Hassenger observes in his final chapter, efforts at interinstitutional cooperation are minimal, with the characteristic narcissism of minor academic differences — minor as seen from the outside — operating to prevent any intellectual common market. Here the most interesting venture is the plan of Immaculate Heart College to locate itself among the Claremont cluster, thus obtaining the advantages of greater facilities and wider interchange while retaining, it is hoped, its own virtues of smallness and a certain spirited serenity.

Robert Weiss, S.J., in "The Environment for Learning on the Catholic College Campus," and Hassenger's chapters present evidence that perhaps the majority of young men and women coming out of the Catholic

---

[5] This is my own observation, but it is supported by a thorough although non-quantitative, survey of Catholic higher education by Father Andrew Greeley, as yet unpublished (Andrew M. Greeley, William Van Cleve, and Grace Ann Carroll, *The Changing Catholic College* [Chicago: Aldine Publishing Co., 1967]).

colleges still fit the piously parental image of them. The fact that, as Father Robert McNamara's research illustrates, they are somewhat readier than their secular counterparts to cheat on examinations, only demonstrates that they see their education as external; possibly it also demonstrates that the conventional Catholic preoccupation with sexual morality and religious adherence tends to drive other moral issues to the periphery. In comparison with evangelical Protestant colleges, the residential Catholic colleges are probably no more puritanical or image-conscious and maybe less so, while the big urban commuter schools, Jesuit and otherwise, of course cannot supervise their students closely. But here, too, atmospheric constraints remain, as in a minatory attitude toward the student press, and perhaps especially for those undergraduates who have come up through parochial schools, a superficially obedient posture toward religious in and out of the classroom has become habitual. It is just this mantle of indifference parading as propriety that many of the abler faculty, both religious and lay, try on the better campuses to subvert. A few theology departments expose their captive audiences to a range of theological speculation and criticism radically at odds with the simple Catholicism brought from home and the local diocese. (The contrast has been known to turn some students to the Young Americans for Freedom or to the John Birch Society for intellectual support against the faculty.) In their essay, "The Student," Hassenger and Gerald Rauch, a senior at Notre Dame, quote some savage commentary by Notre Dame undergraduates concerning the institution's increasingly residual restraints; they also attack their priest-mentors for being too wrapped up in their research or in the educational enterprise. And with the idealism characteristic of some of the best young people, one senior remarks that there may be as many as ten Christians at Notre Dame and certainly no more than twenty, who are not only seeking something but have perhaps found it. Although not all these critics attack from the same point of the compass, their unflattering picture of alma mater is good testimony to the latter's quality.

Reading such criticisms, I am reminded, as I have often been, of the ability of Catholicism since the Reformation to contain "Protestant" elements within it more or less successfully. Indeed, a few of these young men have the desire to return to a primitive noninstitutional Christianity which would make them at home in a Pentecostal sect. Some of these student criticisms, *pari passu*, resemble those by students at other large liberal arts colleges who are angry with their faculty for getting involved in research and administration rather than in intimate student-teacher relations.

Indeed, reading this book one comes to realize the conflicting pressures under which the Catholic colleges are proceeding: to try to become more spiritual, more academic — and more solvent. These colleges want to become among the best in the United States not only so that their students are not handicapped in their chances of further work by attending them, but also to be able to attract top-flight faculty, both Catholic and non-Catholic, in the mad scramble for good people that has been brought about by the boom in the professorial marketplace. But the drive for academic quality by going academic definitions has raised the questions — heard on so many Catholic campuses — as to what is "Catholic" about a Catholic college and whether the teaching orders should perhaps devote themselves to Newman Club work at the state colleges and universities where the bulk of Catholics already go.[6] (Father John Whitney Evans has a spirited and interesting chapter on his own experience as just such a chaplain.)

The religious who try to answer the question of what is Catholic at their institutions have a difficult time because they are in doubt about this themselves; the old certainties have evaporated. This, of course, does not mean that the older oppressions of every variety have evaporated. Even in the oldest Catholic college, Georgetown University, a lay exile, Francis E. Kearns, presents devastating evidence bearing on his own *cause célèbre*, although he ends up pointing out how greatly Georgetown now reflects the increasing social-action consciousness of the best Catholics which leads them, for example, to enter the Peace Corps out of all proportion to their numbers.[7] Kearns is aware that Catholic colleges are caught in a dilemma because they are seeking support as well as students from inside the more traditional Catholic world while also seeking grants, faculty, and status in the larger world of national and international scholarship. In contrast to the situation in Europe, where originally all education was Catholic, in this country the Catholic population as a whole and the colleges in particular (as Philip Gleason demonstrates) are latecomers. In the past, being a latecomer provided an alibi for those moderate dosages of double talk, combining religiosity with ethnic defense, nationalism, and materialism, that other less-favored groups in America have also employed.[8] Correspondingly, the administrators

[6] There are analogies here to the process of desegregation at the predominantly Negro colleges, which are losing some of their best students and superior faculty to previously all-white institutions.

[7] Kearns suggests that charity rather than justice is the motive for social action among some of the Georgetown students; and indeed, the Peace Corps can be entered for a variety of motives, among them, mixtures of philanthropic, reformist, revolutionary, apostolic, escapist, nationalist, and internationalist ones. The last of these would seem to be rare. For example, it is my impression Catholic undergraduates concerned with peace in Viet Nam are a small minority; however, a few of the most radical students on this, as on other fronts, are to be found not at the larger, more emancipated places like Georgetown, but in desperate isolation at the more constricted ones, from which they may emerge to join the Catholic Worker Movement or even to burn their draft cards. Even in the more conventional and conservative Catholic colleges, in my own observation, there is almost invariably a faculty nucleus, lay or religious, for whom not faith nor learning nor life itself has been routinized.

[8] For a critical description of one aspect of this process, namely the fervent Americanism of the whole series of leading bishops and cardinals from Carroll to Spellman, see Dorothy Dohen, *Nationalism and American Catholicism* (New York: Sheed and Ward, 1967).

of Catholic colleges have felt they had to say different things to different constituencies. But the younger religious and lay faculty and the more idealistic and sensitive students are demanding ruthless honesty (so that the term "Jesuitical" sounds quaint today), and they expect their colleges to set standards of candor and openness judged by their scrupulously individual consciences even while these institutions are trying to win respectability in the conventional mode.

For the contributors to this volume, whether of reports on research or critical essays, that goal is itself suspect. They are not satisfied to have the Catholic colleges simply "make it" according to current definitions of academic success. These contributors would like the colleges to "overtake and surpass," providing a milieu that is secular and experimental rather than secular and imitative, yet in some sense still "Catholic." But their own evidence suggests that such experiments are seldom going on. That contributors like Paul Reiss clarify the inevitability of these dilemmas hardly makes them more tolerable for the individuals caught in them.

I do not want to overestimate the uniformity of tone or approach in these chapters, however. They differ very much in method and in the balance between hope and apprehension. But overall what the book illustrates for me is the simply tremendous energy liberated on the Catholic campuses in recent years and the kind of excitement that many Catholics are finding in examining their own institutions with what Daniel Callahan in his book of collected essays called "the third eye." [9]

I have indicated above a certain skepticism (which I know Daniel Callahan shares) [10] about what might be called the agenda beyond renewal; for all social advances, all liberations turn out to be problematical — which is of course no reason for not pursuing them, and certainly no reason for trying to head them off. Furthermore, precisely because so many American Catholics are moving out from encapsulation toward a wider world view, less ethnic, less ethnocentric and nationalistic, what will happen to them and their movements is tied up with the fate of America itself. If we Americans cut ourselves off still more completely than at present from the rest of the world, both by our violence and our affluence, we will force some of our critics back into an inner immigration and others to become catholic in the original and broadest sense of the word, and hence non-American if not actively anti-American. It is a lot to ask of the Catholic prophets of today to hope that they can retain their sanity in the face of so many competing expectations, so many overpowering pressures abroad and at home, so many disappointments in the very face of growing openness and success.

DAVID RIESMAN

[9] *Generation of the Third Eye* (New York: Sheed and Ward, 1965).
[10] See Callahan, "The Renewal Mess," *Commonweal*, 85 (March 3, 1967), 621–25.

PREFACE

As this volume is written, there are more than eight hundred higher educational institutions in the United States associated with religious bodies, comprising more than a third of the colleges listed in the United States Office of Education directory. Located in every state but Nevada and Wyoming, these institutions are affiliated with sixty-four denominations and enroll more than one-sixth of the total American college population.

Great differences among these schools can, of course, be found, as well as a wide range of relationships with their churches. Ties at many of the campuses are only the most tenuous, so that "church-sponsored" is perhaps the most appropriate description for many schools that could scarcely be called "church colleges." The largest single group of these institutions is affiliated with the Roman Catholic church. This book will attempt to illuminate this segment of American higher education.

The Catholic colleges and universities may be the least understood group of American higher educational institutions, with the possible exception of the small liberal arts colleges that have kept their Protestant denominational ties (e.g., Wheaton, Denison, Earlham). Probably no sector of American higher education has experienced so convulsive a series of recent shocks as the Catholic one. And yet, despite the upsurge in critical examination of Catholic higher education during the past decade, there has been very little published work going beyond an impressionistic accounting of isolated incidents and lay-clerical atrocity stories. When first-rate investigations are done, results are often served in forms unpalatable to the layman interested in the social sciences. The intent of this volume is to collect the most significant of the published and unpublished research on Catholic higher education and to present the data in forms meaningful to the intelligent non-specialist.

The primary and secondary branches of the vast Catholic educational enterprise will not be treated here. Nor will graduate education, except briefly in the final chapter. "Catholic higher education," in the chapters ahead, will be limited to the undergraduate years. In attempting to do a volume at once soundly grounded in fact and limited in interpretation, yet meaningful to the non-social scientist, we may be missing both audiences. If we had any prototype in view, it was Nevitt Sanford's volume, *The American College* (New York: John Wiley & Sons, Inc., 1962), although data on Catholic higher education is much less plentiful.

I should make it clear that I do not consider eleven largely independent chapters an ideal way to do this kind of volume; a book integrated by an all-encompassing theoretical perspective would have been in many ways preferable. The independence might have been made less obvious by agreement on a common vocabulary, although this would have forced at least some of our thoughts into strange and unfamiliar molds. While we would undoubtedly have survived, no such guarantee could have been made for the book.

A brief word ought to be said about the selected bibliography. The criteria for selection were primarily two: (1) accessibility; and (2) the direct relevance of the work either to Catholicism in America or to higher education in the United States. Many empirical studies have been outdated by later work; often the original sources are referred to in full in the chapter footnotes but do not appear in the selected bibliography. Nor does unpublished work appear in the latter (although it, too, will be found in the former). When a number of books are available on the same topic (e.g., Jesuit education), we have chosen a representative sample, weighted with more recent publications. If particular types of work receive an undue emphasis in the bibliography, these are probably historical and empirical studies. There seems to be a dearth of first-rate historical and empirical research, and I have listed a variety of sources in the hope of stimulating more work of this type. Also included are some of the widely influential books of a decade and even thirty years ago, although these will strike many readers as wholly anachronistic today. They had great influence in their time, however, and if they do not stand the test of experience so well as, say, George Shuster's *Catholic Spirit in America*, they need to be read for an appreciation of how far we have come.

The book's title has been deliberately chosen: we attempt here to discern the *shape* of Catholic higher education. We do not claim a definitive book. The recent interest in this area — and in the sociology of religion and education generally — will generate increasingly more sophisticated research and publications. Nor can this volume answer such Big Questions as Are Parochial Schools the Answer? The contributors do not pretend to know. They wish they did. But their chief concern at this point is to present a series of portraits and snapshots; some are largely based on data, others are of a more reportorial — and even personal — character. In each approach, however, we have endeavored to draw only the inferences that seem clearly fair. We have not, of course, been able to abstain from criticism and suggestion where these seem appropriate, perhaps even inescapable. To neglect these would be irresponsible. And what young Catholic priest or layman can afford to be called *that* again?

Our debts are many. I can only acknowledge some of my own. For their encouragement and criticism at various stages of this work, I thank Charles Bidwell, Jim Buckley, Dave Burrell, Mike Crowe, Bill D'Antonio, Whitney

Evans, Phil Gleason, Andy Greeley, Terry Hassenger, Robert Havighurst, Norb Hruby, Herb Johnston, Suzanne Kelly, Tom Lorch, Lewis Mayhew, Nevitt Sanford, Charles Sheedy, Joe Shoben, George Shuster, Jim Trent, and particularly David Riesman, not only for his gracious foreword and his thoughtful comments on the drafts of these chapters, but for his immense care and concern for excellence and civility, virtues which, for myself, David Riesman will always himself best exemplify.

A collective dedication here seems most appropriate. To those students at Fordham, Georgetown, Marquette, Mundelein, Notre Dame, Rockhurst, Saint Louis, San Francisco, Saint Xavier, and Santa Clara, whom we have taught and been taught by, we dedicate this book.

ROBERT HASSENGER

CONTENTS

THE FUTURE OF CATHOLIC HIGHER EDUCATION

APPENDIXES

General Perspectives

I. COLLEGE AND CATHOLICS: AN INTRODUCTION

Robert Hassenger

Despite the escalating discussion of the "time bomb" in Catholic higher education, its "identity crisis," and the possibility that Catholic colleges and universities may be "contradictions in terms," there is a paucity of solid information available about the largest higher educational "system" in the United States. The quotation marks are used advisedly. Unlike the Catholic elementary and secondary schools, the church's colleges and universities have never been an official Catholic project. Broad guidelines have long existed, of course.[1] But, as Philip Gleason points out in chapter 2, no overall plan for

Robert Hassenger received his B.A. from Notre Dame in 1959, and his Ph.D. from the University of Chicago in 1965. He is an assistant professor of sociology at Notre Dame, and has contributed to the *American Journal of Sociology, Sociological Quarterly, Sociological Analysis, School Review, Educational Record, Thought, Commonweal, America, Ave Maria,* and *The National Catholic Reporter.*

[1] One of the most widely quoted sources of the Catholic viewpoint on education is Pius XI's encyclical on "The Christian Education of Youth" (1929). In it he stated: "The proper and immediate end of Christian education is to co-operate with divine grace in forming the true and perfect Christian, that is, to form Christ Himself in those regenerated by Baptism, according to the emphatic expression of the Apostle: "My little children, of whom I am in labour again, until Christ be formed in you. . . ." For precisely this reason, Christian education takes in the whole aggregate of human life, physical and spiritual, intellectual and moral, individual, domestic and social, not with a view of reducing it in any way, but in order to elevate, regulate, and perfect it, in accordance with the example and teaching of Christ. Hence the true Christian, product of Christian education, is the supernatural man who thinks, judges, and acts constantly and consistently in accordance with right reason illumined by the supernatural light of the example and teaching of Christ; in other words, to use the correct term, the true and finished man of character." Recent official statements are no more precise. In the section on Catholic colleges and universities of the Second Vatican Council's Declaration on Christian Education, proclaimed by Paul VI on October 28, 1965, hope was expressed that the church's higher educational endeavors would exert "a public, enduring and pervasive influence [on] the Christian mind in the furtherance of culture, and [that] the students [in] these institutions [would be] molded into men truly in their training, ready to undertake weighty responsibilities in society and witness to the faith in the world. . . ." There are, however, some important statements in the Constitution on the Church in the Modern World, from the same Council.

3

Catholic higher education was ever drawn up. Each college seems to have been founded and to have grown in response to various local situations, under the direction of numerous religious orders. Indeed, the loosely structured system of American Catholic higher education can be accused of following too literally the biblical injunction to increase and multiply. It is a continuing vexation of quality-conscious Catholic intellectuals that small colleges are still founded, often drawing on the already limited resources and talent available in some religious orders.

As any history of Catholic higher education will show, the colleges and universities [2] were founded to serve an immigrant, working-class, self-conscious minority; it is thus not surprising that these institutions served largely as — David Riesman puts it well — "decompression chambers for those edging their way out of the ghetto." [3] Unabashedly intent on "saving the faith" of their young Catholic clients, the colleges were characterized by something resembling a "rescue operation" approach, which often manifested itself in an embattled, defensive stance.[4] But as the American church — with Roman Catholicism in general — moves into the *aggiornamento* of the mid-twentieth century, an increasing number of criticisms are being leveled at various aspects of Catholic higher education. The critics of the church's schools are no longer a small and lonely band. If anything, the volume of current criticism runs the risk of overkill. Controversy surrounding the educational system is most often focused on two issues: (1) the purported poverty of Catholic intellectualism and scholarship, and (2) the possibility that Catholic schools are failing even in their avowed purpose of religious education.

There is no real Catholic intellectual tradition in the United States. Orestes Brownson lamented this fact more than one hundred years ago. As Denis Brogan wrote three-quarters of a century later: "In no Western society is the intellectual prestige of Catholicism lower than in the country where, in such respects as wealth, numbers, and strength of organization, it is so powerful." [5]

Into the early 1950's research supported these charges. The Knapp [6] indices of the "productivity" of scientists and humanists by various higher educational institutions showed Catholic schools to be in a "conspicuously inferior position." Interestingly enough, although "exceptionally unproduc-

---

[2] It is tedious to use continually the phrase, "colleges and universities." When we intend to distinguish between these different types of institutions, we shall try to make it clear; otherwise, the terms will be used interchangeably to avoid repetition.

[3] In chapter 7 of the draft of *The Academic Revolution* by Christopher Jencks and David Riesman (in preparation).

[4] More will be said about this in the final chapter.

[5] Denis W. Brogan, *U.S.A.: An Outline of the Country, Its People and Institutions* (New York and London: Oxford University Press, 1941).

[6] R. H. Knapp and H. B. Goodrich, *Origins of American Scientists* (Chicago: University of Chicago Press, 1952); and R. H. Knapp and J. J. Greenbaum, *The Younger American Scholar* (Chicago: University of Chicago Press, 1953).

tive in all areas of scholarship," Catholic colleges and universities achieved a better record in the sciences than in the humanities, despite the prevalent stereotype to the contrary. But the over-all picture seemed unquestionably bleak.

Analysis of Catholic intellectual impoverishment took a new turn with the penetrating survey by John Tracy Ellis in 1955. Addressing the national meeting of the Catholic Commission on Intellectual and Cultural Affairs in St. Louis, Msgr. Ellis threw down the gauntlet to Catholic educators, with a challenge given widespread publicity.[7] A flood of self-criticism was thereby unleashed, often taking rather curious forms. Some seemed preoccupied with nose-counting, asking where the Catholic Rhodes Scholars, *Who's Who* members, and "leaders" were to be found.[8]

It would be a disservice to the Roman church to suggest that Catholics have a monopoly on anti-intellectualism in America. As Richard Hofstadter has clearly shown, they have not.[9] And there are some extenuating circumstances, related in large part to the lower-class, immigrant origins of the American Catholic population. A number of fine discussions about this factor are available, including that of Philip Gleason in chapter 2, so I shall not treat it further here.

But the self-critics have made it clear that much of the responsibility for the inadequacy of scholarship is inescapably American Catholics' own. As Msgr. Ellis wrote

> It lies in their frequently self-imposed ghetto mentality which prevents them from mingling as they should with their non-Catholic colleagues, and in their lack of industry and habits of work, to which Hutchins alluded in 1937. It lies in their failure to have measured up to their responsibilities to the incomparable tradition of Catholic learning of which they are direct heirs, a failure which Peter Viereck noted, and which suggested to him the caustic question: "Is the honorable adjective 'Roman Catholic' truly merited by America's middle-class-Jansenist Catholicism, puritanized, Calvinized, and dehydrated. . . ?"[10]

Thomas O'Dea was no less critical of his fellow Catholics, noting that the inhibition of intellectual activity was owing to the formalism, authoritarianism, clericalism, moralism, and defensiveness that have characterized Amer-

[7] Published in *Thought*, 30 (Autumn, 1955), 351–88; and as *American Catholics and the Intellectual Life* (Chicago: The Heritage Foundation, 1956).

[8] Most of the Catholic response up to 1960 has been summarized in Frank Christ and Gerard Sherry (eds.), *American Catholicism and the Intellectual Ideal* (New York: Appleton-Century-Crofts, 1961).

[9] Richard Hofstadter, *Anti-Intellectualism in American Life* (New York: Alfred A. Knopf, 1964).

[10] Ellis, "Catholic Scholarship," pp. 385–86.

ican Catholicism.[11] The caustic commentary continued unabated until the early 1960's, leading some to lament the "orgy of self-criticism" and to plead for a halt in the exercises of "mass masochism." But the increased volume of the controversy had positive effects; criticism — whether orgiastic or not — stimulated real educational soul-searching and resulted in definite upgrading. It also generated the empirical research necessary for meaningful evaluation.

Although the vast majority of Catholic colleges had long since met the requirements of basic academic respectability,[12] there were few indications of quality among the nearly three hundred institutions. Only four American Catholic schools have Phi Beta Kappa chapters at the time of this writing,[13] compared to approximately 170 secular institutions. As late as the mid-1950's, the existing data all pointed to a dearth of Catholic scholars and researchers. Of 775 fellowships distributed by the National Science Foundation in 1956, 17 went to Catholic colleges; in 1957, 19 out of 845 fellowships were awarded to students from Catholic schools. Progress, of course, can only occur in stages; college attendance itself was not part of the traditional background of the vast majority of American Catholics. Donovan showed that, in 1957, only five per cent of the American bishops had college-educated fathers, and his later data on the educational levels of Catholic college professors' fathers are directly comparable.[14] Wagner *et al.* found that only about one-third of the Catholic college students they studied had college-educated parents, compared to about half of the Protestant students.[15] This is to some extent, of course, a reflection of the later arrival in America of the ethnic groups comprising a large part of the Catholic population.[16]

[11] Thomas F. O'Dea, *The American Catholic Dilemma: An Inquiry into the Intellectual Life* (New York: Sheed and Ward, 1958), p. 60.

[12] Edward Wakin (*The Catholic Campus* [New York: Macmillan, 1963]) reports that by 1960, 87 per cent of the four-year Catholic colleges and universities had met the regional accrediting organizations' standards, compared with 73 per cent of the Protestant and 41 per cent of all other private institutions.

[13] Catholic University, Fordham, Georgetown, and The College of St. Catherine.

[14] John D. Donovan, "The American Catholic Hierarchy: A Social Profile," *American Catholic Sociological Review*, 19 (1958), 98–113; and J. D. Donovan, *The Academic Man in the Catholic College* (New York: Sheed and Ward, 1964), p. 35.

[15] H. R. Wagner, V. Doyle, and Kathryn Doyle, "Religious Background and Higher Education," *American Sociological Review*, 24 (1959), 852–56.

[16] Although the peak years of immigration for the Irish and Germans were 1851 and 1882, respectively, the largest number of Italians came in 1907, and Poles in 1921 (John L. Thomas, "Nationalities and American Catholicism," in *Catholic Church, U.S.A.*, ed. L. Putz, C.S.C. [Notre Dame, Ind.: Fides Press, 1956]). More recent data (Andrew M. Greeley and Peter H. Rossi, *The Education of Catholic Americans* [Chicago: Aldine Publishing Co., 1966]) seem to indicate that although Italians are increasingly found in Catholic schools according to their length of stay in the United States, later generations are not found in as great proportions as Irish, German, French, and Polish Catholics.

But things have changed very rapidly. The work of Andrew Greeley of the National Opinion Research Center (NORC) is so widely quoted that it will not be treated extensively here; references to his research appear throughout this volume. As Greeley has shown, Catholics now appear to be attending college and graduate school in proportion to their representation in the United States population. Further, the NORC researchers were able to find no significant difference between Protestants and Catholics in various measures of "intellectualism" (e.g., academic performance, career plans, occupational values). Catholics from both secular and Catholic schools are as likely to go to graduate school as Protestants (although both lag behind American Jews). Catholic colleges are less likely to produce graduate students than Ivy League or other high quality schools (Table 1), but they are more likely to do so than either the Big Ten schools or other middle-western colleges and universities.[17] In this, they are slightly above the national aver-

TABLE 1

PERCENTAGE OF STUDENTS ATTENDING GRADUATE SCHOOL,
BY COLLEGE TYPE (AFTER GREELEY, 1962).[a]

Subject Area	Ivy League	Other Prestige	Mid-western	Big Ten	Catholic	National Average
Arts and science	21	25	15	9	15	12
All graduate schools	52	63	32	26	36	31

[a] A. M. Greeley, "Anti-Intellectualism in Catholic Colleges," *American Catholic Sociological Review*, 23 (1962), 350–68.

age, although Robert McNamara did find that the Fordham and Notre Dame seniors he studied were more likely than Cornell and Columbia men to be willing to stop with a master's — in lieu of a doctoral — degree.[18] But Greeley states that a follow-up of the sample he studied showed that, three years into graduate school, directly comparable proportions of Catholics and Protestants had obtained master's degrees and were candidates for the Ph.D.[19]

The Greeley data also show that public administration is the most popular field for Catholic college graduates, with accounting and corporate administration close behind; almost one-third of the students were attracted to these fields in 1961. Even the best of the Catholic schools send higher proportions to professional schools than to arts and science graduate schools. Notre

[17] Andrew M. Greeley, "Anti-Intellectualism in Catholic Colleges," *American Catholic Sociological Review*, 23 (1962), 350–68; also Andrew M. Greeley, *Religion and Career* (New York: Sheed and Ward, 1963).

[18] Robert J. McNamara, S.J., "The Interplay of Intellectual and Religious Values," (Ph.D. dissertation, Cornell University, 1963).

[19] Personal conversation, Autumn, 1965. But see Seymour Warkov and Andrew M. Greeley, "Parochial School Origins and Educational Achievement," *American Sociological Review*, 31 (1966), 406–14.

Dame, for example, is the only Catholic college or university among the top twenty schools in numbers of Woodrow Wilson Fellowships received;[20] yet, the entering freshmen in 1965 were considerably more oriented toward professional careers (49%) than toward teaching, research, or other scholarly work (11%). Perhaps these students, who were much more talented than those of earlier vintage,[21] will be socialized to academic pursuits by Notre Dame faculty or peers. But apparently even these students from fairly affluent families were relatively unexposed to influences pointing them toward academic pursuits prior to college.

So there remain a number of difficulties in attempting to ascertain the present state of Catholic intellectualism. Despite the reasoned plea by Philip Gleason that much of the discussion tends to befog the real issues at stake,[22] articles continue to be written and brickbats thrown. One of the primary intentions of the present volume is to summarize the most pertinent of the available data bearing on this problem.

The second major theme in the debate on Catholic higher education involves its religious character. Numerous angry charges have been made in recent years; the following will serve as a sample of the type of criticism often leveled:

> . . . the whole complex of Catholic higher education, presented with the American educational market . . . has found justification for subsequent and imitative patterns of study in "Catholicizing" them. It argues educational wisdom for professional skills out of the tatters of apologetics. The most serious effect is the disintegration of Theology into the role of a "service" department, bid by the divergent aims of students in a diverging society to offer "service" courses aimed at Catholicizing all skills, jobs, and professions. Theology has watched its concern grow literal and its wisdom catechetical. It has stood somewhat helplessly by as it has been made to try to make apologists of all

[20] With an average of about ten a year, for a total of 122 by 1966.

[21] College Board mean scores for entering Notre Dame freshmen dramatically illustrate this:

	Verbal	Math
1955–56	481.78	528.61
	(1,095)	(1,095)
1960–61	532.32	576.86
	(1,536)	(1,536)
1965–66	576.31	629.51
	(1,550)	(1,550)

Although the 1965–66 scores are still considerably below the 650–700 range of the top colleges and universities, the ten-year period shows a rise of about 100 points in both Verbal and Quantitative CEEB means.

[22] Philip Gleason, "Catholic Intellectualism Again," *America*, 112 (January 23, 1965), 112–19.

men, much like the tiring efforts of Freshman English have aimed at making all men writers. . . .

Religion becomes a series of answers, often to questions the student has yet to learn, questions nobody really asks, questions whose intent is out of focus with other academic issues. It is often sadly true that the theology department develops into a huge chaplaincy, more pastoral than academic in function, more kindly in its respect for students than academically disciplined.[23]

The primary reason for statements of this type is the belief "that the schools have failed their Christian purpose or at least have achieved scandalously poor results."[24] Many would take serious issue with such criticism, whereas others might judge the statement too mild. But an increasing number of such comments can be found. Although most research has found that Catholic college students, on the whole, maintain a more positive attitude toward their schools than Protestant students,[25] a recent investigation by Greeley shows that the Catholic undergraduates intending to enter the academic life are more critical of their schools than their secular college counterparts.[26]

It is difficult to determine the extent to which this rising tide of criticism is a function of the changing role of religion in American life.[27] Probably no institution faces greater uncertainty than the church in our society. College-age Americans may never again take institutionalized religion as seriously as their parents have, or even their older brothers and sisters. Ferment is no longer absent from the Catholic campus, as the fall-out from student-publication censorship actions, faculty dismissals, speaker-bans, and perceived administration paternalism indicates. Some Catholics have even raised serious questions about the necessity and practicality of a separate educational system in the America of the space age. As one of the most controversial of the recent writers put it:

> In the past, we have considered the Catholic school and college to be the central means — and the normal one — of providing religious formation. We have not seriously tried to think of any other approach. The

[23] John Mahoney, "The American Catholic College and the Faith," *Thought*, 39 (1964), 243–45.

[24] Daniel Callahan, "The Schools," *Commonweal*, 71 (1965) 476.

[25] John T. Fox, "The Attitude of Male College Students Toward Their Church," *American Catholic Sociological Review*, 24 (1963), 127–31; Greeley and Rossi, *Education of Catholic Americans*.

[26] Andrew M. Greeley, "Criticism of Undergraduate Faculty by Graduates of Catholic Colleges," *Review of Religious Research*, 6 (1965), 97–106.

[27] The entire system of higher education is coming in for more careful scrutiny, as was reflected in the 1966 Conference of the Association for Higher Education, March 13–16, 1966, in Chicago.

new outlook clearly implies that the school will no longer be central; its function now appears as ancillary.[28]

The case made by Mrs. Ryan is a cogent one, although her book did not always receive a fair hearing from some of the more defensive Catholic educators. Whether her argument can stand in the face of the data — particularly the Greeley-Rossi findings showing the importance of the interaction of parental religiousness and Catholic education, the cumulative effects of the school, and the apparent ineffectuality of programs sponsored by The Confraternity of Christian Doctrine — remains to be seen.[29]

Here, in fact, is the essence of the problem and the principal reason for this book. It is relatively easy to criticize Catholic education — or indeed, American education generally. But the Catholic self-critics tend to offend at least two quite different groups. The first are oversensitive to any criticism. Catholic schools have been, as Callahan notes, "the rallying point for Catholic jingoists, that place where tribal loyalty, group myth-making, and minority passions have met and concentrated their power."[30] For a second group, assertions of Catholic intellectual inferiority are provoking because they appear to be just that: assertions, backed only by anecdotal evidence. These people demand that such accusations be supported by data. And empirical evidence is in short supply.

Most discussions of Catholic higher education proceed unencumbered by results of research. The bulk of these are rather glibly superficial, often based on a few days spent visiting several campuses. Such largely anecdotal accounts are sometimes enlightening, occasionally even insightful. But they can also be misleading.

Social scientists must shoulder much of the blame for the paucity of hard data. As Hansen pointed out:

> . . . education, guidance, counselling and other human arts suffer from sociological malnutrition. Today elements of sociological knowledge have only incidental impact on education, for the educator is interested in whole, complex, dynamic worlds. Of such human beings and such worlds the sociologist today says little.

[28] Mary Perkins Ryan, *Are Parochial Schools the Answer?* (New York: Holt, Rinehart and Winston, 1964), p. 150.

[29] The Confraternity of Christian Doctrine (CCD) is a volunteer group of young men and women, often college and high school students, who spend time teaching Catholic beliefs and practices to Catholic children attending public schools. Some pastors make enrollment in a CCD class a condition of approval for public school attendance, although it is, of course, very difficult to enforce such strictures. A few critics of the Catholic schools have suggested that sufficient religious training could take place in an expanded CCD program, increasing the weekly time spent in such sessions from the present one or two hours to four or five. Some would make radical qualitative changes in the CCD as well.

[30] Callahan, "The Schools," p. 473.

. . . the educator, as a human artist, is faced with daily decisions that demand use of every intellectual tool available. He has mastered some sociological tools, but he has done so with little help from the sociologist. He has recognized the potential usefulness of some other tools, but also that the tools must be modified or used with some unspecified care, modifications and care that the sociologist could instruct him in, warn him about.

But few sociologists bother. They create tools, they publish reports — but they give little help, few warnings, few suggestions, to the educator. They are indifferent.[31]

Not all are. In 1962 the massive volume edited by Nevitt Sanford summarized the best of the available research on *The American College*,[32] and the Educational Testing Service has recently inaugurated a comprehensive program of student and institutional assessment, which will greatly facilitate college and university self-studies. The Carnegie Corporation has undertaken a study of the future of the liberal arts college,[33] and government money has funded the establishment of a number of centers for research and development in higher education. This trend augurs well for future understanding of what actually happens (or fails to happen) on American college campuses, including Catholic ones.[34] By the time the present volume appears, the report of the National Opinion Research Center will have been reviewed and discussed (and one hopes, read),[35] and the results of two other extensive surveys will be available.[36] But they will have little to say about the Catholic colleges and universities, and this is the focus of our collective effort, the

[31] Donald Hansen, "The Responsibility of the Sociologist to Education," *Harvard Educational Review*, 33 (1963), 312–25.

[32] Nevitt Sanford (ed.), *The American College* (New York: John Wiley & Sons, 1962). This is still the most important single sourcebook on higher education in early 1967.

[33] Administered through Antioch College and directed by Dean Morris Keeton.

[34] The Berkeley Center for Research and Development in Higher Education has several Catholic institutions in its sample of colleges and universities; some of the Catholic college findings will be reported in a forthcoming volume by James Trent, to be published by The University of Chicago Press shortly after the present book.

[35] Greeley and Rossi, *Education of Catholic Americans*.

[36] The other half (Greeley and Rossi being the first half) of the Carnegie-financed research on Catholic elementary and secondary education became available in late 1966: Reginald Neuwien (ed.), *Catholic Schools in Action: The Notre Dame Study of Catholic Elementary and Secondary Schools in the United States* (Notre Dame, Ind.: University of Notre Dame Press, 1966), as did the final report of the Danforth Commission on Church Colleges and Universities: Manning M. Pattillo, Jr. and Donald M. Mackenzie, *Church-Sponsored Higher Education in the United States* (Washington, D.C.: American Council on Education, 1966).

purpose of which is to gather what data are presently available to provide substance for the debate now raging with a poorly stocked armamentarium.

There are, of course, many varieties of Catholic higher education. School sizes range from less than two hundred students to the huge five-figure enrollments of such urban (and largely commuter) universities as St. John's, Detroit, and Loyola. The nearly three hundred colleges and universities differ enormously, and the roughly 360,000 students enrolled in these institutions come from radically diverse backgrounds and have widely divergent talents, motives, and life plans. Christopher Jencks and David Riesman deal with some of the factors accounting for the differences among the Catholic colleges.[37] The most obvious of these are sex and social class. Five out of six Catholic colleges are segregated by sex, compared with less than one out of six Protestant colleges, and one in ten secular schools. Nearly half of the Catholic colleges admit women only, with an additional third serving men exclusively. But the big coeducational urban universities enroll such large numbers that considerably more than one in six Catholic students is in a coeducational setting. And even the traditionally segregated schools appear to be moving toward increased cooperation with their counterparts.[38]

Qualitative differences among Catholic institutions are enormous, as any quick comparison of College Board scores, National Merit Scholar enrollment, Woodrow Wilson, Danforth, NDEA, and Rhodes fellowship figures, or similar indexes suggest.[39] For example, out of the 5,996 National Defense Graduate fellowships allocated for 1966–67, Catholic universities were awarded 147; Notre Dame led the Catholic group with 45 fellowships, followed by Catholic University with 40. Or consider College Board scores. The largest number of Catholic schools are the women's colleges. Yet many degrees of ability can be found among them, as the CEEB scores for 20 of these schools indicate (Table 2). Those familiar with Catholic higher education will not be surprised to find Manhattanville, Trinity, New Rochelle, and Newton College of the Sacred Heart leading the list. But they may be caught off balance at the data in later chapters indicating that Catholic college women in general appear more intellectual than the men in Catholic schools. (The women's colleges are in many ways more interesting than the coeducational and men's institutions.) They may find other surprises in the following pages, although such was not the principal objective of this volume.

Because "Catholic higher education" is not of a piece, we have placed the chapters with empirical data first, so that the reader will become accustomed to thinking in terms of the diversity they illustrate, as less rigorous

[37] In their extensive exploration of the American higher educational scene now in preparation and tentatively entitled *The Academic Revolution*, Jencks and Riesman have devoted one section to church-affiliated institutions.

[38] Some of the forms these take are described in the final chapter.

[39] The perceptive observer quickly becomes aware of varying atmospheric conditions, as well.

approaches are taken in the second half of the book. In chapter 2, Philip Gleason discusses the historical forces that have shaped the Catholic colleges and universities. The institutional patterns these forces have generated, and the effects of the diverse schools, are seen in the four chapters comprising Parts II and III.

Chapters 7 and 8 are concerned with some of the problems of Catholic higher education. We make no claim that these chapters are entirely objective; they report some of the conflicts that have become so evident in the past few years. The writers would not state that they have presented evidence that such problems are "typical" of Catholic higher education; they have discussed several situations that illuminate the particular difficulties faced by at least some schools.

Paul Reiss considers some of these built-in conflicts more systematically in chapter 9, and John Whitney Evans takes a look at Catholics on secular campuses in the tenth chapter. The editor has addressed himself to some of the issues surrounding the future of Catholic higher education in chapter 11, and Anthony Seidl provides a guide for planning in Appendix A.

TABLE 2

DISTRIBUTION OF CEEB SCORES FOR ENTERING FRESHMEN
AT TWENTY CATHOLIC WOMEN'S COLLEGES, 1964.[a]

COLLEGE (NO. ENTERING IN PARENTHESES)	VERBAL [b]			QUANTITATIVE [b]		
	650+	600–649	−450	650+	550–649	−450
Barat (120)	9	12	4	8	20	15
Clarke (215)	3	11	39	4	13	39
Dunbarton (141)	7	11	5	6	18	20
Immaculate Heart (108)	13	16	18	6	25	31
Loretto Hts. (338)	5	5	9	2	15	14
Manhattanville (234)	38	27	0	18	58	0
Marygrove (301)	13	11	9	7	24	17
Marymount at Tarrytown (244)	11	15	3	6	37	9
Mount Mercy (227)	3	7	34	2	17	35
New Rochelle (250)	28	17	2	13	37	7
Newton College of Sacred Heart (222)	20	28	1	10	58	3
Rosary (215)	20	16	7	6	37	17
Rosary Hill (332)	5	8	27	5	19	36
St. Catherine (354)	9	12	15	6	24	33
St. Joseph, Pa. (140)	5	9	23	2	25	10
St. Mary's of Notre Dame (303)	16	12	6	10	37	12
St. Xavier, Ill. (197)	11	15	7	9	27	16
Seton Hill (209)	12	13	10	7	27	14
Trinity (270)	11	25	0	16	40	1
Webster (230)	29	9	24	2	17	40

[a] In percentages. Source: *Manual of Freshman Class Profiles*, 1965–67, College Entrance Examination Board.
[b] Since women are typically higher in verbal scores and lower in quantitative scores, it was thought to be more useful to concentrate on the distribution at the upper end of the latter, and at the high and low ends of the former.

II. AMERICAN CATHOLIC HIGHER EDUCATION: A HISTORICAL PERSPECTIVE

Philip Gleason

Catholic colleges and universities have historically departed in some degree from prevailing norms in three areas: (1) *socially*, in that most of the teachers and students came from groups who in one way or another were different from other American teachers and students; (2) *institutionally*, in that the patterns of educational organization, administration, and so on were not the same as those in vogue in other institutions of higher learning; and (3) *ideologically*, in that the ideas, beliefs, and attitudes of Catholic educators were not the same as those of other Americans. But since Catholic colleges and universities exist in American society, and since they must prepare young people for roles in that society, they have had to accommodate themselves to the norms and requirements of that society. This accommodation naturally involved the three areas of divergence; hence, the whole story may be understood in terms of the social adjustment made by the Catholic population and of the institutional and ideological adjustments made by the colleges to adapt to the American scene without compromising their Catholicity.

Other kinds of adjustments could perhaps be listed, but these three will serve our purpose in the present investigation. Before taking up any of them, however, a few preliminary points should be clarified. The first concerns the topical approach adopted here. My original intention was to combine with the discussion of the social, institutional, and ideological adjustments a brief narrative history of Catholic higher education, but the project soon grew out of all bounds. What follows, then, is not a history of Catholic colleges and universities but an analytical essay on their development, using the historical record to illustrate the principal types of adjustments they have made.

Secondly, the three categories of social, institutional, and ideological adjustment were adopted because of their usefulness in analysis and exposition; and although it is possible to distinguish conceptually among them, it would

Philip Gleason spent his undergraduate years at Ohio State and at the University of Dayton, and received his doctorate from Notre Dame in 1960. An assistant professor of history at Notre Dame, Mr. Gleason has published in *Religious Education*, *American Quarterly*, *Review of Politics*, *William and Mary Quarterly*, and other scholarly journals.

be quite misleading to think of them existing in nature as separate entities that are independent of each other. In actuality, the Catholic colleges and universities have developed and changed in response to a great number of different forces acting and interacting together; and in using the categories social, institutional, and ideological, I wish merely to indicate three classifications or perspectives that may help in examining the interaction of the many variable factors. That social, institutional, and ideological factors continuously influenced one another becomes clear when we recall, for example, that one of the reasons Catholics constituted a distinct social group was that they held different ideas and beliefs from other Americans, while at the same time the social factors of ethnicity and class background colored Catholic attitudes and beliefs.

A third preliminary point concerns the American environment to which Catholic higher education had to adjust itself. For the American environment itself was in a constant condition of flux; consequently, Catholic colleges were never able to take their bearings in a fixed landscape and work out with slow precision an appropriate permanent relationship between themselves and their American surroundings. Rather their adjustment was a continual process of accommodation, responding to this pressure or that need as it came to demand action. Catholic educators have always been struggling to keep up with the situation; they have never been able to get on top of their problems or to dispose matters according to some ideal scheme. The same is largely true of all American educators, of course, but there are some special complexities involved with the Catholic institutions. All colleges and universities had to adjust themselves to the changing needs of American society, but Catholic educators had the additional problem of adapting their adjustments to the general pattern followed by non-Catholic institutions.[1] In other words, the majority educational system itself constitutes a momentous element in the environment to which Catholic institutions must adjust. And as the non-Catholic colleges and universities have evolved in response to the changing needs of American society, they have constituted for Catholic institutions a sort of second-level problem of adjustment — an ever changing pattern from which Catholics could not depart too far in their own efforts to respond to the primary changes in the Catholic population and in American society generally.

The following discussion stresses the divergence of Catholic institutions from the American norm and their efforts to bring themselves into line; but this stress should not be taken to mean that they were totally different from

[1] An excellent recent survey is Frederick Rudolph, *The American College and University* (New York: Alfred A. Knopf, 1962); also very useful are George P. Schmidt, *The Liberal Arts College* (New Brunswick, N.J.: Rutgers University Press, 1957); and Richard Hofstadter and Walter P. Metzger, *The Development of Academic Freedom in the United States* (New York: Columbia University Press, 1955).

the rest. The difference was always one of degree, and since the Catholic schools existed in the same society and were subject to the same basic pressures, there are many parallels between them and non-Catholic institutions.[2] The development of Catholic higher education has, in fact, followed the same general pattern as that of non-Catholic colleges and universities, but has lagged chronologically. This lag is partly owing to the simple fact that, since there were so few Catholics in this country until the second quarter of the nineteenth century, higher education was naturally slow to develop; other factors involved will be discussed in the remainder of the essay. But this is perhaps as appropriate a place as any to present a few statistics, since they illustrate the similarity between Catholic institutions and others, and because they will provide some basic data on the extent of Catholic activity in higher education.

Reliable statistical information is lacking for most of the nineteenth century, but it is clear that until after the Civil War the characteristic American college was small, denominational, and had a very uncertain life expectancy. Catholic colleges resembled the others in these respects. The first, Georgetown, opened its doors with just one student registered in 1791; by 1850, forty-one more colleges had been founded, but only twelve (including Georgetown) endured to the present day. With the massive immigration of the mid-century, the founding of Catholic colleges accelerated. The single decade of the 1850's saw as many new institutions (42) as had been founded in the previous sixty years; and between 1860 and 1920, no fewer than 156 Catholic colleges were established, of which thirty-six survived as permanent institutions. New schools were less numerous during the 1920's and 1930's, but have increased somewhat in the post-World War II educational boom. Catholic women's colleges, particularly, have grown phenomenally in the twentieth century, but we can say little about them in this essay. The *Official Catholic Directory* for 1965 gives 304 as the grand total of American Catholic colleges and universities today.[3]

In the twentieth century, the most significant growth in Catholic, as in

---

[2] Rudolph speaks of the "remarkable degree" to which Catholic institutions resembled "any other denominational colleges." *Amer. College and Univ.*, p. 514. My colleague Bernard J. Kohlbrenner has called my attention to the fact, as deserving of emphasis here, that Catholic colleges differed from Protestant ones in that they could not train ministers directly, whereas this was the chief function of the early Protestant colleges. Edward J. Power, *A History of Catholic Higher Education in the United States* (Milwaukee: Bruce Pub. Co., 1958), pp. 35–36, discusses this point. The development of American Catholic seminaries will not be treated in the present essay. For a recent general study, see *Seminary Education in a Time of Change*, eds. James Michael Lee and Louis J. Putz, C.S.C. (Notre Dame, Ind.: Fides Publishers, 1965), especially the first two chapters of historical background by John Tracy Ellis.

[3] John M. Daley, S.J., *Georgetown University: Origin and Early Years* (Washington, D.C.: Georgetown University Press, 1957), pp. 64, 67–68; Power, *Hist. of Catholic Higher Ed.*, pp. 333–39. Richard O. Poorman, C.S.C., "The Small

secular, higher education has been in the size of enrollments rather than in the numbers of institutions. No Catholic university rivals the great public universities in size, but compared to their earlier proportions a number of Catholic schools have experienced tremendous growth. In 1900, for example, Boston College was the largest of the Jesuit schools, having just over 400 students in its high school and college departments combined; today it has nearly 10,000 students. St. John's University (New York) had a total of 550 students in 1916, of whom 351 were in the preparatory department; now it has a total enrollment of upwards of 13,000 and is experiencing some very severe growing pains.[4]

Enrollment statistics for the whole range of Catholic institutions of higher education are treacherous because one can never be sure that uniform categories and procedures are being used everywhere; for the same reason, comparisons between Catholic enrollments and totals for all colleges and universities are uncertain. In view of these complications, we are especially fortunate to be able to draw on a careful comparative study covering the quarter-century in which the massive expansion in higher education began. Table 1 sets out the principal findings of the study.[5] This survey, made by the Catholic Educational Association in 1916, shows that in the decade of the 1890's, the pace of Catholic collegiate growth was lagging sadly behind the national average; after 1900, however, the Catholic growth rate caught up to and then exceeded the over-all rate. According to a study made in the 1950's, Catholic college enrollments continued to grow faster than the national average during the period 1920–50.[6]

But leaving aside the question of comparative growth rates, the increase

Catholic College; A Second Look," *Catholic Educational Review*, 63 (March, 1965), 149 n., discusses the wide variation in enumerations of American Catholic institutions of higher education.

[4] David R. Dunigan, S.J., *A History of Boston College* (Milwaukee: Bruce Pub. Co., 1947), p. 179; *Catholic Educational Association Bulletin*, 12 (Aug., 1916), 14; Francis Canavan, S.J., "Academic Revolution at St. John's," *America*, 113 (Aug. 7, 1965), 136–40. *Catholic Educational Association Bulletin* hereafter cited as *CEAB*, or *NCEAB* after 1929 when the word "National" was added to the name of the association.

[5] Adapted from James A. Burns, C.S.C., and Francis W. Howard, "Report on the Attendance at Catholic Colleges and Universities in the United States," *CEAB*, 12 (Aug. 1916), 7, 9; hereafter cited as "Burns-Howard Report, 1916." The figures given for total enrollment in all institutions are much lower than those in U.S. Bureau of the Census, *Historical Statistics of the United States, Colonial Times to 1957* (Washington, D.C.: Government Printing Office, 1960), pp. 210–11, because Burns and Howard excluded all categories of students not comparable to the ones they were using from Catholic colleges. The presence of secondary level students in Catholic colleges swelled the total enrollments much above what is given for "collegiate" enrollment. Respectively, for each of the years given above, the total enrollment in Catholic colleges and universities was: 8,487; 11,703; 21,174; and 32,256.

[6] *NCEAB*, 50 (Aug., 1953), 201.

in absolute numbers has been tremendous since World War I. In 1930 there were approximately 102,000 students in Catholic colleges and universities; it is likely the method of counting was different from that employed in the earlier computations, but even including secondary-level students there were only some 32,000 enrolled in Catholic colleges for men in 1916, and the few real colleges for women would not have raised the total very much.

TABLE 1
CATHOLIC AND TOTAL COLLEGIATE
ENROLLMENT, 1890–1916.

	1890	1900	% Increase over Previous Date	1907	% Increase	1916	% Increase
Catholic collegiate enrollment[a]	2,972	4,220	42.0	6,689	58.5	14,846	121.9
Total collegiate enrollment[b]	60,259	101,483	68.4	129,416	27.5	190,278[c]	47.2

[a] Includes undergraduate, graduate, and professional students; excludes summer school and engineering students and duplicates.
[b] Includes Catholic and non-Catholic schools in categories that can be compared with figures used for Catholic institutions. Women are excluded.
[c] For 1915 instead of 1916.

Hence, by 1930 there was a threefold increase in actual numbers of students, and an important qualitative change since the preparatory departments were a thing of the past, and high school students were no longer counted as part of the Catholic college population. By 1940 the Catholic enrollment figure stood at about 162,000, and the postwar tidal wave brought it to 293,000 in 1948. There was a temporary decline after the veterans passed through, but by 1962 enrollments had exceeded the previous high water mark, and the trend seems steadily upward.[7] The *Official Catholic Directory* gives an enrollment figure of 384,526 for 1965.

The tremendous expansion of Catholic higher education has been a response to the changes going on in American society at large and in the Catholic sector of the population. It is, therefore, an aspect of the social adjustment of Catholic higher education and we now turn to a fuller consideration of some of these social factors.

THE SOCIAL ADJUSTMENT

Aside from the Spanish and French, who were on the fringes of the mainstream of development in what was to become the United States, the first

[7] For the 1930 figure see, *America*, 44 (Jan. 3, 1931), 313; for the later years, *National Catholic Almanac*, 1944 (Paterson, N.J.: St. Anthony's Guild, 1944), p. 336; *National Catholic Almanac*, 1951 (Paterson, N.J.: St. Anthony's Guild, 1951), p. 363; *Official Guide to Catholic Educational Institutions* (Rockville Centre, N.Y.: Catholic Institutional Director, 1963), p. 3.

American Catholics were a handful of colonists in Maryland and Pennsylvania. Although they were few in number — no more than 35,000 in 1790 — and labored under severe legal and social disabilities in the colonial era, by 1800 these Anglo-American Catholics were becoming accepted as a legitimate, but numerically insignificant, segment of American society. Their leaders were old settlers of English derivation who had participated in the struggle for independence and had achieved some wealth and status; hence Catholics could claim to be birthright partners in the new republic, and except for religion, they did not diverge too markedly from the cultural norms of the larger society. This situation changed dramatically with the onset of massive immigration, for the immigrants not only vastly enlarged the Catholic population, they also changed its character radically.[8]

The cultural assimilation of the church was delayed for generations by the coming of the immigrants because they made it an entirely different kind of social organism. Instead of remaining a small group much like other Americans in social background and outlook, little disposed to call attention to themselves in matters where they differed from the majority, Catholics became almost overnight a throng of foreigners who were poor, uncultivated, and sometimes aggressive in demanding that their religious rights be respected. Although it furnished the nucleus around which the American church was to grow, the Anglo-American group seemed to be swamped by the hordes of Irish and Germans, and the church threatened to become an Irish rather than an American institution.

This prospect gave rise to the first explicit "Americanization" crisis in Catholic history, the first time a controversy arose among Catholics themselves over the proper cultural adjustment to American society, and specifically over the need to eliminate foreign nationalism to permit the development of a truly "American" Catholicism. The chief critic of the tendency to equate Catholicism with Irishism was Orestes A. Brownson, the most distinguished thinker and writer to arise among American Catholics in the nineteenth century. Brownson, a convert of New England stock, was offended by the distaste for Yankees openly avowed by many Irish Catholics, and by the assumption, which they seemed to hold implicitly, that an American could not embrace Catholicism without turning his back upon his own nationality and culture. Brownson bluntly told his fellow Catholics that the American nationality was already set in a basically Anglo-Saxon mold, that they would have to conform to it whether they liked it or not, and that the sooner they dissociated their faith from their alien nationality, the better would Catholicism thrive in the United States. Brownson's argument was to the point, but the

---

[8] I am following here the interpretation advanced by Thomas T. McAvoy, C.S.C., "The Catholic Minority in the United States, 1789–1821," *Historical Records and Studies*, 39–40 (1952), 33–50; "The Formation of the Catholic Minority in the United States, 1820–1860," *Review of Politics*, 10 (Jan., 1948), 13–34.

timing was unfortunate: coming at the height of the Know-Nothing furor and sharing, as Brownson conceded, much of the nativists' perspective, his criticism only aroused resentment in Irish Catholics.[9]

The crisis of the 1850's was brief, and by the time the issue came up again thirty years later the Irish were the leading champions of Americanization and the Germans, who had not taken part at all in the earlier skirmishes, were the chief resisters of "Americanism." But the episode of the 1850's is significant because it reflects a recurrent problem for the American church; and it is of special interest here because it reveals how closely education is related to the complex matter of the cultural assimilation of Catholics in American society. For Brownson realized that Catholic opposition to the common schools sprang as much from ethnic and cultural as from religious grounds, and he asserted that many of the weaknesses of Catholic education were traceable to its foreign coloration and to the fact that the immigrants came from "the more uncultivated classes of the Old World." Indeed, Brownson's lack of sympathy with the ethnic purposes of Catholic education gave him a detachment that made his analysis remarkably penetrating and allowed him to anticipate many of the criticisms now being made by Catholics who no longer have ethnic interests that they expect Catholic schools to serve.[10]

The situation in the 1850's was, of course, very much more complicated than these brief remarks may suggest, and it would be interesting to linger here and explore the matter in greater detail. Instead we must be content to look quickly, and in a very general way, at three aspects of the social evolution of the Catholic population. These aspects, which were operative in the fifties and for a long time after, are: (a) the educational implications of the fact that the Catholic immigrants came from "the more uncultivated classes"; (b) the relationship between higher education and efforts to preserve ethnic identity; and (c) the effect on higher education of improvements in the social and economic status of Catholics.

Not only the Irish and, to a lesser degree, the Germans, but also the later Italian and Slavic Catholics came predominantly from peasant, agricultural backgrounds. It is an understatement to say they had no intellectual tradition. Fewer than half of Ireland's pre-famine population could read or write,

[9] "Native Americanism," *Brownson's Quarterly Review* (3d ser.), 2 (July, 1854), 328–54; "The Know-Nothings," *ibid.* (Oct., 1854), 447–87; *Celts and Saxons . . . A Complete Refutation of the Nativism of Dr. Orestes A. Brownson. By the Catholic Press of the United States* (Boston: Thomas Sweeney, 1854).

[10] Cf. "Schools and Education," *Brownson's Quarterly Review* (3d ser.), 2 (July, 1854), 372–73; "Catholic Schools and Education," *ibid.* (3d N.Y. ser.), 3 (Jan. 1862), 66–84, which is reprinted in Neil G. McCluskey, S.J., *Catholic Education in America* (New York: Columbia University Press, 1964), pp. 95–120; "Public and Parochial Schools," *Brownson's Quarterly Review* (N.Y. ser.), 4 (July, 1859), 324–42; "Conversations of Our Club," *The Works of Orestes A. Brownson,* ed. Henry F. Brownson (Detroit: T.-Nourse, 1884), XI, 410–31.

and adult Polish and southern Italian immigrants had illiteracy rates of 35.4 per cent and 54.2 per cent, respectively. Formal education simply did not figure at all in the background of many Catholic immigrants; moreover, the peasant culture from which they came probably habituated them to acceptance of traditional ways and inhibited the development of high educational aspirations. Unless one aspired to the priesthood, education beyond the most basic skills served no functional purpose in peasant society; and the antagonism of the Irish and the Poles toward their foreign rulers spilled over into suspicion of the national schools. Since they were at the mercy of natural forces, of landlords, or of foreign political oppressors, peasants often developed a fatalistic outlook or despaired of their capacity to control their own destinies. The sense of inadequacy or inferiority fostered by such a heritage was directly opposed to the attitudes most useful in sustaining high educational or intellectual ambitions. Family solidarity, which was stressed in peasant culture, likewise operated to discourage young people from cutting themselves away from the limited intellectual universe in which their families had always dwelt.[11] Thus there was nothing in the family background of most Catholic immigrants to stimulate them to exploit to the fullest the educational opportunities of American society; and a survey taken in 1957 showed that children of the more Americanized, older, immigrant groups had a higher opinion of their own intellectual capabilities and were more likely to take a college education for granted than the children of more recent Catholic immigrant stock.[12]

The traditional peasant societies from which Catholic immigrants came were in the process of dissolution; the influences listed above were modified by others; those who emigrated had already made an important break with tradition, and after the immigrants got to America they had to adapt themselves to a very untraditional society that demanded more positive attitudes toward education. Nonetheless, the peasant heritage did exert a negative influence that should not be overlooked in a review of Catholic higher education in the United States. This does not mean, however, that immigrants were uninterested in education. On the contrary, they were deeply — and some-

[11] Philip Gleason, "Immigration and American Catholic Intellectual Life," *Review of Politics*, 26 (April, 1964), 154–56; George Potter, *To the Golden Door* (Boston: Little, Brown & Co., 1960), pp. 84–85, 433–34, 606–7; Brownson, "Conversation of Our Club," p. 417 ff.

[12] Andrew M. Greeley, *Religion and Career* (New York: Sheed & Ward, 1963), pp. 100, 187. Timothy L. Smith of the University of Minnesota, who read my chapter in draft, believes that this discussion overstresses the negative influence of the peasant background. He points out that there was great variety in the backgrounds of the immigrants, even of those who came from the countryside and small villages. The whole question needs much more study; but I would maintain that the presumption must be disproved that the social and educational background of most Catholic immigrants exercised a negative effect on their intellectual and educational aspirations in the United States.

what ambivalently — concerned about it. The ambivalence arose from the partially contradictory functions they wished the schools to fulfill.

The school faces both past and future: the past in its role as conserver and transmitter of the knowledge and values of the race; the future in its role as preparer of the young for the world that awaits them tomorrow. Insofar as the schools dealt with the past, the immigrant's desires were anti-assimilationist in tendency — the knowledge, values, and traditions he wanted to see preserved and transmitted were those of the ethnic group. Thus the young would grow up with a sense of common identity and an awareness of the links that bound them to the generation of their fathers. But in respect to the preparatory function of education, the immigrant's expectations were assimilationist in tendency — he wanted schools that would give children the best preparation for success in life, and to do that the schools had to transcend the narrow horizons of ethnic consciousness. Just as the individual immigrant was torn between the drive to improve his status and the desire to maintain the familiar ways of the past, so the schools of the immigrants were called on to meet two conflicting requirements — to keep alive an alien past and to prepare the young for the unpredictable demands of a strange and novel society.

The role of the schools in preserving ethnic identity can only be hinted at here, and in any event this function was characteristically centered in the lower schools rather than in the colleges. In fact, higher education was a dubious business from the viewpoint of ethnic interests. On the one hand, the need for leaders was clearly perceived and most Catholic immigrant groups founded separate colleges and seminaries to help create an elite. The German Catholics even talked of establishing their own European-style university in the 1870's and again around 1910; the French-Canadians in New England provided scholarships for young men who showed promise of developing into leaders who would foster "race patriotism" and reinforce "the ranks of the survival propagandists." But it was also clear to the rank and file who were called upon to support the colleges and scholarship programs that higher education often had the effect of moving a person "up and out" of the ethnic group.[13] Such cases illustrated that in their function of promoting social mobility, the colleges were working at cross purposes to the preservation of group identity and integrity: higher education often served to siphon off leaders rather than to return them better prepared to their own people.

Language played a crucial role in all efforts to preserve ethnic identity, and we must pause to examine it, especially in view of the distinctive situation

[13] F. P. Kenkel, "An Extraordinary Project," *Central-Blatt and Social Justice*, 18 (Dec. 1925, Feb., 1926), 305–8, 377–78; *Catholic Fortnightly Review*, 17 (1910), 89; E. B. Ham, "French National Societies in New England," *New England Quarterly*, 12 (1939), 324–25; Gleason, "Immigration and Intellectual Life," pp. 161–62.

of the Irish. For non-English-speaking immigrants, the mother tongue was not merely the most treasured symbol of their identity; it was also an essential element in their identity, and at the same time a powerful agency for preserving it.[14] Language was a more specific, concrete, tangible element in a people's heritage than their nationality or even their religion; and it was also a highly visible indicator of their over-all success or failure in maintaining their culture. But language was not looked upon by the immigrant as a distinct element, separable from nationality or religion; rather, all three were intimately blended together to constitute an undifferentiated whole. Loss of language and loss of faith were presumed to go hand in hand, and it was a religious duty to preserve the mother tongue. Naturally, the schools were expected to make a major contribution to language maintenance. In 1887, to give but one example, the German-American Catholics were told that they must insist on the use of the mother tongue in their colleges because the parochial schools alone were inadequate to insure the survival of the German language.[15]

In these circumstances, cultural assimilation was naturally looked upon as a theological as well as a social problem. Among Polish-Americans this view was still entertained in the 1940's, and almost a century earlier the Irish Catholic *Pilot* of Boston had called attention to "the dangerous process of assimilation" that was reflected in the non-Catholic tone of the commencement orations at Holy Cross College in 1858.[16] But although the Irish were aware of the spiritual perils of assimilation, the process was both easier and more subtle for them because there was no language barrier to overcome; consequently, there was likewise no language shift to serve as a barometer of the changing cultural climate. The Irish had already lost their mother tongue and had discovered as a result that loss of faith did not automatically accompany loss of language. Since they already spoke English on their arrival in America, the Irish were spared the terrible social and psychic expense of resisting linguistic assimilation; and not having a linguistic object upon which to fasten, they focused, as it were, the undiffracted strength of their ethnic loyalty on Catholicism — and to a much lesser degree on Irish political

[14] The most elaborate investigation of language and ethnicity is a mammoth three volume report (dittoed) to the U. S. Office of Education, Washington, D.C., 1964, on *Language Loyalty in the United States* prepared by Joshua A. Fishman *et al.* My discussion owes much to George F. Theriault's analysis in "The Franco-Americans in a New England Community: An Experiment in Survival" (Ph.D. dissertation, Harvard University, 1951); see especially pp. 378–79, 538 ff.

[15] *Verhandlungen der ersten allgemeinen amerikanisch-deutschen Katholiken-Versammlung zu Chicago, Ill., am 6. September 1887* (Cincinnati: Benziger Bros. Inc. 1887), p. 40.

[16] Russell Barta, "The Concept of Secularization as a Social Process" (Ph.D. dissertation, University of Notre Dame, 1959), p. 89; Potter, *To the Golden Door*, p. 606.

nationalism. As a result of this historical accident, the ethnic heritage of the Irish was unusually well suited for adaptation to American life; it had assumed a predominantly religious form and, unlike language, religion was not a sphere of life in which drastic modifications were required for successful acculturation.[17]

As a matter of public policy, the United States was officially hospitable to religious diversity, and the conditions of American life permitted religious diversity to flourish; the state was officially indifferent to linguistic diversity, but in practice social and economic pressures made the adoption of English inevitable sooner or later. In emphasizing their religious heritage and making it the most important symbol of their common consciousness as a people, the Irish were following their ethnic instincts and at the same time acting the part of good Americans; indeed, their very resistance to religious assimilation, i.e., Protestant proselytizing, was defensible on the highest grounds of Americanism itself. Yet in language — the area in which conformity to American practice was in fact inexorably required — the Irish could conform with wholehearted good will, without hesitation or sense of betrayal, and without the language conflicts between older and younger generations that so often occurred in other groups. The very ease with which the Irish assimilated sometimes made them feel more "American" than other immigrant groups; and it is perhaps understandable if they felt baffled as well as resentful when people like Brownson reminded them that they were not yet fully American either.

The special relation of Catholicism and group consciousness among the Irish, along with their freedom from linguistic difficulties, had important implications for Catholic higher education. It meant, first of all, that the immigrants who arrived earliest, and in the largest numbers, and who became the dominant group in American Catholicism, had no trouble at all adjusting to American higher education so far as language was concerned. It also meant that their colleges were never linguistically isolated from the rest of American society. And although there can be little doubt that these colleges enlisted and symbolized ethnic as well as religious loyalties, their status in this regard was peculiarly ambiguous and complex. These institutions could not be thought of as exclusively Irish because Catholicism is, after all, a universal religion and not the unique possession of the Irish people — as their language would have been. Any Catholic who spoke English could attend these colleges because their Irish ethnic complexion was only accidental, whereas their Catholicity was the distinctive quality. Thus the religious dimension of

---

[17] Compare Nathan Glazer, "The Process and Problems of Language-Maintenance: An Integrative Review," in Fishman, *Language Loyalty in the U.S.*, chap. 20. Cf. Colman J. Barry, O.S.B., *Woship and Work; Saint John's Abbey and University, 1856–1956* (Collegeville, Minn.: St. John's University Press, 1956), p. 148, for brief reference to the difficulties of linguistic transition at a German Catholic foundation.

these colleges did not need to contract with the gradual attenuation of Irish self-consciousness. Rather, as the "Irish Catholics" became "American Catholics," it was relatively easy for the colleges to adapt themselves to the change.

The evolution and transmutation of ethnic feeling among the several groups that make up the Catholic population has hardly been studied at all, and we know even less about how all this is related to the functions that colleges and universities have performed.[18] But it seems reasonably certain that these processes are not over and that shifts currently under way in the nature of the group basis of American Catholicism have profound implications for Catholic higher education and deserve much deeper study than they have yet received.

Advancement in occupational status, wealth, and social prestige has accompanied the cultural assimilation of the Catholic population, partially as a cause and partially as an effect, for upward mobility and assimilation are interrelated aspects of the same process. These reciprocating developments are in turn related both to generational change and to education. Again, we know much less about these matters than we should, but perhaps we can glimpse some of the forces at work by looking at the situation around the turn of the century, and again in the 1950's.

By 1900 the American church was entering its second-generation stage, at least so far as its "old immigrant" contingent was concerned. Second-generation Irish outnumbered the foreign-born Irish by two to one in the population at large, and by 52.6 per cent in the male labor force. Among the Germans, the next largest Catholic group, the trend was also clear, although not so far advanced: second-generation Germans were 17 per cent more numerous than first among those the Census Bureau called "male breadwinners."[19] The Catholic college population reflected these transitions and also the ethnic complexion of the general Catholic population. Statistics from nine Catholic colleges gathered by the Immigration Commission in 1908 showed that third-generation students (i.e., those whose fathers were native-born Americans) actually outnumbered the second-generation (native-born of foreign fathers) by 386 to 381. Students of Irish derivation accounted for about 60 per cent (228) of the second-generation total, and Germans just over 19 per cent (73); other nationalities were represented by only a handful of students.[20] The ethnic distribution of the third generation is unknown, but presumably it too would show a preponderance of Irish.

[18] David Riesman and Christopher Jencks discuss the ethnic dimensions of Boston College briefly in "The Viability of the American College" in *The American College*, ed. Nevitt Sanford (New York: John Wiley & Sons, 1962), pp. 147 ff.

[19] Dorothy Ross, "The Irish-Catholic Immigrant, 1880–1900: A Study in Social Mobility" (Master's thesis, Columbia University, n.d.), p. 37; *Reports of the Immigration Commission* (Washington, D.C.: Government Printing Office, 1911), XXVIII, 162.

[20] Derived from *ibid.*, XXXIII, 717, 719, 720, 723, 726, 730, 731.

The coming-of-age of the second generation was accompanied by rapid improvement in the socioeconomic status of American Catholics. The Irish were moving upward with noteworthy speed, thanks in large part, no doubt, to the relative ease with which they assimilated and to their concentration in large cities where educational and employment opportunities were best. The advance between the first and second generations in professional occupations is a conventional index of upward social mobility, and it has obvious connections with educational aspirations. Analysis of the census of 1900 shows that the Irish were outdistancing the Germans in their rate of penetration into professional ranks and had improved their position remarkably since the previous census. In 1890, the only professional category in which the Irish were represented in proportion to their numbers in the labor force was "government officials"; by 1900, they were even more strongly over-represented in this category and in three additional ones: actors, journalists, and lawyers. That same census showed that in the group called "literary and scientific persons," the Irish were represented exactly in proportion to their total presence in the labor force.[21] Young women of Irish descent were also invading the new profession of schoolteaching in such numbers that by 1910 the Irish constituted 20 per cent or more of the public schoolteaching force in New York, Chicago, Boston, San Francisco, and eight other cities.[22]

These social changes affected Catholic colleges and universities in a number of ways. They created a much greater demand for higher education for both men and women; over-all enrollments climbed, and the beginnings of true collegiate work for women — in summer schools, in separate women's colleges, and in coeducational schools — dates from this period.[23] The need to provide professional training caused a number of Catholic institutions to add medical, dental, and other professional schools to their liberal arts colleges. The emergence of a small wealthy Catholic elite led to a limited but symptomatic agitation for more exclusive Catholic colleges [24] and to increased attendance at socially prestigious non-Catholic institutions. But

[21] *Ibid.*, XXVIII, 57–58; E. P. Hutchinson, *Immigrants and their Children, 1850–1950* (New York: John Wiley & Sons, 1956), p. 132; Ross, "Irish-Catholic Immigrant," p. 57. In 1900, only 1.9% of the first-generation Irish male breadwinners were in professional occupations, as opposed to 3.7% of the second generation; for the Germans, the comparable percentages were 2.4 and 3.0.

[22] *Reports of the Immigration Commission*, XXIX, 137–39.

[23] Women's colleges need much more study. Presently available are Sr. M. Mariella Bowler, *A History of Catholic Colleges for Women in the United States of America* (Washington, D.C.: Catholic University of America Press, 1933); Mother Grace Dammann, R.S.C.J., "The American Catholic College for Women" in *Essays on Catholic Education in the United States*, ed. Roy J. Deferrari (Washington, D.C.; Catholic University of America Press, 1942), pp. 173–94; Power, *History of Catholic Higher Education*, chap. 7.

[24] See the communication of Thomas Kernan in *New York Freeman's Journal*, Oct. 8, 1898.

attendance at secular universities was not confined to the very wealthy; on the contrary, it was widespread and reflected a rising level of educational aspirations among rich and poor Catholics alike. Harvard, it is true, had more Catholic students than any other non-Catholic institution, according to a survey made in 1907; but the next highest enrollment of Catholics was at Valparaiso University, an Indiana school that called itself "the poor man's Harvard" and specialized in low-cost education.[25]

The improved social status of Catholics was partially responsible for the drift to non-Catholic institutions of higher education, but it was even more clearly a function of a larger development in American society generally — the vast expansion of secondary and higher education that began in the closing decades of the nineteenth century. Catholic educators, however, were understandably disturbed by the drift to secular universities and placed much of the blame on the materialistic influences of American society; but they also realized that the dissatisfaction with Catholic colleges, which the movement reflected, would have to be remedied by some sort of corrective action on their part. Catholic colleges had to be brought more closely into line with the mainstream of American higher education, their curricula made more flexible and more relevant to the needs of contemporary society, and their facilities enlarged to accommodate a vastly expanded clientele. These tasks were undertaken in a long effort of reorganization that extended from around 1900 until after World War I. This reorganization, which we shall examine more closely in the next section, brought Catholic undergraduate education into line with American practice and set the stage for the tremendous growth it has since experienced.[26]

Social changes in the Catholic population were thus deeply involved in the modernization of Catholic higher education in the present century. But not all American Catholics were equally well situated to take advantage of the newly improved system of higher education. The Italian, Slavic, French-Canadian, and Spanish-speaking Catholics were, because of the lateness of their immigration or for other special reasons, stuck at the first-generation stage of assimilation through the early decades of the twentieth century, and the depression and World War II further inhibited college attendance for many.[27] Consequently, the full assimilation of the Catholic population

[25] *CEAB*, 4 (Nov., 1907), 153–57. Cf. John Strietelmeier, *Valparaiso's First Century* (Valparaiso, Ind.: The University, 1959), chap. 3. Harvard had 480 Catholic students and Radcliffe had 43 Catholic women; Valparaiso, which was not at that time a Lutheran institution, had 300 Catholic men students and 100 Catholic women.

[26] There is no account of the reorganization, but it may be followed in the yearly proceedings of the Catholic Educational Association. James A. Burns, C.S.C., *Catholic Education: A Study of Conditions* (New York: Longmans, Green & Co., 1917), chaps. 6, 8, provides a little information about it.

[27] Cf. Leonard Covello, "The Social Background on the Italo-American School Child" (Ph.D. dissertation, New York University, 1944); Nathan Glazer and

considered as a whole was held back by these groups until very recent times. But now the situation is changing rapidly, and even the fragmentary evidence available indicates unmistakably that American Catholicism has reached a new plateau of cultural assimilation and socioeconomic status. As a result, Catholics now share much more fully in the sophistication, the intellectual orientation, and the educational concern that are characteristic of the American upper-middle class. An immigrant leavening of refugee scholars and intellectuals during the 1930's and 1940's also provided a very valuable intellectual stimulus to Catholic academic life.

The contrasts shown between the generation of Catholic professors recently investigated by John Donovan and the present generation of Catholic undergraduates studied by Andrew Greeley indicate the extent to which the social and educational balance has shifted in the last few years. These studies show that persons derived from the oldest and largest Catholic ethnic stock, the Irish, are most numerous in the ranks of both the professors and the students. But only one-third of Donovan's professors, the older generation, had fathers in professional or managerial occupations, compared to more than half of the 1961 graduates of the Catholic colleges included in Greeley's study. The students of 1961, 42 per cent of whom lived in the suburbs, also came from homes where there was a much higher probability that intellectual and cultural interests would be nurtured — the student in the Catholic college was in fact three times more likely than his professor to be the son of a college-educated man (44% as against 13%). There was still a sizeable group of students whose fathers had only a grade school education (27%), but better than half again as many of the professors (44%) were in the same category. Students in Catholic colleges represented a higher socioeconomic group than the Catholics attending secular schools, but taken together the Catholics were abreast or a little in advance of their Protestant fellow students in occupational and economic — but not educational — background, whereas the Catholic professors lagged behind their Protestant counterparts in these areas.

The differences in the backgrounds of the professors and the 1961 graduates are striking. They become even more so when we consider that the social and educational background of an academically elite group like the professors probably ranged further above the Catholic median than does the background of today's undergraduate. The cream of yesterday's

Daniel P. Moynihan, *Beyond the Melting Pot* (Cambridge, Mass.: Harvard University Press, 1963), pp. 199–202; Theriault, "Franco-Americans in New Engl.," p. 417 ff; Julian Samora points out that among the Spanish-speaking in the U. S., "the *greatest* [educational] need at the moment is not at the university level, but rather at the junior and senior high school level and the freshman college level." See the section headed "Recommendations" of Samora, "The Spanish-Speaking People in the United States," A pilot study prepared for the United States Commission on Civil Rights (Notre Dame, Ind.: dittoed, n.d.)

Catholic academic crop, so to speak, came from much less favorably situated social strata than does the ordinary Catholic collegian of today.[28]

An appreciation of the nature, extent, and implications of these social changes is essential for an understanding of the present situation in Catholic higher education. The studies of Donovan and Greeley clearly suggest that the Catholic population has very nearly completed its social adjustment; the "typical Catholic" now approximates the "typical American" — his sense of ethnic distinctiveness is attenuated, and he does not differ very much from his fellow citizens in occupation, wealth, or status. Today more than ever before in their history, the Catholic colleges are dealing with fully Americanized students.

THE INSTITUTIONAL ADJUSTMENT

Catholic higher education still departs from the American institutional pattern in one important respect, clerical control, and it has already made important institutional adjustments in respect to organizational structure and graduate work. We shall take up these points in order.

The degree of clerical control over Catholic higher education has recently become the object of a good deal of criticism by Catholics, and some modifications are likely in the not-too-distant future. But ecclesiastical control passed from the scene so far as the majority of American colleges and universities is concerned more than a half century ago. That it has taken so long before we have even the beginnings of a movement to change the Catholic pattern indicates that clerical direction has very deep roots in the Catholic system. The very persistence of the phenomenon invites careful analysis of its origin, development, and rationale.

We can give the matter only the most cursory examination here, but even a moment's reflection is sufficient to suggest one reason why Catholic institutions have so tenaciously adhered to clerically dominated control in higher education. That is the fact that the transition to lay control of American colleges and universities in the late nineteenth century was part and parcel

[28] John D. Donovan, *The Academic Man in the Catholic College* (New York: Sheed & Ward, 1964), pp. 52–58; Greeley, *Religion and Career*, pp. 28, 31 ff., 148, 176. John Whitney Evans, "Has the Catholic Intellectual a Future in America," *Sociology of Education*, 38 (1965), 150–63, is a good comparative discussion of these two works. I am aware that Greeley's findings have been challenged on methodological grounds; but so far as I have seen, the critics have not yet proved their case. David Riesman, who read this chapter in draft, questioned whether the academically elite group studied by Donovan was also socially elite, and he speculated that perhaps they came from lower social strata than those of their own generation who became doctors and lawyers. This is, of course, possible; but I leave the original paragraph standing, because the hypothesis advanced there is also plausible and we cannot say which is correct on the basis of the evidence presently available.

of the larger movement of secularization that involved a change in the spirit and outlook of higher education as well as the displacement of ministers from the seats of power.[29] Before the Civil War the characteristic institution of American higher education was the small church-related college that was usually academically inferior, but that took religion very seriously; the characteristic institution in 1900 was the large secular university, under state control or in private but nonecclesiastical hands, that was dedicated to science and scholarship and concerned with preparing students for life in this world, not the next. Since Catholic colleges and universities have retained their deep religious commitment much longer than most other American institutions, it does not seem unnatural that they should also retain the type of ecclesiastical control that obtained generally when religiously oriented education was the rule. Viewed in this light, clerical control may be understood as the institutional reflection of the ideological gap that has separated Catholic from secular higher education.

It is true that Catholic lay educators share the same religious beliefs and values as priests, brothers, or nuns; and there is no reason why a layman cannot be as well equipped from the religious point of view to guide a Catholic college as a cleric. Laymen have, in fact, operated a few Catholic colleges at various times in our history, beginning with Calvert College in Maryland in 1852,[30] but the extent of this activity has been almost infinitesimal.

There are many reasons why lay control of Catholic educational undertakings has been practically nonexistent, but two stand out. The first is that historically the layman's competence in matters religious, if granted at all, has been considered inferior to that of clerics. Priests and "religious" — the term itself is significant — are, after all, specialists in matters religious, and the layman has historically been considered one whose main interests were not religious. There is no need to insist here that this view is unsatisfactory; the point is that only very recently have efforts been made to formulate a more adequate theology of the laity or to clarify the different functions that are appropriate to ordained persons and lay persons. Throughout American Catholic history the accepted view was that if an activity was religious, a priest, or at least a religious, should be in charge of it; and education was viewed as such an activity.

But in addition to the hitherto almost universal opinion that control of higher education should be in the hands of clerics, the historical fact is that nearly all of the Catholic colleges were founded and maintained by religious orders that, as self-perpetuating bodies with a natural disinclination to organizational hara-kiri, have simply retained in their own hands control of the institutions they established. So vital is the role played by religious orders

[29] Cf. Hofstadter and Metzger, *Academic Freedom*, pp. 344–63.
[30] Sebastian A. Erbacher, O.F.M., *Catholic Higher Education for Men in the United States, 1850–1866* (Washington, D.C.: Catholic University of America Press, 1931), p. 34.

in the development of Catholic colleges that it is almost impossible to visualize what the history of Catholic higher education would have been without them. If there had been no religious communities, presumably the religious idealism and spirit of dedication which they mobilized would have found other institutional expressions; and if the Catholic church was to enter the field of higher education at all, much more responsibility for it would necessarily have fallen on laymen, either acting by themselves or in concert with diocesan clergy. But the religious orders did, in fact, already exist when the need arose for Catholic colleges in the United States, and a number of them specialized in educational work. Because of their superior organization and discipline, their experience, their resources of personnel, and the degree of permanence that their corporate character lent to their undertakings, the religious orders were incomparably better equipped to establish and operate colleges than either laymen or the diocesan clergy.

The earliest colleges were founded by bishops who were primarily concerned with preparing priests or recruiting candidates for the priesthood from the lay students, and up to about 1840 the "diocesan influence was supreme"[31] in the development of Catholic higher education. But the early bishops had too few priests to handle the normal pastoral work and they found it extremely difficult to man their colleges; consequently, they were eager to attract religious communities who could take them over, and after the Catholic population began to grow rapidly with the massive immigration, the religious orders became the overwhelmingly dominant element in higher education. By 1866, for example, there were sixty Catholic colleges, all men's schools; three were operated by laymen, ten by diocesan priests, and forty-seven by religious communities. Fifty years later there were no lay-operated men's colleges among the eighty-four surveyed by the Catholic Educational Association, only six were in the hands of diocesan priests, and all the rest — roughly 93 per cent of the total — were run by religious orders.[32]

Such dominance of the field argues convincingly that the religious order was the most effective agency available to American Catholics in carrying on the work of higher education; and it seems highly doubtful that without the orders we would have anything like the extensive system of colleges and universities that exists today. This does not mean of course that their predominance has not involved certain drawbacks. Considerations of community loyalty, if not aggrandizement, are certainly involved to some degree in the excessive proliferation of and lack of cooperation between Catholic institutions of higher education, which a number of critics have lamented.

[31] Francis P. Cassidy, *Catholic College Foundations and Development in the United States (1677–1850)* (Washington, D.C.: Catholic University of America Press, 1924), p. 61.

[32] Erbacher, *Catholic Higher Ed. for Men*, p. 116; "Burns-Howard Report, 1916," *CEAB*, 12 (Aug., 1916), 12–17.

Other writers have pointed out that the rules of obedience and discipline under which the religious teacher functions can militate against commitment to scholarship, and that the pietistic spirit that many teaching communities inherit from their founders often creates an atmosphere that encourages anti-scientific and anti-intellectual attitudes.[33] But prescinding from the question of the advantages and disadvantages involved, it is clear that the persistence of the clerically dominated structure of control is in large part owing to the crucial role played by religious orders in Catholic higher education.

The preeminent role played by the Jesuits is also related to the second area in which Catholic colleges diverged from the institutional norms of American higher education — the organization of the undergraduate curriculum. The situation may be briefly described by saying that whereas the typical American college was patterned after the English model and was conceived as a four-year institution that accepted students who had already completed their secondary-level studies, the Catholic college followed the continental model and combined in the same institution a program of six or seven years duration that began as soon as a boy had the rudiments, and it embraced both secondary and collegiate levels of study. The Jesuit educational tradition is the clearest specific source of this organizational structure, but before tracing its derivation we should indicate the extent to which the Jesuits actually dominated the field of Catholic higher education in the United States.

From the sixteenth century on, the Jesuits were considered the educators par excellence of the Catholic church. The oldest American Catholic college, Georgetown, was established by Bishop John Carroll, who was a Jesuit until the order was suppressed; and when the Society of Jesus was reconstituted, Georgetown was placed under Jesuit control. It served as a model for other American Catholic colleges, and the Jesuits themselves established numerous other institutions. They were in charge of thirteen of the twenty-eight Catholic schools in operation in 1850; nineteen of the sixty existing in 1866; and twenty-six of the eighty-four institutions for men surveyed in 1916.[34] By 1916 the Jesuits controlled seven of the nine schools having a total enrollment (including prep students) of 1,000 or more, and seven of the ten institutions that enrolled at least 100 professional school students. Their continued dominance is indicated by the fact that of the ten Catholic universities that conferred the most doctorates in 1964, six were operated by the Society of Jesus.[35]

[33] Donovan, *Academic Man*, p. 29 ff.; Justus George Lawler, *The Catholic Dimension in Higher Education* (Westminster, Md.: Newman Press, 1959), pp. 58 ff., 108 ff. Cf. also Leo R. Ward, C.S.C., *Blueprint for a Catholic University* (St. Louis: B. Herder, 1949), chap. 16.

[34] Cassidy, *Catholic College Foundation*, p. 72; Erbacher, *Catholic Higher Ed. for Men*, p. 166; "Burns-Howard Report, 1916." 12–17.

[35] *Ibid.*; John L. Chase, *Doctors Degrees Conferred by U. S. Institutions; By State, By Institution, 1954–55 through 1963–64* . . . (Washington, D.C.: n.d.)

Given this degree of institutional preponderance, along with their prestige, whatever the Jesuits did was bound to determine to a considerable extent the whole complexion of American Catholic higher education. And it was precisely the Jesuits who were most firmly committed to the combined secondary-collegiate program; in fact, it was not until after World War I that they fully accepted the typical American undergraduate organization and practices. This subject is much too complex to be treated adequately here, and more investigation is needed to determine the degree of influence that Jesuit practice had on other Catholic colleges; but both Notre Dame and St. John's in Minnesota show unmistakable evidence of Jesuit influence in their early years, and the Jesuit schools themselves constituted so important a group that at least some general remarks are required.[36]

As it developed in the sixteenth century and was crystallized in the famous *Ratio Studiorum* (1599), the Jesuit educational program embraced three broad divisions of study: humanistic, philosophical, and theological. The theological level, designed primarily for members of the order, was the culminating stage toward which the lower studies were oriented, but only the two lower levels are relevant here because the Jesuit college curriculum in the United States developed from the humanistic cycle and a shortened version of the three years of philosophy called for in the *Ratio*. The humanistic cycle comprised a classical-rhetorical education characteristic of the Renaissance, which began as soon as a boy could read and write; it was indefinite in length since promotion was strictly by achievement, but it usually extended for about six years. The material of instruction was so ordered that each of the several stages of the humanistic cycle focused on a specific skill, body of knowledge, or intellectual habit that the student had to master before he could go on; and that skill, knowledge, or habit gave its name to the whole work of that particular level, or term of instruction.[37]

The earliest recorded Georgetown version of the program (1820) was six years in length and corresponds closely to the humanistic cycle set forth

[36] The *Catalogue . . . University of Notre Dame . . . 1855, 1856* (Chicago: n.p., 1856), pp. 4–5, shows that the Jesuit cycle of Humanities, Poetry, Rhetoric, and Philosophy (see below) was followed in the early years at Notre Dame. For St. John's similar pattern see Barry, *Worship and Work*, p. 110. By far the most helpful study of the Jesuit adjustment in the United States is Miguel A. Bernad, S.J., "The Faculty of Arts in the Jesuit Colleges in the Eastern Part of the United States: Theory and Practice (1782–1923)" (Ph.D. dissertation, Yale University, 1951), but also see William McGucken, S.J., *The Jesuits and Education* (Milwaukee: Bruce Pub. Co., 1932), and Roman A. Bennert, S.J., "A Study of the Responses of Jesuit Education in Theory and Practice to the Transformation of Curricular Patterns in Popular Secondary Education Between 1880 and 1920" (Ph.D. dissertation, University of Wisconsin, 1963).

[37] See the first section of Bernad, "The Faculty of Arts"; George E. Ganss, S.J., *Saint Ignatius' Idea of a Jesuit University* (Milwaukee: Marquette University Press, 1954), and Allan P. Farrell, S.J., *The Jesuit Code of Liberal Education* (Milwaukee: Bruce Pub. Co., 1938).

in the *Ratio*, except that it added a preliminary course called Rudiments that was designed to make up deficiences in elementary reading and writing. After Rudiments came Third Grammar, Second Grammar, First Grammar, Humanities, and Rhetoric. In 1835, Georgetown's A.B. program was stretched out to seven years by the addition of a year called Philosophy at the upper end; an earlier revision had also changed the names of the three Grammar courses, which then became Third, Second, and First Humanities, and the original Humanities year was renamed Poetry.[38] The situation was to become even more confused later when some of the Jesuit schools rechristened the first three years Third, Second, and First Academic, and the designation Belles Lettres was occasionally substituted for Humanities.[39] This may appear to be a bewildering maze of exotic terminology — as, of course, it is to those familiar only with such straightforward and meaningful terms as freshman, sophomore, junior, and senior. But the strangeness of the terms accurately reflects the major difficulty of the system as far as the institutional adjustment of Catholic higher education was concerned: the terms were outlandish, and the system was foreign; structurally it did not mesh at all with the American pattern of four years of secondary work in one institution and four years of collegiate work in another.[40]

A number of critics have pointed out that nineteenth-century American colleges resembled the Gymnasium, lycée, or English public school in the academic level of their coverage.[41] But with the Catholic colleges the correspondence was even closer; they derived directly from the same educational tradition and institutional source as these European secondary schools and had to adapt themselves to the American 4-4 system of secondary and collegiate study in the course of their development. This was a slow process even in the non-Jesuit schools, which were less closely identified with the seven-year program by virtue of the educational traditions of their orders. The earliest modification was that the first two or three years of the program were simply styled "preparatory" or "academic," and the last four were called "collegiate." Notre Dame, according to one student, "purged" its curriculum of preparatory features in 1873 and has been called the first Catholic school to do so; but all that was done then was that the final four

[38] Daley, *Georgetown University*, pp. 221–24; compare the first program with that outlined in Farrell, *Jesuit Code of Liberal Ed.*, pp. 344–45.

[39] Gilbert J. Garraghan, S.J., *The Jesuits of the Middle United States* (New York: America Press, 1938), III, 505–6. On the introduction of the term "Belles Lettres" see Augustus J. Thebaud, S.J., *Forty Years in the United States of America* (New York: United States Catholic Historical Society, 1904), p. 349.

[40] The difficulties caused by an anomalous 6-6 organizational structure still plague many seminaries. See Paul D'Arcy, M.M., "The 4-4-4 Arrangement of Seminaries," *NCEAB*, 57 (1960), 106–12.

[41] Cf. Richard J. Storr, *The Beginnings of Graduate Education in America* (Chicago: University of Chicago Press, 1953), pp. 30, 35–36, 82, 84, 112, 124, 126, 133.

years of the course were renamed freshman, sophomore, junior, and senior. The preparatory years remained integrally related to the last four; it was not until 1883 that a "sharp distinction" was made between the prep department and the "collegiate department," and the "preps" were not finally eliminated from Notre Dame until the 1920's.[42]

During roughly the first three-quarters of the nineteenth century, the Catholic college was not as clearly a misfit as its anomalous structure would seem to make it because nearly all American colleges had preparatory departments, although they were not thought of as constituting an organic part of the collegiate curriculum as in the Catholic schools.[43] But with the simultaneous growth of the public high school and the development of graduate education, it became imperative for the Catholic college to redefine its position and to bring itself into line with generally accepted norms of American education. With secondary education provided by the free public high schools and with higher education taking on its present-day university character, the Catholic college could not indefinitely remain an institution that ambiguously straddled these areas.

It has been said that the modern American university consists of a German university superimposed on an English college.[44] This educational hybrid may be a novel one, and its development involved some difficult adjustments for all American colleges; but the problems were multiplied for the Catholic institutions because when the process began they had not yet completed their evolution into English colleges of the standard American variety. Catholic higher education had, therefore, to respond to challenges on different levels at the same time, and the pace of adjustment differed considerably from one institution to another. The establishment of the Catholic University of America in 1889 was an early response to the need for a graduate-level institution, but taken as a whole, the Catholic institutions first had to bring their undergraduate programs into line.

The process of adjustment assumed the dimensions of a general movement at the turn of the century when the formation of the Association of Catholic Colleges inaugurated the period of reorganization referred to earlier in connection with the social evolution of the Catholic population. This reorganization represented a "rationalizing" of the system of Catholic educa-

[42] Compare Bernard J. Lenoue, "The Historical Development of the Curriculum of the University of Notre Dame" (Master's thesis, University of Notre Dame, 1933), p. 24, and Philip S. Moore, C.S.C., "Academic Development: University of Notre Dame: Past, Present and Future" (Mimeographed; University of Notre Dame, 1960), pp. 6, 13–14. Cf. also Arthur J. Hope, C.S.C., *Notre Dame, One Hundred Years* (Notre Dame, Ind.: Notre Dame University Press, 1948), p. 347.

[43] Rudolph, *American College and University*, pp. 281 ff.

[44] See, for example, Bernard Berelson, *Graduate Education in the United States* (New York: McGraw-Hill, 1960), p. 10.

tion; the structure and practices of the Catholic schools were clarified, defined, and rearranged to bring them into closer correspondence with American patterns and into greater harmony with the needs of American society. The whole movement was comparable to changes that had been under way for some time in secular higher education.

Before Catholics could overhaul their system — which was at that time not a "system" at all — they had to have some means of exchanging information and undertaking common action; for this reason the formation of a professional association may be considered the first significant step in the reorganization. The Association of Catholic Colleges, which met first in 1899 at the suggestion of Rector Thomas J. Conaty of the Catholic University of America, merged in 1904 with groups representing the parochial schools and seminaries to form the Catholic Educational Association. The CEA was a prerequisite to further educational reforms: it overcame the isolation that had previously paralyzed concerted action; it stimulated the entire body of Catholic educators; and it provided the organizational vehicle for tackling the complex problems of articulation between the various levels of Catholic education. Two specific instances can be cited in which Catholic colleges (Marquette and St. John's in Minnesota) undertook important curricular reforms as a result of a single talk given at the 1901 meeting of college men; and as the CEA continued its work, similar reforms were introduced throughout the whole system of Catholic education.[45]

The reform of the combined secondary-collegiate curriculum was the most important aspect of the reorganization. It involved two major tasks that were distinct but interrelated: separating the high school from the college and standardizing the college.

There were at that time three approaches to secondary education as far as Catholic institutions were concerned. The colleges were of course involved in it; a number of parochial schools were gradually adding high school classes, and there were also a relatively small number of institutions that

[45] For Marquette, see Raphael N. Hamilton, S.J., *The Story of Marquette University* (Milwaukee: Marquette University Press, 1953), p. 53; for St. John's, Barry, *Worship and Work*, p. 231. There is no history of the Catholic Educational Association. The background of its formation is discussed in Peter E. Hogan, S.S.J., *The Catholic University of America, 1896–1903: The Rectorship of Thomas J. Conaty* (Washington, D.C.: Catholic University of America Press, 1949), pp. 69 ff., and Colman J. Barry, O.S.B., *The Catholic University of America, 1903–1909: The Rectorship of Denis J. O'Connell* (Washington, D.C.: Catholic University of America Press, 1950), pp. 214 ff. Anne B. Whitmer and F. G. Hochwalt, "The National Catholic Educational Association: 1903–1951," *Catholic School Journal*, 51 (April, 1951), 127–29 is a brief sketch. Constance Welch, "The National Catholic Educational Association; Its Contribution to American Education: A Synthesis" (Ph.D. dissertation, Stanford University, 1947) is schematic and unhistorical.

specialized in high-school-level work.[46] In general, however, the high school was the weakest segment in the whole range of Catholic education; in 1900 there was only one institution of the most efficient sort — the central high school serving a number of different parishes. James A. Burns, C.S.C., the historian of Catholic education and a keen observer of educational trends, pointed out the serious weakness of Catholic education in this respect. He also demonstrated that the colleges were not meeting the need for high school instruction because they were too expensive; because they had no links with the Catholic elementary schools; and because they made "no attempt whatever . . . to reach out after the great mass of boys of secondary grade, by providing courses of instruction that . . . fit [students] more directly for active life." [47] Many Catholic college men opposed the independent high schools for which Burns campaigned, both because they feared these institutions would dilute the quality of secondary education, and even more because they foresaw that the high schools would draw off their prep students and thus destroy, or at least greatly injure, the colleges. But the trend was irresistible because of the continued development of public and Catholic high schools and because of the pressure exerted by accrediting agencies. By the early 1920's, the prep departments were clearly separated from the colleges, and the latter were thus enabled to adjust their development to the American pattern.

The accrediting agencies, which became a major force on the educational scene around the turn of the century, also exercised a powerful influence on the standardization movement in the Catholic colleges. The colleges were facing an acute crisis, for while the high schools were absorbing the lower portion of their traditional function, the new graduate and professional schools were demanding some sort of uniform standard of undergraduate preparation they could assume on the part of applicants with a bachelor's degree; and at the same time, the rise of the elective system and the proliferation of academic specialties had destroyed the older, commonly accepted

[46] This discussion follows the analysis in James A. Burns, C.S.C., in *Report of the Third Annual Conference of the Association of Catholic Colleges . . . 1901* (Washington, D.C.: Catholic University of America Press, 1901), pp. 25–40. See also John T. Murphy, C.S.Sp., "Catholic Secondary Education in the United States," *American Catholic Quarterly Review*, 22 (1897), 449–64; Edward F. Spiers, *The Central Catholic High School* (Washington, D.C.: Catholic University of America Press, 1951), chap. 2; Sr. Mary Janet Miller, *General Education in the American Catholic Secondary School* (Washington, D.C.: Catholic University of America Press, 1952), pp. 11–22; and James A. Burns, C.S.C. and Bernard J. Kohlbrenner, *A History of Catholic Education in the United States* (New York: Benziger Brothers, Inc., 1937), chap. 10.

[47] *Report . . . 1901*, p. 34. On opposition to the high schools and gradual acceptance, see Spiers, *Central Catholic H. S.*, pp. 19 ff., and Miller, *General Ed. . . . Secondary School*, pp. 11–22, and Michael J. McKeough, O.Praem., "Catholic Secondary Education, 1900–1950," *Catholic School Journal*, 51 (April, 1951), 113–15.

agreement that a prescribed set of readings in the classic authors constituted the essential collegiate experience. Catholic educators were thus compelled to determine, as one of them put it, "how we stand on the question of what constitutes a college." This speaker added, with the accrediting agencies in mind, "if we do not standardize our own work, it may be standardized for us."[48]

The Catholic college men touched on these problems in their earliest meetings, but it was not until 1909 that a special session was devoted to standardization. Matthew Schumacher, C.S.C., became the champion of standardization in the CEA, and by 1915 the organization had developed a set of standards including the requirement of sixteen high school units for college admission, 128 semester hours for graduation, and six other provisions dealing with administrative organization, faculty, library facilities, and so on. The College Department of the CEA adopted these criteria in 1915, but no sanction for failure to live up to them was to be invoked because of protests that they were inflexible and worked a hardship on small colleges. Schumacher attacked the inconsistency of adopting standards without requiring that they be met, and in 1917 the College Department came around to his view; a year later, the CEA issued an approved list of fifty-two standard Catholic colleges.

The modernization of the Catholic undergraduate college also included the acceptance of some degree of electivism, a deemphasis of the classics, and some modification of pedagogical techniques, at least among the Jesuits.[49] As a result of all these changes, the Catholic schools were brought into line with the general pattern of American college education, and their development since then has been similar to other colleges. But while the reorganization of the undergraduate program was being consummated, other new developments were also gaining ground. We have already referred to the increasing enrollments. The growth of women's colleges, the introduction of coeducation, and the expansion into "true" university work through the affiliation of professional schools with Catholic liberal arts colleges,[50] and

[48] *CEAB*, 10 (Nov., 1913), 175, 177. For an excellent contemporary analysis of the implications of standardizing agencies for Catholic education see James P. Fagan, S.J., "Educational Legislation," *CEAB*, 4 (Feb., 1908), 8–40; there is no history of the accreditation movement in Catholic colleges, but the early stages are sketched in Campion R. Baer, O.F.M.Cap., "The Development of Accreditation in American Catholic Seminaries, 1890–1961" (Ph.D. dissertation, University of Notre Dame, 1963), pp. 108–19. Cf. also, John F. Nevins, *A Study of the Organization and Operation of Voluntary Accrediting Agencies* (Washington, D.C.: Catholic University of America Press, 1959), pp. 21–25.

[49] Bernad, "The Faculty of Arts," pp. 150 ff., 318–95; Garraghan, *Jesuits of the Middle U.S.*, III, 508–11. Cf. also Robert I. Gannon, S.J., *The Poor Old Liberal Arts* (New York: Farrar, Straus & Cudahy, 1961), chaps. 1–2; and Hope, *Notre Dame*, p. 365.

[50] Hamilton, *Story of Marquette*, chap. 4, gives a good account of the addition of professional schools to the liberal arts college at Marquette.

the assumption of graduate-level instruction to some extent overlapped the reorganization of the colleges.

The assumption of graduate work overshadowed the other developments in importance. Advanced degrees were awarded by Catholic institutions from their earliest days, but these M.A.'s may be regarded as reinforced bachelor's degrees; they signified merely that the student's liberal education had been informally prolonged a year or two and were not intended to certify that he had been trained as a research scholar, or that he expected to devote his life to academic and scholarly pursuits. This sort of degree — and it was *the* graduate degree in all American colleges and universities through most of the nineteenth century — was characteristically awarded, as the *Bulletin* of Duquesne University put it as late as 1923, to "graduates of the college who, for two years after receiving the degree of B.A., devote themselves to literary studies or some learned profession, and make timely application for the same."[51]

The modern conception of graduate study as strict technical training in research scholarship was not firmly planted in American academic institutions until the last quarter of the nineteenth century. The Catholic University of America (1889) was the first and, for upwards of half a century, the only institution where graduate education of the German-inspired, research-oriented type was conducted under Catholic auspices on a significant scale at the doctoral level.[52] The Catholic University was patterned more upon the model of Louvain than of the German universities, and its transplanted European form of organizational structure caused some difficulties; moreover, it was almost crippled at the outset because it became deeply involved in the bitter ideological quarrels raging among American Catholics in the 1890's. But it did survive and eventually prospered moderately; and it

[51] *Duquesne University Bulletin . . . 1923* (Pittsburgh, n.p. 1923), p. 25. On the history of graduate education see Berelson, *Grad. Ed. in U.S.*, pp. 6–42; Storr, *Beginnings of Grad. Ed.*, *passim*; Roy J. Deferrari, "The Origin and Development of Graduate Studies under Catholic Auspices," in *Essays on Catholic Education*, edited by Deferrari, pp. 195–215; and Power, *History of Catholic Higher Education*, chap. 8. Speaking of the M.A. degree in the nineteenth-century American college, Schmidt writes: "Almost any college graduate who remained alive and kept out of jail could have it." *Liberal Arts College*, p. 71. Cf. also Joseph T. Durkin, S.J., *Georgetown University: the Middle Years (1840–1900)* (Washington, D.C.: Georgetown University Press, 1963), pp. 71, 146–47, 253.

[52] On CU see, John Tracy Ellis, *The Formative Years of the Catholic University of America* (Washington, D.C.: Catholic University of America Press, 1946); Patrick H. Ahern, *The Catholic University of America, 1887–1896: The Rectorship of John J. Keane* (Washington, D.C.: Catholic University of America Press, 1948); and the works by Hogan, *C.U.A., 1896–1903*, and Barry, *C.U.A., 1903–1909*. Roy J. Deferrari, *Memoirs of the Catholic University of America, 1918–1960* (Boston: Daughters of St. Paul, 1962), contains much useful information.

would be difficult to overestimate the importance of the Catholic University as a major breakthrough in the institutional adjustment of American Catholic higher education. Although exclusively a theological school at first, it was designed from the outset to do university work on the graduate level, whereas the other Catholic institutions were still in the process of growing into the organizational pattern and instructional grade of American four-year colleges. The Catholic University, therefore, became the principal channel through which the methods and spirit of modern university work were diffused into the world of Catholic higher education.

The very foundation of the Catholic University stimulated a lively emulation in other institutions: an observer noted in the year it opened that neighboring Georgetown seemed to be putting special stress on its own "*university character.*" Within a short time, Georgetown launched a graduate program that, according to one authority, marked a notable advance over the previous practices of Catholic colleges. But in the embattled atmosphere of the 1890's, the Jesuit authorities in Rome were fearful of seeming to compete with the papally approved Catholic University, and they deliberately curbed the development of graduate work at Georgetown.[53] The establishment of Houses of Study by religious orders in the environs of the Catholic University no doubt exerted a more healthy and positive influence in diffusing an appreciation for scholarship in other religious congregations. Catholic University itself became the great center of graduate education for Catholics, especially in its earlier decades when there was no other Catholic graduate school of comparable standing and when Catholics attended secular institutions less freely than at present. So extensive was this dimension of its influence that by 1931 there were 750 of its alumni teaching in colleges that enrolled more than 80 per cent of the young men in Catholic institutions of higher learning.[54]

Although the Catholic University remained the leading graduate center, other Catholic institutions also entered the field as graduate degrees became more valuable and the demand for them grew. The Ph.D. was the preeminent graduate degree; by comparison, the older type of M.A. seemed shoddy stuff indeed. But instead of being allowed to expire decently, the master's degree was retained in bastardized form — partly a glorified undergraduate degree and partly a junior-grade Ph.D., the M.A. became a stepchild. Unlike the stepchild of storybooks, however, the master's remained very popular because it was a graduate degree of sorts, because it made fewer demands

[53] Ellis, *Formative Years*, p. 344, quotes the observer on Georgetown. Power, *History of Catholic Higher Education*, pp. 213 ff., discusses Georgetown's graduate program; Durkin, *Georgetown University*, pp. 146–47, 253–55, passes a considerably less favorable judgment on the graduate program. Durkin (pp. 215–26) also discusses Georgetown's tense and unprofitable relations with the Catholic University.

[54] Cf. James H. Ryan, "The Catholic University of America: Focus of National Catholic Influence," *Ecclesiastical Review*, 85 (July, 1931), 25–39.

on the student who earned it and the institution that offered it than did the Ph.D., and because of its value as the passport to a teaching career, first on the undergraduate level and now, increasingly, on the secondary level. The Ph.D. also acquired the character of a license to teach, and one of the requirements of the accrediting agencies was that department heads in a "standard" college had to hold Ph.D.'s.[55] In view of these circumstances, it is understandable that Catholic institutions felt that they had to provide graduate education for an expanding clientele, and that their graduate programs at the master's level were developed earlier than at the doctoral.

Systematic graduate work at the master's level was well begun in Catholic universities by the 1920's, although the example of Duquesne reveals that even then it was not universally understood in the modern sense. But doctoral preparation is the distinguishing mark of institutions regarded as "real" universities, and it was not until after World War II that doctoral work assumed very sizeable proportions at Catholic universities — other than at the Catholic University of America and, possibly, at Fordham — or established the dominant tone of these institutions. In 1929, for example, Catholic schools conferred 646 master's degrees, but only 64 doctorates; ten years later the comparable figures were 1,124 and 99.[56] The general lines of development of Catholic graduate education at the doctoral level are indicated by Table 2.[57]

Professor Berelson remarked that we need to remind ourselves how young the institution of graduate study is in American higher education. This is true ten times over if we consider only Catholic graduate education. In fact, if we use Berelson's criterion for "genuine entry" into graduate study — the conferral of about 1 per cent or more of the doctorates awarded annually — the Catholic University of America was still the only Catholic

[55] Walton C. John, *Graduate Study in Universities and Colleges in the United States* (Washington, D.C.: U.S. Office of Education, 1935), pp. 59–60; Roy J. Deferrari, "The Master's Degree and Catholic Institutions of Higher Learning," *NCEAB*, 35 (Aug., 1938), 226–35; Berelson, *Grad. Ed. in U.S.*, pp. 21, 30.

[56] *NCEAB*, 26 (Nov., 1929), 67; *ibid.*, 38 (Aug. 1941), 144–45. The 1929 doctorates are exclusively Ph.D.'s; the 1939 figures include 5 doctorates in canon law or sacred theology. The 1929 report (pp. 85–86) shows that 24 of the Ph.D.'s were earned at Catholic University, which had 279 full-time and 76 part-time graduate students; but 27 of the Ph.D.'s were earned at Fordham, which had 8 full-time and 562 part-time students. The 1941 report (pp. 117–19) discusses the part-time student problem.

[57] *NCEAB*, 26 (Nov., 1929), 67; *ibid.*, 38 (Aug., 1941), 119–20; Chase, *Doctors Degrees Conferred . . . 1954–55 through 1963–64. . . .* The figures for 1922–23 and 1931–32 are for Ph.D. degrees only; the last three include doctor's degrees in special fields, such as canon law. Comparison with total doctoral conferrals (given in *Historical Statistics of the United States*, p. 211) indicates the percentage awarded by Catholic institutions has consistently hovered between 2.5 and 3.5. In 1940, Catholic University awarded 43 of the 103 Catholic doctorates; in 1964, 107 of the total of 409.

TABLE 2
DOCTORATES CONFERRED BY CATHOLIC INSTITUTIONS

Year	Number
1922–23	35
1931–32	68
1939–40	103
1954–55	252
1963–64	409

institution that had achieved genuine entry by 1960, and it did not do so until some thirty years after it began to offer graduate work.[58] Statistics for the decade 1955–64 show that of a grand total of 104,139 doctorates, only 3,277 (or 3.14%) were conferred by the fifteen Catholic institutions included in the survey. And although the number of "Catholic doctorates" increased by almost two-thirds between 1955 and 1964, Catholic universities were barely keeping pace with the general increase in conferral of doctorates; in both years the percentage represented by Catholic institutions was just under 3 per cent.[59]

The marked quantitative growth of Catholic graduate education has been accompanied by a qualitative improvement. In a comprehensive study reported in 1934, only six departments in Catholic universities — five at the Catholic University and one at Notre Dame — were rated as capable of offering adequate doctoral programs; none was listed as distinguished. In Berelson's 1960 study of graduate education, no Catholic university is included among the top twenty-two, but five are numbered in the next highest group of twenty-five, all but one because they had recently received accomplishment awards from the Ford Foundation.[60] The very weak showing in the 1934 report created a flurry in Catholic educational circles and doubtless helped to stimulate the improvements that have been registered since. No one would deny that there is still room for much more improvement, but it is equally important to recognize, in evaluating the present situation, that graduate work on the doctoral level is hardly older than yesterday in Catholic universities.

THE IDEOLOGICAL ADJUSTMENT

All the major shifts we have mentioned in the social and institutional evolution of American Catholic higher education have involved ideological shifts as well — changes in the attitudes, values, and ideas of Catholics as

[58] Berelson, *Grad. Ed. in U.S.*, pp. 39, 93.
[59] Chase, *Doctors Degrees Conferred . . . 1954–55 through 1963–64 . . .* , *passim.*
[60] "Report of the Committee on Graduate Instruction," *Educational Record*, 15 (1934), 192–234; Berelson, *Grad. Ed. in U.S.*, pp. 126, 280; Deferrari, *Memoirs*, pp. 115 ff, 427–28.

they bear on the process of education. The revolution in educational thinking entailed by the transition from a predominantly secondary-collegiate involvement in higher education to the present research-oriented, university approach has occurred in the present century. We are presently in the midst of a critical phase of this intellectual reorientation, and an earlier crisis coincided with the period of reorganization mentioned several times already, so we must begin by reverting again to that era.

The difficulties of Catholic educators at the turn of the century arose in large measure from the problems created for all undergraduate colleges by the vast increase of knowledge and the conversion of the leading secular institutions into universities of the German-inspired type, dominated by graduate schools dedicated to research. As a result of these developments, many new specialized disciplines grew up and were introduced on the undergraduate level as academic subjects, which students were permitted to "elect" at will. At the same time, the needs of a rapidly growing, democratic, urban, industrial society dictated the introduction of other new specialties in the colleges so that trained personnel would be capable of assuming new social functions. Hence, the colleges were called upon to offer more and more subjects to larger and larger student bodies; gone was the unity of vision and purpose that undergraduate education had possessed when the classical curriculum reigned supreme; and, as institutional growth continued and became more complex, the congeries of new specialties was united only by the bureaucratic structure of external administrative control.[61]

The introduction of the credit-hour system is a highly symptomatic aspect of the general academic revolution and is of particular interest because of its key role in the standardization movement to which so many Catholic college men objected.[62] The credit hour and related units were devised to help the standardizing bodies answer the question "What does a college education consist of?" at a time when there was no common agreement that mastery of certain specified subjects was essential to qualify a student for a baccalaureate degree. The accrediting agencies in effect answered this question by saying that it made no difference what subjects one studied, provided he studied them long enough. All subjects — if they were taught

[61] Speaking of this period at Yale, G. W. Pierson writes: ". . . in a single generation the world of knowledge exploded. The hierarchy of values was upset. Experience came under a cloud. Orderliness disappeared. And, like other faculties of like purpose, they found themselves caught up in what can be understood only as one of the greatest disturbances that the world of higher education has ever known." Pierson, "The Elective System and the Difficulties of College Planning, 1870–1940," *Journal of General Education*, 4 (1949–50), 166–67. Cf. Schmidt, *Liberal Arts College*, chaps. 7 and 9; Rudolph, *American College and University*, chap. 20.

[62] See Dietrich Gerhard, "The Emergence of the Credit System in American Education Considered as a Problem of Social and Intellectual History," *AAUP Bulletin*, 41 (1955), 647–68; Bernad, "The Faculty of Arts," pp. 278 ff., 303 ff.

by qualified persons in institutions that met certain standards in respect to facilities and financial resources — were regarded as equally educative; hence the really crucial question was: "How long must one study these subjects to earn a degree?" The credit hour, and other such measuring units as the "academic counts" of the New York Regents and the "Carnegie unit," were introduced to facilitate the reckoning of study time. The standard college was defined as an institution that accepted students who had completed sixteen high school "units" and then exposed them to 128 credit hours of instruction on the higher level.

The credit hour and other academically neuter units of quantification served as all-purpose counters and may be looked upon as the interchangeable parts of the modern educational enterprise; they were the natural complement to the academic division of labor and intellectual specialization that had already been introduced. They symbolize tellingly the extent to which higher education was undergoing the same processes of Weberian rationalization and bureaucratization that were at work in the world of capitalistic business and industry, and in society in general. The accrediting agencies became, as it were, the quality-control inspectors of the educational enterprise; and all the students informally became bookkeepers as they built up a credit-hour account to be cashed in for a degree.[63] Although specialization and bureaucratization were, and are, inseparable from the advancement and widespread diffusion of knowledge, they also brought into the academy an atmosphere of impersonality and big-business-like efficiency that critics of American higher education have denounced from the time of Thorstein Veblen through Robert M. Hutchins to the Berkeley rebels of today.

Catholic college men at the turn of the century shared much of the viewpoint of the critics just mentioned; they too objected to the depersonalized atmosphere, the materialistic commercialism and vocationalism, the extremes of electivism, and the fragmented confusion of American higher education. But to the Catholic critics, these weaknesses were but a faithful reflection of the chaos and confusion of the modern mind, which had lost its anchorage in religious and philosophical truth.[64] Their own educational approach, Catholics believed, effected a synthesis of classical humanism, sound philosophy, and the true religion. The Jesuits, who were among the severest critics of the modern trends, had most fully elaborated what might be called the classic Catholic pedagogical theory, and the Jesuit colleges embodied it in practice most satisfactorily. A sketch of their position highlights the

[63] Compare James A. Schellenberg, "The Class-Hour Economy," *Harvard Educational Review*, 35 (Spring, 1965), 161–64.

[64] Cf., for example, Fagan, "Educational Legislation," pp. 20, 35 ff.; and the attack of Timothy Brosnahan, S.J., on electivism in *Report of the Second Annual Conference of the Association of Catholic Colleges . . . 1900* (Washington, D.C.: 1900), pp. 22–44.

contrast in values and purposes between the Catholic colleges and the leading secular institutions.

John Courtney Murray, S.J., has recently given us a concise summary of the "fourfold structure" of aims that the traditional liberal arts education proposed, and that Catholic educators accepted almost universally at the turn of the century. The traditional ideal of humanistic education, Murray writes, "has been to put the student in the way of developing a power of diction, a view of reality, a set of values, and a sense of style." [65] To achieve these aims, the Jesuits relied on a modified version of the literary-rhetorical program of studies that had been adapted by the Renaissance humanists from Quintilian and Isocrates. Although the natural sciences were not neglected altogether, the program concentrated on a systematically arranged progression of analytical and stylistic study of literary models that not only "trained the mind," but also gave the student mastery of language, the vehicle of thought and expression. At the same time, the literature itself — the Greek and Latin classics, studied in the original — furnished him with the noblest models of human conduct and aspiration. In the final year of the program, the student's humane learning was climaxed by Thomistic philosophical studies designed to provide an intellectually integrated vision of the natural order and its relation to the order of transcendental truth. The whole experience of learning took place in a religious context and was marked by close personal relations between the instructor (who ideally taught all the subjects at each level) and the student.

To an age whose education was secular, scientific, and technical in spirit, particularized in vision, flexible in approach, vocational in aim, and democratic in social orientation, the Jesuits thus opposed a system that was religious, literary, and humanistic in spirit, synthetic in vision, rigid in approach, liberal in aim, and elitist in social orientation. There was no place in it for interchangeable parts, electivism, or vocationalism. These were simply the educational heresies that sprang from the radical defect, the loss of a unified view of reality. To tell a student that he could "elect" anything was to admit that one was no longer sure of what was worth knowing or of the order in which it should be learned; to award a degree to those who elected this, that, and the other thing until the whole collection added up to 128 "credits" was utter academic and intellectual irresponsibility.

Yet the new trends were irresistible, and the Jesuits were carried along

[65] John Courtney Murray, S.J., "On the Future of Humanistic Education," in *Humanistic Education and Western Civilization*, ed. Arthur A. Cohen (New York: Holt, Rinehart, & Winston, 1964), p. 235. For the characteristics of Jesuit education, see the works cited above in notes 36 and 37, especially those of Bernad and Ganss; also Francis P. Donnelly, S.J., *The Principles of Jesuit Education in Practice* (New York: P. J. Kenedy, 1934); John W. Donohue, S.J., *Jesuit Education* (New York: Fordham University Press, 1963); and Robert Schwickerath, S.J., *Jesuit Education* (St. Louis: B. Herder, 1903).

with all the other Catholic colleges in the reorganization brought about by the social and institutional exigencies we have already discussed and by the increasing prestige of the modern view. Many Catholic educators, however, accepted these changes with great reluctance; they had been too deeply attached to the traditional ideal to adapt themselves rapidly and whole-heartedly to the new directions that even their own institutions were com-pelled to follow.[66] This is hardly surprising, since it is not unusual for educational theory to lag behind practice; moreover, the adoption of modern American practices in higher education involved real losses in precisely that area which Catholic educators were disposed to regard as most valuable — the liberal arts. Indeed, non-Catholic critics like Abraham Flexner and Robert M. Hutchins in the 1930's roundly attacked the over-specialization, vocationalism, and other vices of American higher education that Catholics had found repugnant from the beginning; and the movement to reinstate solid "general education" in the colleges and universities represented a movement Catholics could heartily endorse.[67] These currents in the larger world of higher education improved the morale of Catholic college men and probably had the effect of reinforcing their dedication to the classic humanistic-religious theory of Catholic undergraduate education.

But Catholic schools were no longer the same sort of undergraduate colleges they had been; as we have seen, they were becoming much larger, more complex, and more like the secular universities in respect to the growing emphasis on graduate education. The older Catholic pedagogical ideal was badly out of touch with the practical realities of college and university life; it did not come close to explaining or justifying the sort of activities that were actually going on in the Catholic universities. But some spokesmen seemed to feel that, in spite of the fact that it was in practice outmoded and was in danger of becoming completely irrelevant, the traditional one was the only Catholic educational theory possible, and that wherever current prac-tices departed from the traditional norms those practices should be brought into line or abandoned. Perhaps the clearest instance of this sort of thinking was furnished by George Bull, S.J., chairman of the department of philoso-phy at Fordham in the 1930's.

[66] See, for example, Francis P. Donnelly, S.J., "Is the American College Doomed?" *Ecclesiastical Review*, 40 (April, 1919), 359–65; *Report of the . . . Second Annual Meeting of the National Benedictine Educational Association . . . 1919* (Beatty, Pa.: Archabbey Press, 1919), pp. 23–33; and Gannon, *Poor Old Liberal Arts, passim.*

[67] So far as I have been able to discover, there are no scholarly studies of these movements in Catholic higher education. Some information is provided in Russell Thomas, *The Search for a Common Learning: General Education, 1800–1960* (New York: McGraw-Hill, 1962) pp. 200–208, 244–50; and in Willis Rudy, *The Evolving Liberal Arts Curriculum* (New York: Columbia University Press, 1960), chap. 9.

In a famous address to "the assembled Faculties of the largest Catholic University in the world," Father Bull argued that Catholicism was a culture, a way of life, a view of reality; that the characteristic mark of this view of reality was its totality of vision, the way it ordered all knowledge and values into a comprehensive organic unity; and that it was the function of the Catholic college to impart to students this Catholic culture, this synthetic vision. A few years later, Bull argued in another essay that the function of the Catholic graduate school was precisely the same as that of the Catholic college, only on a higher level; he specifically denied that research was the function of the graduate school. In fact, he asserted, to accept the primacy of research would be to attempt "the impossible task of being Catholic in creed and anti-Catholic in culture." Research, as an *"attitude,"* Bull declared, was concerned not with truth, but with the *"pursuit of truth"*; its tendency was vocational and particularistic, "its spontaneous bent [was] toward the apotheosis of the principle of disintegration," and its ultimate consequence was dehumanization. Between the Catholic view and the research view there were only antinomies — organic unity *vs.* disintegration; the "sense of tradition and wisdom achieved *vs.* 'progress'; . . . principles *vs.* fact; . . . contemplation *vs.* 'research.' " Education at the graduate level, as elsewhere, was for Bull, "the enrichment of human personality, by deeper and deeper penetration into the velvety manifold of reality, as *Catholics possess it.*"[68]

Here the classic Catholic theory of undergraduate education is stated in extreme form and applied to the graduate school where its inapplicability and opposition to the spirit of autonomous scholarship are glaringly revealed. Not all Catholic educators agreed with Father Bull, and one of his fellow Jesuits wrote a rebuttal.[69] And of course Catholic universities, including the ones run by the Jesuits, continued to build up their graduate schools, foster more research, multiply their undergraduate offerings, and branch out into new directions — they had to do these things or they simply could not be taken seriously as institutions of higher education. Yet all of this was going on in contravention to the prescriptions of the traditional educational theory outlined by Bull; nor was there any new Catholic pedagogical theory that adequately accounted for it. Catholics, in other words, found themselves at midcentury deeply committed to a kind of educational activity that is unprovided for in their classic pedagogical tradition and that has had the practical effect of destroying the intellectual synthesis of which their pedagogical tradition was a part.

For although some might dismiss Bull's "strange ideas" as not even re-

[68] The two discussions are, "The Function of the Catholic College" (pamphlet; New York: America Press, 1933), and "The Function of the Catholic Graduate School," *Thought*, 13 (1938), 364–80. All italics in original.

[69] See the letter of Thurber W. Smith, S.J., *ibid.*, 638–43.

quiring refutation,[70] they undeniably accorded with the generally prevailing Catholic world-view — the world view that, put in its crudest form, holds that the Catholic church already has the truth, that we know all the answers to the questions that really matter. Bull was also correct in emphasizing that "research as an attitude" was antithetical to the integrity or even the preservation of this view and to the religious-philosophical synthesis upon which it rested. And, in fact, the older synthesis has been subjected to increasing strains by the dynamism released by Catholic acceptance of the spirit of modern scholarship and has been well-nigh, if not completely, overwhelmed by the vast accumulation of new knowledge — Bull's despised heaps of "facts." These developments in large part explain why educated Catholics are presently so impatient with the smugness of the traditional attitude that "we have the truth."

Obviously, the Catholic world view is right now in the process of change; and a fundamental aspect of this process is a reexamination of the previous understanding of the relationship between secular knowledge and religious truth. One of the principle reasons for the reexamination is that Catholics have actually been doing more research, accepting more of the results of the researches of others, and finding that their earlier views stand in need of considerable modification. Yet when they were urged by a number of Catholic "self-critics" to do more research and to be more scholarly, little attention was given to the possibility that this activity would lead to a radical revision of the Catholic view of reality. More often than not, these exhortations to Catholics were animated by the essentially apologetical motive of improving the church's image by showing that Catholics could produce their quota of scientists and scholars. The implicit assumption seemed to be that the findings of the researchers would bolster the intellectual structure of Catholicism by being assimilated into the existing synthesis.[71]

But as the structural outlines of the organic unity of vision of which Bull spoke become ever more obscure, it becomes correspondingly more pressing to develop a theory of research, and of Catholic higher education in general, that goes beyond what might be called the pedagogical fideism of saying

[70] Martin R. P. McGuire, "Catholic Education and the Graduate School," in *Vital Problems of Catholic Education in the United States*, ed. Roy J. Deferrari (Washington, D.C.: Catholic University of America Press, 1939), p. 112.

[71] I am not implying that the work of the self-critics was not necessary and very valuable, or that the critics themselves, many of whom were or are distinguished scholars, were not genuinely concerned with the intellectual, as opposed to the apologetical, aspects of the problem. Nonetheless, the apologetical motivation seems to me the dominant one in the whole corpus of Catholic self-criticism. See the materials gathered in *American Catholicism and the Intellectual Ideal*, eds. Frank L. Christ and Gerard E. Sherry (New York: Appleton-Century Crofts, 1961); and especially the "Preface" by Archbishop John T. McNicholas in John A. O'Brien's *Catholics and Scholarship* (Huntington, Ind.: Our Sunday Visitor, 1939).

that truth is one and that the findings of research, insofar as they are true, cannot conflict with faith. Discussion of these issues, however, is usually carried on in terms of the need for more Catholic scholars and not infrequently loses itself completely in the semantic mazes that surround the terms "intellectualism" and "anti-intellectualism."[72] Moreover, these discussions are apt to be hortatory or polemical rather than analytical; and they often simply *assume* research and scholarship as good things without establishing for them a theoretical rationale, or explaining why they should be made the dominant activities of Catholic higher education, or showing how they fit in with a larger view of reality that harmonizes with faith.

There are, of course, important exceptions to this perhaps too-sweeping generalization; a number of Catholics have recently addressed themselves to the manner in which faith and knowledge are to be integrated in Catholic education, and writers like Msgr. Ellis, Fathers Ward, Weigel, and Murray, and Professors Gilson, Von Hildebrand, Lawler, and O'Dea have done much to clarify the issues.[73] But perhaps Walter J. Ong's brief essay on "Research and American Catholic Education" deserves special notice here because it grounds the appeal for research so firmly in an over-all developmental context that accords with some of the newer trends in theological thinking, and because it contrasts so starkly with the position taken just twenty years earlier by Ong's Jesuit confrere, Father Bull. Where Bull based his argument on a view of reality as fixed and already comprehended, Ong bases his on a view of reality and our knowledge of it as undergoing a continuous process of development. Research is therefore justified in itself because it is participation in the evolving understanding of reality; in addition, research is justified pedagogically because unless a teacher participates by research in the growing body of knowledge that his subject represents, he cannot adequately convey to his students a full appreciation of the radically developmental character of that area of knowledge.[74]

Most Catholic scholars today would probably agree that Ong's dynamic view represents a marked advance — or "development" — as compared to

[72] For the semantic problem see Philip Gleason, "Catholic Intellectualism Again," *America*, 112 (Jan. 23, 1965), 112–18.

[73] John Tracy Ellis, "American Catholics and the Intellectual Life," *Thought*, 30 (1955), 351–88; Ward, *Blueprint of a Catholic University*, chap. 18; Gustav Weigel, S.J., "American Catholic Intellectualism — A Theologian's Reflection," *Review of Politics*, 19 (July, 1957), 275–307; John Courtney Murray, S.J., "The Christian Idea of Education" in *The Christian Idea of Education*, ed. Edmund Fuller (New Haven, Conn.: Yale University Press, 1957), pp. 152–63; Etienne Gilson, *Christianity and Philosophy* (New York: Sheed & Ward, 1939), chap. 5; Dietrich von Hildebrand, *The New Tower of Babel* (New York: P. J. Kenedy, 1953), pp. 129–63; Lawler, *Catholic Dimension in Higher Education*, esp. chap. 5; Thomas F. O'Dea, *American Catholic Dilemma* (New York: Mentor Paperback Books, 1962).

[74] Walter J. Ong, S.J., *American Catholic Crossroads* (New York: Collier Paperback, 1962), chap. 5.

Bull's essentially static view. It has the undoubted merit of addressing itself directly to the sort of activity that actually goes on in Catholic universities today, and it furnishes a rationale for this activity as it is in fact carried on. For these reasons, it seems to me that the line of thinking sketched out by Ong offers greater promise than any other yet proposed for the elaboration of a theory of Catholic higher education that meets contemporary needs. But although Ong's analysis is a notable contribution to the most recent phase of the perennial effort to effect a satisfactory ideological adjustment between Catholic higher education and the American environment, there are still some critical problems, and a few concluding remarks about them may not be out of place.

CONCLUSION

The most critical problem today is in the area of ideological adjustment — it is a crisis of purpose, a question of the fundamental raison d'etre of Catholic higher education. The social adjustment of Catholics as it bears on higher education seems to be very near satisfactory resolution: Catholics are now fairly well abreast of their fellow Americans in wealth, status, and commitment to education. Institutional problems still remain, but they are hardly greater than the problems that have already been overcome. And the major institutional divergence of Catholic schools from the American norm — clerical control — is closely related to the fundamental ideological problem of secularization. The successful social adjustment of Catholics also bears on this problem. For as the demand for higher education taxed the religious communities beyond their resources of manpower, the faculties of the larger institutions especially were to a very considerable extent laicized.[75] Thus the very social advance of the Catholic population replaced the religious teachers with laymen who were the beneficiaries of these advances in wealth and educational opportunity; and mounting demands that laymen be granted a larger role in academic administration and policy-making are a natural consequence of these developments.

In the last decade, however, these social aspects of secularization have been conjoined to the beginnings of a profound shift in Catholic attitudes toward secularization. Fifteen years ago, secularization — or usually "secularism" — was regarded as an undoubted evil. Today that is no longer the case. Rather, there has been a growing insistence on the distinction between "secularism" and "secularity" and a growing acceptance of the notion that "the secular" is an autonomous sphere which is in itself good.[76] By an

[75] In 1958 over 80 per cent of the faculties of six fairly representative medium to large-sized Catholic institutions were composed of laymen. See John Tracy Ellis, *Perspectives in American Catholicism* (Baltimore: Helicon, 1963), p. 237.

[76] This more positive reappraisal of the meaning of secularization and its relation to education is not confined to Catholics. Cf. Ralph C. Raughley (ed.), *New*

analogous development in the Catholic academic world, disciplines formerly considered to be dependent on religion for their value orientation have asserted their self-sufficiency and demand to be freed from any tutelage to extraneous authority. Sociology is a striking example. Here is a discipline in which Catholic scholars have, in the quarter-century since the formation of their professional association, reversed the original determination to create a "Catholic sociology" and are now determined to establish the autonomy of their subject as independent of any non-sociological "Catholic" prescriptions. The very term "Catholic sociology" is now repugnant to them, and the name of their journal has recently been changed from *American Catholic Sociological Review* to *Sociological Analysis.*[77]

But the question naturally arises: In what sense is a Catholic university Catholic if it is composed predominantly of lay professors who employ, in their teaching and research, the same methods and norms as their counterparts in secular universities, and who are engaged in the pursuit of knowledge in autonomous spheres that are in no way dependent upon any over-all "Catholic position"? What, in short, is the reason for being of the *Catholic* college or university?[78]

This question is a radically new one when asked by Catholics themselves in a tone that bespeaks genuine puzzlement as to the raison d'etre of Catholic colleges and universities. American Catholics have often in the past been critical of their institutions of higher learning, and Catholic educators have confessed to many weaknesses in their schools. What they have never really doubted was that these institutions had a reason for being, a vitally important function to fulfill. Now that they are in a fair way of overcoming many of their historic defects, it is clear that they must confront the challenge of justifying their existence as Catholic institutions, regardless of their educational quality.

For the historian, the most distressing aspect of the matter is that American Catholics — for it is not just educators who are involved — must grapple with this fundamental question about the identity and purpose of their colleges and universities without anything approaching an adequate understand-

Frontiers of Christianity (New York: Association Press, 1962), pp. 113–15; and Harvey Cox, *The Secular City* (New York: Macmillan Paperback, 1965), chap. 10.

[77] Cf. Paul Facey, S.J., "Aggiornamento," *Sociological Analysis*, 25 (Fall, 1964), 137–40; and Paul Mundy, "Some Convergences and the Identity-Crisis in the American Catholic Sociological Society," *ibid.*, 26 (Fall, 1965), 123–28.

[78] Cf. Donovan, *Academic Man in Catholic College*, pp. 196–97; Canavan, "St. John's," *America*, 113 (Aug. 7, 1965), 137; Daniel Callahan, "The Catholic University: The American Experience," in *Theology and the University*, ed. John Coulson (Baltimore: Helicon, 1964), p. 74 ff; Richard Horchler, "The Time Bomb in Catholic Education," *Look*, 30 (April 5, 1966), 25; Edward Wakin, "How Catholic Is the Catholic College?" *Saturday Review*, 49 (April 16, 1966), 92 ff.

ing of the past evolution of those institutions. It is hardly an exaggeration to say that Catholic higher education is entering its identity crisis in a state of virtual amnesia, with no meaningful grip on the history that has played so crucial a role in forging its present identity. It is supremely ironic that a Catholic academic community that is more and more disposed to accept a developmental view of reality has only the sketchiest notion of the pattern of its own development. What is even more unfortunate, and from a developmentalist viewpoint simply bewildering, is the disposition sometimes manifested to treat the earlier efforts of Catholic educators with condescension or scorn because they are not what we are doing, or trying to do, today. The simple lack of information is bad enough. There is only one book, Edward J. Power's, that attempts to deal comprehensively with the history of Catholic higher education in this country; and although it is invaluable as matters stand, it tells us almost nothing about what has happened since 1900. About the recent social history of the Catholic population and the intellectual history of American Catholicism, we are likewise almost completely in the dark. Such ignorance is a grievous handicap to understanding the present situation. We can permit it to continue only at our peril.

Profiles of Catholic Colleges and Universities

III. THE ENVIRONMENT FOR LEARNING ON THE CATHOLIC COLLEGE CAMPUS

Robert F. Weiss, S.J.

Catholic higher educational institutions in the United States have frequently found themselves, particularly in recent years, at the center of intra- and extramural controversy stemming from the vast changes sweeping through the church and society. Explosions over speaker policies, various kinds of freedom, social involvement, a greater voice for the layman, and the like seem to have a tendency to erupt more often and more violently on Catholic campuses than in chanceries, parishes, or other locales in which the visible church works.

In the mid-fifties, critics of Catholic higher education often pointed to the lack of scholarly production in making their case, but their attention has gradually shifted to the climate for learning, research, and intellectual creativity. Until recently, however, most of the available research on Catholic higher education failed to differentiate among schools of diverse quality and clientele. Farwell and Warren's study of National Merit Scholarship finalists showed that Catholic colleges appeared to draw those who were less intellectual and more authoritarian than the Merit scholars choosing other colleges and universities.[1] Campbell found that Canadian Protestants attending Catholic universities were "significantly less permissive" than those at nonsectarian schools in matters of civil liberties and of tolerance for questioning what their churches taught; Mundi expressed some concern at the pattern of "moralistic" responses he obtained from Catholic college students in Minnesota.[2] Whether one chooses to interpret such results as owing pri-

Robert F. Weiss, S.J., is academic dean at Rockhurst College in Kansas City. His undergraduate and ecclesiastical degrees were obtained from Saint Louis University and his Ph.D. from the University of Minnesota in 1964. Father Weiss served as administrative assistant to the president at Saint Louis, and has been an associate editor of the *Review for Religious*. An earlier version of this chapter appeared in *School Review*.

[1] Less than half of the Catholic students winning National Merit Scholarships in the years 1956–59 attended Catholic colleges (E. D. Farwell and J. R. Warren, "Student Personality Characteristics Associated with Types of Colleges and Fields of Study" [Mimeographed paper, Center for the Study of Higher Education, Berkeley, California, 1959]).

[2] D. F. Campbell, "Religion and Values Among Nova Scotian College Stu-

marily to college influence, or to the selecting of Catholic colleges by those already "less permissive," it can be inferred that a less liberal climate prevails in these institutions.

But relatively little is learned from the lumping together of Catholic colleges and universities. Despite the convenience of the phrase, "Catholic higher education" is not of a piece. Obvious differences of cost, quality, purpose, and extent of student freedom can be found among the heterogeneous collection of Catholic colleges and universities. Institutional quality is probably the most elusive of these dimensions, yet several objective criteria are available. Considering only the college clientele, for example, there are vast differences in College Board scores and in numbers of National Merit scholarships among the entering freshmen at the various schools;[3] conversely, there are wide variations in awards to graduating seniors. Wakin notes that Notre Dame has been given "more Woodrow Wilson scholarships, Danforth Fellowships, Marshall Fellowships and Rhodes Scholarships than all other Catholic universities combined."[4] More recently, there has been a tendency toward more even distribution among the top Catholic institutions, with Notre Dame and Saint Louis University, for instance, receiving about ten or eleven Woodrow Wilsons annually. (These are the only two Catholic universities, incidentally, to share in the Ford Foundation's mammoth Special Program in Education.)

As a variety of research shows, there is a wide range of differences among the climates of American colleges and universities. Different environments have diverse effects on their students.[5] For example, it has been shown that scientific and humanistic achievers thrive in different college atmospheres.[6] But little systematic information is available. It is the aim of this chapter

dents" (Paper read at the Meetings of the American Catholic Sociological Society, Chicago, 1965), p. 10; Joseph P. Mundi, "Variations in the Opinions, Practices and Attitudes of Selected Samples of Minnesota Catholic College Students Toward Catholicism in America" (Ph.D. dissertation, University of Minnesota, 1964).

[3] Consider, for example, the CEEB means for the freshmen entering seven Catholic women's colleges in 1964: Barat College of the Sacred Heart, 516 (V), and 500 (M); Manhattanville, 632 (V) and 599 (M); Marylhurst, 479 (V) and 450 (M); Marywood, Pa., 524 (V) and 498 (M); Mundelein, 535 (V) and 505 (M); Rosary, 570 (V) and 529 (M); Seton Hill, 546 (V) and 532 (M). — Ed.

[4] Edward Wakin, *The Catholic Campus* (New York: Macmillan Co., 1963), p. 35.

[5] The reader is referred to Rose K. Goldsen, M. Rosenberg, R. M. Williams, and E. A. Suchman, *What College Students Think* (Princeton, N.J.: Van Nostrand, 1960); Philip Jacob, *Changing Values in College* (New York: Harper Bros., 1957); David Riesman and Christopher Jencks, "The Viability of the American College," in *The American College*, ed. N. Sanford (New York: John Wiley & Sons, Inc., 1962), pp. 74–198 and *passim*.

[6] A. W. Astin, "An Empirical Characterization of Higher Educational Insti-

to describe the development of current methods for measuring the educational climate or environment and to summarize the available data for Catholic colleges and universities.

ENVIRONMENTAL STUDIES

For as long as society has been interested in education, it seems, men have been concerned with the influence of the environment of the learner. Plato urged his fellow countrymen, for example, to fill their beloved Athens with works of art so that young men growing up surrounded by such sights might come to love beauty:

> . . . we must seek out these craftsmen whose instinct guides them to whatsoever is lovely and gracious; so that our young men, dwelling in a wholesome climate, may drink in good from every quarter, whence, like a breeze bearing health from happy regions, some influence from noble works constantly falls upon the eye and ear from childhood upward, and imperceptibly draws them into sympathy and harmony with the beauty of reason, whose impress they take.[7]

With increasing interest in the learning process, greater attention has been given recently to the influence that the environment exerts on the development of the individual. Sociologists, for their part, have studied the campus as a miniature society. Learning theorists and psychologists, on the other hand, have focused on the idea that behavior is the reaction between an individual person and his environment. In an attempt to study more systematically these environmental factors, educational researchers have developed methods of categorizing and measuring the various types of influence produced by the campus culture.

These instruments are based on the theory that the values, customs, traditions, rules, regulations, even physical features of the campus, and a host of other characteristics play a more important part in determining behavior patterns and the type of learning that goes on in college than had previously been suspected. The college curriculum may be accurately described in the catalogues and admissions office brochures, but other elements of the environment may be influencing students in ways scarcely envisioned by those who framed the college objectives.

tutions," *Journal of Educational Psychology*, 53 (1962), 224–35; D. L. Thistlethwaite, "College Press and Changes in Study Plans of Talented Students," *Journal of Educational Psychology*, 51 (1960), 222–34; and "College Press and Student Achievement," *Journal of Educational Psychology*, 50 (1959), 183–91.

[7] Plato, *The Republic*, trans. F. M. Cornford (New York: Oxford University Press, 1945), p. 90.

In the mid-1950's, an instrument designed to measure such influences, the College Characteristics Index (CCI), was developed by Stern and Pace.[8] Students themselves act as reporters in describing the situation in which they live and learn. The three hundred items in the questionnaire describe various aspects of the college environment, with the student indicating whether or not he thinks they are characteristic of his own college. The items are scored along thirty scales that can then be combined into clusters or factors, facilitating comparisons among various institutions. Research of this kind has shown that institutions may differ with respect to their environmental profiles even though they are similar in program, size, administration, the types of students they enroll, and in other such characteristics.[9]

It is worth noting at this point that in the research on college environments there is a deliberate attempt to resist value judgments about which emphases are good or bad, which should be fostered or discouraged. The purpose is to identify what is actually going on so that the institution may make its own decisions after achieving a better understanding of the influences affecting the behavior and learning of the students. Such information may be of considerable interest to admissions officers and high school counselors in helping college-bound students choose an appropriate institution. Administrative officers and faculty may also find the data valuable as they attempt to understand their own institution and the ways in which it molds its students. Those concerned in a more general way with the status and influence of Catholic higher education may well find that these studies throw new light on the distinctive atmosphere (or lack of it) found on Catholic campuses.

The College Characteristics Index has been further refined by C. Robert Pace in the College and University Environment Scales (CUES), which consist of 150 items from the original index.[10] CUES is scored along five scales, patterned not on the basis of the students' psychological characteristics (the CCI scales describe the "press" of the institution in terms corresponding to individual "needs"), but rather on the over-all institutional environment. The five dimensions of the campus measured by CUES are its stress on Practicality, Community, Awareness, Propriety, and Scholarship. This instrument has been incorporated into Educational Testing Service's Institu-

[8] C. R. Pace and G. G. Stern, "An Approach to the Measurement of Psychological Characteristics of College Environments," *Journal of Educational Psychology*, 49 (1958), 269–77.

[9] A research project currently in progress at the Center for the Study of Higher Education of the University of California at Berkeley is turning up some fascinating information about the kinds of students attracted to certain institutions and about the image of the institution the freshmen brought with them. See *Carnegie Corporation of New York Quarterly* (Jan., 1966), 1–4.

[10] C. R. Pace, *CUES, College and University Environment Scales: Preliminary Technical Manual* (Princeton, N.J.: Educational Testing Service, 1963).

tional Research Program for Higher Education, introduced in the fall of 1965.[11]

A third method of measuring the "psychological climate" or environment of the college is called the Environmental Assessment Technique (EAT), developed by Astin and Holland.[12] The EAT attempts to assess the college environment in terms of eight characteristics of the student body: its size, average intelligence, and six "personal orientations" based on the proportion of students in each of the six categories of major fields. This method assumes a relationship between the type of student attracted to the campus and the characteristics of the college environment; it is concerned almost exclusively with the academic aspects of college life.

These three assessment devices differ considerably, both in the method of arriving at the environmental measure and in the significance of the scores. Although lengthy comparisons will not be attempted here, it should be noted that the CCI is scored on the basis of the percentage of an individual's responses that agree with the key for a given statement.[13] CUES scores, on the other hand, are obtained by determining for each item whether two-thirds of the total group answered in the keyed direction. The EAT, finally, employs a method that does not involve the students' evaluations of the environment at all; instead, the score is established from the percentage of baccalaureate degrees conferred in particular fields. Consequently, strategies of the three techniques are different. The psychological orientation of the CCI is contrasted with the more sociological approach of the CUES. The former is concerned with a study of personal satisfaction and performance in an environment in relation to individual needs and the latter with environmental differences between institutions without reference to personality factors.[14] The EAT is even less influenced by individual perceptions. Based as it is

[11] The program includes three types of instruments that "yield information about biographical and attitudinal characteristics of students, the atmosphere of the college as students perceive it, and student academic achievement." *The Institutional Research Program for Higher Education* (Princeton, N.J.: Educational Testing Service, 1965).

[12] A. W. Astin and J. L. Holland, "The Environmental Assessment Technique: A Way to Measure College Environments," *Journal of Educational Psychology*, 52 (1961), 308–16. See also A. W. Astin, *Who Goes Where to College?* (Chicago: Science Research Associates, Inc., 1965).

[13] It should be noted that, with all of the social scientist's instruments, the "right" answer in the key is not determined a priori, but is part of an empirical criterion. That is to say, it reflects the way students at institutions known to be high in a given dimension — determined in advance by independent criteria — have characterized their own college climates. — Ed.

[14] For a discussion on the differing strategies of the CCI and CUES, cf. Pace, *CUES*, pp. 7–8.

on the curriculum, this instrument reflects little of the subtle, and perhaps contradictory, influences that may be revealed through the participant-reporter methods of the CCI and CUES.

ENVIRONMENTAL RESEARCH IN CATHOLIC COLLEGES

Not all studies of college environments, however, follow the patterns indicated by these newer instruments. The findings of the Knapp-Greenbaum and Knapp-Goodrich researches not only unleased a wave of self-criticism among Catholic educators, but they stimulated various analyses of the causes, some of which were concerned especially with environmental factors.[15] Scholars outside the Catholic community also participated. One pioneering effort was the bold attempt of David Riesman and Christopher Jencks to describe three colleges from an "ethnological" point of view, a conscious departure from the historical studies common in the past as well as from the more recent "quantitative appraisals of logistic problems in contemporary higher education." [16] They based their findings on the personal observations of outsiders, as they described these themselves. Their work was accompanied by a plea for further research, which has indeed been gradually forthcoming. But as yet little is available for church-related colleges and universities.[17]

[15] R. H. Knapp and H. B. Goodrich, *Origins of American Scientists* (Chicago: University of Chicago Press, 1952); R. H. Knapp and J. J. Greenbaum, *The Younger American Scholar: His Collegiate Origins* (Chicago: University of Chicago Press, 1953).

[16] Riesman and Jencks, "The Viability of the American College," p. 75. This approach appears to be more concerned with the type of students who will be attracted to the college because of the directions consciously taken by the faculty and administration than because of the prevailing atmosphere, the implied (as opposed to explicit) objectives, and the non-curricular elements of the environmental influences. These comments apply to many other analyses of higher education in general and Catholic schools in particular.

[17] One promising study, of which only a preliminary report has appeared at the time of this writing, is the research conducted by the Danforth Foundation's Commission on Church Colleges and Universities (Manning M. Pattillo, Jr. and Donald M. Mackenzie, *Eight Hundred Colleges Face the Future*, [1965]). The complete report will be published in late 1966 by the American Council on Education under the title, *Church-sponsored Higher Education in the United States*. The commission set out to appraise the major assets and liabilities of church-related colleges and universities in the United States and then to make recommendations based on these findings. The study employed various methods of assessment, and data have not as yet been published in detail. One of the criteria used was the "atmosphere of intellectual ferment," and some of the background information presented in summary fashion suggested a generally favorable appraisal, but not much attention was given at this stage of the reporting to pointing up specific characteristics of Catholic institutions.

A few Catholic institutions participated in the study of college environments when Pace and Stern were developing the College Characteristics Index. In the Sanford volume, Stern reported his findings on three individual but unnamed schools. School 19 was described as "an outstanding Roman Catholic women's college in a small Northwestern city."[18] The most striking contrast between this Catholic girls' college and an elite New England women's college was that orderliness, planning, and deliberation were emphasized at the Catholic institution, whereas nonconformity and personal autonomy were encouraged by the private school atmosphere. Stern's conclusion, based on study of the girls' personality scores, was that students in either college would find the atmosphere at the other school somewhat incompatible with their own needs.

To determine the extent of institutional research in Catholic colleges and universities, I surveyed four-year Catholic higher educational institutions in the United States. Of the 224 schools to which brief questionnaires were sent, 169 returned them. One hundred and twenty-one of the responding institutions (72%) indicated that they had conducted no systematic "climate" studies of the kind described, although a large number expressed interest, noted that studies were being planned, or mentioned related types of research. Information was also obtained directly from Pace, Stern, and the Educational Testing Service. A total compilation indicates that at least 51 (23%) of the American Catholic four-year colleges and universities have either conducted some kind of environmental study or participated to the extent of having groups of their students complete the questionnaires.[19]

CATHOLIC COLLEGES AND THE COLLEGE CHARACTERISTICS INDEX

In the few years that the College Characteristics Index has been in use, eight Catholic institutions have administered it and have made their findings available. In several of these instances the CCI was employed as part of extensive research projects. The eight institutions range from a small seminary with only fifty students to large universities enrolling over ten thousand. They include men's, women's, and coeducational colleges and are located in widely separated parts of the country. The data will be reported here in terms of eleven factors that describe various aspects of the educational climate; some of the factors are more concerned with intellectual, others with nonintellectual aspects. Scores were also obtained, for purposes of compari-

[18] G. G. Stern, "Environments for Learning," in *The American College*, pp. 690–730.

[19] Long-term programs for the study of Catholic education have been established at St. Louis University (with the cooperation of the National Catholic Educational Association) and at Notre Dame (in conjunction with The Center for the Study of Contemporary Man directed by George N. Shuster). — Ed.

son, for eleven other denominational or church-related institutions. Seven of these have been classified as major Protestant colleges, the remainder as minor Protestant schools.[20] One of the Catholic institutions, Saint Louis University, will be treated in greater detail later in this chapter, since research there focused on differences among the various undergraduate schools, between faculty and student perceptions of the environment, and among the perceptions of the climate by different categories of students.

Catholic institutions, as represented by the schools included in this study, tend to stand out in the characteristics described by the factors called Group Life, Academic Organization, and Social Form (see Fig. 1).[21] This means, first of all, that there is a tendency on these campuses to encourage various forms of mutually supportive group participation. Activities of a warm friendly character, more or less typifying adolescent togetherness, would be looked on with favor, especially if these also reflect a more serious side of the culture, such as might be found in projects devoted to the welfare of fellow students and less fortunate members of the community. There is a strong group spirit and close rapport among students and with the faculty.

These colleges are also strong in what might be regarded as the environmental counterparts of the needs for orderliness and submissiveness in the individual. They tend to stress a high degree of organization and structure about the campus and in the academic environment. Neatness, regularity, and order are highly valued.

In addition to the interest in human welfare already noted, these schools seem to offer above-average opportunities for the development of formal social skills. Politeness, protocol, proper forms of dress and address are considered important.

On the other hand, the chances are that institutions such as those studied would be noted for the absence of activities associated with dating, athletics, and other kinds of collegiate play and amusement in their more or less exaggerated forms. Although these schools do not differ greatly from the normative group in their emphasis on practical or applied activities, their rejection of aesthetic experiences, and in the orderliness and conformity characterizing students' relations to faculty, peers, and studies, the Catholic colleges are higher then might be expected in vocationalism.

In both Aspiration Level and Intellectual Climate, the Catholic institutions are below the normative group averages. The first of these factors

[20] "Major Protestant schools" are those founded by the larger denominations and include Denison, Earlham, Emory, and Southern Methodist; schools affiliated with smaller religious groups are termed "minor" here (e.g., Heidelberg, Messiah College, Northwest Christian College).

[21] For further details on the use and interpretation of the College Characteristics Index see G. G. Stern, *Scoring Instructions and College Norms: Activities Index — College Characteristics Index* (Psychological Research Center, Syracuse University, 1963). I am indebted to Stern for making his data available.

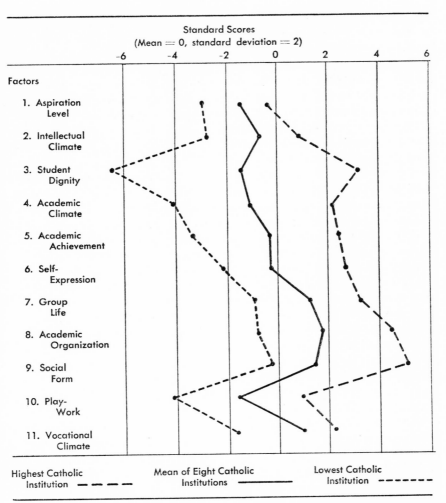

Fig. 1. Highest, mean, and lowest scores among eight Catholic institutions on each of the CCI factors. The mean standard score is 0 and the standard deviation is 2. Thus, approximately two-thirds of the norm group is included between the lines at −2 and +2. The lines at −4 and +4 include 95 per cent of the scores.

indicates the extent to which the colleges provide opportunities for students to participate in decision-making processes involving administrative matters or to be introduced to individuals and to ideas likely to serve as models of professional and intellectual achievement.

The Academic Climate score, reflecting the stress on academic excellence in staff and in facilities in the natural sciences, social sciences, and the humanities, is also lower than for the normative group. The Academic Achievement factor (indicating high standards of achievement in course work, examinations, honors, and the like) and the Self-expression factor (concerned with opportunities offered for the development of leadership potential through open debates, discussions, projects, and other forms of public expression), are both close to the normative group's average.

The factor on which there was the widest variation among the institutions is termed Student Dignity. The highest-scoring Catholic school ranked above 95 per cent of the institutions in the normative group, and the lowest scoring Catholic college was in the lowest one per cent of schools. The low average of the Catholic institutions in general indicates relative weakness in institutional attempts to preserve student freedom and maximize personal responsibility. Schools with high scores on the Student Dignity factor tend to regulate student conduct by means other than legislative codes or administrative fiat; there is a minimum of coercion and students are generally treated with the respect expected among mature adults. Low scores here seem to indicate that Catholic schools in this sample are unconvinced of their students' maturity.

It is interesting to note that mean scores for the seven so-called major Protestant institutions are all closer to the mean of the normative group than are the scores of the Catholic schools, except for the Self-expression factor. In this dimension, which deals with opportunities for the development of leadership potential and self-assurance, the Protestant institutions were lower than the Catholic. The four "minor" Protestant institutions do not follow the same pattern. They tend to be even more extreme than the average of the Catholic schools on such factors as Group Life, Academic Organization, Play-Work, and Vocational Climate. But this group ranks about the same as the normative group on student dignity; they are, however, considerably below the Catholic schools on Academic Climate and somewhat above them on Academic Achievement. On the other factors they are very close to the major Protestant institutions. Further analysis of these findings and their significance for Catholic schools will be postponed until the results obtained from other instruments have been reported.

CATHOLIC COLLEGES RATED ON THE COLLEGE AND UNIVERSITY ENVIRONMENT SCALES

We have data for twenty-seven Catholic institutions where the College and University Environment Scales have been administered.[22] CUES provides a measure of the environmental influences of five dimensions or variables that are expressive of certain major ways in which colleges and

[22] The writer wishes to express his appreciation to C. Robert Pace for supplying the data on two-thirds of these institutions and to the individual colleges for their cooperation in furnishing their own scores in the other cases.

universities differ from one another. In explaining the use of CUES, Pace emphasizes:

> The total feeling or atmosphere that characterizes a particular college campus is best estimated and defined by the pattern of its scores on all the five scales. Although there tend to be some general relationships among the scores, as suggested above, any one college may differ from the general pattern. The special character of a college is revealed by its own unique profile of scores.

In the present study, however, an effort was made to discover characteristics that might be typical of Catholic institutions.

The normative group on which the standard scores are based consists of fifty institutions selected from various regions of the United States, including large, medium, and small institutions, some privately and some publicly controlled.[23] The only Catholic colleges or universities included among the fifty were Seton Hill College and the University of Detroit. Many of the Catholic schools among the twenty-seven on which data are now available have administered the CUES as part of the research being conducted by Pace and the Educational Testing Service to establish new norms. Every area of the United States is represented and institutions of widely diverse size, student bodies, and orientations are included. The CUES items were selected and the scales structured with a view toward reflecting as clearly as possible the differences among environments. Factor analysis was employed in deriving the scales, and names were assigned in a way that, it was hoped, would make the five dimensions, or sets of items, educationally significant to students, educators, and others.

The reader will find that some of the common stereotypes of Catholic institutions will not be borne out by the data in this rather comprehensive sample of twenty-seven widely diverse schools. For example, although the pattern of a highly organized, bureaucratic structure with emphasis on the pragmatic at the expense of the aesthetic appears to be somewhat characteristic of the coeducational colleges and universities in this sample, it is not nearly so pronounced as one might expect. Although these are the types of patterns usually described by some of the Catholic self-critics, the "typical" Catholic college will not be seen to be unusual in this regard. It would not be surprising to find such a syndrome at the large, urban Catholic universities, given the class and ethnic backgrounds of many of their students. But these schools may undergo major changes in the years immediately ahead.[24] At present, however, their failure to emphasize scholarly and intellectual values is pointed up only too clearly by the findings presented here.

[23] The schools are listed by name, and the basis of selection is explained in Pace, *CUES*, pp. 9–14.
[24] Some of these matters are discussed in the final chapter. — Ed.

In Figures 2 to 5 the composite profile for the twenty-seven Catholic institutions is given, and then comparisons are made among schools grouped according to student clientele, size, and the highest degree offered.

Interpretation of the data, of course, depends upon the meaning of the five

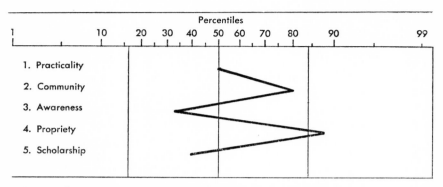

FIG. 2. Composite CUES profile for 27 Catholic institutions.

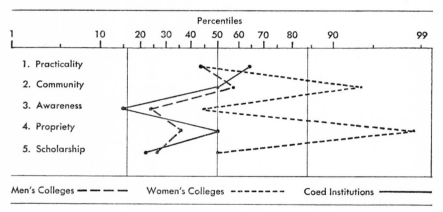

FIG. 3. Composite CUES profiles for 5 Catholic men's colleges, 15 Catholic women's colleges, and 7 Catholic coeducational colleges.

scales or dimensions, which will be discussed in connection with the findings and with frequent reference to the figures.[25]

The items on the *Practicality Scale* deal with the practical-instrumental emphasis in the college environment, particularly such matters as personal status, "going along" with what is expected, order, regularity, and looking toward practical goals. A high score indicates that knowing the right people

[25] For a more complete description of the College and University Environment Scales, see C. R. Pace, *CUES, Preliminary Manual*, pp. 2–4, upon which the explanation in these paragraphs depends heavily.

is important, that orderly procedures are stressed in both administrative and academic areas, and that good fun and strong student leadership are usually present. A low score points to the opposite emphases — that abstract and theoretical considerations are more valued than concrete, applied, practical approaches and that status and procedures are of relatively little importance in the campus community.

The Catholic institutions appeared to be middle-of-the-road on this

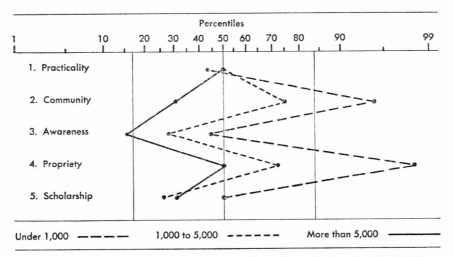

FIG. 4. Composite CUES profiles for 11 Catholic institutions under 1,000 enrollment, 12 between 1,000 and 5,000, and 4 with more than 5,000 enrollment.

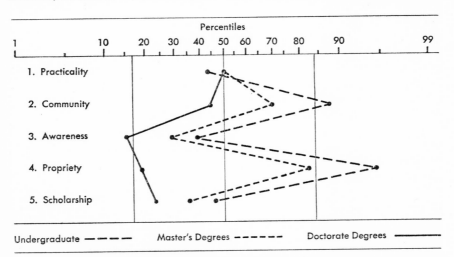

FIG. 5. Composite CUES profiles for 15 Catholic undergraduate institutions, 9 colleges granting MA's, and 3 granting Ph.D.'s.

dimension, and this seems to be generally true, regardless of size or of the level of the degree program. There is somewhat more stress on these practical elements in the coeducational schools, however, than in the all-male or all-female colleges. Of course, the lower scores of the men's and women's colleges, which are generally more committed to the liberal arts, tend to offset the higher scores.

The *Community Scale* is concerned with the extent to which the campus is friendly, cohesive, group-oriented. A high score points to a supportive and sympathetic type of environment with a strong sense of group loyalty and group welfare. A low score, on the other hand, reflects an atmosphere in which privacy, personal autonomy, and detachment are predominant and highly valued.

Catholic institutions score high on this scale; their mean is 29 per cent above the mean of the normative group. But there is a wide variation among the twenty-seven institutions surveyed. Women's colleges were much above the all-male and coed institutions; in fact, they scored higher than 93 per cent of the comparison group. Smaller colleges also had scores at this high level, whereas the largest schools were considerably below the over-all group average. The same pattern is evident when comparisons are based on the type of degree programs, with the undergraduate schools having the highest scores.

The *Awareness Scale* has an extremely wide scope. It reflects a concern and emphasis upon personal, poetic, and political meaning, upon understanding and identity, upon a sense of personal involvement with the world's problems. In a high-scoring institution, the atmosphere is aesthetically both expressive and appreciative; intellectually it is both contemplative and idealistic. A low score suggests an environment with less emphasis on psychological soul-searching, aesthetic opportunities, and concern for the condition of man.

Catholic schools tend to be low on this scale; their mean was 17 percentage points below that of the norm schools. There is no reversal of this trend in any of the three groupings of the Catholic schools, but it is noteworthy that the lowest-scoring schools were the men's colleges, the larger institutions, and those granting the highest degrees.

The combination of items on the *Propriety Scale* measures the degree to which the environment emphasizes politeness, consideration, caution, and thoughtfulness. A high score indicates that group standards of decorum are important, whereas a low score suggests an atmosphere that is generally demonstrative and assertive, more rebellious than cautious, more freewheeling than considerate, more individualistic than concerned about decorum.

The average Catholic campus is high on this scale, above 87 per cent of the normative group. Nevertheless, there are some striking differences among the varieties of Catholic institutions. Catholic women's colleges are outstandingly high — only two per cent of the normative group are above them; male institutions are low — only one-third were below them. The smaller schools also scored high, and the larger ones were about average. On the basis of the type of degrees awarded, the doctorate-granting schools were low, and all the others were high.

The *Scholarship Scale* describes the stress placed on high academic achievement and a serious interest in scholarship. An institution scoring high would be expected to encourage intellectual speculation, an interest in ideas as ideas, knowledge for its own sake, and intellectual discipline. A low-scoring school would tend to be less concerned with the rigorous pursuit of knowledge and theories, either scientific or philosophical.

The typical Catholic institution is somewhat below the middle of the norm group on this scale, that is, below about sixty per cent of them. But although the women's colleges and the small institutions are average on the scholarship scale, the all-male and medium-sized schools rank below three-fourths of the colleges and universities in the entire group, and the coeducational and large Catholic institutions are rated only slightly higher. The Catholic colleges granting only undergraduate degrees are close to the normative group mean, but the doctorate-granting schools rank above only 22 per cent of the institutions.

Following the approach used by Trent, another perspective can be gained by grouping these data differently. This allows comparison of the mean scores on the five institutional environment scales for eighteen Catholic colleges and universities on which Trent had data, six Jesuit institutions, a first-rate Catholic women's college, and the normative group of forty-eight diverse higher educational institutions.[26] This has been done in Table 1. The heavy entrepreneurial, "practical" emphasis in the Jesuit college environments, with a corresponding order and supervision, is especially significant in view of the liberal educational goals claimed by these schools, although it is consistent with the research findings currently available on specific Jesuit institutions.[27]

Particularly disturbing are the low scores on the intellectuality scales, which simply corroborate the findings presented above. Since Jesuit institu-

[26] J. W. Trent, "Religious and Dispositional Characteristics of Catholic Intellectuals" (Paper read at the Meetings of the American Catholic Sociological Society, Chicago, 1965).

[27] Gordon DiRenzo, "Student Imagery at Fairfield University, 1963–64" (Department of Sociology, Fairfield University, 1965, mimeographed); J. Foster, R. Stanek, and W. Krassowski, *The Impact of a Value-Oriented University on Student Attitudes and Thinking* (Santa Clara, Calif.: University of Santa Clara, and Cooperative Research Project No. 729 [Washington, D.C.: Office of Education, Department of Health, Education, and Welfare, 1961], mimeographed); R. F. Weiss, S.J., "Student and Faculty Perceptions of Institutional Press at Saint Louis University" (Ph.D. dissertation, University of Minnesota, 1964).

TABLE 1

COMPARISON OF MEAN SCORES REPORTED FOR STUDENTS IN CATHOLIC COLLEGES AND IN
NORMATIVE SAMPLES ON THE COLLEGE AND UNIVERSITY ENVIRONMENT SCALES
(AFTER TRENT, 1965)[a]

SCALES	INSTITUTIONAL GROUP			
	Normative (48)[b]	Total Catholic (18)	Jesuit (6)	Select Catholic (1)
Practicality	11.2	12.7	13.5	6.0
Community	11.4	11.9	9.2	24.0
Propriety	10.0	12.7	11.1	21.0
Awareness	11.9	6.5	5.6	18.0
Scholarship	11.5	6.6	5.5	17.0

[a] Catholic and, specifically, Jesuit mean scores were weighted by Trent on the basis of the 1964 enrollment reported by the institution represented.
[b] Numbers of institutions in parentheses.

tions enroll over one-third of all Catholic college students, it is distressing to find that their scores were lower than the general Catholic mean for this sample.[28] The high intellectuality scores of the select Catholic women's college are consistent with its characteristics as a resident, high-tuition, upper-middle class institution staffed by a religious order priding itself on quality. There is a pervading sense of belonging at this college, and it is also interesting to note the apparently great emphasis on decorum, manners, and conventional behavior (as measured by the Propriety Scale), which follows the pattern already manifest in the larger sample. And while its students seem to place as high a value on intellectuality and sensitivity as those at the best of the women's liberal arts colleges such as Smith, Radcliffe, Wellesley, and Vassar, there is considerably less tolerance for deviant, off-beat, convention-flouting behavior.[29]

CATHOLIC INSTITUTIONS AND THE ENVIRONMENTAL ASSESSMENT TECHNIQUE

In his recently published book, *Who Goes Where to College?* Alexander Astin has applied his Environmental Assessment Technique to 1,015 four-year colleges and universities. For each of these he reports estimated scores for five characteristics of the entering student body and scores for the eight scales of the EAT. These eight are: Estimated Selectivity, Size, Realistic Orientation, Scientific Orientation, Social Orientation, Conventional Orienta-

[28] It would, of course, be presumptuous to infer that *all* Jesuit or *all* urban universities would manifest these same patterns, and we make it clear that this is not suggested here.

[29] Andrew Greeley found that self-identification as "conventional" (choice of this term in a list of adjectives the respondent felt characterized himself) seemed to be somewhat associated with Catholic college attendance (Andrew Greeley, *Religion and Career* [New York: Sheed and Ward, 1963]).

tion, Enterprising Orientation, and Artistic Orientation. Mean scores have been computed on all of these scales for the 178 Catholic institutions included in the Astin volume. These Catholic institutions have also been classified (Figs. 6–9) on the same bases as in the preceding analyses. A brief description of each of the scales as the data are presented will make the profiles on the following pages more meaningful.[30]

Estimated Selectivity (or the ability level of the student body) is a measure

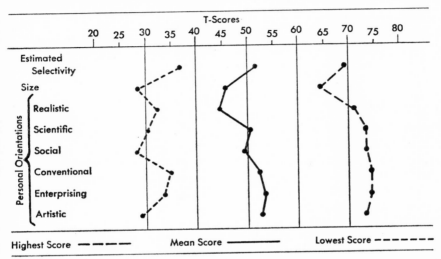

FIG. 6. Profiles for the highest, the mean, and the lowest scores among 178 Catholic higher educational institutions on the Environmental Assessment Technique (EAT). The mean T-score is 50 and the standard deviation is 10 in this figure and in Figures 7, 8, and 9. Thus, about two-thirds of the T-scores are between 40 and 60; about 95 per cent of them between 30 and 70.

of the total number of highly able students who want to enroll at the college divided by the number of freshmen actually admitted. The scores were determined on the basis of the number of National Merit semi-finalists and commended students who expressed interest in the institution compared with the total entering class. Although the suitability of this measure is open to question, Astin found a high correlation (.88) between this scale and academic ability as measured by the Verbal and Mathematical Scholastic Aptitude Test scores.

The mean score of the Catholic colleges placed them just slightly above the average for all schools. The only two classes of Catholic institutions showing notable variations were the large universities and those granting

[30] For a more complete explanation of these measures and how they are obtained, along with the scores of 1,015 individual institutions, see Astin, *Who Goes Where to College?* The following paragraphs are based on these data.

doctorate degrees. These would, on the average, rank higher than about eighty per cent of the other colleges and universities in the study.

Since *Size* is included as a significant measure in Astin's method of assessment, it is reported here although it is based simply on total full-time enrollment. Large institutions tend to be characterized by an impersonal atmosphere, says Astin, with personal contacts between faculty and students

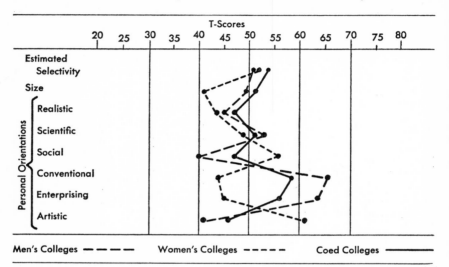

Fig. 7. Composite EAT profiles for the mean scores of 43 Catholic men's colleges, 93 Catholic women's colleges, and 42 Catholic coeducational colleges.

at a minimum; they also have highly organized student sub-cultures and a fairly well-defined status hierarchy of social groups. Catholic institutions tend to be somewhat smaller than the average colleges in Astin's research.

The six personal orientations that comprise the remaining scales are based on the proportion of baccalaureate degrees awarded by the institution in various fields of study. Each major field has been classified according to one of the six broad types. These six orientations thus suggest the nature of the institution's curriculum and at the same time reflect some characteristics of the college environment. They are interpreted as follows.

A *Realistic Orientation* is characterized by a preference for the practical and the concrete rather than the abstract and by an aversion to intense emotional experiences. It reflects the proportion of baccalaureate degrees awarded in such fields as agriculture, engineering, physical education, forestry, and industrial arts. It is probably not surprising to find Catholic institutions generally scoring considerably below the over-all mean on this measure.

The *Scientific Orientation* reflects the environments of colleges that tend to deemphasize interpersonal relationships and social activities and to stress the acquisition of intellectual skills. It is based on the proportion of degrees

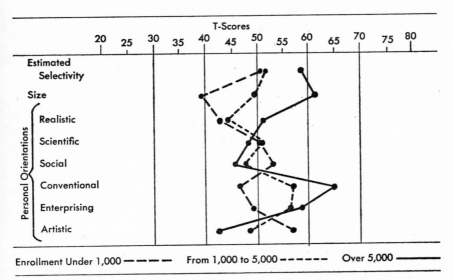

FIG. 8. Composite EAT profiles for the mean scores of 92 Catholic colleges with enrollments under 1,000, 70 with enrollments of 1,000 to 5,000, and 16 with enrollments over 5,000.

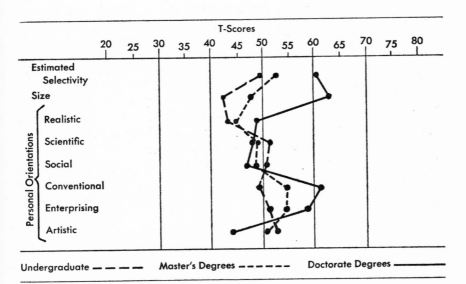

FIG. 9. Composite EAT profiles for the mean scores of 111 undergraduate Catholic colleges, 54 colleges granting MA's, and 13 granting Ph.D.'s.

awarded in the natural sciences. The typical Catholic college, regardless of size, sex of student body, or type of degree is close to the mean for all institutions.

Social Orientation indicates an environment that is likely to emphasize social interaction and service to others. It is based primarily on the proportion of degrees awarded in such fields as education, nursing, social work, and social science. The mean of all the Catholic institutions is close to that of the entire group; but there is considerable divergence, as might be expected, between the all-male and the all-female colleges, with the latter scoring higher.

A *Conventional Orientation* is characterized by a high degree of conformity among the students and a relatively authoritarian attitude on the part of the faculty and administration. It is determined by the proportion of degrees awarded by the institution in accounting, business, economics, and library science. Although the mean of all the Catholic schools is only slightly above the mean of all the institutions studied, the Catholic men's colleges are above 90 per cent of the group. The large Catholic institutions are also strongly oriented this way as are those granting doctoral degrees, but women's colleges scored lower than the average.

An *Enterprising Orientation* signifies an environment that tends to encourage the development of verbal and persuasive skills and to foster an interest in power and status. It depends upon the proportion of degrees awarded in such fields as advertising, business administration, history and political science (pre-law), journalism, international relations, and foreign service. Again, the mean of all Catholic institutions is only slightly above the normative group's mean, but several types of colleges stand out prominently. The men's schools rank above 90 per cent of the other institutions; larger Catholic schools and those granting doctorates also tend to rank high on this scale, whereas women's colleges are generally low.

The *Artistic Orientation* describes a climate emphasizing aesthetic and humanistic pursuits and deemphasizing sports and similar activities that require the use of gross physical skills. It is based on the proportion of degrees earned in such fields as fine arts, writing, languages, music, and speech. Catholic colleges generally are slightly above the mean in this respect, with the women's colleges standing out most prominently. In general, the small institutions are ranked above the large ones, the undergraduate colleges above those granting higher degrees.

A CASE STUDY—SAINT LOUIS UNIVERSITY

The data reported thus far have dealt with Catholic colleges and universities in general or in groups. Thus it seems appropriate now to look at an individual institution in terms of its educational environment. During the

Fall semester of the 1963–64 academic year, Saint Louis University conducted an extensive "Climate of Learning" study to discover more about the environment it was providing for the students in its five undergraduate divisions. The study had several purposes: to furnish the university's faculty and administration with some indexes for judging the extent of correspondence between stated objectives and those implicit in the environment; to compare the "press"[31] profile of the university with that found in institutions of similar orientation; to identify any differences in the climate for learning in the undergraduate schools; and to find out how closely student and faculty perceptions agreed as well as how various groups within the student body and the faculty described their learning environments. The research project had as its distinctive focus the differences that might be discovered on the campus or campuses of a large, complex institution.[32]

Background information was obtained by means of a comprehensive questionnaire administered to the students and a briefer one completed by the faculty. The freshmen were asked to respond to the College Characteristics Index during Orientation Week — before they had had an opportunity to experience campus life firsthand — in an effort to assess their expectations. Toward the end of the first semester they replied again. Sophomores and seniors also participated, bringing the total number of respondents to 3,024 students and 282 full-time faculty members.

In the over-all view, the environment of Saint Louis University does not seem to be characterized by an exceptionally strong or weak press in any particular dimension, such as tended to distinguish some of the smaller and less complex institutions in the original normative sample. Instead, the university's scores were clustered fairly close to the standard score mean. Relatively speaking, however, there were somewhat higher scores on the Vocational Climate, Academic Organization, and Social Form factors and lower scores on those dimensions reflected by the Student Dignity and Intellectual Climate factors. Significant differences were discovered between Saint Louis University's environment and other university colleges or denominational colleges in the normative group, for St. Louis appeared to place greater stress on the academic and intellectual elements of the environment than did these institutions. On the other hand, when St. Louis scores

[31] A term used by social scientists to describe the environmental counterparts by individual needs. Thus, a college emphasizing order, neatness, punctuality, conventionality, and the like will be more attractive to individuals with corresponding personal needs than to more free-wheeling individuals. — Ed.

[32] For a full report on this study see R. F. Weiss, S.J., "Perceptions at Saint Louis University." The problems involved in studying the environments of complex universities have recently prompted the development of "a diagnostic version of CUES aimed at studying the different subenvironments in large universities." Pace reports that this test is now being used experimentally. See C. Robert Pace, "When Students Judge Their College," *College Board Review*, 58 (Winter, 1965–66), 26–28.

were compared with those of seven elite liberal arts colleges included in the normative group, the latter proved to have much higher scores.[33]

The most striking results of the study were those pointing up differences within the institution itself. For example, the five undergraduate schools were found to differ significantly on every one of the eleven factors. The environment in the College of Aeronautical Technology (an almost totally residential division on a separate campus), for example, places comparatively little emphasis on academic excellence in staff and facilities and stresses practical, applied activities along with a high level of orderliness and conformity in the student's relations with faculty, peers, and studies. But the School of Nursing and Health Services appears to have a climate that strongly stresses excellence in areas of the natural and social sciences and humanities, but that presents a lack of opportunities for students to engage in theoretical, artistic, and other "impractical" activities. The School of Commerce and Finance followed closely the pattern of similar schools in the normative group, having rather low scores on the factors concerned with the academic and intellectual emphases in the environment and a high score on Vocational Climate, indicating encouragement of the practical and applied. The Institute of Technology departed from the profile of the group of engineering schools in the normative sample by scoring about average rather than above average on the Aspiration Level and Academic Achievement factors, and by scoring higher than the norm schools on Academic Organization and Social Form. The College of Arts and Sciences, by far the largest of the undergraduate schools, had a profile parallel to that already described for the university as a whole.

Revealing in this study were the differences between student and faculty perceptions of the environment. The two groups agreed about the opportunities offered for the development of formal social skills and related influences. In most other matters, however, particularly those dealing with institutional attempts to preserve student freedom and maximize personal responsibility, there was wide disagreement. The faculty judged that there was a minimum of coercion; the students often felt otherwise. For example, only 17 per cent of the facuty agreed with this statement: "Faculty members are impatient with students who interrupt their work," but 44 per cent of students marked it true. It was interesting that only 59 per cent of students labeled his statement true: "The school has an excellent reputation for academic freedom," whereas 78 per cent of the faculty thought it was true.

The responses of freshmen during Orientation Week presented an interesting contrast with the ones they gave toward the end of the first semester; on every factor the differences were statistically significant. On all except

---

[33] As Astin would be the first to point out, these scores are owing in large measure to student "input" at the elite colleges. That is to say, the intellectual climate reflects the aspirations and abilities of the students. — Ed.

two factors the scores on the second administration of the CCI were lower, indicating that academic standards and pressures were not as great as the freshmen had anticipated. On the other hand, the two dimensions that deal with student freedom or personal responsibility and with the atmosphere of collegiate play or social life were rated higher the second time freshmen responded. Thus, there was more encouragement of student initiative and also more of the lighter side of college life than they had expected.[34]

Freshman, sophomore, and senior responses were also compared. The tendency was for the senior evaluations to be lower than the freshman ratings. Again the dimension about which there seemed to be most disagreement was the Student Dignity factor; the seniors reported significantly higher scores than the others, whereas the sophomores' ratings were lowest. Other studies have also found that upperclassmen tend to be more critical and demanding, so the lower scores were to be expected in such measures as that assessing the concern for academic excellence.

Perceptions of students — classified according to sex, to whether they lived on campus or at home, to the type of high schools they graduated from, and the like — were also subjected to analysis. Differences in background or status were not generally reflected in significantly diverse responses, but there were differences between the evaluations of the men and women. On all of the six factors dealing with intellectual aspects of the climate (and on one of the others), the scores based on the women's perceptions were significantly higher than those of the men. This finding may throw new light on the data presented elsewhere in this chapter concerning the higher ratings given to some of the women's colleges on scales dealing with intellectual orientation. It should be noted that the men and women in the Saint Louis University College of Arts and Sciences were reporting on many identical influences. This is obviously an area that will require further investigation.

That an institution would permit itself to be analyzed and allow the results to be published as Saint Louis University has done in this study seems to be a sign of the maturation of this Catholic campus and a measure of the determination of an already good school to strive for even greater excellence. In a recent article in the *College Board Review*, Pace notes the Antioch profile, published in the *Antioch College Bulletin* for 1965–66, as the first instance, although more than 150 institutions that have administered the CUES, of a college releasing its environmental profile for the benefit of

[34] Regarding the comparison of student and faculty perceptions of the environment, the experience of a midwestern Catholic college for women is interesting. In a study using the College Characteristics Index, students were asked to report on the situation as they thought it existed, and faculty were requested to respond in the way that they thought it should be. A follow-up study several years later revealed a greater change in the faculty views of what they considered desirable than in the students' evaluations of the actual state of affairs.

prospective students.[35] Pace also calls attention to the vast discrepancies that have been discovered between freshman expectations and their realizations at schools that have studied their environments in the way described in this chapter. Greater knowledge about the educational atmosphere might go a long way toward preventing both the groundless fears that seem to paralyze some incoming students and the exaggerated hopes that lead to disillusionment and frustration on the part of many others.[36]

THE CLIMATE FOR LEARNING
AT CATHOLIC COLLEGES

Any attempt to generalize from the findings discussed in the preceding pages involves considerable risk. There is, first of all, the problem of vast differences, as the data clearly indicate, among Catholic as well as among other institutions. Secondly, the findings summarized in this review do not represent a scientifically selected sample, nor do they take into account more than a few of the many possible variables that might influence the scores. Although studies so far have not shown that the results are greatly affected by the representativeness of the sample, such research is still in its early stages and much remains to be done in the way of refining and comparing the results with knowledge from other sources. Nevertheless, with these cautions and qualifications, some general patterns may be noted.

When the Catholic four-year accredited colleges and universities are compared with other institutions on the basis of Astin's EAT data, the differences are not outstanding. But it must be remembered that these scores reflect only the types of baccalaureate degrees conferred, and therefore the Catholic schools understandably show few differences except in Realistic Orientation, which indicates the proportion of degrees granted in agriculture, engineering, physical education, forestry, and industrial arts. Thus, although the other two techniques are more open to bias insofar as they originate in personal judgments, they may offer greater insights into the more intangible varieties of environmental influences.[37]

[35] Pace, "When Students Judge Their College." It may be easier, of course, to publish profiles pointing up the high intellectual climate of an institution than those showing less positive results.

[36] Mundelein College in Chicago has recently undertaken a follow-up study to investigate the effects of the massive overhaul following the self-study of the college in 1962–64. The reader is referred to Norbert J. Hruby, "The Mundelein Self-Study: An Experiment in Reorientation," *North Central News Bulletin*, 22 (March, 1963), pp. 2–10 and "Truth and Consequences: Mundelein College Emerges from Analysis," *ibid.*, 24 (March, 1964), pp. 2–23.

[37] Astin has been developing an instrument which attempts to incorporate the best of both the subjective and objective approaches. In a paper read at the 1965 Meetings of the American Psychological Association, Chicago, as part of the symposium, "Recent Research on the Characteristics of College Environ-

Probably the most noteworthy over-all finding to emerge from this study is the confirmation that Catholic institutions do vary widely among themselves, particularly in such sensitive areas as the encouragement of student freedom and of individual responsibility, and participation in the development of policy.[38] There is a definite tendency, however, for Catholic colleges and universities to rate somewhat lower in this regard than most other institutions. On measures reflecting the encouragement of academic excellence and scholarship, the typical Catholic institution definitely ranks below the average of the norm group of schools.

There has been no attempt to compare Catholic institutions in these areas with the truly outstanding American colleges whose environments would be exceptionally high on the factors and scales dealing with intellectual aspiration and achievement. The Catholic campus appears, however, to place greater emphasis on social awareness, politeness, and more formalized relationships with the faculty and among the students themselves than other schools. There is a serious atmosphere of work with little tolerance for extreme forms of amusement in the Catholic environment, where propriety and conventionality also tend to weigh heavily.

The research on college climates is geared to describing rather than evaluating the environment, and in this respect, the available instruments present special difficulties for the church-related college. Although the CCI and the CUES include individual items about religious practices and values, the "blindness" of the current devices to religious influences, as evidenced by the lack of scales referring to the moral and spiritual impact of the college on the student, leaves an important area of human life — and one of special concern for the value-oriented school — unexamined.

Nevertheless, even the information now attainable can enable the young people entering college to know more clearly the style of life they can expect at a particular college. And the findings of such studies can be revealing for those immersed in the day-to-day life of the institution. One Catholic liberal-arts college dean remarked in responding to the writer's survey, "[The report] is anything but something of which we are proud, but on the other hand, it

ments," Astin described his Inventory of College Activities, an elaboration of Environmental Assessment Technique to pick up some of the more subtle stimuli impinging on students, while still concentrating on observable events. (One of the difficulties with self-reported climate scores is determining the reference groups of reporters.—Ed.)

[38] Similar results can be found in E. G. Williamson and J. L. Cowan, "The Role of the President in the Desirable Enactment of Academic Freedom for Students," *Educational Record*, 46 (1965), 351–72; in his preliminary report of the Carnegie-financed study of the growth of Catholic colleges and universities, Andrew Greeley also emphasized the differences to be found in Catholic higher education ("Changing Intellectual Standards in Catholic Colleges and Universities" [Paper read at the 1966 Meeting of the American Catholic Sociological Society, Miami]).

has forced a bit of thinking as to the causes for such a poor climate of scholarship." He went on to add:

> As an unsolicited comment I might mention that [our] study tends to establish the dichotomy between the strictly academic endeavors and the non-academic, and for this reason it was worthwhile for the faculty to see that though the students work very hard in their classes, their commitments do not go beyond the courses in which they are involved.

Respondents such as this would undoubtedly plead for a greater congruity between the expressed objectives of a college and those implied by the values, customs, and protocol that govern campus life. It is not to be denied, of course, that many institutions would hardly be pleased to find that they are not nearly as academically oriented as the faculty and administration like to think. But not only will such studies provide a spur to improving this environment and the corresponding image, but they will also furnish fairly exact hints about some of the practices that may need changing if the climate itself is to be modified.

IV. PORTRAIT OF A CATHOLIC WOMEN'S COLLEGE

Robert Hassenger

In the preceding chapter, Robert Weiss has presented a broad overview of the Catholic college climate and indicated some of the intra-institutional differences within a large Catholic university. In the present chapter, a portrait of one college will be sketched. Women's colleges comprise the largest segment of Catholic higher education;[1] their growth has been the most conspicuous feature of Catholic college development in this century. No claim is made that *the* Catholic women's college is portrayed here — if indeed there is such an animal. "Mary College"[2] may be similar to some, vastly different from others. But it would appear useful to portray a specific institution at close hand and to try to show how some of the historical forces discussed by Philip Gleason have led to the types of climate uncovered by Robert Weiss.

CLIENTELE: PAST AND PRESENT

In the late 1920's, the archbishop of a major midwestern city requested an order of sisters to open a women's college to provide a good liberal education for local girls of moderate means. As with Catholic schools generally, the college was founded more "to create a center for missionary activities" and to provide a place where young ladies "might be given an opportunity to cultivate the moral virtues"[3] than to foster intellectual development. With its comparatively low tuition, the college has always been something of a melting pot, enrollment at a given time reflecting the mobility patterns of American Catholics.

Confronted by certain changes in its situation,[4] the college administration decided, in midsummer, 1962, to embark on an institutional analysis, gathering information on which decisions could be based regarding

[1] According to F. A. Foy (editor, *National Catholic Almanac*, St. Anthony's Guild, 1961), 53% of the Catholic institutions of higher learning are women's colleges.

[2] "Mary College" is a fictitious name and does *not* refer to the institution in Bismarck, North Dakota, or any other college so named.

[3] From Edward Power's *History of Catholic Higher Education in the United States* (Milwaukee: Bruce Publishing Co., 1958), p. 34.

[4] To be discussed at the conclusion of this chapter.

the school's future. An experienced educator was engaged as director of the analysis and was given the rank of vice-president, the first layman to serve as an administrator there. Data reported in this chapter were obtained from the student and alumnae questionnaires of the "Mary College" self-study.

STUDENT BACKGROUNDS

The ethnic origins of the college's clientele during the four decades of its existence are portrayed in Table 1. The reader notices at a glance the steady decrease in Irish and Anglo-Saxon enrollment, with corresponding increases

TABLE 1
PRIMARY ETHNICITY OF "MARY COLLEGE"
CONSTITUENCIES, BY DECADE[a]

Decade	Anglo-Saxon	German	Irish	Italian	Polish	Total
1930's	17	17	56	1	4	95
1940's	13	22	49	5	8	97
1950's	6	22	44	9	16	97
1960's	8	22	36	11	20	97

[a] In percentages.

among the Italian and Polish groups; the number of German students has remained constant since the 1940's. Indeed, a kind of watershed can be found in the enrollment of the early 1960's. Of the 1963 Seniors, 34 per cent were Irish and 21 per cent Polish; but the 1963 freshman class was 28 per cent Polish, 26 per cent Irish, and 23 per cent German, with subsequent entering classes also reflecting this change. Italians, by 1965, comprised about 10 per cent of the student body,[5] Anglo-Saxons had dropped to 8 per cent, Belgian-French students averaged 5 per cent, Spanish and Negro students 2 per cent each. An indication of how close some of these students remained to traditional backgrounds in 1963 was the finding that foreign languages were still sometimes spoken in one-quarter of the homes; about half of these (12 per cent) were Polish homes, five per cent were Italian, four per cent German, and the remaining two per cent were primarily Spanish-speaking homes.

It is also instructive to compare the occupations and educations of the parents of students in the early 1960's with those of earlier decades. Tables 2 and 3 indicate that in 1963 the college was enrolling students of somewhat lower social class than at the time of the school's founding; there were fewer

[5] Fewer than might be expected. In this regard, it is interesting that Glazer reports that there were fewer Italian girls at New York's Hunter College than would be expected on the basis of the city population of Italian origin ("The Italians," *Beyond the Melting Pot*, eds. Nathan Glazer and Daniel P. Moynihan [Cambridge, Mass.: Harvard University Press, 1964], p. 201). Perhaps these figures reflect the attitude toward education of daughters in Italian families.

of these girls' fathers in the professional and proprietor/manager categories and more in the skilled and semi-skilled occupations, than in the 1930's and 1940's. Further, there were no more college graduates (although slightly more college attenders among students' fathers) than in the school's earlier days, despite the greatly increased proportion in the population as a whole. The majority of the 1963 student body would probably be best labeled lower-middle class, in comparison with the earlier middle-middle class constituency.

TABLE 2

OCCUPATIONS OF FATHERS OF VARIOUS
"MARY COLLEGE" CONSTITUENCIES, BY DECADE[a]

	Profes-sional	Proprietor Manager	Sales/Clerical	Service	Skilled	Semi-skilled	Don't Know or No Answer	Total
Students in 1930's	15	44	11	6	12	4	8	100
Students in 1940's	10	41	13	6	13	5	12	100
Students in 1950's	9	35	13	10	16	7	10	100
Students in 1960's	8	38	7	8	20	11	8	100

[a] In percentages.

But the fathers of 1963 "Mary College" students had often been themselves upwardly mobile. When asked to rate their fathers' present (1963) occupations compared with their occupations at the times of the students' births, 22 per cent indicated that it was "considerably higher now," and an additional 45 per cent stated it was "somewhat higher now." Respondents were also asked to indicate the occupations of their fathers' fathers. About one-third of these grandfathers had been in semi-skilled occupations, whereas only 11 per cent of the students' fathers were in this category. But these

TABLE 3

EDUCATIONAL LEVELS OF FATHERS OF "MARY COLLEGE"
CONSTITUENCIES, BY DECADE[a]

	Less than 8 Grades	Less than HS Diploma	HS Diploma	1–3 Yrs. College	College Graduate	Total
Students in 1930's	38	15	20	11	16	99
Students in 1940's	32	16	26	13	15	100
Students in 1950's	27	20	25	12	16	100
Students in 1960's	16	20	30	17	17	100

[a] In percentages.

fathers seemed to be bunched in skilled labor and sales/clerical positions and were found with only slightly greater frequency in the professional and proprietor/manager categories.[6] Following Lipset and Bendix,[7] it can be suggested that the fathers of the 1963 students had been upwardly mobile by about one step in the occupational hierarchy. The median family income was $9,060, with 12 per cent of the families under $5,000, and 13 per cent making more than $15,000 a year. In the early 1960's, "Mary College" still tended to serve students who were the first in their families to go to college; but, in a time of more widespread educational opportunities, this meant a somewhat lower average socioeconomic level than in the 1930's and 1940's.

The economic situation of these students is illuminated by the data on employment and educational finances obtained from the student questionnaire. All but about sixty of the 1963 students worked at least part-time. Only 41 per cent of the students stated that their families paid for all or "most" of their education; 11 per cent of the underclassmen and 17 per cent of the juniors and seniors paid for all of their schooling, with an additional 14 per cent paying for "most." In response to a query about their "primary reason" for working, approximately 70 per cent of the underclassmen, and 60 per cent of the upperclassmen, gave as their reply "to pay school expenses." Almost a third of the student body worked ten or more hours a week (29% of the freshmen, 35% of the seniors), more than a tenth of the underclassmen and approximately a fifth of the juniors and seniors more than twenty hours a week. The median income for those working was about $750 during the school year, and an additional $450 during the summer; many, of course, earned considerably more. When asked what "event or circumstance would most likely make [them] leave the college," 25 per cent stated "financial problems."

Considering the social-class level of the majority of "Mary College" students, the reader will not be surprised to find a high percentage with social or vocational rather than "liberal" educational objectives. Asked to indicate which of eleven "purposes or goals of a college education" they felt were most important "for a majority of the students" and for themselves, both at college entrance and "now" (1963), about two-thirds in each class stated that "getting career training" was most important for the majority; about one-fifth judged the others to be in search of "economic security," and approximately one-sixth believed that the "better marriage opportunity in college" was a motivating factor. For comparison, almost two-thirds of the seniors admitted that "career-training" was their most important educational objective when they first entered college, but only 43 per cent chose this objective shortly before graduation. In the Spring of their freshman year,

[6] There are, of course, proportionately fewer of these positions in the mid-twentieth century.

[7] Seymour M. Lipset and Reinhard Bendix, *Social Mobility in Industrial Society* (Berkeley and Los Angeles: University of California Press, 1959).

first-year students were closer to upperclassmen than to entering freshmen, 48 per cent indicating "career-training" as their primary educational objective. Only 10 per cent of the students admitted that "economic security" was of first importance for themselves, and a few honest girls (3 per cent) confessed their interest in a "better marriage opportunity." Less than 10 per cent stated that they first came for such noninstrumental, "liberal" reasons as "an opportunity to read interesting books," "an opportunity to examine ideas and argue with people," or "an opportunity to examine political, social and moral questions,"[8] and about the same number felt this was a goal for the others. But approximately 17 per cent of the upperclassmen claimed these goals for themselves. The frequency of choice of "learning to get along with different types of people" remained about the same (20 per cent) whether students were judging others or stating their own freshman or present objectives. Fully one-quarter, both at college entrance and later, chose "gaining true knowledge from instructors," another 10 per cent picked "gaining an understanding of true moral principles from teachers," each alternative expressing a rather unsophisticated view of the educational process. So while there is some decrease of the more pragmatic and social goals and an increase in choice of "liberal" objectives, aspirations toward the former remained high, and there was some uncritical belief that "true knowledge" and "true principles" can be gained from one's teachers.[9]

Historically, "Mary" has been a commuter college, drawing students from the metropolitan area. The largest single contingent in 1963 came from the northwest side of the city (23%), with an additional 15 per cent from the south side, 14 per cent from the western suburbs, 8 per cent from the west side, 4 per cent from the central city area; approximately one-fifth were from out of town, although more than half of these were from other communities in the same state.

Only a handful of the college's 1,100 students had been residents prior to the construction of a new dormitory and the acquisition of a neighboring apartment building in 1962–63.[10] During the 1963–64 academic year, about

---

[8] These three statements were used in place of the usual "basic education and appreciation of ideas" because of the generally high response rates of virtually all college populations to this obviously "right" choice.

[9] This does not mean that objective truth and morality do not exist but refers to the rather passive expectation of "receiving" these from superiors.

[10] The dormitory built in 1962 provides double rooms for 206 students. The six-story apartment hotel purchased by the college in 1963 houses 300 students in one-, two-, and three-room units. A counselor (almost always a religious sister, but occasionally a single woman) lives on every floor of each building. Residence life is generally governed by the students themselves, acting through an elected group called the House Council. Freshmen are assigned rooms in either hall by the Resident Director (a sister); upperclassmen choose their own rooms and roommates. The new hall has a student-lounge area and snack bar in the basement, and a more formal parlor on the first floor. Meals are taken together in the college dining room.

22 per cent of the lay student body[11] were residents: 34 per cent of the freshmen, 24 per cent of the sophomores, and 19 per cent of the upperclassmen. Most of these residents stayed at the college between Sunday evening and Friday afternoon, returning to their homes on weekends; about 80 out-of-city women remained in full-time residence.

The great majority of the student body has always been, not surprisingly, Roman Catholic, coming from Catholic families (77 per cent of the fathers and 87 per cent of the mothers were practicing Catholics in 1963; 14 and 8 per cent more, respectively, non-practicing Catholics). Sixty-two per cent of the student body were from the city's Catholic high schools, 15 per cent from suburban Catholic schools, 10 per cent from city public high schools, with suburban public and out-of-city Catholic high schools contributing about 7 per cent each.

The "Mary College" student of 1963 was, then, a Catholic, lower-middle class girl, from one of the more recently arrived ethnic groups. Along with her brothers and sisters, she belonged to her family's first educational generation. To pay for her education, she worked part-time, and commuted at least twice a week. But she was also interesting in other ways.

STUDENT TRAITS

Additional data from the college self-study can be used to flesh out this sketch. A list of forty-eight adjectives was included in the questionnaire, with respondents instructed to use these to describe the "typical 'Mary College' student" and themselves. The most often chosen qualities were, in order of their frequency:

Typical MC student: Sense of humor, intellectual, genuine, happy, energetic, out-going, religious, cultured.

Self: Sense of humor, fun-loving, cooperative, easy-going, ambitious, religious.

Fully 82 per cent described themselves as having a sense of humor. Whether or not the reader agrees with the faculty wag who remarked that such a description might be that of a pious waitress, he will undoubtedly find these self-portraits interesting.

A more objective indication of the personal attributes of "Mary College" students can be obtained by considering results of the *Activities Index*,[12]

[11] Approximately one-hundred members of the religious community sponsoring the college also take their junior and senior years at "Mary College," but are not included in the data reported here.

[12] This instrument, a companion device to the *College Characteristics Index* described in chapter 3, was used to assess student traits. The thirty scales correspond to the thirty CCI scales, as Robert Weiss noted. Further description can be found in George G. Stern, "Environments for Learning," in *The American College*, ed. N. Sanford (New York: John Wiley & Sons Inc., 1962), 690–730.

administered as part of the self-study. Scoring procedures made available four polarities: independent-dependent, sociable-unsociable, impulsive-controlled, and intellectual-unintellectual.[13] Table 4 shows the percentage of freshmen, sophomores, and seniors characterized by these qualities.

TABLE 4
"MARY COLLEGE" STUDENTS CHARACTERIZED
BY VARIOUS TRAITS, BY CLASS[a]

Traits	Freshmen (269)[b]	Sophomores (232)	Seniors (185)
Independent	23	18	14
Dependent	5	5	9
Sociable	36	44	37
Unsociable	13	13	10
Impulsive	27	28	24
Controlled	3	3	6
Intellectual	23	25	28
Unintellectual	16	11	10

[a] In percentages. Since it is possible for students to be characterized by more than one trait, percentages may total more than 100%.
[b] Number of students in parentheses.

The *Activities Index* indicated some interesting differences among ethnic groups. German students were somewhat higher (39%) and Polish girls slightly lower (20%) in impulsivity, compared to about 30 per cent with Irish and Italian backgrounds. The Italian girls were comparatively high in independence (34%), and Irish students were conspicuously lower in intellectuality (21 per cent, compared to about one-third of the other three groups).

In political identification, German girls were predominantly Republican, Polish students clearly Democratic. The Irish women were slightly more Democratic than Republican, and Italian students were almost equally divided between the two parties. The reported politics of the parents were only slightly correlated with their income and educational levels but were clearly related to the fathers' occupations, with a steadily diminishing Democratic identification as fathers moved up the occupational pyramid.

Students with vocational educational objectives were not disproportionately represented in any of the ethnic groups. Nor were graduate-school plans apparently related to ethnicity, income, or parental occupation. A fairly large number of Irish seniors reported that "friendship with other students" was their most important college experience, whereas Polish students were

[13] For an explanation of the modified scoring used in the "Mary College" investigation, the social scientist is referred to Robert Hassenger, "The Impact of a Value-Oriented College on the Religious Orientations of Students with Various Backgrounds, Traits, and College Exposures" (Ph.D. dissertation, University of Chicago, 1965).

much more likely to choose "career preparation" or an academic experience, such as a particular course or professor.

When queried about how important college graduation was to their parents, Polish girls reported considerably less parental interest than those with other ethnic backgrounds. The average educational and occupational levels of these parents was also clearly lower, as would be expected for a group more recently arrived in the United States.[14] Since these families are often less persuaded of the importance of college for their daughters than for their sons, a self-selection process may operate to send the brightest and most critical of the Polish (and perhaps Italian) women to colleges with relatively low tuition, such as the institution described here.[15] At the same time, these girls might be expected to be more interested in the marketability of their college degrees, justifying the investment of time and money to somewhat skeptical parents.

Keeping this in mind, it is interesting to note the higher percentage of "Mary College" freshmen, compared to seniors, characterized by independence (Table 4). It might be suggested, of course, that the more independent women drop out of such colleges.[16] But the possibility of a changing ethnic constituency being associated with changing student characteristics remains an intriguing one.[17]

[14] The peak year of Polish immigration to America was 1921, compared to 1851 for the Irish, 1882 for the Germans, and 1907 for the Italians (John L. Thomas, S.J., "Nationality and American Catholicism," in *Catholic Church, U.S.A.*, ed. Louis Putz, C.S.C., [Chicago: Fides Press, 1956]).

[15] Kosa *et al.* have shown that aptitude and achievement test performances were just as high for college women from the newer immigrant stock as from "first-wave" families, although "first-wave" college men were significantly higher than "second-wave" men. (Researchers often dichotomize students into "first-wave" [English, Germans, Irish] and "second-wave" [Italians, Poles, and other southern and eastern Europeans] for investigating possible effects of ethnicity.) They suggest that girls from the newer stock who fail to channel their energies into the traditional feminine patterns of housewifery and motherhood are characterized by distinctive motives and attitudes. When such girls attend college despite the absence of parental support, the cogency of this suggestion is increased (John L. Kosa, "Religious Participation, Religious Knowledge and Scholastic Aptitude: An Empirical Study," *Journal for the Scientific Study of Religion*, 1 [1961], 88–97; John L. Kosa, L. Rachiele, and C. Schommer, "Psychological Characteristics of Ethnic Groups in a College Population," *Journal of Psychology*, 46 [1958], 265–75.

[16] Although Trent found "an increase in docility" for senior women in five West Coast Catholic colleges, in both cross-sectional and longitudinal studies (James W. Trent, "The Etiology of Catholic Intellectualism" (Ph.D. dissertation, University of California, 1964).

[17] As the more recent arrivals among American Catholics become increasingly assimilated, larger numbers will be enrolling in Catholic (and even more, in non-Catholic) colleges. This may cause some interesting changes in the Catholic schools; a brief discussion of this possibility is found in the conclusion of this volume, p. 308.

Many "Mary College" students of the 1930's and 1940's are mothers of college-age girls today. But they do not, typically, send these daughters to their alma mater. Now several rungs up the social ladder, often ensconced in a comfortable suburb and alert to status considerations, they encourage their daughters to attend the Manhattanvilles, Trinitys or Newtons, or perhaps a coeducational Catholic college or university, where they can meet aspiring physicians, dentists, and lawyers — but *not* their alma mater, which remains something of a first stop on the way up the social pyramid.

Thus, an increasing segment in 1963 was from the second ethnic wave, or from working-class first-wave families. The middle-class first-wave girl who came to the college was more than likely a less gifted student, or one having a particularly pressing need to stay close to home. Middle-class second-wave students, on the other hand, although the first in their families to go on for higher education, come from more upwardly mobile, less traditional backgrounds. But their concern for social status makes this segment, too, unlikely to be strongly attracted to "Mary College."

Some data are available that throw further light on the differences within the college clientele. Built into the self-study questionnaire was the *Marquette Religious Approach Scale*;[18] several interesting differences can be seen, when scores on this scale are grouped by students' backgrounds. College women from Polish families were found to be high in apostolic Catholicism; Irish girls were somewhat apostolically religious and were high in moralistic Catholicism as well; German college women were intellectually and humanistically religious. In addition, a random sample of freshmen entering the college in the Autumn of 1963 were given instruments measuring authoritarianism and dogmatism.[19] Initial authoritarianism scores of middle- and working-class students were practically identical; but when retested in the Spring, the working-class women were found to drop considerably, while middle-class girls had remained the same; these scores were virtually un-

[18] Paul J. Reiss and Bernard Cooke, S.J., *The Religious Approach Scale* (Milwaukee: Marquette University, 1960). This instrument investigates the basic approach to Catholicism that a student possesses and that is operative in his daily life. Four such general approaches are suggested: moralistic — the approach of one who sees religion as primarily an ethical system, as a code for right and wrong that should be followed to attain heaven and avoid hell; apostolic — the orientation to religion viewing the Catholic church as the Mystical Body of Christ and one's role in the church as integrated with its mission; intellectual — approaching religion as a body of dogma, with both central and peripheral aspects; humanistic — the orientation of one who sees religion as a means for making himself a better human person and contributing toward the fulfillment of various human needs. This scale is discussed again in chapter 5 and in more detail in Robert Hassenger, "Varieties of Religious Orientation," *Sociological Analysis*, 25 (1965), 189–99 and in Hassenger, "Impact of a Value-Oriented College."

[19] The social scientist will be familiar with these often-used instruments. More extensive discussion of them can, however, be found in the following two chapters.

changed ten months later, toward the end of the students' sophomore year. The same differences were revealed by the dogmatism scores, although a different rate of change resulted in little freshman decrease. Entering middle-class women had a dogmatism mean of 176, which decreased to 164 eighteen months later; comparative scores for working-class girls were 151 and 143.[20] There were no consistent differences related to ethnicity, but class and ethnicity interact to produce an interesting pattern of change, which will be discussed in the chapter on college impact which follows.

Some information about students' ability levels can be presented. Although 58 per cent of the 1963 freshmen were in the top fifth of their high school classes, and another 29 per cent in the second fifth, a better indication of the clientele's intellectual power can be obtained by consideration of the Verbal and Quantitative Scores of the College Entrance Examination Board tests. Mean CEEB scores for the 1963 freshmen were 543.1 (Verbal) and 496 (Quantitative), with less than a third scoring above 600 on the Verbal section, and less than 15 per cent on the Quantitative section (Table 5). When the College Board exams were first required of "Mary College" applicants in 1961,[21] the Verbal and Quantitative Scores were 514 and 457, respectively. By 1965, scores of entering freshmen were 535 and 505, respectively. The quality of the average student seems to be inching upward. As enrollment pressures allow the college to be more selective in the last third of the century, even greater increases will probably be found.

Students, of course, are only part of a college — necessary, but not sufficient. What kinds of faculty are they likely to encounter at "Mary College"?

TABLE 5
DISTRIBUTION BY CEEB SCORES,
1963 FRESHMEN

CEEB SCORES	VERBAL		QUANTITATIVE	
	No.	%	No.	%
700–749	6	2.3	5	1.0
650–699	25	9.5	17	6.2
600–649	45	16.7	17	6.2
550–599	49	17.7	36	13.2
500–549	53	19.7	54	20.1
450–499	59	21.9	62	23.1
400–449	23	8.5	39	14.3
350–399	9	3.3	31	11.6
300–349	1	.4	9	3.8
		100.0		100.0

[20] The slower rate of change in dogmatism might suggest that this is a "deeper" dimension than authoritarianism. That working-class students were low on dogmatism but not on authoritarianism at college entrance would be difficult to reconcile with such a suggestion, however.

[21] American Council on Education examinations had previously been used.

FACULTY

Like most Catholic women's colleges, the school functioned for years staffed almost entirely by members of a religious community. The slow "invasion"[22] of lay faculty members began with women at first, but the number of men teachers has increased steadily since the mid-1950's. The self-study found that there were in a sense two faculties at "Mary College," but the lines of cleavage were not drawn as some readers might expect. In 1963, of the forty-six sisters, fifty-two laymen, and two priests, the clearest division was on the basis of age, not religious or lay status. This can be better understood if the educational backgrounds of the various groups[23] are described.

There were about ten middle- to advanced-age laywomen, usually alumnae with bachelor's or master's degrees who had been with the college for some time, or who had retired from another institution, such as a city junior college. Two or three from the latter group had the doctorate.

Older sisters or lay men tended to have either master's degrees from state universities or doctorates from Catholic universities; they had also been with the college a number of years. The men were concentrated in the humanities, education, and philosophy; the older sisters were primarily in the physical sciences, the humanities (although not philosophy), history, and education.

About ten younger sisters and twenty young men and women were typically fresh Ph.D.'s or doctoral candidates at good secular universities (e.g., Wisconsin, Northwestern, Chicago, and even one from Harvard). The young sisters were more likely actually to have the doctorate; when the lay men and women acquired their degrees, they usually left for greener pastures, unless they were wives of professors at the neighboring university. A few of these women were in the sciences, but most were in English, history, psychology, or philosophy.[24]

In 1963, about a third of the full-time sisters and 22 per cent of the lay faculty had Ph.D.'s. All four full-time sisters in the sciences had the doctorate, three from good non-Catholic universities.[25] As data from the self-study showed, communication barriers were not between sisters and laymen,

[22] This is the term used by John Donovan in his description of *The Academic Man in the Catholic College* (New York: Sheed and Ward, 1964), p. 24.

[23] "Group" as used in this section does not imply a formally or informally existing collection of people who consistently interact. It is used to mean category or collectivity here, but the less technical word is in deference to readers other than social scientists.

[24] A number of part-time faculty were also in and out of the college, from high school teachers participating in the teacher-supervision of the Education Department and instructors of art and home economics to a distinguished mathematician and an eminent Jesuit theologian teaching small seminars in their specialties.

[25] The effects of their more professional orientation are described below.

or between female and male faculty members, but between the younger and older faculties. The young nuns who had been to secular universities were often much more liberal than the older sisters, but in many ways the sisters as a group were less conservative than the lay faculty. This statement is not made rashly. It is based on careful analysis of faculty responses to fifty items taken from several past studies of the attitudes and values of college students, for example, the Inventory of Beliefs, the Cornell Values Survey, the Berkeley Authoritarianism, Ethnocentrism, and Conservatism Scales.[26] The fifty statements were included in the student questionnaire to sample attitudes in areas such as civil liberties, politics, economics, race, social problems, education, and personal responsibility.[27] Although no norms exist for this particular collection of items, intra-college comparisons are possible.[28] Mean "liberalism" scores for the fifty items were 69.3 for the religious sisters, and 58.7 for the lay faculty, which seemed to indicate a greater "liberalism," or at least "criticalness," on the part of the former group.

As an additional indication of the different orientations of these two "Mary College" populations, it is noteworthy that the religious faculty was found to be 76 per cent Democratic, 13 per cent Republican, and 7 per cent politically independent; the lay faculty was 33 per cent Democratic, 46 per cent Republican, and 19 per cent independent. So, although the younger and better-educated sisters and lay men and women are probably the most "pro-

[26] The most accessible source for brief descriptions of these instruments is Philip Jacob, *Changing Values in College* (New York: Harper Bros., 1957).

[27] Taken together, these items comprise a "fundamentalism" or "liberalism" index, depending on the scoring procedure. A respondent was given a score of 2 for each item with which he "disagreed" or "strongly disagreed," i.e., took the "liberal" position. There was no attempt to weight these responses differentially on the Likert-type items. Thus, a perfect "liberal" score would be 100, a perfect "conservative" score, O. Some sample items and percentages of disagreement (the "liberal" position) were: "Democracy depends fundamentally on the free enterprise system," 28% disagreement by religious faculty, 16% by the lay faculty; "People who plead the Fifth Amendment before Congressional committees may usually be presumed guilty," 78% disagreement by the religious faculty, 52% by the lay faculty; and "The way they are now run, labor unions do this country more harm than good," 70% of the religious faculty disagreed, 57% of the lay faculty.

[28] Since the self-study was directed by the vice-president and me and run by the student council, faculty members had not previously seen the instrument. It was suggested they work through the questionnaire to better prepare for discussion of results, and this provided an excellent way of collecting data on faculty, which would otherwise have been difficult. Since the study was done, an exciting instrument has been developed by Sr. Marie Augusta Neal (*Values and Interests in Social Change* [Englewood Cliffs, N.J.: Prentice-Hall, 1964]), and future studies would be enhanced by use of this instrument.

gressive" groups, particularly with regard to discipline and student freedom, the sisters in general were more "liberal" in matters of political and economic policy and civil liberties.[29]

THE COLLEGE CLIMATE

Asked if there was a "certain type" of ("Mary College") student who was "rewarded with grades, offices and honors," approximately half (42% of the freshmen, 58% of the seniors) agreed that there was. The percentages of students checking various characteristics to describe her were: "intellectually sharp" (51%); "hard-working" (39%); "out-going" (29%); "tactful" (26%); and "looks good in public appearances" (23%).

There was also general agreement that the positions with "greatest prestige" were: Student Activities Council President (91%);[30] Senior Class President (70%); Woodrow Wilson or National Science Foundation Fellowship winner (53%, but 49% of the freshmen and 64% of the seniors[31]); and Social Chairman (48%). The newspaper editor was further back (31%), and the Sodality Prefect (president) was checked by only 15 per cent.

In another question, students were asked "in what ways 'Mary's' freshman year was different from senior year in high school"; their responses are

TABLE 6
WAYS IN WHICH THE FRESHMAN YEAR AT "MARY COLLEGE"
DIFFERED FROM HIGH-SCHOOL SENIOR YEAR [a]

No major difference between them	15%
Intellectual challenge greater at MC	49%
Students at MC work harder	36%
Students at MC given more responsibility	27%
More personal freedom at MC	41%
More independent study required at MC	35%
Friendships at MC on more mature basis	17%
Freshman year at MC easier	5%

[a] In percentages. More than one response was permitted, so percentages total more than 100%.

[29] One of the older, and yet most progressive, of the sisters noted that it may be relatively easy for those with vows of poverty to proclaim their encouragement of Negroes in the neighborhood, their support of the welfare state, and so on. There were other indications that the differences were genuine, however; one possible reason for this is the greater exposure to liberal orientations for the older sisters by living with the younger ones, a situation with few parallels for the older lay faculty members.

[30] The "Activities" is important; in 1963, "Mary College" did not have a genuine student council or senate.

[31] Which is probably fairly typical of most colleges: the more scholarly students ranking near, but not at, the top of the prestige hierarchy. This may be changing, however, as the numerous disaffiliations from "Who's Who" may indicate.

presented in Table 6. A cross-tabulation was then run to determine what high schools were attended by those who stated there was no major difference between high school and freshman year at the college; these were overwhelmingly from Catholic high schools. Another questionnaire item yielded similar data. Responding to a question about whether they had ever felt "out of it" at "Mary College," students from Catholic high schools gave a disproportionately low number of negative answers, whereas those from suburban public high schools and from Polish families were clearly more likely to assent.

An increasing amount of research indicates that a variety of subcultures exists within American colleges, attracting different types of students who have differing perceptions of the campus climate.[32] Even schools the size of "Mary College" can be expected to have several such subcultures. One of the most common determinants of membership in a campus group is a student's major field.

Like most Catholic women's colleges, "Mary" followed in 1963 a traditional liberal arts curriculum, with required sequences in English, the natural sciences, mathematics, history, and the social sciences. The last area was probably weakest, but was fast improving. Majors were chosen in the Spring of one's sophomore year, and each of these fields required 24 to 30 hours of course work, most of which was prescribed. Considering the backgrounds of many "Mary College" students, it is perhaps not surprising that a majority believed that their educations — often acquired at considerable sacrifice — should result in a marketable skill.[33] It appeared that many of these women would have preferred to major in education — often to teach on the primary level — and chose fields such as English, psychology, and sociology only because they had to have a major, and one was not available in education. Twenty-two per cent of the 420 junior and senior laywomen in 1963 were science or mathematics majors, 24 per cent chose English, 16 per cent psychology or sociology, 12 per cent economics or history, 10 per cent home economics, speech, or speech correction, and 8 per cent each, art and languages. More than half of the upperclassmen minored in education.

Data are available to illustrate some interesting differences among the fields, both in students' perceptions of the college and in their personal traits. Four groups of twenty students each, from the humanities (English, art, and languages), the social sciences (psychology and sociology), mathematics and the natural sciences, and a group minoring in education,[34] filled out the *Col-*

[32] Indications of this can be found in the preceding and following chapters.

[33] A strong vocational orientation — more than a quarter of the student body indicated "career plans" as their primary motive to study — was undoubtedly linked to a strong desire for upward social mobility in this population.

[34] In each group there were ten junior and ten senior students; the education minors were stratified by major field as well.

lege Characteristics Index, an instrument designed specifically to assess the environment or "climate" of an educational institution.[35]

The data for "Mary College" are summarized in Table 7. In general, the four college groups can be seen to rank[36] between the liberal arts colleges, which are highest in intellectual climate and lowest in nonintellectual climate, and the denominational schools and teachers' colleges, which ranked lowest

TABLE 7

RANKINGS IN COLLEGE CHARACTERISTICS INDEX FACTORS,
BY COLLEGE TYPE AND "MARY COLLEGE" MAJOR[a]

Type of College	Work	INTELLECTUAL CLIMATE						
		Non-vocational Climate	Aspiration Level	Intellectual Atmosphere	Student Dignity	Academic Climate	Academic Achievement	Self-expression
Liberal arts colleges	4	1	1	1	1	1	1	2
"Mary Col."								
Science	2	6	2	4	4	2	3	5
Humanities	1	3	6	3	2	6	4	4
Soc. science	3	5	7	5	3	7	5	3
Education	5	4	3	2	5	5	2	1
Denominational schools	6	7	5	7	7	4	7	6
Teachers' colleges	7	2	4	6	6	3	6	7

	NON-INTELLECTUAL CLIMATE					
	Self-expression	Group Life	Academic Organization	Social Form	Play	Vocational Climate
Liberal arts	2	7	7	7	4	7
"Mary Col."						
Science	5	4	3	2	6	2
Humanities	4	5	1	4	7	5
Soc. science	3	2	4	5	5	3
Education	1	3	2	3	3	4
Denomination-al schools	6	1	5	1	2	1
Teachers' colleges	7	6	6	6	1	6

a "Rank" refers to "how much" of a factor a group reports. See footnote 36.

35 Stern, "Environments for learning." In the preceding chapter, Robert Weiss explained that the three-hundred items to which students respond describe commonplace daily activities, school policies, procedures, attitudes, and impressions that might be characteristic of various types of undergraduate college settings. There has been considerable research carried out with this instrument in the past few years, so that it is now possible to compare students' descriptions of their school with the responses given by those in other colleges. By analyzing scale means, a profile of the institution can be sketched, which takes its meaning from contrast with or similarity to other environmental descriptions.

36 Rank refers to how much of a factor a group reports. Thus, liberal arts colleges rank first on six of the eight dimensions of the Intellectual Climate; "Mary College" humanities majors rank first on Work, third on Non-vocational Climate, etc.

in intellectual climate, highest in non-intellectual climate. There were interesting departures from this pattern, however. Humanities and social science majors reported a very low "aspiration level" (college encouragement of self-prescribed high student standards) and "academic climate" (institutional stress on academic excellence), while science majors ranked immediately behind the liberal arts colleges here. Education students reported numerous opportunities available for the development of leadership potential and self-assurance ("self-expression"), and ranked second in both "academic achievement" and in perceived "intellectual atmosphere." In the non-intellectual climate, "Mary College" groups held the first four ranks on "academic organization" (a highly structured academic environment, with little freedom to substitute courses and make other changes), with humanities majors first. The school was also high in "vocational climate," an emphasis on practical, applied activities with comparative rejection of esthetic experience, and all but the education students were conspicuously low on "play," activities associated with dating, athletics, or other forms of collegiate amusement.

These student perceptions of the college, then, seem to support the picture that began to emerge from the data presented earlier in this chapter: that of a college catering to lower-middle class commuting students, many of whom must sacrifice to obtain their degrees, and who may be expected to show some concern over its market value. Science majors reported the most intellectual college climate.

This is particularly interesting because women in the sciences at "Mary College" were also found to be higher in the corresponding *Activities Index* variables contributing to the intellectualism dimension.[37] The remaining college groups differed only slightly from one another.[38] Other self-study data are consistent with these findings. When queried about whether they would take the same major again, for example, only 13 per cent of the science seniors indicated they would not, compared to 40 per cent of the psychology and sociology seniors, and one-quarter of those in English.[39] In ranking their "most important college experiences," 30 per cent of the science seniors checked "preparation for graduate school," compared to 22 per cent each for the English and psychology-sociology seniors. Another 31 per cent of the science seniors ranked "knowledge of God" first, compared to 24 per cent and 21 per cent, for psychology-sociology and English seniors,

[37] Stern has presented evidence that these instruments are independent of each other. College press is not a function of students' needs, i.e., personal traits do not significantly distort perceived press.

[38] It is interesting that even science majors were higher than the normative group in Deference, Order, Succorance, Aggression, and Sensuality, along with the remaining three "Mary College" groups. So their intellectualism is coupled to a rather deferential, authoritarian trait pattern.

[39] Education minors are also much less likely to be dissatisfied with their college work.

respectively. Twenty-five per cent of the science upperclassmen actually had graduate-school plans, compared to an average of 16 per cent for the upperclassmen in the humanities and social sciences (although one-quarter of the English majors also planned to go to graduate school). Only 13 per cent of the science seniors stated they were consistently bored in class, compared to one-third of those in English, and one-fifth of the psychology-sociology seniors.

Science seniors participated more in their departmental clubs (33%, compared to 22% and 17% for humanities and social science seniors), but had less time for other student affairs. This seemed to be owing more to the press of work than to lack of interest. When indicating why they did not participate, one-quarter of the senior science majors checked "class work" (compared to 15% and 11% of the non-participating seniors in humanities and social sciences), 62 per cent indicated "lack of time" (as against 50% and 43% of the humanities and social science people), and 18 per cent claimed "conflicting schedules" (8% and 6%, in humanities and social sciences). Only one-fifth claimed a "lack of interest," whereas one-third of the humanities and social science non-participants indicated this to be the reason.

Finally, there were better teacher-student relationships in the sciences. One hundred per cent of the science seniors claimed to have made use of the advice of a faculty member, compared to 84 per cent of the humanities and three-fourths of the social science seniors. Only 16 per cent of the science seniors felt that no faculty member "cared about" them, compared to one-quarter of both social sciences and humanities seniors.

Little additional data allowed the majors in social science and humanities to be characterized; these two groups seemed to provide the background against which those in science stood out. One set of findings helps describe the former groups, however. Although 61 per cent of all the seniors minored in education, only one-quarter of the science upperclassmen did so, and all but three of these girls were in secondary education. This means that considerably more than two-thirds of the social science and humanities upperclassmen took an education minor, with more than half concentrating in primary education.

It was shown earlier that the sisters were, collectively, more liberal than the lay faculty. Science majors had virtually all of their courses from four full-time sisters and interacted frequently with them outside of class, as the above data indicate. More highly intellectual than "Mary College" students generally, and sharing immediate objectives both with each other and with the more professionally oriented sisters[40] with whom they interacted rather intensely, science majors might be expected to have undergone greater

[40] All four had the doctorate from good schools, three published regularly in the professional journals, and two received national fellowships for their research activities.

change during their college years than many of their peers. This was, indeed, the case. Other data on the differential impact of "Mary College" can be found in chapter 5 on Catholic college effects. But it is appropriate to indicate here that seniors in the sciences at "Mary College" were consistently liberal in virtually every measure of the self-study, an outcome not found for "Mary College" students generally.

It would be possible to present other data that would furnish a more complete picture of this Catholic women's college. But the foregoing should be sufficient to indicate both the diversity and homogeniety of one specific institution. No claim is made that it is typical; but parallels with many colleges can undoubtedly be found.

Nor is the "Mary College" of 1963 that of 1966–67. Some extensive changes had occurred in the three short years between the self-study and the time of this writing, but these cannot be discussed in detail without compromising the anonymity of the college.[41] The two decades preceding 1963 had witnessed a revolution in the educational situation in the metropolitan area within which "Mary College" is located. The Catholic men's universities had become completely coeducational; several other Catholic women's colleges were performing essentially the same functions; and two additional colleges were scheduled to open within a few years. New municipal teachers' colleges were built, and an extension of the state university was greatly expanded. All of these institutions were or soon would be offering the same educational opportunities that were furnished by "Mary College" in 1963. Confronted by this prospect, the administration decided on a radical restructuring of their operation; the new program is still in its early infancy in 1966, but is being watched with real interest by many Catholic educators.

Other colleges would have chosen different paths. Many undoubtedly will.[42] By 1970, there may be great diversity among the Catholic women's colleges. Even in 1966, these schools can no longer be counted on to "assure the parents of a safely hermetic, if not ascetically uncomfortable, education for their daughters."[43] Some may be positively "dangerous" places in the 1970's for those who believe the function of these colleges is to "save the faith" of their students.

All such speculation is outside our scope here. This chapter has attempted to introduce empirical data to sketch the portrait of one among the almost three-hundred institutions of Catholic higher education.

[41] Some will already have decided on its identity; they may be correct, but it is likely that at least a dozen schools are considered.

[42] Immaculate Heart College, for example, will formally affiliate with the Claremont Colleges of California in the near future. And, of course, Webster College is undergoing "secularization."

[43] David Riesman and Christopher Jencks, "The Viability of the American College," in The American College, ed N. Sanford (New York: John Wiley & Sons, Inc., 1962), p. 91.

Effects of Catholic Higher Education

V. THE IMPACT OF CATHOLIC COLLEGES

Robert Hassenger

Despite an almost universal acceptance of the importance of college in contemporary American society, there has been little investigation of the real effects of the higher educational experience. Only in the past few years have certain college populations been given close attention, as efforts are made to measure precisely what is being modified in their students, and how these changes are taking place. Results have not been entirely encouraging. One comprehensive review of research on student values noted that few significant changes could be attributed to what Veblen called the higher learning in America.

> College does make a difference — but not a very fundamental one for most students. Basic values remain largely constant through college. The changes which do occur bring greater consistency into the value patterns of the students and fit these patterns to a well-established standard of what a college graduate in American society is expected to believe and do. . . . College socializes, but does not really liberalize the students.[1]

Although the Jacob report received extensive criticism,[2] his general conclusion has been little challenged. There are some indications that a few colleges and universities — usually characterized by the liberal arts curricula, small enrollments, and a high academic reputation — effect some value and attitude changes in their students; but these colleges seem exceptions.

Little is known about the impact of the vast majority of colleges and universities, including the Catholic higher educational institutions. It is the intent of this chapter to consider the available data on the effectiveness of Catholic colleges.[3] Already a value term has been introduced. The results

---

[1] Philip E. Jacob, *Changing Values in College* (New York: Harper Bros., 1957), p. 38.

[2] Most notably, those of Allen H. Barton, *Studying the Effects of College Education* (New Haven, Conn.: The Edward W. Hazen Foundation, 1959); and David Riesman, "The Jacob Report," *American Sociological Review*, 23 (1958), 732–39.

[3] Here, as throughout the chapter, "college" is used to refer to both four-year institutions and undergraduate colleges within universities.

summarized in this chapter will be interpreted differently by various readers. Data will not "mean" the same thing to all who work their way through the statistical thickets to follow. Nor is the presentation totally free from a kind of bias. Although I have tried to control the influence of my own value stance, it will undoubtedly show through at times. Social scientists find it difficult to look with dispassion on certain results, particularly if they care deeply about the subject of their investigation. It is better to make this bias explicit here and indicate its foundation.

We understand little about changes of values in college. This is matched by the existing ignorance about the developmental changes of later adolescence. Sanford refers to this period as "the largest barren area in the field we have sought to map," and only recently has a theory developed concerning these changes. Sanford has summarized the situation:

> Psychologists, for their part, have in their consideration of personality development tended to neglect the period of late adolescence or young adulthood. The prevailing opinion has been that the personality is pretty well formed by the age of eighteen, and what happens after that is to be understood mainly as expression of dispositions established earlier, usually much earlier.[4]

The result, he noted, has been "a lack of concepts and theory relevant to the actual changes that may be observed to take place during the college years or shortly thereafter."[5]

A number of theorists have pointed up the attitudinal and behavioral changes that can be expected to accompany the developmental processes of later adolescence. Piaget, for example, describes the movement away from adult constraint through the "moral realism" of uncritical acceptance of external rules to an autonomy based upon cooperation with others, as each individual separately examines and rationally validates his own moral decisions.[6] This is accomplished largely because the adolescent "extends his conceptual range to the hypothetical, the future, and the spatially remote."[7] Erikson writes of the "identity crisis," because "new and often conflicting social demands all make previous adjustments appear insufficient, and, in fact, makes previous opportunities and rewards suspect."[8] Other theorists

---

[4] Nevitt Sanford, "Research and Policy in Higher Education," in *The American College*, ed. N. Sanford (New York: John Wiley & Sons, Inc., 1962), p. 1010.

[5] Nevitt Sanford (ed.), "Personality Development During the College Years," *Journal of Social Issues*, 12 (1956), 61.

[6] Jean Piaget, *The Moral Development of the Child* (New York: Harcourt, Brace, 1932).

[7] John Flavell, *The Developmental Psychology of Jean Piaget* (New York: Basic Books, 1964).

[8] Erik Erikson, "The Problem of Ego Identity," *Psychological Issues*, 1 (1959), 116; perhaps more widely known is Erik Erikson, *Childhood and Society* (New York: Norton, 1950).

could be cited; thus, Anna Freud's discussion of ego-defenses;[9] Maslow's distinction between "deficiency motivation" and "growth motivation";[10] White's outline of "natural growth trends"[11] — all these are relevant. But perhaps the most interesting explanation of personality growth in college is the theory advanced by Sanford, which arose to considerable extent from his Mellon Foundation investigation at Vassar.[12]

Sanford proposes "a stage of late adolescence that intervenes between adolescence proper and early adulthood."[13] The college freshman is somewhere in this stage of development.

> The freshman tends to be like a convert to adulthood, an enthusiastic supporter and imitator of adult ways who knows what it is to backslide — which he sometimes does. The achievement of flexible control, an arrangement in which there is genuine freedom of impulses because there is little danger of their getting out of hand, lies ahead; nevertheless, impulses are now inhibited or contained with sufficient effectiveness so that the young person can turn his attention to other matters. He is now ready to concentrate upon his relations with the external world — to improve his understanding of that world and find a place within it.[14]

Work such as the Vassar research has indicated that growth can be charted along several dimensions, among which are impulse expression, enlightenment of conscience, and differentiation and integration of the ego. Considerable development between the freshman and the senior year was observed at Vassar:

> Evidence from the MMPI scales [the Minnesota Multiphasic Personality Inventory, a commonly used assessment device], and from the Development and Impulse Expression scales [scales of the Omnibus Personality Inventory, discussed below] leave no doubt that seniors are more unstable, more disturbed, or . . . "upset," than are freshmen. . . . Seniors are most unstable because there is more to be stabilized, less certain of their identities because more possibilities are open to them.[15]

[9] Anna Freud, *The Ego and the Mechanisms of Defense* (New York: International Universities Press, 1946).

[10] Abraham H. Maslow, *Toward a Psychology of Being* (Princeton, N.J.: D. Van Nostrand and Co., Inc., 1961).

[11] Robert W. White, *Lives in Progress* (New York: Dryden Press, 1952).

[12] First presented systematically in N. Sanford, "Personality Development," and turning up frequently in the volume edited by Sanford, *The American College.*

[13] Nevitt Sanford, "Developmental Status of the Entering Freshman," in *The American College,* ed. N. Sanford (New York: John Wiley & Sons, Inc., 1962), p. 260.

[14] *Ibid.,* p. 260.

[15] Sanford, "Personality Development," p. 42.

To explain these findings, Sanford outlines a theory resting upon "a conception of a *course* of development, that is to say, an order of events defining progress from lower to higher levels of development."[16] The freshman is characterized by a pattern "in which strong impulses are directly opposed by an alert, rigid, and punitive conscience,"[17] resulting in a certain degree of ambiguity intolerance, conventionality, and impulse repression. With further development there will be a movement toward freer expression of impulses, greater flexibility and nonconformity in actions and values, and a less uncritical acceptance of the institutional authority of family, state, and organized religion. This "differentiation and integration of the ego" will have as a correlative the reexamination of values, attitudes, and behavior.

A summary statement of the changes found to occur at Vassar has been presented by Brown.

> As a group, seniors are more able to tolerate and express their inner lives; they are capable of self-insight; they admit what others might call bizarre or neurotic experiences as part of their inner life. They are more emotionally and intellectually flexible; they are able to accept ambiguity and complexity in the world of events and in art objects; they are freer of compulsive and driven trends to perform or do the "right thing"; they are tolerant of the shortcomings of others; they are critical and discerning toward rules and institutions, but accepting of individuals. On the whole, seniors have mature interests, place value on intellectual processes, tend to be less conventional and conforming to social pressures, tend to reject traditional feminine roles in favor of more broadly defined roles, are concerned and even anxious about the future, and wonder whether they haven't been educated for the best of all non-existent worlds.[18]

An attempt to represent this course of development is presented in Figure 1.

One of the results of this maturation is a liberalization of values and attitudes: political, social, economic, and religious.[19] It is possible, of course, that limitations will impede this growth, preventing the modification of atti-

[16] Sanford, "Status of the Freshman," p. 259.

[17] *Ibid.*, p. 262.

[18] Donald Brown, "College and Value Conflict," *American Association of University Women Journal*, 55 (1962), 219.

[19] In the latter domain, notes Pierre Babin ("Rethinking the Life of Faith," *Lumen Vitae*, 15 [1960], 233–46), it often happens that the adolescent will, as he advances toward young adulthood, "leav(e) behind childhood supports such as simplistic, subjective forms of his childhood faith; purif(y) certain artificial links between the life of the Church and the morality of his environment, secondary religious practices, nonessential forms of devotion; recogniz(e) the human and sinful dimension of the Church on earth; (be) conscious of a personal vocation and commitment of charity. . . ." See also P. Babin, *Crisis of Faith* (New York: Herder and Herder, 1963).

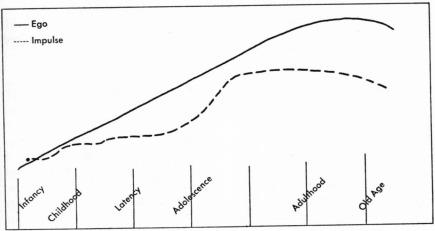

FIG. 1. Development of the ego and of impulse according to Sanford's theory of personality (with the permission of N. Sanford).

tudes and values. If, for example, value and attitude change poses a threat to students, such growth is unlikely to take place. The theory and research of Adorno *et al*, Katz and Stotland, Plant, Trent, Wagman, and others make it clear that ego-defensive attitudes are particularly resistant to modification,[20] since they "give the ego security through the belief that the individual is superior to others."[21]

Early learning experiences may cause defensiveness. One of the most frequent correlates seems to be a rigid, punitive family atmosphere. For the present investigation, it is important to note that many Catholic students come from homes that, for a number of historical reasons — as Philip Gleason has shown — tend to maintain strict, unpermissive patterns of relationships.[22] As a variety of research indicates,[23] this very often leads to an

[20] T. W. Adorno, Else Frenkel-Brunswik, Daniel Levinson, and Nevitt Sanford, *The Authoritarian Personality* (New York: Harper and Bros., 1950); Donald Katz and Ezra Stotland, "A Preliminary Statement to a Theory of Attitude Structure and Change," in *Psychology: A Study of a Science*, ed. Sigmund Koch (New York: McGraw-Hill, 1961), vol. III; Walter Plant, "Changes in Ethnocentrism During College," *Journal of Educational Psychology*, 49 (1958), 112–65; James W. Trent, "The Etiology of Catholic Intellectualism" (Ph.D. dissertation, University of California, 1964); M. Wagman, "Attitude Change and the Authoritarian Personality," *Journal of Psychology*, 40 (1955), 3–24.

[21] Katz and Stotland, "Theory of Attitude Structure," p. 442.

[22] Cf. John D. Donovan, *The Academic Man and the Catholic College* (New York: Sheed and Ward, 1964); John Kane, "Social Structure of American Catholics," *American Catholic Sociological Review*, 8 (1947), 209–18; and Thomas F. O'Dea, *American Catholic Dilemma* (New York: Sheed and Ward, 1958).

[23] Some of the most important of this is summarized in Bernard Berelson and Gary Steiner, *Human Behavior* (New York: Harcourt, Brace and World, 1964).

authoritarian defensiveness characterized by rigid value and attitude structures. Perhaps their working-class, immigrant origins had much to do with
this. As Greeley *et al.* suggested, a largely immigrant church had emphasized
the preservation of certain elements of creed, code, and cult as symbols of
the faith.

> Regular church attendance was a manifestation of loyalty to the Church
> of one's ancestors; acceptance of Church authority distinguished one
> from other Americans who did not vest their Church with very much
> authority. Strict sexual morality not only preserved the rigorous morals
> of the old world; it also marked Catholics as being different from other
> Americans. . . . By emphasizing external devotion, authority, and
> chastity, the Church not only preserved its distinctiveness, but also de-
> fended its members from what it took to be the most serious threats
> of the New World culture — moral, doctrinal, and cultic indifferent-
> ism.[24]

There are indications that such days are largely over, and that the Catholic
college students of the 1960's will be less resistant to change. If the colleges
are effective, seniors should look different from freshmen. They should be
more open to new ideas and attitudes, less "sure" of themselves in many
ways, having uncovered their many selves within. They should value more
highly what can be called intellectual pursuits; they will of course not all be
intellectuals, but they will not harbor the stereotypes held by many freshmen.
They will be more tolerant of deviation, less willing to condemn. Deeply
committed to personal beliefs themselves, they will also be receptive to other
value systems. Seniors will be more self-reliant, less willing to accept uncriti-
cally the cliches, canards, and bromides of the larger society. In short, they
will be more mature. This may be asking too much. But it is the ideal, and
if results indicate some colleges effect such changes in their students more
successfully than others, these schools can be called — at least by the criteria
outlined here — "better."

Before the results of the available research are reviewed, some prefatory
comments need to be made. First, it must be clear that studies of Catholic
higher education are of greatly diverse quality. Few investigations of the
caliber of the National Opinion Research Center's surveys are available. It
is difficult to convey to the non-social-science oriented reader the vast differences among studies summarized here. The more sophisticated research —
which means, primarily, work in which care has been taken to "control" for
extraneous factors — is more reliable and is, in this sense, "worth" more.

---

[24] Andrew M. Greeley, Peter H. Rossi, and Leonard J. Pinto, *The Social
Effects of Catholic Education: A Preliminary Report*, National Opinion Research
Center, 1965.

We shall try to make clear which of the investigations are more valuable, but the really good studies are so few that they will sometimes appear buried within a mass of less sophisticated research.

Second, the random and even haphazard ways in which research on Catholic campuses has been done makes it necessary to keep in mind the many varieties comprising Catholic higher education. Certain difficulties of orderly presentation of this meagre data result in some blurring of these differences. The reader is asked to keep these in mind, as well.

Third, few studies purportedly assessing college impact really do so. Strict adherence to an ideal investigatory design would involve comparable groups of students followed throughout their post-high school years. Instead of such longitudinal research, the bulk of the studies of "college effects" compare concurrent freshmen and seniors, in what is termed a cross-sectional investigation. Usually no evidence is available that seniors were at the same stage or level three years previously as are the freshmen against whom comparison is made. Nor are controls available for the possible effects of differential drop-out, which might well influence the freshman-senior comparisons.

Fourth, the easiest way of approaching individuals' attitudes and opinions is to ask them, usually with an instrument of numerous items that are responded to as true or false. The obvious difficulties need not be elaborated here. Until a less risky way is devised (and many of the suggestions for improvement turn out to be fraught with even greater dangers), this procedure will necessarily be followed; most of the data summarized in this chapter were obtained by this method.

Fifth, difficulties of definition abound. When attention is directed to the phenomena that can be lumped under such broad headings as "beliefs," "values," and "opinions," it is quickly seen that these have been variously defined, described, and denoted.[25] Problems of definition must remain outside our scope here. Since the primary concern of this chapter is with the effects of a Catholic college education, concentration will be on summarizing the work that has been done and on presenting comparative results whenever possible, however diverse are the definitions of beliefs, values, attitudes and opinions from one study to another.

Finally, since the content of attitude items is soon outdated in a fast-changing society, only research done since the late 1950's will be considered in any detail here. Some early investigations will be mentioned, however, when they lend perspective to the more recent research.

[25] As Berelson and Steiner note in their recent "inventory of scientific findings on human behavior": "Opinions are sometimes called impressions or guesses, attitudes are sometimes called views or convictions, and beliefs are sometimes called values or sentiments. There are, however, no hard-and-fast boundaries for the terms, so that one man's opinion may be another man's attitude and still another man's belief" (*Human Behavior*, p. 558).

POLITICAL, SOCIAL, AND ECONOMIC VALUES AND ATTITUDES

Several sets of data exist for matters that can be placed under the broad heading of political, social, and economic attitudes and values. One of the most interesting studies is the survey of twelve colleges and universities by *The Educational Reviewer*.[26] Growing out of a study done by the editors of the Harvard *Crimson* in collaboration with David Riesman in the spring of 1959, a poll of institutions chosen to typify certain styles of education was conducted. The students responding were from Sarah Lawrence, Williams, Yale, Marquette, Boston University, Indiana, South Carolina, Howard, Reed, Davidson, Brandeis, and Stanford. In this widely quoted survey, it was found that nearly half of the Marquette students identified themselves as liberal, although more students claimed to have moved "from liberal to more conservative" than "from conservative to more liberal" during college,[27] and their liberalism was combined with an anti-Communism more militant than at any of the other schools surveyed. For example, only 10 per cent of the 1960 Marquette students were favorably disposed to admitting Communist China to the United Nations, compared to 13 per cent at South Carolina, 17 per cent at Indiana, a quarter of the Davidson students, about a third of the Yale, Harvard, Stanford, and Boston University students, and majorities at Sarah Lawrence (58%), Williams (68%), Brandeis (70%), and Reed (82%). It is interesting that this militant stance appeared less related to distrust of Communist economic doctrines than to students' religious beliefs. Although Marquette undergraduates were considerably less likely to favor the welfare state than those at such bastions of liberalism as Reed and Sarah Lawrence, they did not differ greatly from the remaining schools on this matter. But 54 per cent at Marquette saw religious beliefs as a "central issue" in the cold war, compared to less than 26 per cent of the other students. On such matters as right-to-work laws, social security, anti-trust legislation, wage and price controls, and federal assistance of various

[26] The Educational Reviewer, "Survey of the Political and Religious Attitudes of American College Students," *National Review*, 15 (October 8, 1963), insert.

[27] Catholic college populations undoubtedly differ greatly in this regard. Where only 11% of the student body at a women's college in North Dakota typed themselves as liberal (Sr. Anne Burns, O.S.B., "Values in a Campus Culture" [Paper read at the 1964 Meetings of the American Catholic Sociological Society, Montreal]), about a fifth of those at a midwest metropolitan women's college (Robert Hassenger, "The Impact of a Value-Oriented College on the Religious Orientations of Students with Various Backgrounds, Traits and College Exposures" [Ph.D. dissertation, University of Chicago, 1965]), and more than half at Notre Dame (William V. D'Antonio directed a senior honors paper of Fred O'Connor, "Values on the Campus," [Sociology Department, Notre Dame, 1960], which uncovered this data), considered themselves liberal in political and economic philosophy.

kinds, Marquette students were little different from those in colleges other than the most vociferously liberal. They did show a firmer opposition to unilateral suspension of atomic testing by the United States, however, a stand undoubtedly related to their strong anti-Communism.[28]

An association between Catholic college attendance and what might be called "conservatism" or at least "non-liberalism" can also be seen in the work of Greeley, who found that students in Catholic schools were less likely to identify themselves as "liberals," with this reluctance clearly related to amount of Catholic schooling. Of those who attended Catholic high schools, but secular colleges, 61 per cent claimed to be "liberals," compared to 47 per cent of those with Catholic college backgrounds and to 44 per cent of those with their entire education in Catholic institutions.[29]

Other available data also point to a pattern of more conservative attitudes for Catholic college students.[30] Selvin and Hagstrom attempted to assess support for civil liberties by development of a "libertarianism" scale. There was little difference between Protestants and Catholics at Berkeley (although both groups were much less libertarian than Jews), but when control for

[28] Comparable results were obtained in the Cornell survey of college students (Rose K. Goldsen, M. Rosenberg, Robin Williams, and E. A. Suchman, *What College Students Think* [Princeton, N.J.: Van Nostrand and Co., Inc., 1960]), and in Lenski's research on Detroit-area Catholics (Gerhard Lenski, *The Religious Factor* [New York: Doubleday, 1961]). The relation of anti-communism to Catholic religious beliefs was also found by Robert McNamara, S.J., in a dissertation study ("The Interplay of Intellectual and Religious Values" [Cornell University, 1963]); in a comparison of Fordham and Notre Dame with Cornell and Columbia men, Catholic students appeared to believe that those who do not profess belief in God cannot be convinced of the dignity of the individual. Further, while Fordham and Notre Dame men in general supported civil liberties, they did so less strongly than the Cornell-Columbia seniors.

[29] Andrew M. Greeley, *Religion and Career* (New York: Sheed and Ward, 1963).

[30] Political identifications of variously educated Catholics will not be considered here. The Catholic proclivity toward the Democratic Party in the U. S. has been often demonstrated, although there are a number of indications this was due more to ethnic than religious factors, and that the pattern may be changing. Lenski (*The Religious Factor*), for example, found a direct relationship between the amount of Catholic education and Republican political affiliation. This may be social class operating, since it is known that the extent of Republican affiliation increases with social class level, and the data of Greeley and Rossi (*Social Effects of Catholic Ed.*) show that Catholic school students are from higher-income families.

The expected "back-lash" of certain Catholic ethnic groups in the 1964 election failed to materialize, but there were indications in the 1964 primaries of some anti-Negro voting in heavily Catholic areas, and the New York mayoralty campaign in November, 1965, showed Catholics deserting the Democratic Party for both the conservative and liberal Republican candidates, with the conservative doing especially well in Italian and Irish, and some Polish and German, precincts.

church attendance was introduced, nonattending Catholics were clearly more libertarian than nonattending Protestants, scoring about as high as the Jewish group.[31]

Rose concluded that those attending the Catholic women's college in his sample of eleven New England schools were most opposed to allowing a professor to express his ideas and convictions on any subject, even if they were contrary to accepted beliefs,[32] and that Catholics in all eleven colleges were

> a) most opposed to the Supreme Court decision regarding prayers in the schools; b) most favorable to the aims (although not the methods) of the John Birch Society; c) most supportive of federal aid to parochial schools; d) highest in anti-Castro feeling; e) more likely to agree that "sooner or later we will have to fight the Russians." More than two-thirds of the Catholic women's college students believed that a Communist take-over would follow unilateral disarmament [compared to about a quarter at colleges such as Smith and Mt. Holyoke].[33]

Such outcomes of research on Catholic colleges have often been reported,[34] but in a longitudinal study begun in 1963, Hassenger found that the libertarian scores of students in a Catholic women's colege were significantly

[31] Hanan Selvin and Warren Hagstrom, "Sources of Support for Civil Liberties," *British Journal of Sociology*, 11 (1960), 51–73. Such differences might be expected; since nonattendance is more serious from the point of view of the orthodox Catholic, those staying away are most likely strongly disaffected and cannot be directly compared to Protestants or Jews with similar records of religious participation. The definitions of expected religious behavior also vary from country to country for Catholics. A Gallup poll in England in the autumn of 1965 showed only 50% of the British Catholics attending Mass "most Sundays," and were also almost evenly split on the question of "artificial birth control."

[32] Peter I. Rose, "The Myth of Unanimity: Student Opinions on Critical Issues," *Sociology of Education*, 37 (1963), 129–49. Seniors, however, were higher than freshmen, sophomores, and juniors.

[33] *Ibid.*, p. 147.

[34] In a Canadian study, D. F. Campbell ("Religion and Values among Nova Scotian College Students" [Paper read at the 1965 Meetings of the American Catholic Sociological Society, Chicago]) found Catholic university students to be significantly lower in support of various democratic values than non-sectarian college attendants. It is noteworthy, however, that Campbell found seniors somewhat more supportive of these values, including an atheist's right to free speech. Further, the highly religious students were significantly less tolerant than the less religious Catholic Canadians, a finding closely paralleling those of Seymour M. Lipset ("Opinion Formation in a Crisis Situation," in *The Berkeley Student Revolt*, eds. S. M. Lipset and S. S. Wolin [New York: Doubleday Anchor Books, 1965], pp. 464–93) and of C. O'Reilly and E. J. O'Reilly ("Religious Beliefs of Catholic College Students and their Attitudes Toward Minorities," *Journal of Abnormal and Social Psychology*, 49 [1954], 378–80). As late as the Summer

higher at the end of sophomore year than they had been at college entrance, with a mean score approaching the range labeled "highly libertarian" by Selvin and Hagstrom.[35]

Finally, in perhaps the best-planned and most carefully controlled national survey, Greeley and Rossi[36] showed that Catholics who had attended Catholic colleges were significantly lower than secular college Catholics in anti-Semitism and in opposition to civil liberties (although the support of civil liberties was little higher for this group than for those educated in Catholic grade and high schools). So, while the bulk of the available data on attitudes and values which have here been called political, social, and economic show a pattern of more conservative response for Catholic college students, the most recent research indicates this trend may be changing.

RELIGIOUS VALUES, ATTITUDES, AND BEHAVIOR

Turning to data available on aspects of religious beliefs and behavior, it might be expected that a conservative secular orientation would mean a similar religious one. Things are not always so clear cut. Wiley and Basil found that these were closely related for priests and sisters, but that the religiously liberal Catholic layman was as often as not politically and economically conservative.[37] Religious liberals, however, were more likely to be libertarian in matters of civil rights and civil liberties than in foreign affairs or domestic economic matters. So perhaps judgment should be suspended until the available data are considered.

Research on religious attitudes is meager, and the results of the little work that has been done are somewhat inconsistent. From Starbuck's classic study showing that education led to doubts about religious belief,[38] through the research of Leuba, Katz et al., and Wickenden, there seemed to be clear indications of a decreased religious involvement, both in terms of church

of 1966, Richard Braungart of Pennsylvania State University found that only nine of 180 participants in the 1966 congress of the liberal Students for a Democratic Society (SDS) were Catholics, compared to 36 of 155 (23%) attending the convention of the conservative Young Americans for Freedom (YAF) ("SDS and YAF: Backgrounds of Student Political Activists" [Paper read at the 1966 Meetings of the American Sociological Association, Miami]).

[35] Hassenger, "Impact of a Value-Oriented College."

[36] Andrew M. Greeley and Peter H. Rossi, The Education of Catholic Americans (Chicago: Aldine Pub. Co., 1966).

[37] Norbert Wiley and Thomas Basil, "Religious and Political Liberalism Among Catholics" (Paper read at the 1965 Meetings of the American Catholic Sociological Society, Chicago).

[38] Edwin D. Starbuck, The Psychology of Religion (London: Walter Scott, 1899).

participation and orthodoxy of belief, for college students.[39] Jones, for example, detected a decline in religiosity on three scales: "attitude toward the church," "religion as an influence on conduct," and "the reality of God."[40] Similarly, Allport *et al.* found that about three-fourths of the non-Catholic postwar Harvard students and about three-fifths of the Harvard Catholics had reacted against their religious upbringing, moving toward a more liberal set of attitudes and a nonpersonal concept of God.[41] After reviewing the literature and conducting their own investigation, Kuhlen and Arnold concluded that more highly educated individuals were less likely to accept orthodox beliefs or to have pro-religious attitudes.[42] Such results are supported by the data cited in Argyle and Hoult and in the recent investigations of Burchard, Havens, and Stark.[43] As Sanford, summarizing a variety of pertinent research, wrote in *The American College*:

> recent studies, as well as those performed twenty-five years ago, show that between the freshman and senior years in college there is, in general, change in the direction of greater liberalism and sophistication in political, social and religious outlook.[44]

There is not, however, a unanimity of results. The early Thurstone and Chave, Whitely, and Gilliland studies found no significant religious changes associated with the college experience.[45] This was the conclusion of Eddy,

[39] J. H. Leuba, *The Belief in God and Immortality* (S. French and Co., 1916); D. Katz, F. H. Allport, and M. B. Jennes, *Students' Attitudes* (Syracuse, N.Y.: Craftsman Press, 1931); A. C. Wickenden, "The Effects of the College Experience Upon Students' Concepts of God," *Journal of Religion*, 12 (1932), 242–67.

[40] V. Jones, "Attitudes of College Students and the Changes in Such Attitudes During Four Years in College," *Journal of Educational Psychology*, 29 (1938), 14–25, 114–34.

[41] Gordon W. Allport, J. M. Gillespie, and Jacqueline Young, "The Religion of the Post-War College Student," *Journal of Psychology*, 25 (1948), 3–33.

[42] R. G. Kuhlen and M. Arnold, "Age Differences in Religious Beliefs and Problems During Adolescence," *Journal of Genetic Psychology*, 65 (1944), 291–300.

[43] Michael Argyle, *Religious Behavior* (London: Routledge and Kegan Paul, 1958); Thomas F. Hoult, *The Sociology of Religion* (New York: Dryden, 1958); Waldo W. Burchard, "Religion at a Midwestern University: An Interim Report" (Paper read at the 1964 Meetings of the Society for the Scientific Study of Religion, Washington, D.C.); Joseph Havens, "The Changing Climate of Research on the College Student and his Religion," *Journal for the Scientific Study of Religion*, 3 (1963), 52–69, and "A Study of Religious Conflict in College Students," *Journal of Social Psychology*, 64 (1964), 77–87; Rodney J. Stark, "On the Incompatibility of Religion and Science: A Survey of American Graduate Students," *Journal for the Scientific Study of Religion*, 3 (1963), 3–20.

[44] Nevitt Sanford, "The Effects of College Education," in *The American College*, ed. N. Sanford (New York: John Wiley & Sons, Inc., 1962), p. 806.

[45] L. L. Thurstone and E. J. Chave, *The Measurement of Attitude* (Chicago: University of Chicago Press, 1929); P. L. Whitely, "A Study of the Allport-

who noted that "religion to many college students appears to have little direct relationship to higher learning."[46] Jacob summarized his review with the comment that

> students normally express a need for religion as part of their lives and make time on most weekends for an hour in church. But there is a "ghostly quality" about the beliefs and practices of many of them. . . . Their religion does not carry over to guide and govern important decisions in the secular world.[47]

Part of the explanation for the divergent findings is no doubt due to the difficulties of studying the phenomena in question. Dukes and Barton have pointed out the variety of ways in which values can be defined,[48] and Glock has considered some of the requirements for a "comprehensive and operationally useful definition of religion" and has suggested a research strategy for meeting them.[49] Although religious participation is probably the most readily assessed type of religious involvement, few would assert that data on frequency of church attendance tell anything like the whole story.[50] At a time when the death-of-God theologians are becoming increasingly influential, the social psychologist of religion must concern himself with each of the dimensions delineated by Glock.[51] Unfortunately, however, very few research projects have been done with such care. In attempting to evaluate the impact of Catholic colleges on religious attitudes and values, we must be content to summarize the available data from investigations of widely varying quality and sophistication.

The results of research on Catholic students are remarkably consistent. Despite the decrease generally found in religious concern among college students, Cavanaugh reported an increase in church attendance and ritual

Vernon Test for Personal Values," *Journal of Abnormal and Social Psychology*, 28 (1933), 6–13; A. R. Gilliland, "Religious Attitudes of College Students," *The Christian Student*, 39 (1938), entire issue.

[46] Edward D. Eddy, Jr., *The College Influence on Student Character* (Washington, D.C.: American Council on Education, 1959), p. 115.

[47] Jacob, *Changing Values in College*, p. 2.

[48] Walter F. Dukes, "Psychological Studies of Values," *Psychological Bulletin*, 52 (1955), 24–50; Barton, *Studying the Effects of College Ed.*

[49] Charles Y. Glock, "On the Study of Religious Commitment," *Religious Education*, 62 (1962), S–98–110.

[50] Glock suggests that the religiosity expressed on one dimension may not be manifested in other dimensions, and this is supported by the work of N. J. Demerath (*Social Class in American Protestantism* [Chicago: Rand McNally, 1965]); Lenski, *The Religious Factor*; and Glock's own work with Rodney Stark (*Religion and Society in Tension* [Chicago: Rand McNally, 1965]).

[51] The dimensions suggested are: experiential, ideological, ritualistic, intellectual, and consequential.

participation for Catholic students,[52] and both Ferman, and Brown and Lowe showed that, although college students generally moved in the direction of a more liberal religious stance while in college, Catholics remained consistently more orthodox in belief and behavior.[53] In his dissertation study, Flanagan found a clear association between having had some Catholic schooling (whether high school or college: the superiority of either level was not shown) and possessing religious attitudes "that conform to Catholic expectations," and in her research Sister Helen Veronica concluded that attend-

TABLE 1
RELIGIOSITY OF COLLEGE GRADUATES,
BY RELIGION[a]

	Protestant	Catholic	Jew
Very religious	18	32	4
Fairly religious	52	52	36
Neither	13	6	19
Fairly nonreligious	12	6	23
Very nonreligious	5	5	17
	100 (1,972)[b]	101 (816)	99 (268)

[a] In percentages. From *Religion and Career* by Andrew M. Greeley, © Sheed and Ward, Inc., 1963 (p. 152).
[b] Sample sizes in parentheses.

ance at Catholic schools was associated with "religious maturity" for the Catholic college women in her sample.[54]

There are, of course, some differences of opinion about what religious maturity may mean for Catholic college students. If religious participation were the appropriate criterion, Catholic students — whether in Catholic or other institutions — would be clearly the most religious. Greeley's study of a national sample of 1961 college graduates indicated that it was Catholics who most diligently attended religious services, and this appeared to be directly related to the level of Catholic education, with those in church colleges attending most frequently.[55] Hadden found a higher level of religious

[52] John J. Cavanaugh, C.S.C., "Survey of Fifteen Surveys," *The Bulletin of the University of Notre Dame*, 34 (1939), 1–128.

[53] L. Ferman, "Religious Change on a Campus," *Journal for College Student Personnel*, 1 (1960) 1–12; in this study of religious change at Cornell University, Ferman noted that "the great secularization of religious values which some Catholics often attribute to secular education . . . simply does not exist in the Cornell case" (p. 10); Donald G. Brown and M. L. Lowe, "Religious Beliefs and Personality Characteristics of College Students," *Journal of Social Psychology*, 33 (1951), 103.

[54] George F. Flanagan, "An Investigation of Religious Attitudes Among Catholic Seniors in College Who Have Had Varying Amounts and Levels of Catholic Schooling" (Ph.D. dissertation, University of Minnesota, 1957); Sr. Helen Veronica, S.S.J., "Religious Attitudes and Personality Traits," *Journal of Social Psychology*, 54 (1961), 279–88.

[55] Greeley, *Religion and Career*.

performance for Catholics at the University of Wisconsin.[56] Since weekly formal worship is of considerably greater importance to Catholics than to Protestants or Jews, however, one might suggest that students' self-judgments of their religiosity are a better indicator than churchgoing. But by this measure, too, Catholics are "more religious" (Table 1). When queried about their anticipated greatest satisfactions in life, Catholics were clearly higher than Protestants (who were in turn higher than Jews) in choice of "religious beliefs and practices," with Catholics in Catholic colleges almost three times more

TABLE 2
RELIGIOUS CHANGES BY RELIGIOUS
GROUPS (PER CENT IN EACH CATEGORY)[a]

ORIGINAL RELIGION	PRESENT RELIGION					TOTAL
	Protestant	Catholic	Jew	Other	None	
Protestant	85	2	0	2	11	100 (2,007)[b]
Catholic	2	91	0	1	6	100 (833)
Jew	1	0	84	2	13	100 (272)
Other	13	2	2	67	16	100 (108)
None	24	2	1	7	66	100 (110)

[a] From *Religion and Career* by Andrew M. Greeley, © Sheed and Ward, Inc., 1963, p. 189.
[b] Sample sizes in parentheses.

likely to make this choice than their coreligionists in other colleges.[57] Perhaps what is sometimes termed apostasy (religious change) is the best indicator; by this measure Catholic students are still "most religious" according to the Greeley data (Table 2).

These findings are consistent with other research. In the national sample of Goldsen *et al.*, it was found that, of all American college students, "the Catholics are most agreed on the necessity for a religious or ethical belief system to be based on absolute or traditional values."[58] As did Stark,[59] these investigators found a lower rate of apostasy for Catholic students both in Catholic and secular institutions (although the apostasy rates found for the latter are higher than for the former, they are still far below those of Protestant and Jewish students).

Further support for the above findings can be found in the 1960 *Educational Reviewer* poll.[60] Comparing the single Catholic institution, Marquette,

[56] Jeffrey K. Hadden, "An Analysis of Some Factors Associated with Religious and Political Affiliation in a College Population," *Journal for the Scientific Study of Religion*, 2 (1963), 209–216. Catholic students were, however, found to be doing less well scholastically.

[57] Greeley, *Religion and Career*; but, as with Protestants and Jews, religion as a primary life value is outranked by the values of family and career. The same pattern was found by W. S. Salisbury (reported in *Religion in American Culture* [Homewood, Ill.: Dorsey Press, 1964]).

[58] Goldsen *et al.*, *What College Students Think*.

[59] Stark, "Incompatibility of Religion and Science."

[60] Educational Reviewer, "Survey of College Students."

to the other eleven schools, a clear pattern emerges. Twice as many at Marquette as at any other colleges stated that religion had a "very marked" influence on their upbringing (67%, compared to 34% at Davidson, 33% at Howard, 19% at Stanford, and 16% at Yale). There was considerable stated apostasy at most of the colleges. At Davidson, for example, where 74 per cent were raised as Protestants, 53 per cent remained affiliated with Protestantism, for a 28 per cent defection rate. For other schools, some of the apostasy rates were: 72 per cent at Reed; 25 per cent at Boston University; 19 per cent at Yale; 12 per cent at South Carolina; at Marquette, the rate was 2 per cent of those polled.[61]

But formal disaffiliation does not tell the whole story. Even at schools where vast numbers of students consider themselves Christians, there was considerable rejection of basic Christian beliefs. At only four colleges did a majority accept the idea of "God becoming flesh": Marquette (94%), South Carolina (67%), Indiana (56%), and Howard (51%). At Williams, only 45 per cent did; at Yale, 36 per cent; and at Reed, only one-quarter.

As for belief in "the Gospel account of Jesus' resurrection as an historical event which occurred as concretely as Lincoln's assassination," fewer still agreed: about one-quarter at Yale and Williams; two-fifths at Boston University and Stanford; half at Indiana. At Marquette, however, 84 per cent agreed.

Another item read: "Do you believe in immortality, if this is taken to mean the continued existence of the individual soul as a surviving entity after the end of organic life?" At Jesuit Marquette, 95 per cent did, 3 per cent did not; at Jewish Brandeis, 15 per cent did, 81 per cent did not. Other undergraduates not believing were: at South Carolina, 22 per cent; at Sarah Lawrence, 36 per cent; at Indiana, 38 per cent; and at Williams, Yale, and Stanford, more than half.

The student samples were also asked if they agreed that "there is a wise, omnipotent, three-person God Who created the universe and Who maintains an active concern for human affairs?" The proportions at the various colleges who did so believe were: at Marquette, 90 per cent; at South Carolina, 51 per cent; at Indiana, 43 per cent; at Howard, 38 per cent; at Davidson, one-third; at Boston University and Yale, one-fifth; and Sarah Lawrence, 14 per cent; at Reed, none of those polled.[62]

In the preliminary report of the Danforth Commission on Church Colleges and Universities, it was noted that students in Catholic and "conservative

[61] It is clear, of course, that those giving up their Catholicism would be more likely to transfer from a school such as Marquette.

[62] It must be noted, however, that other concepts of God were assented to by students at the various schools; e.g., "I believe in a God about whom nothing definite can be affirmed except that I sometimes sense Him as a mighty spiritual presence permeating all mankind and nature"; those agreeing to this were, at Sarah Lawrence, 31%; at Yale, 24%; at Boston University, 27%. Another state-

Protestant" colleges did better on a "test" of religious knowledge.[63] Recent data collected for the National Opinion Research Center (by Greeley and Rossi in 1964) show that a national sample of Catholics from Catholic colleges were higher than those from non-Catholic schools in measures of religious knowledge, acceptance of the church as teacher, religious participation, doctrinal orthodoxy, and ethical orthodoxy.[64] (Only on the latter two

ment about "a vast, impersonal principle of order or natural uniformity working throughout the whole universe and which, though not conscious of mere human life, I choose to call God," received a fair number of votes, although only 2% at Marquette. Still more students stated that "because of our ignorance in this matter, I see no adequate grounds for either affirming or denying the existence of God," the agnostic position: none at Marquette; but 18% at Sarah Lawrence; 20% at Williams; 21% at Yale; 8% at Indiana; 37% at Reed. Relatively few agreed with the statement: "I reject all belief in anything that could reasonably be called 'God' and regard every such notion as a fiction unworthy of worship": 4% at Sarah Lawrence; 6% at Williams; 7% at Yale; 1% at Boston University; 3% at Indiana; 22% at Reed; 10% at Brandeis; 6% at Stanford; none at Marquette. Although not outright apostasy, a considerable revision of classical Christian beliefs was found at practically every school (in varying extremes, from South Carolina to Reed) but Marquette.

Even with the questioning of religion which occurred, the majority of students saw religion as a "good thing" and planned to raise their children "according to religious tradition." (What form this might be is left to the reader to speculate.) Only a few termed it "unwholesome and dangerous": about one-seventh at Reed and Brandeis. There would seem to be some support for the assertion that "God is dead," at least with regard to the classical Christian deity.

Taking Marquette students alone, 27% claimed to have sometime "reacted partially or wholly against" Catholicism; of these, 6% did so in grade school, 39% in high school, 30% in freshman year, 19% later in college. And, again for Marquette alone, 11% "experienced a sudden resurgence of faith" in adolescence, another 47% in college. Only 41% of the "reactors" did not find this later resurgence of religious interest (so only 41% of 27%, or 11%, felt no resurgence of interest and faith).

[63] Manning M. Pattillo, Jr., and Donald M. Mackenzie, *Eight Hundred Colleges Face the Future: A Preliminary Report of the Danforth Commission on Church Colleges and Universities* (St. Louis: The Danforth Foundation, 1965); the complete report will be published in late 1966 by the American Council on Education, under the title, *Church-Sponsored Higher Education in the United States*. The recent findings of Glock and Stark, *Religion and Society*, point up the importance of carefully specifying the Protestant denominations investigated in religious research.

[64] Lenski (*The Religious Factor*) found a similar pattern in his study of Detroit-area Catholics: those with a Catholic education were more regular in attendance at Mass, and were more "doctrinally orthodox," i.e., agreed with traditional Catholic teachings; even on such peripheral matters as family planning, Burchard ("Religion at a Midwest Univ.") showed that Catholics in a midwestern state university were higher than Protestants in "religious fundamentalism." Perhaps this fundamentalism is in fact Catholic orthodoxy, involving matters with which, if one were to disagree, he would no longer be considered a Catholic.

indexes were they higher than Catholics with elementary and secondary Catholic educations, however, and only slightly so.) Catholic college students were also lower in measures of "Manichaeanism" and "religious extremism," but did not differ from those with Catholic elementary and secondary educations on the latter index.[65]

Similar data are available from less widely known studies. In his research on seniors from Catholic and nonsectarian colleges, McNamara found four-fifths of the Fordham and Notre Dame students asserting that logical reasoning can establish the existence of God, compared to 17 per cent of the Columbia-Cornell group.[66] Fifty-nine per cent of the latter expressed greater confidence in science than in religion, compared to 10 per cent of the Catholic college seniors. And, where 28 per cent of the nonsectarian seniors thought that "people with strong religious beliefs [were] usually politically intolerant," only 17 per cent of the Catholic sample agreed.[67]

Research at other Catholic universities show comparable results. In an undergraduate honors thesis that he directed at Notre Dame, D'Antonio found that 28 per cent of the 1960 seniors rated themselves better Catholics at that time than before attending Notre Dame, with an additional 45 per cent rating themselves "very good" or "good" Catholics, although they did not believe they had changed during college.[68] Only 6 per cent rated themselves less religious. Almost identical figures were reported by Weiss for undergraduate men at St. Louis University;[69] St. Louis women, however, were more likely to agree that their religious lives had "improved considerably" during college. About half of the St. Louis women, and a third of the men, attributed these changes to regular courses taken in college (not necessarily, however, courses in theology). At the same time, it should be noted that almost half of the Notre Dame seniors admitted their religious efforts

[65] "Manichaeanism" refers to a heresy of the early church, which held that material things were basically evil and that Christians ought to concentrate their efforts on gaining salvation, instead of fighting poverty and injustice on earth. Readers can see this attitude reflected in St. Augustine's *Confessions*.

"Religious extremism" is a kind of "more Catholic than the pope" scale, containing items such as "The Catholic Church teaches that large families are more Christian than small families." To hold this and similar attitudes is, of course, not more Catholic, or more Christian. It represents an overconcern with what some would call the letter of the law, at the expense of the spirit.

[66] McNamara, "Interplay of Values."

[67] But as Professor Riesman suggested after reading the draft of this chapter, both of these figures are low, since it *would* be intolerant to assent to this statement.

[68] D'Antonio and O'Connor, "Values on Campus." Of these 45%, however, two-fifths were found to show an increased religious participation during college, and three-fourths reported they appreciated and understood their religion more.

[69] Robert F. Weiss, S.J., "Student and Faculty Perceptions of Institutional Press at St. Louis University" (Ph.D. dissertation, University of Minnesota, 1964).

were weaker when away from the campus, where facilities were less accessible; and Weiss found considerable opposition from both men and women at St. Louis to the suggestion that campus religious activities might be increased.

Other criticism of Catholicism was evident in the results of a survey conducted by the Notre Dame *Scholastic* in late 1964. About 6 per cent of the Notre Dame students felt that the Mass was superfluous in their lives, and nearly 8 per cent thought that other students did not believe in God. More than a third felt that Christianity had considerable influence in their lives, but only 13 per cent believed it significant in the lives of their acquaintances. Forty-seven per cent admitted that the spirit of Christianity played "only some" part in their own lives. In judging the effectiveness of Notre Dame in preparing students for a Christian life, less than a third believed the university was doing an acceptable job. Even greater antipathy was expressed toward the church as an organization: more than a third stated that it had only "some" influence in their lives.[70]

All of the above data indicate a pattern of higher religiosity for Catholics than for Protestants or Jews in college, with those from Catholic institutions highest in these criteria of religious commitment.[71] As Herberg, after summarizing survey results from a variety of sources, concluded:

> In all of these respects, the pattern is very much the same: Catholics come closest to the religious norm, to what is usually regarded as the beliefs and attitudes proper to religious people; Protestants come next . . . Jews are most remote.[72]

Carrier and Schneider have reminded the sociologist, however, that he must take into account the specific milieu within which studies of religious attitudes are made.[73] Unlike the Protestant or Jewish student, the Catholic is rarely able to consider religious commitment apart from direct participation in "official" religious services. Adherence to doctrine and religious practice "means" Catholicism for those brought up to feel the necessity of institutional affiliation. Since a Catholic defines laxity in religious belief and participation as "falling away," such behavior is less likely to occur,

[70] Perhaps this is because, as Riesman suggests, Notre Dame students set high standards for themselves. If so, these results may be in their favor.

[71] Less than one per cent of the graduates from Catholic colleges in graduate school no longer considered themselves Catholics, whereas 12% of the Catholics who had graduated from other colleges were "apostates" (Greeley, *Religion and Career*).

[72] Will Herberg, *Protestant, Catholic, Jew* (New York: Doubleday Anchor Books, 1959), p. 220.

[73] H. Carrier, *Psycho-sociologie de l'appartenance religieuse* (Rome: Presses de l'Universite Gregorienne, 1960); L. Schneider, "Problems in the Sociology of Religion," in R. E. L. Faris (ed.), *Handbook of Modern Sociology* (Chicago: Rand McNally and Co., 1964), 770–807.

except for the strongly disaffected.[74] Accordingly, there are bound to be disagreements as to what the above results "really mean."

Clearly, the social scientist will remain unable to give final answers about the nature of religiosity. But whatever one's persuasion in this regard, it would be difficult to disagree that genuine Catholic religiosity will typically issue in commitment, manifesting itself to some extent in the public order and in attitudes toward it.

It is on such aspects of religiosity that research on Catholic college impact becomes most interesting. For, despite the greater incidence of religious participation and lower frequency of apostasy among Catholic students, there is virtually no evidence pointing to a deeper concern with what might be called the social apostolate — an involvement with social, political, and moral questions in the Secular City.

Rossi and Rossi discovered differences between those educated in parochial and nonparochial schools primarily in areas where the church has traditionally taken the strongest stands, such as in the performance of religious duties; but along dimensions such as community participation, differerences were minimal.[75] This can also be seen in the work of Fichter[76] and is supported by Foster's study of a Catholic, "value-oriented" university that uncovered no greater political and social consciousness than in a neighboring non-Catholic institution.[77]

The preliminary report of the National Opinion Research Center on the "social effects" of Catholic education suggested that the church schools in this country have tended to emphasize certain desiderata that, because of their social and historical predicament, "have crucial symbolic importance for American Catholicism — church attendance, sexual morality, and organizational 'loyalty' (to the Papacy and to the teaching authority of the Church)."[78] In the final report of Greeley and Rossi, a more careful analysis uncovered differences for those who had attended Catholic colleges after Catholic grade and high schools, particularly if they came from highly reli-

---

[74] The dangers of such definitions will be discussed in the concluding chapter.

[75] Alice S. Rossi and Peter H. Rossi, "Some Effects of Parochial School Education in America," *Daedalus*, 90 (1961), 300–323.

[76] Joseph H. Fichter, *Parochial School: A Sociological Study* (Notre Dame, Ind.: University of Notre Dame Press, 1958).

[77] Julian Foster, R. Stanek, and W. Krassowski, "The Impact of a Value-Oriented University on Student Attitudes and Thinking" (Mimeographed; Santa Clara, Calif.: University of Santa Clara, 1961); the results of this study are summarized in chapter 6. In an unpublished paper, Gordon De Jong and Joseph Faulkner ("The Church, Individual Religiosity, and Social Justice" [Paper read at the 1966 Meetings of the American Catholic Sociological Society, Miami]) found that Catholics at Pennsylvania State University were less likely than Protestants to support the involvement of clergy in social action movements.

[78] Greeley *et al.*, *Social Effects of Catholic Ed.*, p. 54.

gious families.[79] But, while Catholic college students were significantly lower than Catholics from secular colleges in anti-Semitism and anti-civil liberties, there was very little difference on the latter index between those from Catholic colleges and the sample members who attended Catholic grade and high schools. That is to say, although Catholic college attendance appeared to lower significantly anti-Semitism scores from high-school levels, there was little similar effect on support of civil liberties.[80] Nor did those from Catholic and secular colleges differ on the community involvement and racism indexes.[81] Further, when separate results are presented for those who attended Catholic schools only at the college level, it can be seen that this group is higher on all three indexes: racism, anti-Semitism, and anti-civil liberties. Apparently the Catholic colleges had little effect on these students' attitudes.[82]

A similar pattern of results can be found in Hassenger's study of the impact of one college on the religious attitudes and values of its students. Seniors in a Catholic women's college were minimally different from freshmen, moving only slightly away from a preoccupation with doctrinal and ethical orthodoxy, and ritual performance.[83] As in virtually all of the research to date, there seemed to be indications that the Catholic educational system was having its greatest impact "in precisely those areas where the adults can be expected to adhere to the norms even without such education."[84]

[79] Greeley and Rossi, *Ed. of Catholic Americans.*

[80] Comparing Tables 7.1 and 7.8 of *ibid.*

[81] It might be asserted that an expectation of higher scores is unrealistic, but the *Commonweal* readers for whom results are separately presented in Greeley and Rossi are considerably higher in the various indexes of social and cultural liberalism, regardless of whether they attended Catholic or secular colleges.

[82] It is only fair to warn the reader that only twenty-three subjects are involved here — in the "Catholic-college-only" group — making inferences a risky matter; but of course results reported for this group are not necessary to the suggestion of slight Catholic college impact, which can rest on the other data reported above.

[83] Based on data collected by Hassenger ("Impact of a Value-Oriented College") in the early 1960's. By late 1965, in a more recent longitudinal study, there were indications of a considerable decrease in moralistic religious orientations.

[84] Greeley *et al., Social Effects of Catholic Ed.,* p. 79. As Greeley has later shown (in "The Religious Behavior of Graduate Students," *Journal for the Scientific Study of Religion,* 5 [1965], 34–40), even the Catholic Ph.D. candidates in the top secular graduate schools are faithful religious participants. But in matters other than doctrinal-ethical orthodoxy and ritual performance, the available data lead researchers to conclude, as did Rossi and Greeley in an earlier article, that there is "little in the way of evidence to prove that the graduates of the Catholic school system excel their coreligionists who have not gone to Catholic schools in the practice of the virtue of charity, that they are any more opposed to racial injustice, any more concerned with the suffering people of new nations,

MORAL AND ETHICAL STANDARDS

Only scattered data are available on matters perhaps best termed moral and ethical. One interesting piece of research is the work of Robert McNamara, S.J., which allows comparison of the moral values of students on two Catholic and two secular campuses. Eighty-nine per cent of the Catholic college (Fordham and Notre Dame) students based their moral norms on "supernatural values," i.e., saw their criteria of action determined by the existence of a supreme being; only 23 per cent of the other (Columbia and Cornell) men held supernatural values. Yet, there is evidence that it was the students' religious affiliation and not their attendance at Catholic colleges that was the key element here, for 72 per cent of the Catholics on the secular campuses held supernatural moral values.[85]

A fascinating comparison of relative value strengths for these two groups is also available. Cheating on term papers and examinations was taken much more seriously on the Cornell and Columbia campuses, whereas academic integrity was more lightly regarded at Fordham and Notre Dame. Further, great differences in cheating behavior existed. At both Catholic colleges, more than 40 per cent admitted to cheating more than once, while less than 20 per cent on the Cornell and Columbia campuses (and 27 per cent of the seniors attending the eleven colleges in the 1952 survey of Goldsen *et al.*) did so.[86] (It is interesting that Weiss also found cheating a fairly common occurrence: 41 per cent of the Saint Louis University men and 42 per cent of the women stated that copying was common on assigned papers, with

any more inclined to agree with the teachings of the papal social encyclicals. . . ." Greeley and Rossi, "The Impact of the Catholic School," p. 38.

There has been a great deal of speculation about whether the highly religious person is more or less likely to be prejudiced, and a number of investigations show contradictory findings. Several early studies appeared to show that Catholic college students were anti-Semitic (John Kane, "Anti-Semitism Among Catholic College Students," *American Catholic Sociological Review*, 8 [1947], 209–18) and anti-Negro (Bro. D. Augustine, F.S.C., "The Catholic College Man and the Negro," *ibid.*, 204–8), with highly religious students more inclined to anti-minority attitudes (cf. O'Reilly and O'Reilly, "Religious Beliefs and Minorities)." But Lenski reported he could find no indication that attendance at Catholic schools had any such influence on Catholics' attitudes toward Negroes. Allport, summarizing the literature, noted that the issue has not yet been resolved: "The role of religion is paradoxical. It makes prejudice, and it unmakes prejudice" (*The Nature of Prejudice* [New York: Doubleday Anchor Books, 1958], p. 413).

[85] McNamara, "Interplay of Values."

[86] Even if it is argued that only the admission is greater, with the incidence of cheating not necessarily higher on the Catholic campuses, the rejoinder can be made that this higher frequency of admission indicates that fewer Catholic campus students think this behavior seriously wrong. But it is perhaps worthwhile to consider the suggestion of Riesman in this regard: "Are the exams in the Catholic colleges more factual, less free-wheeling, and therefore easier to cheat on?"

those in the business college apparently the most flagrant violators.[87]) The Cornell-Columbia group, however, is less concerned about sexual morality than the Catholic college men, who are consistently more likely to judge various types of sexual behavior (e.g., necking, prostitution, homosexuality, sexual relations with one's fiancée) more harshly. Catholics on the nonsectarian campuses fall between the two groups.

One final value- and attitude-area for which sufficient data is available to present briefly here is that of marriage and the family. In recent years, the volume of criticism surrounding the traditional Catholic stance on family limitation has steadily increased.[88] Correspondingly, surveys show a decreasing percentage of Catholics supporting the church's opposition to use of "artificial" contraceptives. When the Gaffin survey was done in the mid-1950's,[89] only about half of the Catholics in the sample were in agreement with the Catholic stand. Lenski found 68 per cent of those Catholics who had been educated in the church's schools in favor of the traditional view, compared to 54 per cent of the Catholics with secular educational backgrounds.[90] Approximately the same level of support was found among Catholic Nova Scotians, with little difference between Catholic college

[87] Weiss, "Student and Faculty Perceptions." It is difficult to know how to evaluate such data. One item on the *College Student Questionnaire* of the Educational Testing Service asks students to indicate which of several actions they would take if a classmate were found cheating on an examination. Twenty-two per cent of the 1965 Notre Dame freshmen would take no action at all, and another 76 per cent would express concern only to the student himself. Only 2 per cent would take stronger action. But most likely similar results would be found on virtually all college campuses, in light of the strong American taboo against "ratting," and the more general fear of "getting involved." ("Fink" — the all-purpose word used by American adolescents in the mid-1960's — originally meant an informer or "squealer.")

[88] For recent discussion of the birth control issue see Anne Biezanek, *All Things New* (New York: Harper and Row, 1964); William Birmingham (ed.), *What Modern Catholics Think About Birth Control* (New York: New American Library, 1964); Louis Dupre, *Contraception and Catholics* (Baltimore: Helicon Press, 1964); G. G. Grisez, *Contraception and the Natural Law* (Milwaukee: Bruce Publishing Co., 1964); Michael Novak (ed.), *The Experience of Marriage* (New York: Macmillan Co., 1964); L. Pyle, *The Pill and Birth Regulation* (Baltimore: Helicon Press, 1964); Archbishop Thomas Roberts (ed.), *Contraception and Holiness* (New York: Herder and Herder, 1964); and the magnificent summary of official Catholic teaching over the centuries in John Noonan, *Contraception* (Cambridge, Mass.: Harvard University Press, 1965). The reader is also referred to the statement of thirty-five prominent Catholics in *The National Catholic Reporter*, 2 (August 18, 1965).

[89] Reported in John L. Thomas, *Religion and the American People* (Westminster, Md.: Newman Press, 1963).

[90] Lenski, *The Religious Factor*. Percentages of Catholic- and secular-educated Catholics agreeing that divorce was "always or usually" wrong were 73 and 60 per cent, respectively.

freshmen and seniors (although Catholic men were less favorable than Catholic women).[91]

Westoff *et al.* seemed to show a clear relationship between Catholic education and both desired family size and fertility-planning success. The number of children desired was directly related to the extent of the individual's education in the Catholic school system, with both family religiousness and ethnicity controlled. The more Catholic education, the greater was the desired family size.[92]

With the escalation in public discussion of the church's stance since the early 1960's, however, it may be determined in later research that increasing numbers of college-educated Catholics call this (and other) traditional positions into question. Two recent studies provide empirical support for this suggestion. A survey of 283 Catholic couples in fifteen states found that between one-fifth and one-fourth[93] of these highly educated men and women reported having used contraceptive pills, and about 8 per cent indicated they had used other contraceptive devices.[94] Apparently many of these couples

[91] Campbell, "Religion among Nova Scotian Students." Further light can be thrown on the values of the Nova Scotian students by noting that Catholics were significantly more likely to agree that "the father is the head of the family," and that "a woman's place is in the home" than non-Catholic students, although Catholic seniors were somewhat more inclined to question the traditional role of women than were freshmen.

[92] Charles Westoff, Robert Potter, and Philip Sagi, *The Third Child* (Princeton, N.J.: Princeton University Press, 1963). Although religious preference was apparently the most important predictor of family size, according to the Westoff data, the degree of religiosity worked in opposite ways for Catholics and Protestants, with more religious Catholics having more, and Protestants *fewer*, children. A recent follow-up study requires some modification of these conclusions, however. Westoff and R. H. Potvin ("Higher Education, Religion and Women's Family-Size Orientations," *American Sociological Review*, 31 [1966], 489–96), found that the "college effects" reported in Westoff *et al.* are more accurately seen as differential selectivity of women with larger-family orientations into Catholic colleges. But these colleges apparently counteract influences that might otherwise prevail: women from Catholic high schools attending non-Catholic colleges desired smaller families as seniors than as freshmen. The interaction effects uncovered by Greeley and Rossi, *Ed. of Catholic Americans*, appear to be operating with regard to fertility as well.

[93] Husbands and wives reported different frequencies, with husbands higher. This survey is presently being conducted on a more comprehensive basis and thus cannot be further identified at this time. We wish to express our appreciation to Dennis J. Geaney, O.S.A., for making results available to us.

[94] These 8 per cent may also be included in the 20 to 25 per cent using "the pill." That is to say, it may be misleading to add the 8 per cent to the previous figures for a total of about one-third of the Catholics sampled using some "artificial" methods, since the same couples more than likely have tried both pills and devices. But the more recent data of Westoff, with Norman B. Ryder, would suggest that, in 1965, a majority of married Catholic women aged 18–39 were not conforming to Catholic doctrine on birth control (paper presented at the Notre Dame Population Conference, November, 1966).

turned to more reliable methods after having attempted the rhythm method unsuccessfully. Some of the effects on their religious behavior and on their relationships with each other and with their children were reported by these Catholics; negative effects appear to outweigh positive results for those trying to follow traditional Catholic teaching. Very few were satisfied with the rhythm method, and 86 per cent indicated they would use other methods if they were approved by the Catholic church.[95]

Further interesting results can be found in my study, which showed that in 1963 about four-fifths of both freshmen and seniors in a Catholic women's college assented to the birth-control teaching. But a sample of forty members of the class of 1967, with this same level of support at college entrance, showed a decrease to about 25 per cent support by the end of their sophomore year.[96]

To date, however, the findings have been more consistent with the data of Westoff *et al.* than with the more recent results for Catholics with higher educational backgrounds. In Greeley and Rossi's national sample, 68 per cent of the Catholics with all of their education in Catholic schools supported the traditional Catholic position (compared to 52 per cent of those with some Catholic education, 44 per cent of those with no Catholic education, and 8 per cent of a comparative Protestant sample).[97] And this is the pattern of virtually all such research. Catholics receiving their entire education in Church schools are considerably more likely to engage in behavior that has been associated with traditional Catholicism, such as greater "willingness to accept the Church as authoritative teacher in controversial areas, in loyalty (especially to symbolically crucial doctrines such as birth control and Papal authority), and in their financial contributions to the church (though not in organizational memberships)."[98] But on matters of prejudice and civil liberties — what some would call the social apostolate — Catholic college impact is more limited. It has been asked whether these results do not reflect an inward-looking Catholicism — one which has been rather unconcerned with its temporal mission, preferring to concentrate on orthodoxy of belief and behavior.[99] The difficulties in evaluating such suggestions are legion. Greeley

[95] Apparently some Catholics are already acting as their own theologians in this regard; of those who reported using "the pill," there was a greater reported increase in their reception of the sacraments — and less reported decrease — than those using the rhythm method. In the group using other devices, however, a much greater decrease occurred. Perhaps those using "the pill" have been advised to do so for medical reasons, and have thus rationalized any doubts they might have had.

[96] Hassenger, "Impact of a Value-Oriented College." This is a longitudinal study (the same students polled as freshmen and sophomores), compared to the earlier cross-sectional survey.

[97] Greeley and Rossi, *Ed. of Catholic Americans.*

[98] Greeley *et al., Social Effects of Catholic Ed.*, p. 78.

[99] See, for example, Daniel Callahan, "The Schools," *Commonweal*, 71 (1965), 473–76.

et al. warn against demanding too much of Catholic education, in light of the stability of characteristics resulting from early learning,[100] and Bloom has extensively documented his thesis of the need for a powerful environmental impact to overcome the salient interpersonal influences of one's past.[101] If, as was suggested above, many Catholic colleges serve a clientele only recently removed from working-class, immigrant family settings, this would be reflected in the attributes of their students. It is to this question that we now turn.

THE CHARACTERISTICS OF CATHOLIC COLLEGE STUDENTS

Although there has been little systematic investigation of the Catholic college clientele, several recent studies contain relevant data. Perhaps the somewhat controversial Greeley research is the most appropriate place at which to begin. Since this study was largely focused on career plans,[102] the data relate to occupational values and anticipated satisfactions; but some general conclusions can be drawn.

In rating a number of possible job satisfactions by their relative importance, Catholics placed "money" higher than students from any of the Protestant denominations; "originality and creativity" were apparently less important for Catholic students than for Episcopalians, Lutherans, and Congregationalists (although more so than for Baptists, Methodists, and Presbyterians). Neither of these choices was affected by the level of Catholic education.[103]

Another of the findings of the NORC survey was widely cited: Catholic students were more likely to prefer working for a large company, with this preference higher for those in Catholic colleges (33%, compared to 26%

[100] Greeley *et al.*, *Social Effects of Catholic Ed.*; Greeley and Rossi, *Ed. of Catholic Americans.*

[101] Benjamin Bloom, *Stability and Change in Human Characteristics* (New York: John Wiley & Sons, Inc., 1964).

[102] Greeley, *Religion and Career.*

[103] McNamara ("Interplay of Values") found Jesuit seminarians relatively uninterested in "the opportunity to be creative and original" as a key occupational value (45%), compared to the opportunity to help others (94%). More than four-fifths considered the development of "moral capacities, ethical standards and values" as their central educational concern, compared to about two-thirds of the Fordham and Notre Dame seniors and two-fifths of the Cornell-Columbia sample. Among the seminarians intending to get Ph.D.'s, however, priority was given to intellectual goals to nearly the same extent as the Catholic and nonsectarian campus groups. Donovan also found a high interest in the moral aspects of teaching in his sample of Catholic college professors (*Academic Man*).

for Catholics in secular schools).[104] Regardless of the type of college attended, Catholics chose business as a future career more often than Protestants from all denominations except Congregational. The business orientation of Catholics in college has been noted by critics as diverse as Ellis, Lawler, O'Dea, Riesman and Jencks, Trent, and Ward.[105] Explanations for this phenomenon differ, but a common thread running through them all is the suggested absence of critical inquiry. This is variously formulated, but the statement of Lenski is typical: "Especially influential is the basic intellectual orientation which Catholicism develops: an orientation which values obedience above intellectual autonomy."[106] Lenski in fact found that Catholics with a college education were more aware of "conflicts" between religion and science than either college-educated Protestants or Catholics who did not attend college. Mundi, on the other hand, found that Catholic college students were less likely to perceive an incompatibility of science and Catholicism as upperclassmen than as freshmen.[107] Such conflicting findings can be due to a number of factors, including the wording of the items, possible biases in sampling, regional differences, test sophistication, and so on.[108] Attempts

[104] Some have tried to link this to a presumed desire to be enmeshed in a bureaucratic structure after years of experience in a hierarchical religious organization. This is at best hypothetical. A more sophisticated explanation has been suggested by Riesman, who wondered about a possible "hesitation to strike out on one's own entrepreneurial track, leaving him in a bureaucratic setting by default." This is, of course, also hypothetical, but it is more accessible to empirical test. Some relevant research is found on pp. 131 ff.

[105] John Tracy Ellis, *American Catholicism* (Chicago: University of Chicago Press, 1956); Justus G. Lawler, *The Catholic Dimension in Higher Education* (Westminster, Md.: Newman Press, 1959); Thomas F. O'Dea, *American Catholic Dilemma* (New York: Sheed and Ward, 1958); David Riesman and Christopher Jencks, "The Viability of the American College," in *The American College*, ed. N. Sanford (New York: John Wiley and Sons, Inc., 1962), 74–192; James W. Trent, "Religious and Dispositional Characteristics of Catholic Intellectuals" (Paper read at the 1965 Meetings of the American Catholic Sociological Society, Chicago); Leo R. Ward, *Blueprint for a Catholic University* (St. Louis: B. Herder and Co., 1949).

[106] Lenski, *The Religious Factor*, p. 255.

[107] Joseph P. Mundi, "Variations in the Opinions, Practices and Attitudes of Selected Samples of Minnesota Catholic College Students toward Catholicism in America" (Ph.D. dissertation, University of Minnesota, 1964).

[108] One's definition of religion — or the aspects of religion one has in mind — may well be the key element here. There seems to be some incompatibility between an explanation of the universe that relies exclusively on theological premises and the general outlook and method of science. If the dimension of religion involving devotion to such values as justice, peace, and love is considered, however, there is no conflict, but a mutual supplementation. Some colleges may be more successful in imparting an understanding of this distinction. Others, with a more apologetic orientation, may provide students with a few formulas to cover perceived incongruities, or by a form of what Lasswell and Riesman term "restriction by partial incorporation."

to isolate possible contaminating variables are beyond the scope of the present summary. At the beginning of this chapter there is some discussion of the relationship between a rigid, authoritarian personality structure and a fundamentalist, ultraconservative attitude system. If one accepts our premise that seniors ought to look different from freshman, the impact of Catholic colleges can be explored indirectly by a consideration of the personality characteristics of their students.[109]

Fortunately, a number of studies are available. Slusser was able to show that students from Catholic and small Protestant "sect" backgrounds were significantly lower in a scale measuring favorable self-concepts than members of the larger Protestant denominations.[110] Bieri and Lobeck noted that Catholics tend to be dependent on external authority,[111] and Trent found a higher level of docility for West Coast Catholic seniors than for freshmen, even in a longitudinal study.[112]

One of the most useful survey items to get at the extent of one's reliance on external authority is a query about what is "most important" for a child to learn.[113] Lenski reported that "attendance at Catholic schools was correlated with a belief that it is more important for children to learn to obey than to think for themselves."[114] Campbell found that 64 per cent of the Catholic Canadian freshmen in his sample and 53 per cent of the seniors valued obedience more, compared to 42 and 23 per cent of the non-Catholic freshmen and seniors, respectively.[115] D'Antonio, on the other hand, discovered that Notre Dame students valued independent thought much more than obedience (although there were no freshmen-senior differences, as might be expected),[116] and Greeley found only slightly fewer Catholic than

---

[109] Comparisons of Catholics in Catholic colleges with those in secular schools is one approach; perhaps even better would be comparisons of Catholic college freshmen and seniors — ideally the same students as freshmen and seniors — but few such studies exist.

[110] G. H. Slusser, "Some Personality Correlates of Religious Orientation" (Ph.D. dissertation, University of Texas, 1960). Definitions of sect differ, but they refer usually to "storefront," revivalist groups, with primarily lower-class membership. Often a "call" is felt to be necessary for acceptance. This risks oversimplification, however, particularly in light of the research showing the transformation of sects into denominations.

[111] J. Bieri and R. Lobeck, "Self-Concept Differences in Relation to Identification, Religion, and Social Class," *Journal of Abnormal and Social Psychology*, 62 (1961), 94–98.

[112] Trent, "Characteristics of Catholic Intellectuals."

[113] Typically, the query reads: "If you had to choose, which thing on this list would you pick as the most important for a child to learn to prepare him for life? (1) to obey; (2) to be well liked or popular; (3) to think for himself; (4) to work hard; (5) to help others?"

[114] Lenski, *The Religious Factor*, p. 252.

[115] Campbell, "Religion among Nova Scotian Students."

[116] William V. D'Antonio, unpublished study of the characteristics of students in Notre Dame campus organizations, University of Notre Dame, 1962.

Protestant college students scoring high on the "Drive" scale of the NORC researchers (47 to 54 per cent).[117]

Most of the discussions of the relative values placed on independence and autonomy by Catholics and Protestants take place within the framework of Max Weber's now classic work dealing with the origins of modern capitalism.[118] Probably no theory has been more consistently misapplied or has evoked more critical response.[119] Those relying on Weber usually suggest that the values of Protestantism better mesh with the disposition and behavior required in a competitive achieving society; they then hypothesize that Catholic parents would place considerably less emphasis on independence training and achievement motivation in their children, which would result in a lower average educational level and less likelihood of upward occupational mobility and social success.

Discussion of the vagaries of the debate would lead us far afield here. But it would be worthwhile to mention in passing some studies that have investigated achievement motivation[120] and the independence training of children, for the light they can throw on the purported absence of an orientation toward upward social mobility among Catholics. The suggestion that something in the nature of Catholicism limits the economic success of its strict adherents seemed to be given some support in the research of Lenski, Mayer and Sharp, McClelland et al., Rosen, and Weller.[121] All of these studies have, however, been cogently criticized, particularly by Greeley, who, in addition to pointing up the inadequacies of this research, cited a number of investigations seeming to show that contemporary Catholic men are, if anything, higher in achievement motivation and mobility striving than Protestants (both,

[117] Greeley, *Religion and Career.*

[118] Max Weber, *The Protestant Ethic and the Spirit of Capitalism*, trans. Talcott Parsons (New York: Charles Scribner's Sons, 1948).

[119] The best known of the criticisms include A. Fanfani, *Catholicism, Protestantism, and Capitalism* (New York: Sheed and Ward, 1935); K. Samuelsson, *Religion and Economic Action* (New York: Harper and Row, 1964); and R. Tawney, *Religion and the Rise of Capitalism* (New York: New American Library, 1958).

[120] Variously defined, but usually some version of "interest in excellence of performance on a unique task or in the pursuit of a long-term career" (R. Hassenger, "The Interaction of Instructional and Picture Cues in the Assessment of Achievement Motivation" [Master's thesis, Marquette University, 1961]).

[121] Lenski, *The Religious Factor*; A. J. Mayer and H. Sharp, "Religious Preference and Worldly Success," *American Sociological Review*, 27 (1962), 218–27; D. C. McClelland, A. Rindlisbacher, and R. C. DeCharms, "Religious and Other Sources of Parental Attitudes Toward Independence Training," in *Studies in Motivation*, ed. D. C. McClelland (New York: Appleton-Century-Crofts, 1955); B. Rosen, "Race, Ethnicity, and the Achievement Syndrome," *American Sociological Review*, 24 (1959), 47–60, and his review of Lenski in *ibid.*, 27 (1962), 111–12; N. Weller, "Religion and Mobility in Industrial Society" (Ph.D. dissertation, University of Michigan, 1960).

however, lag behind American Jews).[122] Although it would be too sanguine to suggest that the controversy is now over, there seems to be considerable evidence that, whatever the orientations of traditional Catholics, those assimilated into American life are little different from their WASP[123] fellows and can be expected to climb the success ladder with at least equal facility. Catholics can take comfort that they are, in Andrew Greeley's only half-facetious remark, "just as greedy as anyone else and indeed a bit more so if really put to the test."[124]

Data are available from some other instruments developed by social scientists in attempts to measure "deeper," more "central" personality traits or tendencies. One of the most widely used of these has been the F-(for pre-Fascism) Scale, which grew out of the Berkeley research on anti-Semitism and general intolerance during the postwar years of reaction. The F-Scale has been used to assess a syndrome characterized by hostility to minority groups, rigid and stereotyped thought, conventionalism, submission, and power-consciousness, usually termed "authoritarianism."[125]

[122] Greeley, *Religion and Career*; and "The Protestant Ethic: Time for a Moratorium," *Sociological Analysis*, 25 (1964), 20–33. Evidence that can be adduced (not all of which is found in Greeley) includes the work of Marvin Bressler and Charles Westoff, "Catholic Education, Economic Values, and Achievement," *American Journal of Sociology*, 69 (1963), 225–33; R. Mack, R. J. Murphy, and S. Yellin, "The Protestant Ethic, Level of Aspiration and Social Mobility," *American Sociological Review*, 21 (1956), 295–300. See also Donald R. Miller and G. E. Swanson, *The Changing American Parent* (New York: John Wiley & Sons, Inc., 1958); Joseph Veroff, Sheila Feld, and Gerald Gurin, "Achievement Motivation and Religious Background," *American Sociological Review*, 27 (1962), 205–17; H. R. Wagner, "The Protestant Ethic Today" (Paper read at the Meetings of the Society for the Scientific Study of Religion, 1960); and H. R. Wagner, V. Doyle, and Kathryn Doyle, "Religious Background and Higher Education," *American Sociological Review*, 24 (1959), 852–56. A good summary of the work to the early 1960's can be found in David McClelland, *The Achieving Society* (New York: D. Van Nostrand and Co., 1961). Greeley presents an intriguing hypothesis of the effects of social marginality on mobility in Greeley and Rossi, *Ed. of Catholic Americans*.

[123] "White Anglo-Saxon Protestants." For an interesting discussion of this group, see E. Digby Baltzell, *The Protestant Establishment* (New York: Random House, 1965); cf. also my review of Baltzell in *Sociological Quarterly*, 7 (1966), 100–102.

[124] Greeley's "plea for a moratorium," in "The Protestant Ethic."

[125] A more complete discussion of the scale, its derivation, and modifications are found in Adorno *et al.*, *The Authoritarian Personality*. Various criticisms have been leveled at this instrument, the most important of which are summarized in R. Christie and M. Jahoda (eds.), *Studies in the Scope and Method of "The Authoritarian Personality"* (Glencoe, Ill.: The Free Press, 1954). Controversy about the "meaning" of high scores on this scale need not concern us here. We are not, that is to say, disposed to worry about what the scale "really measures" in this chapter, but are concerned to provide comparative results of various student groups. A cursory examination of the items in the scale is suffici-

Some interesting comparative results are available from investigations using a modified form of the F-Scale, designed to eliminate those items likely to cause spuriously high scores when used with subjects from minority groups, including Jews and Catholics.[126] The following mean authoritarianism scores were reported by Brown and Bystryn in their research on college women.[127] Descriptions of the students' colleges are found on the left in Table 3; figures in parentheses indicate the number of subjects in each group.

TABLE 3
MEAN AUTHORITARIANISM SCORES OF PROTESTANT,
CATHOLIC, AND JEWISH COLLEGE WOMEN[a]

Sample	Freshmen		Seniors	
Protestant women in "Eastern liberal arts college"	199.	(48)[b]	195.2	(44)
Protestant women in "large Eastern urban coed univ."	214.7	(17)	200.2	(40)
Jewish women in "Eastern liberal arts college"	191.8	(28)	141.7	(25)
Jewish women in "large Eastern urban coed univ."	189.7	(17)	171.4	(17)
Catholics in an "upper-middle class Catholic liberal arts college for women with an enrollment of 450"	243.6	(26)	231.7	(31)

a After Brown and Bystryn, 1956, p. 284
b Sample sizes in parentheses

It can be seen that Catholic college seniors were only slightly less authoritarian than freshmen, and scored higher than the Protestant or Jewish freshmen.[128] But this was a cross-sectional study, comparing concurrent freshmen and seniors. One might suggest that on becoming less rigid and authoritarian the students may well drop out of a Catholic women's college.[129] In an attempt to obviate this possibility, Hassenger did a longitudinal study using the same modified authoritarianism scale; at the time of this writing, data are available for the first two years of the subjects' careers in a midwestern Catholic women's college.[130] A clear difference in the F-Scale means oc-

ent to convince one of the anti-minority, rigidly intolerant, and highly punitive tendencies of the respondent assenting to many of these statements.

126 The reader may object that Catholics are not really a minority group, but one of the criticisms of the original F-Scale was that it caused those who held firm beliefs to appear more rigidly "authoritarian" than they really are. It discriminated, they charged, against those holding firm beliefs. But see note 125.

127 Donald Brown and Denise Bystryn, "College Environment, Personality, and the Ideology of Three Ethnic Groups," Journal of Social Psychology, 44 (1956), 279–88.

128 A number of other investigations have reported Catholics more authoritarian than any but fundamentalist Protestant groups.

129 Although this, too, would tell something about the school.

130 Hassenger, "Impact of a Value-Oriented College."

curred between college entrance and the end of these students' freshman year, with a slightly further decrease occurring in the sophomore year (number of students in parentheses):

September, 1963	May, 1964	March, 1965
205.8 (40)	189.0 (39)	185.4 (37)

All three means are considerably below those found by Brown and Bystryn for Catholic college women, and lower than one of their samples for Protestant women entering as freshmen. Using another measure of authoritarianism (which prevents direct comparison with the above scores), Fox also found a significant difference between freshmen and seniors, this investigation being done in an Iowa Catholic men's college.[131] The climate of liberalism may be more generally widespread in the mid-1950's than when the Brown and Bystryn and other early studies were done, but there are indications that significant student change does occur in at least some Catholic colleges.[132]

One of the more successful efforts to devise a measure of stereotyped thought that did not discriminate against those with conservative political beliefs (another criticism of the F-Scale) is the Dogmatism Scale of Milton Rokeach.[133] The intent of this forty-item instrument is to assess the open or closed nature of one's "belief-disbelief system," i.e., the extent to which

[131] John T. Fox, "Authoritarianism and the St. Ambrose College Student," *Religious Education*, 60 (1965), 272–76.

[132] Which is not to say the college caused the change; it may have taken place had these students worked at Woolworth's for four years. J. C. McCullers and W. T. Plant ("Personality and Social Development: Cultural Influences," *Review of Educational Research*, 34 [1964], 599–610) found significant decreases in dogmatism, ethnocentrism, and authoritarianism for 1,448 San Jose State College applicants, whether they had attended the college for eight semesters, for four, for two, or for none at all. It should also be pointed out that Fox found State University of Iowa men who were paired by sex, college classification, and major field with the Catholic sample to be clearly lower in the authoritarianism scale. But at least the College did not impede some "liberalizing" of its students.

[133] Milton Rokeach, *The Open and Closed Mind* (New York: Basic Books, 1960). This instrument consists of items such as "To compromise with our political opponents is dangerous because it usually leads to the betrayal of our own side," or "It is only natural for a person to be fearful of the future." One indication of how those more inclined to a less permissive, more stereotypical outlook and style of life also tend to score high on dogmatism comes from the research of D'Antonio at Notre Dame. It was earlier noted that students respond differently to a query about the "most important thing a child can learn." It is interesting to compare the dogmatism scores of those with different views (first choice only):

to obey	(42)	155.6
to be well-liked	(5)	172.4
to think for himself	(205)	150.7
to work hard	(54)	156.7
to help others	(45)	153.6

If the much higher scores of the "well-liked" group were found in a larger sample, this pattern would be very suggestive.

an individual uses a set of rigid attitudes or thought categories to ward off aspects of a world he perceives to be dangerous or threatening. Some of the data from the use of this scale in various college settings are summarized in Table 4.

Although differences among colleges exist, a fairly narrow range has been

TABLE 4
MEAN DOGMATISM SCORES FOR VARIOUS
COLLEGE POPULATIONS (NUMBERS IN PARENTHESES)[a]

Source	Freshmen	Mixed Sample	Seniors
Rokeach Research[b]			
Michigan State Univ.			
Protestants (145)		180.1	
Catholics (42)		191.1	
Non-Believers (15)		174.6	
New York Colleges			
Protestants (24)		138.3	
Catholics (46)		147.4	
Jews (131)		139.5	
Lehmann Research[c]			
Michigan State Univ.			
Males (590)	166.9		154.0
Females (461)	162.9		146.7
Male Catholics (262)		174.1	
Plant Research[d]			
San Jose State College			
(1958 applicants)			
Male (1,007)		159.7	
Female (1,343)		155.3	
Foster *et al.* Research[e]			
Santa Clara Men			
1959	166.0 (297)		155.6 (243)
1961	170.0 (241)		155.8 (348)
Hellkamp Research[f]			
Xavier Univ. Men (38)		168.4	
Hassenger Research[g]			
"Mary College" women			
Longitudinal: 1963–65	162.3 (40)	157.5 (39)	146.2 (37)

[a] For the convenience of the interested layman reading this volume, standard deviations are omitted here but can be found in the indicated sources.
[b] Rokeach, *Open and Closed Mind*
[c] Lehmann; Lehmann and Ikenberry, *Critical Thinking, Attitudes and Values*
[d] Plant, "The Impact of College"
[e] Foster *et al.* "Santa Clara University"
[f] Hellkamp, "Catholic College Students"
[g] Hassenger, "The Impact of a Catholic College"

found at each institution. At both Michigan State and in Rokeach's sample of New York colleges, Catholic students were found to be more dogmatic than Protestants, Jews, and non-believers. Men at Santa Clara were found to undergo about the same decrease as Michigan State students, with most of the change apparently occurring in their first college year.[134] At "Mary

134 For further discussion of this finding, which was part of a pattern in the Santa Clara research, the reader is referred to Julian Foster's contribution, which follows (chap. 6).

College,"[135] in contrast, there was little drop in dogmatism between September and May for the forty freshmen in my longitudinal sample, but a clear decrease occurred for the thirty-seven remaining students during their sophomore year.[136] Although it is difficult to interpret the meaning of these scores (especially since they are closer to the D-Scale means of a group pre-selected by judges as being "high dogmatic" rather than "low dogmatic" in the Rokeach research),[137] the more recent data for Catholic college students shows scores comparable to those at other colleges and universities.[138]

Two recent studies by careful researchers would indicate that Catholic educators have little cause for complacency, however. Reporting data obtained from using the *Activities Index* he developed with C. Robert Pace, George Stern[139] summarized the personality patterns he found in student samples from six colleges with "major Protestant" denominational affiliation, four "minor Protestant" colleges, and eight Roman Catholic institutions.[140] There are, of course, considerable differences within the individual colleges

[135] A pseudonym, as explained in chapter 4.

[136] It is interesting to compare this rate of decrease with the three F-Scale means at "Mary College"; the slower rate of decrease in dogmatism may support the contention of Rokeach that the D-Scale gets at a more central dimension than the F-Scale, and is less readily modified. But see note 20, chapter 4.

[137] Rokeach, *Open and Closed Mind*, p. 104.

[138] Although no data are given, Barbara Long ("Catholic-Protestant Differences in Acceptance of Others," *Sociology and Social Research*, 49 [1965], 166–71) also reports that Catholic students at the University of Delaware did not score significantly higher than Protestants on the Rokeach scale. Further, D. G. Dean and J. A. Reeves ("Anomie: A Comparison of a Catholic and a Protestant Sample," *Sociometry*, 25 [1962], 209–12) found 160 women from a Protestant liberal arts college to be significantly higher in anomie or "normlessness" than an equal number of midwestern Catholic women's college students. It may be, of course, that the Michigan State and New York college students would also score lower today than when data was gathered almost a decade ago, so that they would still be less dogmatic than Catholic college students.

[139] George G. Stern, "Psychological Characteristics of Denominational Colleges" (Paper read at the 1965 Meetings of the American Catholic Psychological Association, Chicago, data not available at the time of this writing.) Since the *Activities Index* has been described in the preceding chapter, it will not be treated again here, except to remind the reader that the mean scores on each of the thirty *Activities Index* scales and on the factors deriving from scale combinations are compared to the normative group of students from about forty colleges and universities.

[140] "Major Protestant" colleges are those schools established by such major denominations as Congregationalists, Baptists, and Presbyterians; they include Denison, Earlham, Southern Methodist, and Emory. "Minor Protestant" colleges were established by smaller denominational groups; here, they are Eastern Mennonite, Heidelberg, Messiah, and Northwest Christian College. The Catholic institutions are Barry College, Detroit University, Divine Word Seminary, Mount Mercy, Mundelein, St. Francis, St. Louis University, and St. Scholastica.

and differences among the schools that are not a function of their religious affiliation.[141] But there seem also to be, judging from the Stern data, modal student "types" at the colleges in each of the three groups. For example, men at the minor Protestant denominational colleges tend to be dependent, in need of close fellowship, and are comparatively low in the various scales measuring intellectual interests. Women at these schools are even less intellectually inclined.

A brief summary of Stern's findings for Catholic college men and women give one pause. The men are rather low in achievement orientation and tend to be highly constrained, fearful of aesthetic and sensual enjoyment.[142] The Catholic college women are higher in intellectual orientation than most college women, but this takes an applied, pragmatic form (represented by majors in such fields as education and home economics) for the most part. They are very low on sensuality,[143] appearing to be the most puritanical of the student populations, and are rather constrained, but no more so than Catholic men.[144] Stern is careful to suggest that such patterns may be primarily a function of the social class and ethnic backgrounds of these students and not something specifically Catholic; but whatever the "cause," the findings are intriguing.

One of the most promising instruments that have emerged from recent attempts to understand the variations in student characteristics is the *Omnibus Personality Inventory*, developed at the Center for the Study of Higher Education at Berkeley.[145] The need for improved measures for use with "normal" college populations led to the refinement of scales measuring

[141] There were, that is to say, some Catholic and major Protestant colleges high in academic climate, whereas others from each group were low. A fuller discussion of the *Activities Index* and its dimensions is found in George G. Stern, "Environments for Learning," in *The American College*, ed. Nevitt Sanford (New York: John Wiley & Sons, Inc., 1962), 690–730.

[142] This should not be misinterpreted as sexual gratification; it refers rather to the sort of delight associated with new colors, sounds, tastes, experiences.

[143] The reader is again referred to note 142.

[144] Catholic women are less constrained than Catholic men in these colleges, when compared to the normative groups of college men and women. Comparisons are always relative, and the expected behavior of men and women, of course, differ. What is meant by the above is that Catholic college men are less like "typical" college males than Catholic college women are like "typical" college females. D. C. Dauw and R. C. Pugh ("Creativity and Religious Preferences," *Religious Education*, 61 [1966], 30–35) found that non-Catholic boys were higher in creativity than Catholics, although mean differences for girls were not statistically significant.

[145] *The Omnibus Personality Inventory* (Berkeley, Calif.: Center for the Study of Higher Education, 1961). The description and use of this instrument can be found throughout the 1962 Sanford volume, particularly in Part VII.

general social maturity, intellectual activity, and ego-functioning. There has been extensive validation of the scales with other well-known instruments.[146]

Utilizing data collected by the Berkeley Center in their Study of Selected Institutions and the High School Graduates Study (which he co-directed), Trent compared the scores on a number of the *Omnibus Personality Inventory* (OPI) scales for Catholics in Catholic colleges, California state colleges, and The University of California at Berkeley with non-Catholics at the California state colleges and at Berkeley, and with the scores of students in a number of top-flight liberal arts colleges.[147] Although justice cannot be done to this fine investigation here, a summary of the most important findings will be attempted.

The scores of freshmen at five West Coast Catholic colleges on the scales from the OPI assessing "intellectuality"[148] were compared to those of public and private college students — including Catholics at these schools. With ability and social-class levels controlled, Catholic college students were found to score lower than any of the comparison groups, except state college Catholics in four cases. They seemed to be, according to the OPI scale definitions,[149] less interested in ideas, in critical inquiry and thought, and in matters of aesthetic concern. Scoring lower in non-authoritarianism, they seem more inclined to dogmatism and intolerance. The Catholic students at

---

[146] Including the *Minnesota Multiphasic Personality Inventory*, the *California Personality Inventory*, the *Allport-Vernon-Lindzey Study of Values*, and the *Activities Index*.

[147] Trent, "Etiology of Catholic Intellectualism."

[148] A dimension composed of five OPI scales denoting interest in reflective thought, critical thinking, tolerance for ambiguity, independence, and open-mindedness. The scale definitions are from the *OPI Research Manual* (Berkeley, Calif.: Center for the Study of Higher Education, 1962). *Thinking Introversion*: high scorers indicate a liking for abstract, reflective thought and an interest in a variety of areas such as literature, art and music. Low scorers indicate a preference for overt action and the evaluation of ideas for their immediately practical worth. *Theoretical Orientation*: this scale measures interest in science and scientific activities, including a preference for using the scientific method of thinking. High scorers are generally logical, rational, and critical in their approach to problems. *Complexity*: an experimental or tentative, rather than a fixed, way of viewing the world. High scorers are fond of novel situations, tolerant of ambiguities, more aware of subtle environmental variations. *Estheticism*: the high scorers endorse statements indicating diverse interests in artistic matters and activities — literature, dramatics, music, painting, and sculpture. *Non-authoritarianism*: high scores indicate a sense of independence and freedom from opinionated, rigid, intolerant thinking, emotional suppression, and nondemocratic beliefs.

[149] Definitions for the social scientist are empirical, not a priori; scale content is not derived by the armchair approach, but by testing items with populations known to differ. Only items clearly discriminating between such groups are employed in instruments such as the OPI.

Berkeley scored higher in intellectuality than those in Catholic colleges, but not as high as their non-Catholic classmates.[150]

But do these students perhaps undergo considerable change while attending Catholic colleges? Apparently not; on only one of the five intellectuality scales were senior scores significantly higher than those of freshmen.[151] Although it appeared that four college years had produced a somewhat greater interest in non-pragmatic, reflective thought, the over-all difference was not great, nor were the absolute levels of intellectualism high.

With the recent push toward academic excellence in Catholic higher education, and the parity in graduate school attendance indicated in Greeley's research, it might be expected that Catholic college seniors expressing an intention to attain a higher degree would compare favorably with others on the intellectuality scales. But this was not found to be so. Catholic college seniors planning to attend graduate school scored lower than both groups of beginning graduate students on all but one of the scales.[152] Trent believes this comparative lack of intellectual attitudes is "suggestive of the reason why even those Catholic college graduates who have obtained higher degrees have been found to be under-represented in the world of scholarship."[153] Whether graduate school attendants from other Catholic colleges would fare so badly in comparative intellectuality remains, of course, a moot point.

Catholic college freshmen were compared with their senior classmates on another useful scale from the OPI, Impulse Expression.[154] Low scores on this scale are indicative of a general restrictiveness and docility. Although college seniors are typically found to score higher on the impulse expression scale (i.e., to be less submissive) than freshmen, the reverse was found in the West Coast Catholic colleges. Even with the shortcomings of a cross-sectional design and the danger of selective attrition accounting for this pattern, it is of little help to suggest that the more free-wheeling students are most likely to leave Catholic colleges, and the more docile and moralistic to remain. Such an interpretation would suggest that these students find the Catholic colleges uninteresting, perhaps even constraining. The only factor that might be operating to account for such findings — aside from faculty assessment procedures — would be a fast upgrading of the clientele in these colleges, so that seniors, who were even less intellectually oriented

[150] The reader will recall the different evaluations of intellectual integrity shown in McNamara's research (p. 124).

[151] Thinking Introversion (cf. note 148).

[152] Estheticism, not primarily on "*intellectual*" scale.

[153] James W. Trent, "Dimensions of Intellectual Productivity among Sectarian and Non-sectarian College Students" (Paper read at the Convention of the American Personnel and Guidance Association, 1964), p. 9.

[154] *Impulse Expression*: this scale measures a general readiness to express impulses in overt action or conscious feeling. High scorers work imaginatively, have a rather active fantasy life, and employ freedom of thought. Low scorers are moralistic and authoritarian in thinking and behavior.

and impulse-free as freshmen, could be shown to have undergone some change. The freshmen in the sample might then be expected to undergo similar change during their college careers, scoring higher as seniors than the senior group to which they were compared by Trent. Only longitudinal investigation can determine this.[155]

Data obtained from two other instruments used in the investigation of Trent will be briefly considered here. Students from Catholic colleges were found to be clearly higher than Catholic men and women attending California state colleges or Berkeley on the "Religious Concepts Inventory," a measure of religious knowledge.[156] But on the OPI Religious Liberalism scale,[157] this group is well below all other students. Trent also found minimal differences between Catholic college freshmen and seniors on these two instruments. So, while Catholic undergraduates showed the highest religiosity, it is difficult to interpret what these results mean. Upperclassmen are typically found to score higher than freshmen on religious liberalism, but it is questionable whether Catholic students should be expected to show the same pattern. The opposition to authority usually manifesting itself among college students might be anticipated, and this could lead to higher senior than freshman scores. But to the extent that the scale items appear to be getting at a kind of agnosticism, it would seem unlikely that students remaining in small Catholic colleges would look like religious liberals as assessed by this scale.[158] And indeed, Trent found senior women in these institutions obtaining the same scores as freshmen, with senior men only slightly higher than freshmen.[159] We cannot answer here whether this can be attributed to a

[155] Trent has a longitudinal investigation underway, and the writer has studies in process at "Mary College" (class of 1967) and at Notre Dame (class of 1969).

[156] See Trent, "The Etiology of Catholic Intellectualism," pp. 66–67.

[157] Now termed Religious Orientation by the Berkeley researchers, although high scorers are more critical of traditional beliefs and practices (i.e., they are *not* higher in religious orientation); they are especially opposed to organized, institutional religion. The scale content is still best described as religious liberalism.

[158] Perhaps the dimension being assessed here is really non-theism or a-theism. If one examines the content of the scale, it can be seen that Catholics could not score high without disagreeing with numerous traditional beliefs. Normative data are primarily from California colleges and universities. This points up the need for developing special techniques for assessing religiosity among Catholic students. For discussion of one attempt in this direction, see Robert Hassenger, "Varieties of Religious Orientation," *Sociological Analysis*, 25 (1964), 189–99. The instrument worked out by Sr. Marie Augusta Neal (*Values and Interests in Social Change* [Englewood Cliffs, N.J.: Prentice-Hall, 1964]) has exciting possibilities.

[159] At only one of the five West Coast colleges he studied did Trent find seniors to be significantly more critical and intellectually curious than freshmen. These seniors were at the same time highly religious, which corroborates the impression of Andrew Greeley after visiting the college: "The most Christian college I've even seen!" (Personal communication, Autumn, 1965.)

failure of college impact or is explained by the nature of the Religious Liberalism Scale.

How typical are the five West Coast Catholic colleges in Trent's sample? Until more data are available, we cannot be sure. It is interesting, however, to consider the OPI scores of entering freshmen in a midwest Catholic women's college, for comparative purposes.[160] On two of the OPI scales,[161] scores of the forty students were considerably above the freshmen in Trent's five Catholic colleges and compared directly with the select private college group. Scores on the remaining intellectualism scales, on the other hand, were similar to those of the West Coast Catholic women. The Impulse Expression scores from "Mary College" freshmen were also low.[162] On the Religious Liberalism scale, this group had a "low" mean score, but it was higher than that of the West Coast Catholic college women, and this score had gone up slightly by the end of their sophomore year. At the same time, these students were fairly high at college entrance on the OPI Developmental Status scale, indicating a certain independence and freedom from authoritarianism, and were even higher by the spring of their second college year.[163] With the decreases in dogmatism and authoritarianism in the longitudinal study of "Mary College" students reported earlier in this chapter, it would seem safe to infer that significant personality "growth" occurred during the first two years students spent at a Catholic women's college.

Parallel movements away from a rigid, instrumental religious orientation toward a more "open" stance were minimal however; there was little real autonomy of judgment, despite the inclusion of a number of issues that should have been of considerable concern to the young adult.[164] Apparently slight change occurred to the extent that seniors were more willing to accept some statements of a less authoritarian cast, particularly when couched in general and unspecific terms.[165] But when responding to more concrete queries about religious beliefs and behavior, seniors were little different from freshmen. That is to say, when respondents were asked what they would *do*, they did not respond in ways congruent with the more liberal values they seemingly espoused.

These results are consistent with the work summarized earlier in this chapter. What they mean is less clear. Some will no doubt rejoice that Catholic college seniors' religious attitudes and behavior were apparently similar to

[160] Hassenger, "Impact of a Value-Oriented College."

[161] Theoretical Orientation and Estheticism (cf. note 148).

[162] This is consistent with the profile of "Mary College" sketched in chapter 4, with a clientele largely from working-class homes, who bring a pragmatic, non-academic educational orientation to the campus.

[163] Standard scores were 45 and 50, respectively.

[164] Attitude items on the *Index*, fasting and abstinence, sexual behavior, drinking, and the like, were included.

[165] E. g., support of "greater freedom" for the layman.

those of freshmen, particularly since seniors generally appear "less religious" than freshmen in non-Catholic colleges. Those who demand more of Catholic higher education, on the other hand, are less easily pleased. They would expect four years of Catholic higher education to produce significant differences.

It is difficult to deal with such questions as "Are Parochial Schools the Answer?"[166] To appropriately evaluate the excellence of the Catholic schools, e.g., one would have to pin down precisely what it was one wished to know, and then explore it systematically. Even when data are available, however, those approaching the problem from different directions do not always agree on what the findings mean. One of the most recent controversies, for example, seemed to be structured by some as a battle between the "prophets" and "sociologists."[167] It is not clear who "won." Almost certainly each "side" would claim victory. But the Big Questions will not likely be resolved by polemics. Sociologists tend to concentrate on comparisons of Catholics and non-Catholics with various levels of education, from both Catholic and secular schools. If those with a given amount of time spent in Catholic institutions are shown to do "better" in a particular area of Catholicism, the prophet may reply that "these values are something less than central to Christianity."[168] And, from one point of view, he would be right. But is he realistic? It is extremely difficult to determine the extent to which such presumably dynamic characteristics as values and attitudes can or should change in college. Psychoanalysts have long insisted on the importance of early life experiences. In one longitudinal study, Whitely found little fluctuation in the personal values of college men,[169] and Greeley and Rossi[170] continually warn against demanding too much of church-related education, in view of the other influences operating in students' lives.

Although it is known that young men and women in some liberal arts colleges undergo dramatic value and attitude changes,[171] it has not been demonstrated in the existing research that colleges are agents of this modifi-

---

[166] To use the title of the recent critical work by Mary Perkins Ryan (New York: Holt, Rinehart and Winston, 1964). Strictly speaking, "parochial" refers to parish, and is not interchangeable with "religious." Thus, Catholic higher education cannot be described as parochial (at least in the above sense), although many do use the term in this way.

[167] Callahan, "The Schools."

[168] *Ibid.*, p. 474.

[169] P. L. Whitely, "The Constancy of Personal Values," *Journal of Abnormal and Social Psychology*, 33 (1938), 405–8.

[170] Greeley and Rossi, *Ed. of Catholic Americans*.

[171] The reader is again referred to Jacob, *Changing Values in College*; Goldsen et al., *What College Students Think*; Sanford "Personality Development;" to the classic study of Theodore Newcomb, *Personality and Social Change* (New York: Dryden, 1943); and to the forthcoming *The Impact of College*, by Newcomb and Kenneth Feldman (in preparation).

cation. The so-called college effects may be owing to maturational change, or to differential recruitment, or both.[172]

This chapter has frequently lamented the paucity of research on college impact. The little work that has been done has been based on somewhat simplistic models, with little reflection of the diverse situations of students with various backgrounds, attributes, and college experiences.[173] Yet the key problem in evaluating the schools lies in determining what systematic exposures are likely to produce differential college impact, on what types of students, and for what attitudes and values. Thus, the social scientist would insist that any questions about the impact of the Catholic colleges must remain in large part unanswered. The dimensions to be evaluated must be carefully specified, and only after careful investigation can attempts to answer the query be made. To my knowledge, no such elegant studies have been designed and carried out within Catholic higher education. The differential college effects on students with various characteristics can be gleaned from the existing research, however, and the remainder of this chapter will consider some of the more interesting of these.

DIFFERENTIAL COLLEGE IMPACT

STUDENT BACKGROUNDS

Much has been made of the lower-class, immigrant origins of American Catholics. And rightly so. As a number of commentators have pointed out, a large part of the explanation for the rather dreary record of scholarship that has characterized American Catholicism lies in the fact that both the church as an institution and its adherents were immigrants to these shores.

[172] In recent years, for example, the National Merit Scholarship Corporation has carried out research that led to a revision of the earlier conclusions of Robert Knapp and his co-workers (R. H. Knapp and H. G. Goodrich, *Origins of American Scientists* [Chicago: University of Chicago Press, 1952]); R. H. Knapp and J. J. Greenbaum, *The Younger American Scholar: His Collegiate Origins* [Chicago: University of Chicago Press, 1953]), regarding the colleges most successful in sending students on for higher degrees (Alexander Astin, "A Re-examination of College Productivity," *Journal of Educational Psychology*, 52 [1961], 173–78; and Donald L. Thistlethwaite, "College Press and Changes in Study Plans of Talented Students," *Journal of Educational Psychology*, 51 [1960], 222–34, and "College Press and Student Achievement," *Journal of Educational Psychology*, 50 [1959], 183–91). A. O. Pfnister (*A Report of the Baccalaureate Origins of College Faculties* [Washington, D.C.: Association of American Colleges, 1961]) has also done some interesting work on this problem.

[173] See, for example, Kuhlen and Arnold, "Age Differences in Religious Beliefs"; for a criticism of the psychological models that have been used, see Orville Brim, *Personality Development in Children* (Austin: University of Texas Press, 1960) and J. Milton Yinger, *Toward a Field Theory of Behavior* (New York: McGraw-Hill, 1965).

Philip Gleason has handled his discussion of this so competently (chap. 2) that no further elaboration is needed here.

Most of the research on American Catholics has been influenced — some would say unfortunately so — by the work of Max Weber, leading to a concentration on the influence of religion on occupational values, social class, and social mobility. The importance of social class for religion in America has been long realized.[174] There are indications, however, that ethnicity may be of greater importance than social class in understanding American Catholicism. Indeed, it could scarcely be anything but crucial, considering the great differences in the cultures from which immigrant Catholics came, and their times of arrival in this country.[175] (It would be interesting to speculate on the implications of the changing ethnic "mix" of Catholic colleges, but this would take us far afield here.[176]) Confining ourselves to the existing research, empirical support for the greater relevance of ethnicity than social class for understanding American Catholicism can be found in Cross, Greeley, Lipset and Bendix, McClelland, and Rosen.[177] Both Greeley and Rosen

[174] Although it has been little studied. H. Richard Niebuhr (*The Social Sources of Denominationalism* [New York: Henry Holt, 1962]) and Ernst Troeltsch (*The Social Teaching of the Christian Churches*, trans. Olive Wyon [2 vols.; New York: Macmillan, 1931]) have undertaken exploration of the social forces influencing religious beliefs, behavior, and organization; and Liston Pope ("Religion and the Class Structure," *Annals of the American Academy of Political and Social Science*, 246 [March, 1948], 84–91) did an early study of the social origins of the members of various denominations' members. Demerath has recently approached the problem of religion and social class from a different perspective and with provocative results.

[175] The peak years of immigration for the most visible Catholic ethnic groups: Irish, 1851; Germans, 1882; Italians, 1907; Poles, 1921 (from John L. Thomas, S.J., "Nationalities and American Catholicism," in *Catholic Church, U.S.A.*, ed. Louis Putz, C.S.C., [Chicago: Fides Press, 1956]).

[176] An illustration of how this is occurring in one college is found in chapter 4. Femminella's suggestions about some likely changes in the character and tone of American Catholicism resulting from the increasing visibility of Italian-Americans is worth reading (Francis X. Femminella, "The Impact of Italian Migration on American Catholicism," *American Catholic Sociological Review*, 22 [1961], 233–41). Some implications for the Catholic college are mentioned in the concluding chapter.

[177] Lawrence J. Cross, "The Catholics in Norristown, Pennsylvania" (Ph.D. dissertation, University of Pennsylvania, 1962); Andrew M. Greeley, "Religious Segregation in a Suburb" (Master's thesis, University of Chicago, 1961); S. M. Lipset and R. Bendix, *Social Mobility in Industrial Society* (Berkeley and Los Angeles: University of California, 1959); D. McClelland, *The Achieving Society*; Rosen, "The Achievement Syndrome." This might also be inferred from the work of Kosa and his associates, although less clearly (John L. Kosa, "Religious Participation, Religious Knowledge and Scholastic Aptitude: An Empirical Study," *Journal for the Scientific Study of Religion*, 1 [1961], 88–97; "Patterns of Social Mobility Among American Catholics," *Social Compass*, 9 [1962], 361–71; John L. Kosa and L. D. Rachiele, "The Spirit of Capitalism, Traditionalism, and Re-

have taken Lenski severely to task for his failure to control for ethnic influence among Detroit Catholics.[178]

This hue and cry notwithstanding, little hard data on the meaning of ethnicity in Catholic colleges exist. The available information relates primarily to occupational mobility and college and graduate school attendance. Fosselman and Liu found considerable differences in mobility between Catholic students of Irish and English and those of southern and eastern European origin.[179] In his secondary analysis of data from the National Opinion Research Center, Greeley discovered that Irish and German students were more likely to have taken college for granted than Polish and Italian Catholics (43% of the former, compared to 30% of the latter) and had more positive appraisals of their own abilities (33% and 23%, respectively, had a high estimate of their own competence).[180] Regarding plans for their later careers, however, the split was another way, with 28 per cent of the Poles and 21 per cent of the Germans (compared to 13% and 12% of the Irish and Italians, respectively) indicating an intention to pursue academic fields; Irish and Italians were more interested in professional careers.[181]

The great loyalty to Catholicism among the American Irish has often been remarked. Greeley and Rossi found that Catholic school attendance was much greater among first and second generation Irish (and French) than first or second generation Germans, Italians, or Poles.[182]

ligiousness: A Re-examination of Weber's Concepts," *Sociological Quarterly*, 4 [1963], 243–60; J. L. Kosa, L. Rachiele, and C. Schommer, "Psychological Characteristics of Ethnic Groups in a College Population," *Journal of Psychology*, 46 [1958], 265–75). Mundi ("Attitudes Toward Catholicism"), on the other hand, did not uncover the effects of ethnicity he predicted in his research on Minnesota college students.

[178] Greeley, *Religion and Career*; Rosen, "Review of Lenski."

[179] D. H. Fosselman and William T. Liu, "Social Mobility of Catholic Students in the Northwest," *Social Compass*, 8 (1961), 91–96.

[180] Greeley, *Religion and Career*.

[181] The former would incline toward law, the latter toward engineering. Nathan Glazer reports that the majority of Italian boys graduating from City College in New York (now City University) take degrees as engineers (N. Glazer and Daniel P. Moynihan, *Beyond the Melting Pot* [Cambridge, Mass.: Harvard University Press, 1963], p. 202). As was pointed out in chapter 4, Italians have traditionally been less convinced of the value of education for their daughters. "Do not make your child better than you are," runs a southern Italian proverb (*ibid.*, p. 199). Perhaps the Polish and German students are able to raise their levels of aspiration considerably during college, particularly when helped along by faculty mentors (see Greeley, *Religion and Career*). Or it may be that the Irish and Italian students are from higher income levels, and seek the rewards of professional life. Greeley (*ibid.*) found upper-income level Jewish males (but not females) more interested in professional than academic life.

[182] Greeley and Rossi, *Ed. of Catholic Americans*. Almost half of the Catholic college sample in this study were Irish. It is interesting that third- and later-gen-

Other evidence indicates a greater affinity for Catholicism among the Irish, to the extent that this can be measured. Greeley noted that Irish students were least likely of the Catholic groups to abandon their religion during college and were more faithful church attenders (Table 5). But religious participation may not be the best indicator of religious commitment, as was pointed out early in this chapter. Hassenger found some evidence that Irish students in a Catholic women's college tended to be dogmatic and moralistically religious, whereas Polish girls were more openminded and

TABLE 5
CHURCH ATTENDANCE FOR CATHOLICS OF
FOUR MAJOR ETHNIC GROUPS BY SEX
(PER CENT ATTENDING WEEKLY)[a]

Ethnic Group	Male		Female	
Irish	91	(945)[b]	96	(439)
German	89	(640)	89	(264)
Polish	79	(310)	91	(181)
Italian	68	(773)	83	(370)

[a] In percentages. From *Religion and Career* by Andrew M. Greeley, © Sheed and Ward, Inc., 1963 (p. 189).
[b] Number of students in parentheses

liberal, and appeared to undergo more value and attitude modification during their college years.[183]

Since social class and ethnicity are complementary categories, with classes stratified by ethnic group and ethnic groups by social class, it is possible for cross-pressures to be exerted. The interaction of class and ethnicity must be briefly considered. Kosa and Rachiele suggested that the lower-middle class Irish students in their sample were influenced simultaneously toward religious traditionalism by their ethnicity and toward "the religious spirit of capitalism" by their social class, leading to a "lower mean score on mobility aspiration than the rest of the lower-middle class students."[184] But since Irish families generally are less likely to be from the working or lower-middle class,[185] perhaps such results can be explained in a less risky fashion; it may be, e.g., that these Irish students learned their lower achieve-

eration German and Polish Catholics are found in Catholic schools in as high proportions as are Irish, but Italians are not (although percentages do increase with length of stay in the United States).

[183] Hassenger, "Varieties of Orientation." To some extent, this may be explained by the nature of the clientele of this college (see chap. 4); the reader is referred, however, to Jencks' and Riesman's discussion of the somewhat Jansenist cast of Irish Catholicism in their chapter on Catholic colleges in *The Academic Revolution* (in preparation).

[184] Kosa and Rachiele, "Re-examination of Weber's Concepts," p. 259.

[185] Greeley (*Religion and Career*) found that only 24% of the Irish-German-English students in the NORC survey were from working-class backgrounds, compared to 45% of the Italian-Slavic students.

ment motivations from less successful fathers, who had not followed the upward climb of their compatriots. There are some likely effects of the inter-action of class and ethnicity, however, whether or not these are of the variety Kosa and Rachiele suggest.[186]

The earlier noted difference between "first-wave" and "second-wave"[187] ethnics on expected college attendance and self-confidence can be shown to be partly a function of class; this is seen in Table 6.

It is interesting, however, that self-appraisal of ability seems more closely

TABLE 6
ETHNIC VARIABLES BY FATHER'S OCCUPATIONAL STATUS[a]

	FIRST WAVE		SECOND WAVE	
	College Taken for Granted			
Middle and upper class	52[b]	(424)[c]	45	(80)
Working and lower class	15	(132)	19	(67)
	High Estimate of Ability			
Middle and upper class	35	(286)	27	(15)
Working and lower class	32	(283)	18	(63)

[a] After Greeley, 1963
[b] In percentages
[c] Numbers of students in parentheses

linked to ethnicity, and that planning to attend college is primarily related to social class.[188] On plans for later careers, the relative lack of interest in the academic life found for Irish and Italian students persists even at the upper-income levels of the four major ethnic groups.[189]

In all income categories, Irish students of both sexes are more likely to report weekly church attendance, according to the Greeley data (Table 7). Results for the four groups do not differ greatly from those in Table 5, with social class making a slight difference for German and Italian women (but in different directions: higher income German girls are lower in attend-ance, whereas upper income Italians are higher), and Italian men. The clear sex differences for Poles and Italians persist.[190]

[186] Some highly suggestive data on the relationship of "status inconsistency" to students' sociopolitical belief sytems can be found in Braungart, "Student Political Activists."

[187] Greeley sometimes dichotomized his sample into those arriving in the first-wave of immigration (typically Anglo-German-Irish) and the later arrivals (Italians and Poles).

[188] Greeley found this to persist even when controlling for length of time in American, i.e., first-, second-, third-, or fourth-generation.

[189] Greeley (Religion and Career, chap. 7). There is some indication that German and Polish undergraduates may not go immediately to graduate school, however, even at the upper income levels. This remains puzzling.

[190] Kosa, Rachiele, and Schommer, "Characteristics of Ethnic Groups," found

An interesting illustration of the interaction of class and ethnicity in a college setting can be found in my study.[191] Working-class girls at "Mary College" were lower in authoritarianism and dogmatism and appeared to undergo more consistent value and attitude modification.[192] When this group was dichotomized by ethnicity into "first-wave" and "second-wave," however, it was found that working-class students from the second ethnic wave (primarily Italian and Polish women) were higher at college entrance in the OPI scales of developmental status, autonomy, complexity, and

TABLE 7
CHURCH ATTENDANCE FOR CATHOLIC ETHNIC
GROUPS, BY SEX AND INCOME LEVELS[a]

ETHNIC GROUP	MALE		FEMALE	
	−$7,500	$7,500+	−$7,500	$7,500+
Irish	89 (462)[b]	93 (483)	95 (166)	96 (273)
German	89 (360)	89 (280)	94 (159)	81 (105)
Polish	80 (183)	78 (127)	91 (122)	90 (59)
Italian	66 (468)	72 (305)	78 (204)	86 (166)

[a] In percentages. From *Religion and Career* by Andrew M. Greeley, © Sheed and Ward, Inc., 1963 (p. 189).
[b] Numbers of students in parentheses

higher in the Selvin and Hagstrom libertarian scale.[193] By contrast, the working-class students from the first ethnic wave were lower in Developmental Status and Complexity, and higher in authoritarianism at college entrance. Yet — and this is fascinating — the latter underwent a dramatic increase in Developmental Status and a corresponding decrease in authoritarianism during their first two college years.[194] College effects? Perhaps. But it must be noted that these Catholic women were also high in Autonomy from the start of their college careers, and it may be that this is the key variable here. Considering the nature of the institution,[195] however, it is likely that the

corresponding sex differences in religious attitudes and knowledge, with male Catholic students lower than female.

[191] Hassenger, "Impact of a Value-Oriented College."

[192] Since, as earlier reported, over-all changes were not significant, a criterion of "consistency" of change was introduced for exploratory purposes in the dissertation.

[193] The OPI Autonomy scale assesses independence of thought and behavior. High scorers are independent of authority, nonjudgmental, and greatly concerned with the rights of individuals (Center for the Study of Higher Education *OPI*); Selvin and Hagstrom, "Support for Civil Liberties."

[194] This is a longitudinal study, as noted earlier in the chapter. Data will be collected at the end of the students' junior and senior years and at post-college intervals.

[195] "Mary College," as described in chapter 4, has been since its founding a low-tuition, largely commuter college with a predominantly working-class clientele. Many girls came from families relatively uninterested in higher education

climate was salubrious for these students,[196] with developmental changes at least exacerbated, if not directly caused. With a clear risk of oversimplification, the following profiles of the "Mary College" clientele can be sketched, using a class-ethnicity frame: working-class second-wave women were most autonomous and non-dogmatic at college entrance, changing little during their first two college years; working-class first-wave women were not as mature[197] at entrance, but improved considerably; middle-class second-wave girls underwent some changes during the first half of their college careers; those from middle-class first-wave families were relatively uncritical and dogmatic at entrance and throughout their first two college years. It would appear that "Mary College" had greater impact on students from certain backgrounds, and perhaps this is true for other colleges as well. Without investigation of the institutional mechanisms of such effects, attempts to explain these results will remain in the realm of conjecture.[198]

The reader intrigued with the above findings will be interested in the clear difference in college impact for "Mary College" students from Catholic and from public high school backgrounds. In all of the scales used in my investigation, public high school girls were more "open" and receptive to change. At the same time, they were more religiously mature than Catholic high school students, who tended to exhibit a guilt-centered, moralistic religious orientation.[199] Fox found a similar difference between students with public and Catholic high school backgrounds, using an authoritarianism scale,[200] and some of the data of Mundi also indicated less tolerance on the part of students with Catholic educational backgrounds.[201] I found public high school girls clearly higher in scores on the OPI scales of Autonomy, Impulse Expression, Complexity and Developmental Status, lower in authoritarianism and dogmatism. This raises a question about which is "really more central" in determining differential college impact: backgrounds or personal dispositions? The stability of personal traits is a strongly supported principle of a good many social-psychological theories.[202] Although sophisticated critics

for their daughters; thus a self-selection operated, in that girls who chose college in spite of this weak support were more highly motivated, independent, and often brighter. For reasons primarily of social status, middle-class girls are less eager to attend "Mary College," but rather — as one put it — "end up there."

[196] I.e., providing a non-threatening atmosphere incorporating a pressure to change. See chapter 11.

[197] Perhaps a bias. What is meant is that they appear more rigid and less open-minded, which social scientists find difficult to admire.

[198] The effect of various college experiences is discussed on pp. 155–59.

[199] As determined by the *Marquette Religious Approach Scale* discussed on pp. 91–92 and in Hassenger, "Varieties of Orientation."

[200] Fox, "Authoritarianism."

[201] Mundi, "Attitudes Toward Catholicism."

[202] Bloom summarized a vast array of research buttressing this position, and Weller found, in an examination of the relationship between personality factors

such as Yinger[203] would insist on the basic meaninglessness of the question posed above, it is worthwhile to consider briefly the ways in which various personal dispositions can influence student change in a college setting.

One recent article illustrated how students' concepts of God are influenced by their own needs; Spilka and Reynolds found that highly prejudiced Catholic college women had a picture of God as abstract, distant, impersonal, and inaccessible; another study shows the relationship of personality structures to attitudes about the recent Catholic liturgical changes.[204] This summary will consider only a few findings for the light that they can throw on Catholic college impact.

Greeley has presented data to show that the highest-performing students in Catholic colleges, particularly those who intend to go into the academic life themselves, are more critical of their own faculties than similar students in comparable schools.[205] There was some evidence that such criticism was greatest among those placing considerable importance on "freedom from supervision" as an occupational value, leading Greeley to suggest that their criticism is related to a desire for greater freedom than found in their present setting.

Similar results are available from Trent's research.[206] The OPI "intellective" scales (p. 138) can be combined into a single dimension of intellectuality, and this composite scale can be divided into three equal intervals or levels: high, middle, and low. Those at a high level of intellectuality on the composite scale have been shown to browse more frequently in bookstores, to visit art galleries, and to value more highly modern art and literature; they have also been shown to choose more readily such self-descriptive adjectives as "intellectual," "nonconformist," and "liberal."[207]

Trent has done a useful comparison of Catholic students at each of the

and age, sex, marital status, education, and other of the usual sociological variables, that "not much more is explained by the addition of the 12 nonpersonality variables" (*Stability and Change*, p. 135).

[203] Yinger, *Field Theory of Behavior*.

[204] B. Spilka and J. F. Reynolds, "Religion and Prejudice: A Factor-Analytic Study," *Review of Religious Research*, 6 (1965), 163–68; Gordon Di Renzo, "Personality Structures and Orientations Toward Liturgical Change" (Paper read at the 1966 Meetings of the American Catholic Sociological Society, Miami).

[205] Andrew M. Greeley, "Criticism of Undergraduate Faculty by Graduates of Catholic Colleges," *Review of Religious Research*, 6 (1965), 97–106. Both geographical location and school position on the college quality index developed by the National Opinion Research Center were matched.

[206] Trent, "Etiology of Catholic Intellectualism."

[207] Percentages of Catholic students checking these self-descriptions on Catholic and non-Catholic campuses are comparable, except for "intellectual," which is checked more frequently at the Catholic schools by those high in intellectuality; this suggests they may be more aware of their difference from the "typical" students on Catholic campuses, although there is no conclusive evidence for this hypothesis.

intellectuality levels on both Catholic and non-Catholic campuses. Catholics with a high level of intellectuality are much more likely to express concern for questions of civil rights and civil liberties than Catholics of a low intellectuality level, with little difference between students on Catholic and public campuses. There is considerable difference, however, in their judgments of premarital intercourse and of divorce, with Catholics on the non-Catholic campuses more tolerant of these. Highly intellectual Catholics at the secular colleges are higher in Autonomy and Impulse Expression (OPI scales) than their counterparts on Catholic campuses.[208] Further, there is a clear difference in the religious participation of these Catholic students

TABLE 8

PERCENTAGES OF CATHOLICS REPORTING VARIOUS FREQUENCIES OF CHURCH ATTENDANCE BY TYPE OF COLLEGE ATTENDANCE AND INTELLECTUALITY LEVEL[a]

FREQUENCIES OF ATTENDANCE	INTELLECTUALITY LEVEL IN CATHOLIC COLLEGE			INTELLECTUALITY LEVEL IN NON-CATHOLIC COLLEGE		
	High	Middle	Low	High	Middle	Low
More than once a week	70[b]	63	42	11	18	10
Once a week	25	35	58	50	54	71
At least once a year	0	2	0	25	23	17
Never	5	0	0	14	5	2

[a] After Trent, 1965
[b] In percentages

(Table 8), and in their evaluations of Catholicism, which they report having changed since high school (Table 9). It is apparent from these tables that Catholic college students of all intellectual levels are much more devout and value their Catholicism more than Catholics on secular campuses. At the same time, the intellectuals are more critical of church customs (25% of the "highs," 11% of the "lows"), and are higher on the Religious Liberalism scale of the OPI;[209] Catholics at non-Catholic colleges are, however, higher in Religious Liberalism at each intellectual level.[210]

Very similar findings were obtained in my own research; Catholic college women typed as "intellectuals"[211] were lower in dogmatism and authoritarianism, higher in Developmental Status (OPI) and libertarianism. Even more

[208] Those at the high level of intellectuality in both settings are more autonomous and impulse-expressive than middle- or low-level students.

[209] In Trent, "Dimensions of Intellectual Productivity." But, as Trent elsewhere reports ("Etiology of Catholic Intellectualism"), these students indicate that they feel colleges should place even greater emphasis on religion, with seniors higher than freshmen.

[210] That is to say, those high in intellectualism at the Catholic colleges were ten standard score-points lower than the high intellectuals at the non-Catholic colleges, and this difference persisted at the middle and low intellectualism levels.

[211] From their scores on the *Activities Index*, the set of thirty scales developed by George G. Stern and C. Robert Pace as a companion device to the College Characteristics Index discussed by Robert Weiss in chapter 3.

likely to manifest this pattern were "impulsive" Catholic students, and yet —
unlike the intellectuals who seemed to undergo some modification of values
and attitudes — these women remained impervious to college impact. It may
be that this type of student is least likely to be affected by a Catholic women's
college, whereas intellectual girls will undergo the same kinds of development typically found in college. Without further investigation, we cannot
be sure.

One of the problems in understanding differential college impact on Cath-

TABLE 9

PERCENTAGES OF CATHOLICS REPORTING VARIOUS EVALUATIONS OF CATHOLICISM BY
TYPE OF COLLEGE ATTENDED AND INTELLECTUALITY LEVEL[a]

CHANGE OF VALUE	INTELLECTUALITY LEVEL IN CATHOLIC COLLEGE			INTELLECTUALITY LEVEL IN NON-CATHOLIC COLLEGE		
	High	Middle	Low	High	Middle	Low
Value it much more	55[b]	49	38	25	23	23
Value it more	35	35	36	13	24	30
No change	5	12	25	14	25	32
Value it less	5	4	1	48	28	16

[a] After Trent, 1965
[b] In percentages

olic campuses is that few research instruments exist that could help an
investigator get the "inside view" advocated by Havens.[212] To the extent
that the religious values and attitudes of Catholic students are relatively inaccessible by presently available techniques of assessment, researchers remain
ignorant of their dynamics. There have been several recent attempts to develop measuring devices for use with Catholic populations; two will be
briefly discussed here.

Beginning with the idea that the way in which religious believers relate
to God is of central concern — more central, perhaps, than the manifest
content of the belief — Robert McNamara developed a scale to uncover
what he calls an "instrumental" religious orientation;[213] he defines this as
"the orientation to the transcendent God which the believer manifests when
he values churchgoing, prayer, and the canons of morality as tools which
he can use to build a safe social and psychological shelter for himself."[214]
A similar scale for assessing a "restrictive" democratic ideology was also

[212] Joseph Havens, "The Changing Climate of Research on the College Student and his Religion," *Journal for the Scientific Study of Religion*, 3 (1963),
52–69; Joseph Havens, "A Study of Religious Conflict in College Students,"
Journal of Social Psychology, 64 (1964), 77–87.

[213] Robert J. McNamara, S.J., "Intellectual Values and Instrumental Religion,"
Sociological Analysis, 25 (1964), 99–107. The social scientist will recognize the
influence of Talcott Parsons here; McNamara has also drawn from David McClelland and Gordon Allport in this formulation.

[214] *Ibid.*, p. 101.

developed. McNamara found that low instrumental scores were significantly related to higher intellectual commitment on two Catholic campuses (Fordham and Notre Dame), but not at Cornell and Columbia. The reverse obtained for low restrictive scores, which were related to higher intellectual commitment on the nonsectarian campuses, but not at the Catholic schools. McNamara suggested that this reflects the importance of the campus climate. Where the atmosphere is religiously homogeneous, instrumental or noninstrumental religious orientations are closely related to intellectual values. In an atmosphere with relative ideological homogeneity (in this case, the commitment to democratic values characterizing the Cornell and Columbia student culture), the restrictive scores of an individual are more predictive of his intellectual commitment.[215]

There has already been reference in this chapter to another recently developed instrument for assessing religious orientations. The *Marquette Religious Approach Scale* investigates the basic approach to Catholicism that a student possesses and that is operative in his daily life.[216] Four such general approaches are suggested: moralistic, intellectual, apostolic, and humanistic;[217] depending on the scoring system used, it is possible for a student to be characterized by a single approach, or by a primary and a secondary approach (or, in either method, by no approach).[218] The approaches have been shown to be sufficiently reliable to make the Marquette scale a useful research instrument in attempting to get at various "styles" of Catholic college students.[219]

Some data throw light on the differences among religious orientations. Hassenger found that there was a general decrease in moralistic and humanistic Catholicism and an increase in apostolic orientation, between freshman and senior years in a Catholic women's college. Moralistic students were significantly higher in authoritarianism,[220] and lowest of the four groups

[215] Only a slight relationship was found to exist between intellectual and moral values. The different values placed on sexual misconduct and academic cheating on the Catholic and secular campuses have been mentioned on pp. 124–25.

[216] Developed by Paul Reiss and Bernard Cooke, S.J., at Marquette University, and discussed in Hassenger, "Varieties of Orientation." The areas analyzed are: the meaning of religion; the practice of Catholicism; God and one's reaction to Him; moral principles; virtue and sin; prayer; religious belief.

[217] These approaches are defined in chapter 4, note 18.

[218] Hassenger modified the Reiss scoring system in his investigation. This is described in "The Impact of a Catholic College."

[219] *Ibid.* Better techniques can undoubtedly be developed. The reader is again referred to Sr. Marie Augusta Neal, *Values and Interests in Social Change.*

[220] Mean scores on the modified F-scale described earlier in the chapter (numbers in parentheses):

Moralistic	Intellectual	Apostolic	Humanistic
(40)	(40)	(70)	(30)
215.7	195.6	200.3	216.7

The alert reader will notice some discrepancy between these scores and those

in a measure of social and political liberalism. Intellectually religious Catholic women were lowest in authoritarianism and dogmatism,[221] highest in Developmental Status (OPI) and libertarianism.[222] In Activities Index traits, the moralistically religious were significantly less likely to be independent and intellectual, more likely to be dependent, unintellectual, and sociable, and were the only "Mary College" group not higher as sophomores on the libertarianism scale of Selvin and Hagstrom. It will be recalled that religious approach was also associated with pre-college backgrounds (p. 91).

Arriving at the college with more liberal educational goals, the intellectually religious students were most likely to move toward a more critical view of institutional Catholicism, yet remained high in personal devotion. The more vocationally and socially oriented moralistic girls still displayed as seniors a rather embattled, defensive set of religious attitudes, were less tolerant of others, and most severe in self-judgments of their own religiosity.[223] Parallels with Trent's findings can be seen here.

The reader will not, of course, be deceived by the way results have been reported in this section. Not only is it difficult to adequately describe the interactions no doubt occurring; most of the studies summarized have in fact proceeded as if intellectuality or dogmatism existed in a vacuum. A real grasp of what happens in college will require a variety of subtle investigations considering the possible contaminating variables. Donovan, for example, found a definite and consistent relationship between non-publication and education at Catholic institutions for Catholic college faculty members.[224] But, as he points out, it is difficult to determine whether more achievement-oriented professors chose non-Catholic institutions or were socialized by them. Obviously, different factors operate in individual cases. Students come with years of interpersonal influences and unique experiences; all extraneous factors will not be always and everywhere controlled. It will

reported earlier for "Mary College." These findings are based on the cross-sectional "Mary College" investigation in 1963, which meant that seniors had entered the college in the fall of 1959. Previously reported scores were based on the longitudinal study of forty students entering as freshman in 1963. It was noted that the latter less strongly supported the traditional Catholic stance on birth control as sophomores than did the seniors in 1963. There are other indications that more recent "Mary College" entrants are a brighter and more critical group, which may be a function of the upgrading of the college alluded to in chapter 4. (The above scores were not presented earlier because they would be misleading, since many "Mary College" women did not fall into any of the Marquette scale categories.)

[221] Differences between D-Scale scores were not significant, however: moralistic (162), intellectual (157), apostolic (164), humanistic (162).

[222] Selvin and Hagstrom, "Support for Civil Liberties."

[223] Thirty-three per cent of the moralistic-approach students judged themselves "below-average" religiously, compared to 18% of the humanistic; 17% of the intellectual, and 11% of the apostolic girls.

[224] Donovan, *Academic Man.*

perhaps never be possible to partial out this much of the variance as owing to ethnicity, that to social class; so much to achievement motivation; a little to autonomy, and so on. This is to be fooled by labels, and one theorist's way of slicing his subjects may not be another's. What we aim for is not a kind of brass-instrument technology divorced from warm-bodied undergraduates, but something like the field theory recently discussed by Yinger,[225] which would allow consideration of a number of influences simultaneously, and *within* different settings. It is to a cursory discussion of the last point that we finally turn.

COLLEGE EXPERIENCES

Those who address themselves to the problems arising from the changing nature of American higher education seldom fail to comment on the increasing diversity of the system. The recent volumes by Baskin, McConnell, and Michael have, in different ways, dealt with this phenomenon;[226] Medsker, and Riesman and Jencks have shown how certain colleges are most successful with particular types of students;[227] Gamson illustrated how the two dominant departments within an experimental liberal arts college had distinct educational orientations;[228] and Gusfield and Riesman outlined the different responses of scientists and humanists to the "mass culture" of the first-generation students who appeared on their campus.[229] Although there has been no comprehensive overview of American higher education — even within a given locale — there will be major efforts in this direction during the years ahead.[230]

[225] Yinger, *Field Theory of Behavior.*

[226] Samuel Baskin (ed.), *Higher Education: Some Newer Developments* (New York: McGraw-Hill, 1965); T. R. McConnell, *A General Pattern for American Public Higher Education* (New York: McGraw-Hill, 1962); Donald Michael, *The Next Generation* (New York: Vintage Paperback, 1965). Two of the best recent books are Laurence E. Dennis and Joseph F. Kauffman (eds.), *The College and the Student* (Washington, D.C.: American Council on Education, 1966); and Robert S. Morison (ed.), *The Contemporary University: U.S.A.* (Boston: Houghton Mifflin Co., 1966).

[227] L. L. Medsker, *The Junior College: Problems and Prospect* (New York: McGraw-Hill, 1960); Riesman and Jencks, "Viability of the Amer. College."

[228] Zelda F. Gamson, "Utilitarian and Normative Orientations Toward Education," *Sociology of Education*, 39 (1966), 46–73.

[229] Joseph Gusfield and David Riesman, "Academic Standards and the 'Two Cultures' in the Context of a New State College," *School Review*, 74 (1966), 95–116. See also Rebecca Vreeland and Charles E. Bidwell, "Classifying University Departments: An Approach to the Analysis of their Effects upon Undergraduates' Values and Attitudes," *Sociology of Education*, 39 (1966), 237–54.

[230] An "educational map" of the colleges and universities in the Chicago metropolitan area is being developed as part of a U. S. Office of Education grant to Robert J. Havighurst and others to study the interaction of society and education in that city.

Besides a macrocosmic view, a number of microcosmic pictures are also needed. There is no good reason to expect colleges to have directly comparable effects on their students. Rose's data fly in the face of what he terms the "myth of unanimity" regarding student attitudes.[231] If a pattern is discernible for Catholic schools generally, vis-a-vis other colleges and universities, it is not without modification and embellishments. If, for example, it can be shown from Mundi's investigation that Catholics at St. John's and St. Thomas in Minnesota are more like each other than like Catholics at the state university, data from McNamara's research will suggest that Fordham is not Notre Dame.[232] Nor, perhaps, is St. John's on Long Island much like St. John's in Collegeville. Even greater diversity is likely in the 1970's and 1980's, particularly with varying degrees of "secularization."

To really understand the impact of the Catholic colleges, information will have to be gathered to determine what happens to whom in which settings. One of the most difficult problems facing the social psychologist of education is the isolation of the determinants of change, even when it is known to occur. Wallace's findings point to the importance of peer influence in college, with rapid changes occurring in freshmen's evaluations of grades and graduate school attendance; the work of Newcomb and the Mellon Foundation researchers also provide evidence to suggest that a good part of "college impact" is really "peer influence."[233]

In addition, there are at most schools several subcultures, associated to some degree with institutional processes, that are independent of participating students' characteristics. As a number of investigations have shown, changes in students' attitudes and values are often associated with certain college exposures.[234] Vreeland and Bidwell, for example, found the residents of different Harvard houses to change in ways consistent with house goals

---

[231] Rose, "*Myth of Unanimity.*"

[232] Mundi, "Attitudes toward Catholicism"; McNamara, "Interplay of Values."

[233] Walter L. Wallace, "Institutional and Life-Cycle Socialization of College Freshmen," *American Journal of Sociology*, 70 (1964), 303–18; W. L. Wallace, "Peer Influences and Undergraduates' Aspirations for Graduate Study," *Sociology of Education*, 38 (1965), 375–92. Newcomb, *Personality and Social Change*; Sanford et al., ("Personality Development"). See also the recent volume edited by T. M. Newcomb and E. K. Wilson, *The Study of College Peer Groups* (Chicago: Aldine Publishing Co., 1966).

[234] Goldsen et al., *What College Students Think*; D. Gottlieb and B. Hodgkins, "College Student Sub-cultures," *School Review*, 71 (1963), 291–99; N. Miller, "Social Class and Value Differences Among American College Students" (Ph. D. dissertation, Columbia University, 1958); B. E. Segal, "Fraternities, Social Distance, and Anti-Semitism Among Jewish and Non-Jewish Undergraduates," *Sociology of Education*, 38 (1965), 251–64; Selvin and Hagstrom, "Support for Civil Liberties"; C. H. Stember, *Education and Attitude Change* (New York: Institute of Human Relations Press, 1961); Rebecca Vreeland and Charles E. Bidwell, "Organizational Effects on Student Attitudes: A Study of the Harvard Houses," *Sociology of Education*, 38 (1965), 233–50.

and structures.[235] Selvin suggested that the fraternities he studied seemed to insulate their members from influences changing the career plans of students in other residence settings; in his work with Hagstrom, Selvin concluded that libertarianism was associated with academic major for men and residential experience for women.[236]

Little data are available for students in diverse Catholic college settings. Fox found a significant relationship between authoritarianism and major field of study; those in the seminary associated with the small Iowa men's college he studied were lowest in authoritarian attitudes, while English and sociology majors were highest.[237] Hassenger predicted that seniors majoring in the sciences at "Mary College" would manifest more liberal attitudes than science sophomores or seniors in other majors; this hypothesis was partially — but not spectacularly — confirmed.[238] More successful was the prediction that resident students would show greater value and attitude modification than commuters.

Membership in various campus groups might be expected to mediate college impact differentially. In some 1962 research, D'Antonio analyzed the dogmatism, anxiety, and anomie scores of every eleventh Notre Dame student, grouped by the campus organizations to which they belonged (e.g., Young Democrats, the Sodality, Young Christian Students).[239] It is interesting to compare the profile of the members of the conservative Young Americans for Freedom (YAF) with students in the Catholic International Lay Apostolate (CILA), an organization which concentrates on assistance to those in backward or culturally deprived areas. The YAF students were highest of the Notre Dame groups on the Rokeach Dogmatism Scale (the twenty men had a D-Scale mean of 157), but lowest in measured anxiety.[240] The CILA men were one of the lowest groups in dogmatism, but were higher

235 *Ibid.* For a perceptive account of the Harvard house system, see Christopher Jencks and David Riesman, "Patterns of Residential Education," in *The American College*, ed. N. Sanford (New York: John Wiley & Sons, Inc., 1962), 731–73.

236 Hanan Selvin, "The Impact of University Experience on Occupational Plans," *School Review*, 71 (1963), 317–39; Selvin and Hagstrom, "Support for Civil Liberties."

237 Fox, "Authoritarianism." These findings are contrary to expectation. Mr. Fox points out, however, that the seminary fostered a rather untypically free-wheeling climate, and that the English and sociology majors were intending to teach in high school (Personal correspondence, Autumn, 1965), which may account for the unexpected pattern.

238 Hassenger, "Impact of a Value-Oriented College."

239 D'Antonio. The concept of anomie was originally used to describe a state of normlessness in society, but has come to mean an individual's feeling of not belonging, of being rootless or alienated (anomic).

240 The Taylor Manifest Anxiety Scale was used in D'Antonio's investigation. Rokeach has suggested that one of the functions of a dogmatic belief-structure is to ward off aspects of reality perceived as threatening. It has previously been found that high scores in dogmatism are associated with lower anxiety scores.

in measured anxiety.[241] The twenty-two Sodality members, on the other hand, were high in both dogmatism and measured anxiety.[242] Similar results were obtained from members of the "Mary College" Sodality; seniors were as high as freshmen in a number of conservative and rather defensive religious attitudes (e.g., the most important Vatican Council issue being "return of the separated brethren").[243] Mundi reported that seniors from St. John's University and the College of St. Thomas were significantly higher than freshmen in tolerance for other religious denominations, but these differences were not found for Catholic freshmen and seniors at the University of Minnesota, except for those who were active in the Newman Club.[244]

One of the knotty problems in interpreting such findings is to decide how much of these differences is attributable to differential selectivity, which operates to draw students of certain traits or dispositions into campus organizations. Such differences in recruitment might be more important than differential socialization. Rosenberg, for example, discovered that students changed majors when these were inconsistent with their own values, and both Sternberg and Teevan showed personality types were clustered in certain academic majors.[245] Scott, discussing his failure to uncover clear evidence of value change within college fraternities and sororities, suggested that "(m)embers are already 'pre-socialized' to a sufficient degree for organizational maintenance."[246] In a Catholic college, Kosa and Schommer found that the religious knowledge of students was associated with recruitment to campus religious organizations, but there was no pattern of high or low scorers being attracted to any of the other campus groups.[247] In my own

[241] Sixteen undergraduate men had scores of 147 and 89.8, on dogmatism and measured anxiety, respectively. This group was also lower in anomie, but not significantly so.

[242] Scores of 156 and 98, respectively.

[243] Hassenger, "Impact of a Value-Oriented College."

[244] Mundi, "Attitudes toward Catholicism." The reader is referred to John Whitney Evans' perceptive comments on the Newman Apostolate in chapter 10.

[245] Morris Rosenberg, *Occupations and Values* (Glencoe, Ill.: The Free Press, 1957); B. Sternberg, "Personality Traits of College Students Majoring in Different Fields," *Psychological Monographs*, 69 (1955), 1–21; P. C. Teevan, "Personality Correlates of Undergraduate Field of Specialization," *Journal of Consulting Psychology*, 18 (1954), 212–14. Different academic fields also attract students of diverse ability. One illustration of this comes from the College Board means of 1965 Notre Dame freshmen with various intended major fields:

	Verbal	Quantitative
Science	606	655
Liberal Arts	599	617
Engineering	568	654
Business Admin.	521	581

[246] William A. Scott, *Values and Organizations* (Chicago: Rand McNally, 1965), p. 243.

[247] Kosa, Rachiele, and Schommer, "Characteristics of Ethnic Groups." "High or low scorers" refers to performance on the LeMoyne Religion Test (*ibid.*).

research, it was the students with apostolic religious approaches who were most likely to join the Sodality at "Mary College"; further, women in the sciences were found to be high in intellectuality and independence,[248] which may have been the key variables in determining the greater impact the college apparently had on students in scientific fields.

Interactions may be even more subtle. Personality traits and value commitments, as well as student backgrounds, may be more predictive of change in some settings than in others; support for this suggestion can be found in Bidwell et al., Brown, and MacArthur.[249] It was reported above that resident students at "Mary College" underwent greater attitude and value change than commuters. Among residents, however, it was discovered that working-class girls were the most frequent changers, along with residents from the second ethnic wave who were characterized by independence and intellectuality. Middle-class residents, and first-wave women with the same traits, did not exhibit these socialization effects. There were indications that educational objectives (liberal or vocational) would also be associated with differential college impact *within* certain settings, but insufficient evidence was available to draw definite conclusions here. There is every reason to believe that such results might occur; as Bidwell et al. noted, turning points in college (changes in career plans, for example) are "contingent upon choices among the alternative lines of action presented by a social structure such as a college. These decisions are made on the basis of criteria provided by personal, situation-specific goals, developed within the legitimizing framework of value commitments."[250] Future research on Catholic college students will have to consider the interactions of student characteristics and college exposures.[251]

CONCLUSION

How "good" are the Catholic colleges? Are they "the answer"? One's response depends on his criteria. If the critic of the schools attends only to the magnitude of the measured religiosity for graduates of Catholic colleges,

[248] As assessed by the Activities Index (cf. note 139 and Hassenger, "Impact of a Value-Oriented College").

[249] C. E. Bidwell, S. H. King, B. Finnie, and H. A. Scarr, "Undergraduate Careers: Alternatives and Determinants," *School Review*, 71 (1963), 299–316; Donald Brown, "Personality, College Environment and Academic Productivity," in *The American College*, ed. N. Sanford (New York: John Wiley & Sons, Inc., 1962), 536–62; Charles MacArthur, "Subculture and Personality During the College Years," *Journal of Educational Sociology*, 33 (1960), 260–68.

[250] Bidwell et al. "Undergraduate Careers," p. 314.

[251] It may be that one shortcoming of many Catholic colleges is the lack of a diversity of subcultures to which students may be exposed to expand their own horizons. David Riesman has noted the limitations of rather homogenized settings "in which like-mindedness reverberates upon itself as the potentially various selves within each of us do not get evoked or recognized" (David Riesman, "College

he may be shocked at what is considered a poor showing on matters he deems central. More pessimistic about human behavior, the social scientist may urge the prophet to compare this performance to that of Catholics in non-Catholic colleges, and perhaps note the results for other church-related colleges as well.[252]

But minor skirmishes will continue to occur, and there are undoubtedly latent functions to this. Certainly, as Greeley has pointed out, the Catholic educational system will profit in the long run from the controversies.[253] But hard questions can only be really answered by hard data. Catholic higher education is not a monolith. Effects must be as diverse as the schools. What are most needed are comparative studies, utilizing more than survey techniques. The development of instruments such as the *Omnibus Personality Inventory* and the *College and University Environment Survey*[254] can be profitably utilized. To get at many of the dimensions of particular concern to Catholic education, however, a number of new techniques will have to be devised. A variety of experiments must be tried.[255]

To date, the bulk of the findings available on Catholic college impact are

Subcultures and College Outcomes," in *Selection and Educational Differentiation* [Berkeley, Calif.: Center for the Study of Higher Education, 1960], 1–14). This point will be elaborated in chapter 11.

[252] See, for example, the report of the Danforth Commission, "Church-Sponsored Higher Education." It may well be that religiously affiliated colleges do not change their students so much as they reinforce the formation which has occurred in the home, and to some extent in grade and high school. Greeley and Rossi (*Ed. of Catholic Americans*) found that the Catholic schools were effective reinforcers of the religious training received in highly religious homes, but had little effect on those from less religious backgrounds. Catholic colleges seemed to make a difference only for those who had attended Catholic grade and high schools. Westoff and Potvin ("Higher Ed., Religion, Family Size") demonstrated that attendance at a Catholic college prevented the "secularizing effect" on Catholic women's high-fertility attitudes which occurred for Catholic women not attending Catholic colleges, but the Catholic colleges did not cause the large-family orientations. These institutions attract women who are already large-family oriented, and this selectivity is more important than Catholic college experience in explaining large-family preference.

Parallel findings for the Catholic students in five New York City colleges were reported by Lawrence Menard ("Effect of the Newman Club on the Religious Commitment of its Members" [Paper read at the 1966 Meetings of the American Catholic Sociological Society, Miami]). In this investigation, Catholic students who were involved members of the Catholic organizations (Newman Clubs) on secular campuses were found to undergo less decrease in traditional belief and practice than Catholic non-members. Some attrition from traditional Catholicism occurred, but it was less for Newman participants than non-participants (and of the members, less for women than for men).

[253] Andrew Greeley, "Catholic Education," *America*, 112 (1965), 522–28.

[254] Described in chapter 3.

[255] The first dramatic reforms in years appear to be underway as this volume goes to press.

rather consistent. The church's schools seem to have been most successful at — to quote the preliminary report of the Greeley-Rossi research — "inculcating precisely those norms already reasonably well accepted among American Catholics."[256] This behavior derives from the historical situation of the group: "Parochial school Catholics perform especially well in those aspects of Catholicism — attendance at Mass, sexual morality, acceptance of authority — that were immensely important to the American Church in the last century."[257] The felt necessity to "preserve the faith" in the new world often resulted in an embattled, defensive posture that seemed to resist modification.

It is hoped that the emphasis on credal and cultic symbols was primarily a function of the immigrant status both of Catholicism as an American institution[258] and of its new world adherents. Certainly there are indications in the more recent research summarized in this chapter — including the final report of the Greeley-Rossi research — that movement away from a siege mentality is occurring. Pockets of resistance, of course, remain. Recent shifts of emphasis within Catholicism have not all been reflected in its American schools. A historically inward-looking church is faced with the problem of specifying new educational objectives. What some of these might be will be treated in the final chapter of this volume.

[256] Greeley *et al.*, *Social Effects of Catholic Ed.*, p. 79.

[257] *Ibid.*

[258] This is well described in Will Herberg, "Religious Group Conflicts in America," in *Religion and Social Conflict*, eds. R. Lee and M. E. Marty (New York: Oxford University Press, 1964), pp. 143–58.

VI. SOME EFFECTS OF JESUIT EDUCATION: A CASE STUDY

Julian Foster

In 1959, Dr. Richard Stanek in psychology, Dr. Witold Krassowski in sociology, and I initiated a study of the impact of the University of Santa Clara on its students. This investigation will be described below, after the setting is briefly considered.

The University of Santa Clara is located in a rapidly growing suburban area some fifty miles south of San Francisco. It has been there for more than a century, one of the first academic institutions established west of the Mississippi. It possesses a graduate school of law and a college of engineering — hence the title "university." Santa Clara offers very few advanced degrees other than law. Most of its students are drawn from California and the adjoining states; about half of them come from the San Francisco Bay area. Sixty-seven per cent are housed on the campus; any who cannot live at home or with relatives are required to stay in the dormitories. When this study ended in 1961, the first woman had yet to be admitted as an undergraduate.

The fees, high in comparison to the state colleges or the University of California, ensure that entrants come from middle class or reasonably prosperous homes. Only a small proportion of the students are supported by scholarships. Nearly 40 per cent of the fathers were college graduates, and less than 20 per cent of the students reported that their fathers were in low-status occupations. There are not very many transfers from other schools, most of those who graduate from Santa Clara having spent four years at the institution. In 1961 only 5 per cent of the undergraduates were older than twenty-four.

There is little question about the Santa Clara environment being Catholic. Ninety-four per cent of the students identified themselves as members of this church. Over 90 per cent of them came from families in which at least one parent was a Catholic. More than 70 per cent attended Catholic high schools before coming to Santa Clara. There has never been any evidence of social discrimination on the campus against the non-Catholic minority, nor any

Julian Foster attended Oxford University, England, where he received bachelor's and master's degrees in 1951 and 1955, and UCLA, which granted him a Ph.D. in 1963. After four years as assistant professor of political science at Santa Clara, Mr. Foster became an associate professor at California State College, Fullerton, in 1961. He is the editor of *Reason*, a review of politics.

suggestion that the pressures toward conformity are irresistable. Nevertheless, the student body tends to pride itself on its homogeneity, and there can be little doubt that this environment plays an important part in producing whatever impact the institution has.

The top administrative posts were reserved for Jesuits. At the time the study was conducted, the Dean of Students had always been a priest, and the traditional policies of this office were strongly paternalistic. Each dormitory had one or more priests living in it, and rooms were inspected for infractions of the rules. Discovery of a copy of *Playboy*, for example, could involve certain penalties. In spite of — or perhaps because of — this vigilance, disorders would occasionally occur. I recall arriving one morning to find the faculty offices on the ground floor of one of the dormitories exceedingly damp, owing to some exploits with the plumbing above.

But apart from such spontaneous and good-humored eruptions, the students tended to be docile in their attitudes toward the administrators. Student efforts to affect university policies could easily be classified as troublemaking. The circulation of a petition after some specific grievances had arisen was considered a very daring departure, and the career of the student who initiated the action was somewhat blighted — although extremely able, he was thereafter passed over for any kind of honors. Student government existed more in form than in content, and student elections were generally devoid of any issues more serious than who could run the most efficient dance or picnic. The student newspaper was pious and uncritical; its editor was selected by the administration. Daring journalistic ventures were in disrepute. Social events were usually planned in conjunction with neighboring Catholic women's colleges.

At the time our investigation took place, the university seemed to be entering a period of change. Controversial speakers were beginning to be invited to the campus. The most notable occasion of this kind involved a member of a Young Socialist group. Covering a number of topics, the speaker mentioned almost in passing that he was an atheist; he was later to be nonplussed by a simple freshman who inquired "If you don't believe in God, then how do you account for Adam and Eve?" The emphasis also appeared to be shifting from the social and athletic toward the more scholarly. Grades were becoming a social asset, rather than a liability. Greater efforts were being made to steer good students toward graduate school. The atmosphere of the campus, however, with the Mission Church at its physical center, seemed generally to be conducive to quiet and respectability, rather than to protest or academic competition.

For the faculty, academic freedom was fairly well protected, although one was never sure what the prevailing standards of the institution were in this respect. Once in a while, a student would carry stories of heretical words in the classroom to a counselor or dean, and such reports usually reached the faculty member involved; but in such instances, it was clear that the faculty was given the benefit of every doubt. The present writer, a non-Catholic teaching in the "sensitive" area of political theory, encountered no specific and serious difficulties of this kind. Teaching anything contrary to Catholic faith or morals was, however, a clear breach of the ethics of the institution; one might teach about other doctrines, other faiths, but one could not teach or advocate them as the truth. A few faculty members took an extremely prudent line. One biologist, for example, revealed that he had for years avoided the matter of evolution in the classroom — a restraint that, when the dean involved heard about it, irritated him greatly. Two non-Catholic laymen in the sciences were cited by Karl Prussion, a professional witness, as Communists before the House Un-American Activities Committee in its celebrated San Francisco hearings. The university conducted a brief and informal investigation and issued a statement to the effect that they were not impressed by the charges; in fact, all that the accusation seemed to be founded upon was the membership of the teachers in the liberal California Democratic Council. In this, Santa Clara took a more forthright stand than the neighboring state college, which was confronted with a similar situation and behaved in a somewhat devious and apologetic manner. The faculty members involved, both non-Catholics, retained their positions at Santa Clara.

Yet it was always clear that the faculty had little part in policy-making. There was no faculty senate or council, no organization that could make its weight felt, and although attempts were made to establish one during the period of our study, nothing much happened. But this was more due to the long-existing habits of apathy and acceptance of authority on the part of the lay faculty, rather than to any opposition from the administration. Pay and promotions were on an individual basis, and sometimes appeared rather arbitrary; nor was there any grievance procedure. Hiring was strictly an administrative prerogative. On one occasion, an old friend of the president, whose last academic experience had been the acquisition of a B.A. in 1908, was brought in to teach a course in political science without consultation with the members of that department. When the introduction of anthropology into the curriculum was proposed, the dean made the unwelcome judgment that we must certainly get a good Catholic to teach *that*. Curriculum requirements were firmly in the hands of the Jesuits. Despite the money-raising feats of the lay deans of law, engineering, and business, the proposition that the Jesuits guided the direction of the institution was never publicly questioned.

In the curriculum, the specifically Catholic flavor was concentrated in the courses in philosophy and theology. The normal requirements were 21 units of philosophy and 16 of theology during the four years at Santa Clara. Owing to curricular pressures, majors in engineering and the natural sciences took rather less of both subjects, and non-Catholics were not required to take courses in theology. The great majority of classes in these two departments were taught by Jesuits, and a general homogeneity of viewpoint prevailed. Some attention was paid to the philosophical alternatives to Thomism, and a few instructors tried to offer an objective presentation of these, although the student was seldom left long in doubt about what his teacher considered to be the correct view on any question. Some courses, however, such as those in metaphysics and philosophy of man (taken in the junior year), and in ethics (taken in the senior year), were devoted almost entirely to the explanation and justification of the Thomistic position. The theology department, which was entirely staffed by Jesuits, devoted little attention to the alternatives (Christian or otherwise) to the Catholic position.

In other departments, the value-orientation of the university was far less conspicuous. Most of the teaching was done by laymen; the 1961 catalogue listed 23 Jesuits and 83 laymen teaching undergraduate courses. Many of the laymen were non-Catholics, and most of them had some non-Catholic academic background. Only 12 of the laymen took their highest degree at a Catholic university, while 76 attended some other type of institution. Of the 38 laymen with doctorates, a scant 3 obtained them at Catholic universities. Only 9 Jesuits taught courses other than philosophy of theology, and none was chairman of his department.

Most disciplines other than philosophy and theology were concerned with description and with training skills, rather than with questions of evaluation or ultimate meaning. These courses, it seems safe to say, were taught much as they would be in a secular institution. Yet something in the atmosphere of Santa Clara made a thoroughgoing professionalism, a commitment to one's discipline, somehow a little irrelevant. Those who are so committed will usually say, when asked for comment on the university as a whole, that they have no complaints — that "They leave me alone." The university has made the usual official statements about excellence, but the difference between professional academic quality and "molding character" was never faced, and the possible conflict of these goals was not resolved.

THE SANTA CLARA STUDY

The investigation alluded to above was sponsored jointly by the university and by the U.S. Department of Health, Education, and Welfare, and it took more than two years. The study was stimulated in part by Philip Jacob's *Changing Values in College*, a survey of college attitude studies.[1] The picture of the student that emerged from Jacob's book was unacceptable to those concerned with the traditional purposes of Jesuit education; a collec-

[1] Philip Jacob, *Changing Values in College* (New York: Harper Bros., 1957).

tion of essays by Princeton scholars was even more disturbing.[2] It appeared from these works that the years in college tended to produce students who were self-centered, self-satisfied, uncommitted, conformist, and materialistic. Little data had been available on Catholic colleges, but there was an uncomfortable suspicion that the high purposes so commonly enunciated in catalogs and in commencement speeches were not being attained at Santa Clara, and that despite the specifically Catholic features of education there, its graduates were much like those of secular universities.

A wide range of possible approaches presented themselves. Two principal considerations guided choice in this area. First and foremost, it was hoped that the findings could be of help to administrators and others responsible for the general form of university programs; attention therefore focused on characteristics the university might hope to affect. Needless to say, the selection of traits was somewhat subjective; official statements concerning goals of Jesuit education are too general to be directly translatable into operational terms. Secondly, we wanted to learn about the differences and similarities between the impact of Catholic and of other colleges that would be of interest to educators generally. We were anxious for the results to reach a lay audience, which meant exclusion of some of the more esoteric possibilities: many traits familiar and meaningful to professional psychologists may fail to impress those without such training.

The selection of measuring techniques is necessarily much influenced by the methodological training and experience of those carrying out the work. In this study, written test batteries were preferred to interviews. A further choice lay between inquiry about behavior and inquiry about thinking. The usual problems with frankness of responses and individual rights of privacy that complicate surveys of conduct were in this case reinforced by the sensitivity of the university. The mores of intellectual Catholicism are changing rapidly, but it is perhaps fair to say that Santa Clara Jesuits in the 1950's were not ready to accept any sort of lay audit of their operations. Further, social science seems to receive less understanding or respect in Catholic educational circles than it does in others. These were among the considerations that led us to restrict ourselves to the measurement of skills, beliefs, and attitudes, and to exclude enquiries about intended or actual behavior.

With the cooperation of the university, it proved possible to test virtually all enrolled students at various times over a two-year period. This provided data on impact that could be analyzed in two ways. Cross-sectionally, the freshman, sophomore, junior, and senior classes could be compared one with another. Few students transfer in or out of Santa Clara in the middle of their college careers, so comparisons of the whole freshman and senior classes were more relevant to impact than they would be if applied in an institution with greater turnover. Longitudinally, the performances of the same students

[2] Otto Butz, *The Unsilent Generation* (New York: Rinehart, 1958).

at various points in their educational careers could be compared. As the data presented below will indicate, results obtained by these two methods were generally consistent with each other.[3]

Classes were dismissed for three hours one morning in September, 1959, so that the test battery could be administered to all students. More than 98 per cent of those eligible answered the questionnaires: 1,033 students in all. This provided the first basis for cross-sectional comparisons. Of this group, 209 seniors about to graduate were retested eight months later, in May, 1960. This provided one basis for longitudinal comparison; not, we originally thought, a very good one, but as the study progressed, the results tended to focus attention on the senior year. The freshman, sophomore, and junior classes (599 students) were retested in May, 1961, twenty months or two college years after administration of the initial battery. In addition, 348 freshmen answered the questionnaires on entry in September, 1960, with 322 of these retested in May of the following year. The second major questionnaire administration (in May, 1961) involved 1,011 students, 921 of whom had been tested before; this provided data for a second inter-class cross-sectional analysis. A few of the questionnaires were also given at neighboring institutions for purposes of comparison.

The characteristics chosen for measurement in the study were: authoritarianism, ethnocentrism, conservatism, ability in critical thinking, critical thinking in ethics, and acceptance of or deviation from the doctrine of the Catholic church. Most of these relate to what will be termed the value-orientation of the university. Critical thinking ability, which may seem to be an exception, was included because questions have been raised about whether an attempt to inculcate certain values through appeals to authority might inhibit the student's capacity for critical analysis. Each variable will be discussed in turn, in terms of its nature, importance, and the extent of change observed for the variable among students at the University of Santa Clara.

AUTHORITARIANISM

One of the most elusive variables in social scientific research is the dimension of personality that has come to be termed authoritarianism. Originally isolated by researchers at Berkeley and described in *The Authoritarian Per-*

---

[3] Each type of analysis involved the same statistics: means, standard deviations, standard errors of the means, standard errors of the differences between means, and *t*-ratios of statistical significance. In addition, correlation coefficients (Pearson's *r*) were computed in the longitudinal study, as well as for certain validational purposes. Intercorrelations between the various measures were also computed. A more complete discussion can be found in J. Foster, R. Stanek, and W. Krassowski, *The Impact of a Value-Oriented University on Student Attitudes and Thinking* (Washington, D.C.: Cooperative Research Project No. 729, Office of Education, Department of Health, Education, and Welfare, 1961).

sonality,[4] it has been subject to considerable analysis and refinement since the early 1950's. The dimension includes such negative characteristics as prejudice, intolerance, tendency to think in stereotypes, and even paranoia. Yet it may also involve other traits — firmness of conviction, toughness, belief in a cause — that are not necessarily negative and may even be the desired outcomes of some educational programs. The original California scale for assessing authoritarianism, the F- (for pre-Fascism) Scale, was the by-product of an extensive investigation of the psychological roots of anti-Semitism. The researchers found a general pattern of characteristics underlying not only anti-Semitism but all forms of intolerance:

1. Rigid adherence to conventional, middle-class values.
2. Submissiveness to, and hero-worship of, accepted group leaders.
3. Tendency to be on the look-out for, to condemn, reject, and punish people who violate conventional values.
4. Dislike of anything subjective, imaginative, or "tenderminded."
5. Belief in superstition, in mystical determinants of the individual's fate. Tendency to think in stereotypes, rigid categories.
6. Preoccupation with power and toughness.
7. General hostility, destructiveness, and cynicism about humanity.
8. A belief that wild and dangerous things happen in the world.
9. An exaggerated concern with sexual "goings-on."

Because of a general out-dating of the items in the F-Scale, and because of other methodological shortcomings, which need not concern us here,[5] Milton Rokeach developed a D- (for Dogmatism) Scale that attempts to identify a similar dimension.[6] Rokeach and his co-workers at Michigan State have directed their efforts to uncovering a dimension they feel is more central than the dogmatically conservative authoritarianism of the Berkeley researchers, which in large measure was insensitive to an equally authoritarian stance at the extreme left of the ideological spectrum. They aimed, rather, at uncovering the way in which belief-systems are structured, whatever their specific content, "right" or "left." They present the following composite portrait of the highly dogmatic individual.

1. The authoritarian emphasizes the difference between his own group and all others, at the same time tending to lump all others together, failing to perceive differences that exist among those with whom he disagrees.

[4] T. W. Adorno, Else Frenkel-Brunswik, D. J. Levinson, and R. N. Sanford, *The Authoritarian Personality* (New York: Harper Bros., 1950); see especially pp. 222–79.

[5] See R. Christie and Marie Jahoda (eds.), *Studies in the Scope and Method of "The Authoritarian Personality"* (Glencoe, Ill.: The Free Press, 1964).

[6] Milton Rokeach, *The Open and Closed Mind* (New York: Basic Books, 1960), pp. 117–18.

2. He values loyalty to the group highly and expects people to be able to understand only beliefs that they themselves hold. He is very ready to say that those who are arguing with him are being irrelevant.

3. He tends to avoid people, books, and newspapers that disagree with him. He avoids the facts that are incongruent with his belief system.

4. He tolerates contradictions within his own belief system.

5. He dislikes the present, prefers either past or future; although he tends to think he can reliably predict the future, he may fear it greatly.

6. He is fairly ready to revise his more marginal beliefs on receiving the word from a trusted leader. He searches for such a leader, tending to have heroes.

7. He believes in a cause or crusade and thinks that everyone should do likewise.

8. He is intolerant of those who disagree with him and believes it necessary to force the recalcitrant into line.

9. He sees the world as a hard and lonely place.

10. He has a tendency to doubt his own qualities and to desire martyrdom.

11. He has a feeling of urgency, of much to be done in little time.

12. He desires power and status, sometimes believes he has great potential.

13. He indulges in compulsive repetition of ideas and arguments.

14. He has a paranoid outlook on life, feels persecuted.

Both the D- and the F-Scales have been thoroughly validated, and both have been used extensively with college populations.[7]

Judging from their scores on these two instruments, students entering Santa Clara were more authoritarian than those entering other institutions. The mean dogmatism scores on college entrance of the freshmen in 1959 and 1960 were 166.0 and 169.9, respectively. Means of 159.7 and 155.3 were reported for males and females entering San Jose State College in 1958,

[7] The F-Scale went through a number of forms during the California study, for which reliabilities ranged from .74 to .91. The thirty-item version of the scale used here was developed by H. G. Gough ("Studies of Social Intolerance I — Some Psychological and Sociological Correlates of Anti-Semitism," *Journal of Social Psychology*, 33 [1951] 237–46). Because of the different scale used in the Santa Clara research, the reader should not attempt comparison of the F-Scale scores in chapters 5 and 6. — Ed.

The final forty-item version of the D-Scale had a corrected reliability of .81 for a group of English college students, and .78 for a group of English workers. In college populations at Michigan State, Ohio State, and an unspecified New York university, reliabilities ranged from .74 to .91.

and a study of entrants to six junior colleges reported a mean score of 162.4 for those males who remained in college for at least three semesters.[8] Michigan State University entrants, however, closely approached those at Santa Clara, with mean scores of 166.4 (males) and 162.9 (females).[9] Male Catholics in the MSU group had a mean score of 174.1, however. On the F-Scale, the mean score of Santa Clara entrants in 1960 was 131.1; male students entering San Jose State College in 1958 had mean scores approximately ten points lower.[10] The greater differences found for the F-Scale may have occurred because this instrument detects authoritarianism of a primarily "conservative" cast; perhaps the authoritarianism of the church has more in common with that of the right wing than of the left wing. (The F-Scale would presumably be a better measure than the D-scale of what in the context of European politics is called clericalism.)

During the years spent at Santa Clara, authoritarianism decreases. Cross-sectional analysis showed mean scores on the D-Scale declining steadily, with each class less dogmatic than the one junior to it, both in 1959 and 1961. Only the differences between the freshmen and other classes, however, were statistically significant; freshmen were more dogmatic than sophomores both in 1959 and 1961. The F-Scale, used only in 1961, revealed a similar pattern, save that seniors scored fractionally higher than juniors; again, only the freshmen appeared significantly different from other classes. Longitudinally, the same trend was apparent. Decreases in dogmatism from college entrance to the end of the sophomore year were again found. Those who were sophomores and juniors in 1959 became less dogmatic (although not significantly so) by 1961. During the eight months between the autumn of 1959 and the spring of 1960, however, mean dogmatism scores for seniors increased fractionally. The only group to which the F-Scale was administered twice was the one that entered as freshmen in 1960; after eight months in college, the mean score of this group decreased four points. In summary, then, it was found that authoritarianism declined significantly during the freshman year at Santa Clara and continued to decline gradually thereafter, although there was some evidence that by the senior year the trend was reversed.

A comparison of these results with other data suggests, however, that the decreases in authoritarianism found at Santa Clara were less than elsewhere.

8 Walter T. Plant, *Personality Changes Associated with a College Education* (Washington, D.C.: Department of Health, Education, and Welfare, 1962), pp. 34–37; Charles W. Telford and Walter T. Plant, *The Psychological Impact of the Public Two-Year College on Certain Non-Intellectual Functions* (Washington, D.C.: Department of Health, Education, and Welfare, 1963), p. 45.

9 Irvin J. Lehmann and Stanley Ikenberry, *Critical Thinking, Attitudes and Values in Higher Education* (East Lansing: Michigan State University, 1959); I. J. Lehmann, "Changes in Critical Thinking, Attitudes and Values from Freshman to Senior Year," *Journal of Educational Psychology*, 54 (1963), 305–15.

10 Plant, *Personality Changes and College Ed.*

Mean D-Scale scores of Santa Clara freshmen declined 8.5 points over two academic years. At San Jose State College, Plant found the scores of the corresponding groups down 13.3 points over a similar period.[11] A parallel study of six junior colleges showed a decrease of 10.4 points. Over the full four-year period, D-Scale scores of state college students declined twenty points. Most interesting of all, the D-Scale scores of 133 students who registered to enter junior colleges but did not, in fact, attend any college for two years declined 13.7 points, and 37 students who registered at San Jose State College but did not attend declined 10.4 points. Such data seem to suggest that attendance at a public college is not instrumental in reducing dogmatism, but that such reductions are a function of the general maturation process. So it may even be that attendance at Santa Clara reduced the rate of decline generally associated with maturation. It should be clear, however, that this hypothesis cannot be tested with the limited data available here.

ETHNOCENTRISM

It seems that the reduction of racial prejudice can be considered a goal of Catholic education. From papal encyclicals to diocesan papers, the whole weight of church literature leans toward the liberal position on this matter. There are few social or political issues on which a comparable consensus, or a stronger one, could be observed, although Catholics as a group are probably no less prejudiced than other Americans.

Santa Clara university had never enunciated any policy positions on race. Further, during the period of this study, although there were numbers of oriental, Mexican, and foreign students enrolled, there was at no time more than one Negro student on the campus nor were there any Negro faculty members. Nevertheless, reduction of racial prejudice can be considered at least an implicit goal for the majority concerned with education at Santa Clara, just as it is for American students at large.

Two of the most widely used measures of ethnocentrism are the Bogardus Social Distance Scale[12] and the California E- (for Ethnocentrism) Scale. Both have been used extensively with college populations and have been validated with satisfactory thoroughness. The E-Scale was preferred because it was related, both in format and by statistical analysis, to other scales employed.[13] A thirty-item version, already in use at San Jose State College, was

[11] Plant used the same thirty-item F-Scale, and these results should not be compared with the F-Scale means in chapter 5. — Ed.

[12] E. S. Bogardus, "Measuring Social Distance," *Journal of Applied Sociology,* 9 (1925), 299–308.

[13] For the complete E-Scale, Adorno *et al.* reported a split-half reliability of .91. Each item correlated on the average of .60 with the total scale. As with the F- and D-Scales, the respondent indicates which of three degrees of agreement or disagreement he feels, with high scores indicating ethnocentrism.

selected. Four items were dropped from the original thirty-four item scale as being out of date or otherwise unsuitable.

One point about the definition of the E-Scale, however, should be noted: some items measure preference for one's own group without necessarily defining the group in racial terms. One reason for expecting that Catholics might score higher than non-Catholics on it is that the church, particularly in its more conservative manifestations, has often suggested that Catholics should prefer their coreligionists not only as date and marriage partners, but even as friends. If the group is thus understood in religious rather than in racial terms, many doubts may be raised about the extent to which Catholic education seeks to break down in-group exclusiveness.

Santa Clara students were, on entry, more ethnocentric than those enrolling at the neighboring state college. Those who entered the university in 1960 had a mean score of 94.7 on the E-Scale; males enrolling in San Jose College in 1958 had a mean score nearly ten points lower.

At Santa Clara there was a decline in ethnocentrism. The measure was used cross-sectionally only in 1961. Thus analyzed, freshmen were more ethnocentric than sophomores; their scores were significantly higher. Juniors were less ethnocentric than sophomores, but seniors had a higher mean score than juniors; in neither case was the difference statistically significant. The only longitudinal study was conducted with the freshmen entering in 1960; after one academic year the retest scores averaged 2.7 points higher, although this increase was not statistically significant. In this instance, then, cross-sectional and longitudinal analyses did not yield similar results — one of the very few instances of this problem that occurred.

At San Jose State College, mean scores of male freshmen who stayed in college for two academic years declined 9.1 points. The greatest difference between any classes at Santa Clara was 8.5 points. Over a four-year period at San Jose, the decline in mean scores was 14 points. Test-retest analysis of those who registered at the state college but dropped out before completing two years shows a less impressive decrease (6.7 points), and the decline among a small group who registered but never attended college was 4.8 points. Combining all these results, it appears that education at the public institution produced a decline in ethnocentrism more marked than that at the Catholic one. Ethnocentrism appears to have some tendency to decrease in the college age group, and there is no reason to think that experience at Santa Clara had any marked influence on this variable.

CONSERVATISM

One of the major difficulties in measuring the trait that has most often been called conservatism is the lack of clarity about this orientation. The measures available obviously do not all focus on the same thing. Some have concerned themselves with conservatism as simply a "suspicion of change";

others have seen it as an ideological position. Some tests include only items dealing with contemporary economic and political issues. Others range more widely and include items relating to personal, moral, and theological realms. The latter items may strike many practical politicians as being unrelated to the notion of conservatism. Further, conservatism tends to vary in scope according to an individual's own political stance. For some, conservatism connotes the reactionary views of the radical right, but to the "New Left" it may appear to embrace most of the policies of both the Republican and the Democratic parties. There is no need, however, to become mired in a philosophical discussion of the "true" meaning of the term. Readers interested in pursuing the matter further can refer to the sources indicated below.

The Political and Economic Progressivism Scale (PEP), originated by Stagner and refined by Newcomb in the course of his Bennington study, confines itself to political and economic questions. A major difficulty with it, however, is that the somewhat obsolete references to "the depression," "recovery," and the threat of "war against fascism" are meaningless in a contemporary context. Similar difficulties, though less acute in form, exist in the instrument called the Political and Economic Conservatism (PEC) Scale, from the postwar Berkeley research, but these could be handled by the slight adaptations made for the Santa Clara study.[14] As described by Adorno *et al.*, the main characteristics of the high scorers on the PEC Scale are:

1. The conservative approves the status quo, distrusts reformers.
2. Politicoeconomic problems are regarded by the conservative as in-

[14] The PEP Scale is described in T. M. Newcomb, "The Influence of Attitude Climate upon some Determinants of Information," *Journal of Abnormal and Social Psychology*, 41 (1946), 291–302; the PEC Scale is described in Adorno *et al.*, *The Authoritarian Personality*, pp. 222–279.

The following changes were made in Form 60 of the PEC Scale: "Most government controls over business should be continued after the war," was replaced with, "Most wartime controls over business should be continued." Our item read "No one should be allowed to earn more than $35,000 a year," where the original sum had been $25,000. We replaced Henry Wallace in "If America had more men like Henry Wallace in office, we would get along much better" with William Knowland; in this case, agreement was counted as "conservative," rather than disagreement. The transitory character of such scale items was pointed up in connection with this latter item. In 1959, most respondents appeared to at least know who Knowland was; in 1961, a much larger number of blank answers to this item suggested that he was no longer a symbol of convervatism recognizable by lower-division students. [*Sic transit gloriam mundi.* — Ed.]

Since these changes already violated the strict comparability of our findings and of those reported by the California researchers, we went one step farther, and to their fourteen-item PEC Scale (Form 60), added the only new item in their later Form 45–40. We would hope, however, that although total scores on the scales could no longer be compared with those reported earlier, means would still be roughly comparable.

evitable consequences of human nature, whereas the liberal is anxious to take some action to remedy them.

3. Conservatives value practicality, they regard financial status as an index of social worth, they approve of charity to the poor in a patronizing spirit. Liberals, on the other hand, distrust charity as second best to reform, do not admire millionaires, and they have a great appreciation of idealism.

4. Conservatives tend to see political problems in moral rather than sociological terms; they stress honesty and integrity of candidates, while liberals stress stands on issues.

5. Conservatives value laissez faire, they distrust powerful unions but respect businessmen, and they propose that government should be strictly limited in function, particularly in the economic realm.

Thus racial tolerance, patriotism, militarism, isolationism, and attitudes toward freedoms for unpopular minorities are not measured in this scale. This was no doubt because the Berkeley groups' interest was in correlating this PEC scale with their ethnocentrism, anti-Semitism and pre-Fascism scales. But they may well be missing something.

Fortunately, two other measures of conservatism were available. From the Cornell study, there evolved a four-item Philosophy of Government scale,[15] concentrating on attitudes to state control of the economy. A more traditional approach to conservatism was used by McClosky in his Classical Conservatism scale.[16] The PEP, PEC, and Cornell Philosophy of Government scales depend heavily on the equation of conservatism with rejection of welfare economics. The Classical Conservatism scale is based on the statements of Edmund Burke and later philosophers who are generally recognized as conservatives. The essence of the conservative position, seen in its historical context, lies not in its economic doctrine but in its attitudes toward the nature of man and of society, and the possibility of satisfactory change and reform. The McClosky Classical Conservatism scale was used in the 1961 phase of this study; it contains nine items, all in some way related to problems of change and reform.[17]

[15] Reported in Rose K. Goldsen, M. Rosenberg, R. M. Williams, and E. A. Suchman, *What College Students Think* (New York: D. Van Nostrand Co., 1960), pp. 111–23.

[16] Described in Herbert McClosky, "Conservatism and Personality," *American Political Science Review*, 52 (1958), 27–45.

[17] Agreement with the change-opposed items indicates conservatism; scores can range from zero to nine, with high scores indicating conservatism. McClosky reports that scores on the scale correlate in the predicted way with other measures. A challenge to the validity of the instrument was issued by one of the editors of the conservative *National Review* (Wilmoore Kendall, "Comment on McClosky's 'Conversatism and Personality,'" *American Political Science Review*, 52 [1958], 506–10), and McClosky replied to the criticisms in the same place.

Data from the PEC and Classical Conservatism scales indicate some slight decline in both kinds of conservatism during the years at Santa Clara. Mean scores of the different classes on the PEC scale were also identical in 1959, though in 1961 the freshmen proved significantly more conservative than any other group. On the Classical Conservatism scale, used only in 1961, the freshmen were significantly more conservative than sophomores or juniors, but the trend was reversed at the senior level. Longitudinally, only performances on the PEC scale were available. Over a twenty-month interval, a statistically significant decline in conservatism was found for 1959 freshmen and sophomores, when retested as 1961 juniors and seniors.

Immediately comparable data for other college groups are not available. Various studies have reported the liberalizing tendency of the college experience, however. The University of Santa Clara reflected this tendency but to a very modest degree. A straw poll among the students in 1960 revealed a lopsided majority for John F. Kennedy over Richard Nixon. American Catholicism has traditionally leaned towards the Democratic party, but this has not, in most cases, indicated a thoroughgoing commitment to liberalism, an approach that remains suspect to many Catholics. The bishops' statement on social philosophy, issued forty years ago under the leadership of Monsignor John F. Ryan, placed the church fairly clearly on the side of some sort of welfare-oriented government, as opposed to the laissez-faire philosophy of nineteenth-century liberalism. But neither Ryan nor those who have followed in his footsteps could be easily classified as liberals — Cardinal Cushing, for example, has been generally favorable toward Democrats' social policies, yet could apparently see something in the John Birch Society that met with his approval. There is also evidence that as Catholics have moved up the social ladder, from immigrant status to membership in the middle and professional classes, they have become more conservative. A Catholic presidential candidate obviously had appeal for Santa Clara students, but perhaps the suspicion of those aspects of liberalism that involve emphasis on civil liberties and an opposition to censorship and to aggressive "anti-communism" — all areas in which, as the summary of available data in the preceding chapter indicate, Catholics have not been conspicuously in the forefront — may be reflected in responses to the conservatism measures. When most educators talk of "liberalizing" their students, they mean opening their minds to new and perhaps iconoclastic ideas. It appears doubtful that this is an acceptable goal at Santa Clara, or that it is one which is actualized to any great extent.

CRITICAL THINKING

It has been a commonplace since at least the time of Plato that a prime purpose of education is to teach men to think. The absorption of facts by rote memory may sometimes be necessary, but it will usually be defended as an essential preliminary to the business of training the mind. No one with a serious concern for education suggests that memorization constitutes true learning, and there is a consensus in favor of "real understanding," "training the reason," and so on. The official description of the Jesuit system of education gives "sound judgment . . . the ability to evaluate critically" as its proper goal, along with other aims of a value-oriented nature. Yet, despite so much verbal agreement, there is perhaps a certain ambiguity about exactly what is meant by these terms. Many teachers can accept such worthy goals for their profession without having any very clear idea about how they can be attained.

An outward sign of this lack of clarity is the variety of examinations that are supposed to measure the success of teaching. Until recent times, most such tests confined themselves to specific fields of study. Frequently the emphasis was placed solely on factual knowledge. A perusal of Buros' comprehensive surveys of psychological tests revealed no published tests of critical thinking available for college populations as of 1953.[18] Evidently, this is a difficult concept to make operational; however, there are now some measures available that seek to tap the student's ability to "evaluate critically." We decided to use one of these as an indicator of the university's over-all educational success. There seems little reason to doubt that all colleges, regardless of their value orientation or lack of it, can be compared meaningfully on such a basis.

Dressel and Mayhew,[19] although admitting that other aspects of critical thinking exist, stress its problem-solving nature:

1. Ability to define problems
2. Ability to select pertinent information
3. Ability to recognize unstated assumptions
4. Ability to invent and evaluate hypotheses
5. Ability to make valid inferences and to judge the validity of inferences.

[18] Oscar K. Buros (ed.), *The Fourth Mental Measurements Yearbook* (New Brunswick, N.J.: Rutgers University Press, 1953).

[19] Paul L. Dressel and Louis B. Mayhew, *General Education: Explorations in Evaluation* (Washington, D.C.: American Council on Education, 1954), esp. pp. 177–78. Dressel and Mayhew report adjusted split-halves coefficients of .84 for 97 cases and .79 in a sample of 231. These figures, although lower than expected, were regarded as high enough for research purposes. They also report high powers of discrimination for the items. Scores on Form G of this instrument were correlated with scores on related measures of ability, with coefficients ranging from .38 to .71; performance was also correlated with ratings of teachers, counselors, peers, and the subjects themselves, with coefficients ranging from .42 to .66. The device is comprised of 52 multiple-choice items and takes about fifty minutes to administer.

These abilities are the ones the American Council on Education Test of Critical Thinking was designed to measure. It was decided to use this test, instead of the only alternative, the Watson-Glazer Critical Thinking Appraisal,[20] primarily because of the more extensive use that has been made of it with college students.

The committee that drew up the Test of Critical Thinking included psychologists, mathematicians, logicians, and evaluation experts. The items included in Form G of this instrument represent the best from a series of three experimental forms, selected on the basis of the following considerations: (1) optimum length of the test; (2) item analysis; (3) student interest in the problems presented; (4) familiarity of student with the vocabulary involved; (5) level of information assumed in the items; and (6) face validity.

Little empirical work has been done to determine the relative effectiveness of a value-oriented university in producing critical thinking ability. Some critics of Catholic higher education suggest that any impact is likely to be in the direction of dogmatism and *un*critical thinking. Nevertheless, philosophy, which par excellence is the discipline concerned with critical thinking (although all departments should, of course, contribute to it), has been particularly stressed in the Catholic college. All freshmen at Santa Clara, for example, take a course in logic, described in the catalogue as: "An introductory course in the science of correct thinking, comprising both deductive and inductive inference, and scientific method. Exercises in the various forms of logical inference and in the detection of fallacies." It would seem, therefore, that a test such as Dressel and Mayhew's would be a fair measure of the success of this university in attaining one of its chosen goals.

The findings indicated that a development in critical thinking did take place at Santa Clara. Mean scores over the twenty-month interval increased for each of the three classes tested; the largest gain was among freshmen, but the sophomore and senior gains were also statistically significant. Results from the cross-sectional study also suggested that the greatest improvement in critical thinking occurred during the first year, with freshmen scoring significantly lower than each of the other three groups. No other comparisons of this kind yielded significant results. It seems clear, then, that growth in this ability is concentrated during the years in the lower college division. This conclusion is similar to that reached in many comparable studies.

The extent of change at Santa Clara compares unfavorably with those reported for other college groups. The mean improvement in score among Santa Clara freshmen over their first two academic years was 3.7; Dressel found slightly greater improvements among freshmen at five unnamed colleges over a single year.[21] Lehmann and Ikenberry, also retesting after one

---

[20] G. Watson and E. M. Glazer, *Manual for the Watson-Glazer Critical Thinking Appraisal* (Yonkers-on-Hudson, N.Y., and Chicago: World Book Co., 1952].

[21] Dressel and Mayhew, *General Education*, p. 204.

year, found a 4.6 gain among male freshmen at Michigan State University in 1958.[22] It seems that Santa Clara entrants arrive better prepared, however; their scores on entry are higher than for any of the other groups. It may be that improvement is harder to attain, the higher the base point; what data there are appear to support this. There seems little reason to question, therefore, that the University of Santa Clara was quite successful in teaching its students to think critically, but equally little reason to claim that the heavy dosage of philosophy affects this ability in any special way. If the courses in Thomistic philosophy do serve, as many of their proponents believe, to sharpen capacities for deductive thought, such improvement was not reflected in our results.

CRITICAL THINKING IN ETHICS

What has been said about the outcomes of education in general must surely apply also to value-oriented education; that is, while memorization must play some part in such training, the real aim must be to produce an ability to think critically and to solve problems effectively. This aim is in tune with Catholic doctrine, which insists that man can reach much of the truth in the normative realm by use of his reason, and which presents ethical judgments as parts of a very complex system of objectively knowable propositions. It was decided, therefore, that a test of critical thinking in ethics should be employed.

One test has already been developed that measures the skill and perceptiveness of respondents' moral judgments. The Shields Moral Judgment[23] test was based on conventional morality and the generally accepted social and legal standards of American society. No attempt was made to deal with real philosophical problems; questions about the ultimate source of values or whether they are objective or subjective are not involved; nor are areas explored in which Catholics, Protestants, Jews, and humanists might be likely to differ. Rather, the method was to isolate various generally acceptable norms, and to discover to what extent the individual respondent conformed to them; some items also tapped knowledge of the usual definitions involved in ethical discussion. Different forms of this test were designed for use with various age groups between six and twenty years. The Shields test explicitly avoids measuring the kind of fine distinctions that are emphasized in courses in Catholic philosophy and theology. Further, it has not been used extensively or recently with college populations. It was, therefore, decided that it was not suitable for us in the present study, and instead the research group developed a new measure.

This new measure could not confine itself to an examination of Catholic ethical principles, since this would test mainly memorization, and it would

[22] Lehmann and Ikenberry, *Critical Thinking*, p. 72.
[23] Described in E. A. Lincoln and F. J. Shields, "An Age Scale for the Measurement of Moral Judgment," *Journal of Educational Research*, 23 (1931), 193–97.

be possible to gain a low score as much by being a nonconformist as by being ignorant or illogical. Many textbooks in ethics use the device of hypothetical cases, and it might have been possible to produce a test similar to the one in critical thinking, with ethical issues as its content. But it was decided that a more effective measure could be developed that would yield an inconsistency score. Such a measure would allow persons with contrasting ethical views to be assessed with the same device. Those who rejected a particular position would not be penalized, since all that would be required for a perfect score would be to avoid agreeing with conflicting propositions. This kind of inconsistency has something in common with authoritarianism. Definitions of authoritarianism have included such tendencies as "irrational acceptance of external authority," and "tolerance of conflicts within the belief system."[24] But these qualities are joined in such studies with many others, and for present purposes it seemed desirable to attempt to isolate inconsistency in thinking about values and attitudes. To measure this, an Inconsistency Scale was developed by the Santa Clara researchers.

Inconsistency was not the only measure of critical thinking in ethics employed. Included in the same questionnaire was another scale, given the title Moralistic Perception. This was defined as a tendency to permit values and attitudes to influence and distort perceptions of matters where facts are discrepant with personal predilections.

The precise nature of the links between opinions, knowledge, and personality structure have yet to be discovered. Certainly there is no need to accept the extreme position, which holds that all attitudes and opinions are to be interpreted in terms of personality needs, and that conscious thought can be nothing more than rationalization of a conclusion already reached. Opinions can be, and often are, based on available knowledge, but it also is possible that a person may arrive at what he considers to be knowledge by allowing his opinions to lead him toward comfortable stereotypes and misperceptions. McClosky has written that:

> A process by which cognitions of the external world may be structured (is) through projection of the personality of the observer himself. In this way, an individual creates a set of perceptions that express, or are consonant with, his own needs and impulses. The more ambiguous the thing observed, the greater the likelihood that he will fashion his perceptions of it to accord with his own inner feelings. In other words (they) believe what they do not because the world is the way it is because they, the observers, are the way *they* are.[25]

The group described by McClosky was right-wing conservative, but these comments could apply to many other groups including, perhaps, Catholics.

---

[24] Rokeach, *Open and Closed Mind*, p. 74.
[25] McClosky, "Conservatism and Personality," p. 31.

It therefore seemed desirable to test whether students at Santa Clara seemed to misperceive facts relevant to the value-orientation of the institution.

Other approaches were no doubt possible to an area that seems to have received little attention from behavioral scientists. If the notion of critical thinking in ethics is to be accepted, an assumption that ethical thought should be consistent and coherent and form some sort of system must be made. Many would reject this, believing that values are totally subjective. The teaching of values is disappearing from secular colleges, where philosophy departments are displaying steadily diminishing interest in the content of values and are coming more and more to be preoccupied with linguistic and conceptual analysis. Authorities in such colleges still talk about affecting student values, but they seem to suppose that this cannot be an intellectual or academic function, that it must somehow develop through value-free teaching in a generally open and questioning environment. Catholic colleges have taken a radically different position.

The final form of the Test of Critical Thinking in Ethics contained 150 items, with which respondents were invited to agree or disagree, strongly or slightly. Sixty-nine pairs of items were inconsistent with one another, so that agreement with both halves of a pair increased the subject's inconsistency score. Each pair was approved by all of the six members of the research team, representing six different disciplines. Some of the pairs used were:

a. Loyalty, whether to one's family, political party, or country, is the highest virtue.
b. No really good man would have fought in Hitler's army in World War II.
a. The telling of a lie with intent to deceive can never be justified.
b. Telling a lie to save a life really is morally justifiable.
a. Homosexuals are entitled to the same justice as anyone else.
b. We should not allow the usual legal protection for individuals who commit appalling crimes such as dope peddling or perversion.
a. The American Way of Life is specifically Christian.
b. Western man is on the whole unthinking, materialistic, and superficial.

The items in each pair were widely separated in the test form. Inevitably, some of the pairs could be challenged; it is not easy to insure that such brief statements, devoid of context, are unambiguous. Nevertheless, statistical analysis of the scale, discussed below, seems to provide convincing evidence of its validity.

The moralistic perception scale consisted of 35 items in the test. In each case, agreement signified a tendency to permit values to distort perceptions of fact. Again, it was difficult to develop statements that were both in some degree persuasive and beyond doubt false. An effort was made to seek out prejudices of various kinds. Some examples:

   a. Socialized medicine means that doctors virtually become robots.
   b. While one certainly need not accept any Communist ideas, one should realize that there is no evidence that the American Communist Party would ever participate in any illegal activities.
   c. The divinity of Christ is as historically demonstrable as the existence of Julius Caesar.
   d. To say that a country can have an overpopulation problem is absurd; what it actually may have is an underproduction problem.

Various standard statistical analyses seemed to provide convincing and sufficient evidence that the scales can be useful research tools.[26]

Study results indicated that inconsistency declined with time spent at Santa Clara. In both the 1959 and 1961 cross-sectional studies, freshmen were more inconsistent than sophomores, and sophomores more than juniors; but in both instances the mean for seniors was slightly higher (more inconsistent) than that for juniors. In 1959, only the difference between freshmen and the two upper classes was significant, but in 1961, freshmen were significantly more inconsistent than all other college classes. Since the 1961 testings were at the end of the academic year, this suggests that decline in inconsistency takes place during the second year in college.

The longitudinal analysis supports this suggestion. Freshmen entering in 1960 were markedly more consistent after eight months; over the twenty-month interval, inconsistency among both freshmen and sophomores declined significantly. Seniors were slightly higher than juniors, but this difference was not statistically significant. The seniors who were retested after eight months showed a minute gain in inconsistency.

[26] A number of standard measures of statistical validity and reliability were made. When performance on two halves of the Inconsistency and Moralistic Perception Scales were compared, the split-half reliabilities, corrected according to the Spearman-Brown formula, were .85 and .78, respectively. Scores of 27 upper-division students who took the test twice with a four-month interval correlated .81 on inconsistency, .69 on moralistic perception. For 97 freshmen over a six-week interval, test-retest reliability was slightly lower: .74 for inconsistency, .52 for moralistic perception. Scores of these two measures of critical thinking in ethics were correlated .67 with one another. Both correlated negatively with scores on Dressel's Test of Critical Thinking: $-.32$ for inconsistency, and $-.39$ for moralistic perception; this is, of course, expected since high scores on the Dressel instrument indicate success at problem-solving, whereas high scores on the Santa Clara tests indicate confusion. Similar negative correlations were found with high grade point averages and with high scores on the College Board tests. Correlations with other measures of social and political attitudes were:

	Rokeach, D	Calif., F	Calif., E	Calif., PEC	McClosky
Inconsis.	.55	.63	.49	.17	.46
Mor. per.	.56	.64	.43	.13	.44

When critical thinking was measured in terms of moralistic perception, the same trends appeared. Both in 1959 and 1961, the freshmen were significantly higher on this variable than any other class; otherwise, only the difference between sophomores and seniors in 1961 reached significance. The longitudinal pattern also shows the marked impact of the freshmen year; decline in moralistic perception over this eight-month period was very marked. Over the twenty-month interval, decline in moralistic perception for all three classes was statistically significant. For the class tested at the beginning and end of its senior year, however, the decline in this variable was negligible.

The lack of change during the senior year was of particular interest, since it is then that all the students take a six-unit course in ethics. The emphasis of that course was almost exclusively on the Thomistic approach, with little open-minded attention either to alternatives or to the kinds of linguistic analysis that would be found in most non-Catholic philosophy departments. Whatever the advantages of the traditional approach to ethics, it is apparent that the variables developed in the Critical Thinking in Ethics Test did not tap it.

ACCEPTANCE OF CHRISTIAN TEACHING

The raison d'etre of Catholic higher education clearly lies in the specifically Christian element that is imparted, both in the classroom and throughout the life of the campus. Measurement of effectiveness in this area, however, presented special difficulties. Student attitudes toward religion have been examined in many studies, but there has been considerable ambiguity about the nature of the variable. In the previous chapter, Jacob's comment on the "ghostly quality" of students' religious beliefs was cited, along with his suggestion that beliefs were ritualistic rather than real guides for decision-making. The Cornell study throws further light on this "ghostly quality": "The tendency on the campuses is not away from religion, but toward, perhaps, a view of God and religion that is relativistic rather than absolute, personal rather than dogmatic."[27] The book that resulted from the Cornell study of eleven campuses has a chapter entitled "Secular Religion," in which the authors report that: "About 80 per cent said they felt a need for religion; but 40 per cent meant 'some sincere working philosophy or code of ethics, not necessarily a religious belief.' "[28]

No one familiar with the Santa Clara campus would doubt that religion to most of the students means something far more clear-cut than this "sincere working philosophy." Few practicing Catholics would accept such a definition of religion as adequate. The five-item Religiousness Scale, developed by the Cornell group, was designed to test such attitudes; the Santa

[27] Goldsen, et al., *What College Students Think*.
[28] *Ibid.*, p. 161.

Clara research group decided that it might thus have limited relevance for Catholic students. Levinson has developed a Religious Conventionalism Scale,[29] designed to distinguish those who emphasize faith, tradition, and absolute moral authority from those who are humanistic, non-theistic, and rationalistic; again, it was believed that such a measure might be unrevealing at Santa Clara. Catholics are usually reported as scoring high on the Thurstone attitude scales toward religion, which are designed primarily for use with groups less firm in their formal religious affiliation.[30] Dunkel reports that the Inventory of Religious Concepts, developed in the course of the Cooperative Study of General Education, was not very useful when applied to Catholics.[31] For these reasons, none of the established measures of religious belief seemed to lend themselves to purposes of our research; we decided to construct a measure of the extent to which students understood and accepted the doctrines of the Catholic church.

Catholic doctrine involves propositions in the realms of theology, metaphysics, and ethics. It might be argued that a measure of adherence to Catholic doctrine should cover all these fields, although in what proportions it would be difficult to determine. The research group was interested principally in those attitudes that would most directly affect the individual's life in society, rather than in those relating to his personal spiritual welfare. Attention was focused on ethical matters, and no questions that might deal with problems of metaphysics or theology not comprehensible to the average non-Catholic college student were included. Practically all of the items in the scale developed, therefore, dealt with ethical principles and alternatives.

A tendency toward nonconformity with the doctrines of the church we called deviation. Two kinds of deviation were distinguished. Broad Deviation consisted, in general, in taking a more lax view than that approved by the church; Narrow Deviation, in taking a stricter view. In particular, broad deviation is the acceptance of a theoretical position or the approval of a course of conduct that the church has either condemned or disapproved, or at least considered improper for a Catholic; narrow deviation is the condemning of the theoretical position or the disapproval of a course of conduct as inconsistent with Catholicism when the church has neither condemned nor forbidden or even disapproved of it.

Of the two, broad deviation is — from the church's standpoint — the more serious, since it indicates less interest in (and less good will toward) religion and toward the church as the Catholic's chief interpreter of religion, whereas narrow deviation indicates an abundance of good will but insufficient instruc-

---

[29] Daniel J. Levinson, "Personage Admiration and Other Correlates of Conservatism-Radicalism," *Journal of Social Psychology*, 10 (1939), 81–93.

[30] See L. L. Thurstone and E. J. Chave, *The Measurement of Attitude* (Chicago: University of Chicago Press, 1929).

[31] Harold B. Dunkel, *General Education in the Humanities* (Washington: American Council on Education, 1947), p. 80.

tion or too literal and unintelligent compliance. Broad deviationists tend to transgress the church's precepts, at least objectively, while narrow deviationists fulfill all that the church prescribes and then some. Many of the views that the narrow deviationists condemn are ones that the church does not necessarily approve, but only tolerates, so there is not always a discrepancy of opinion but only of the rigidity with which the opinion is held. Since the purpose of a Catholic university is to produce informed and intelligent Catholics, narrow deviationists do the church a disservice by their ignorance or misunderstanding or lack of intelligent interpretation of the church's positions. Broad deviationists are failures both as Catholics and as intelligent Catholics; narrow deviationists may be excellent Catholics, but are failures as well-educated Catholics.

It was originally intended to combine the two scales to yield an over-all assessment of deviation from Catholic doctrines. Scores on the two were found to be uncorrelated with each other, however, suggesting that a combination of the measures might yield nothing meaningful, tap no behavioral pattern. They were therefore retained as separate scales. The Broad Deviation scale contained 17 items, including some on which positive and some on which negative replies indicated variance from the church's position. The Narrow Deviation scale contained only 7 items. Both scales were put into the Critical Thinking in Ethics Test, with the items separated by others irrelevant to Catholic doctrine. In both instances, a high score indicated deviation, and the ideal score was zero.[32]

The cross-sectional study indicated that deviation of both types declined slightly but steadily with experience at the university. The decrease in broad deviation scores did not reach significance between any two contingent classes; in 1959, only the difference between freshmen and seniors was significant, and in 1961 no class was significantly different from any other. The change in narrow deviation was somewhat more marked. In both 1959 and 1961, the difference between juniors and seniors was significant; in 1961, the freshmen scored significantly higher in narrow deviation than all the other classes.

[32] Statistical analysis for the two deviation scales yielded split-half reliabilities of .64 for the seventeen-item Broad Deviation scale and .45 for the seven items contributing to Narrow Deviation. Test-retest reliabilities over a four-month period were .79 and .48 for broad and narrow deviation, respectively ($N=27$); over a six-week period, the corresponding figures were .60 and .86. Both kinds of deviation correlated negatively with the test of critical thinking, with grade point average, and with CEEB scores. Narrow deviation correlated positively with scores on the Dogmatism Scale, Pre-Fascism (F-) Scale, Ethnocentrism Scale, and the Classical Conservatism scale. Broad Deviation scores were related positively to all of these, but only somewhat. None of the items in the latter instrument had a correlation between item and total test score of less than .36, suggesting that the scale was tapping a genuine variable. Yet this dimension is apparently unrelated to those tapped by the other instruments.

Longitudinal analysis revealed a generally congruent picture. The impact of the ethics course, taken during the senior year, was clarified in the retesting of the class of 1960 just before graduation; the decline in broad deviation was the only significant decrease for any group. Longitudinal results for narrow deviation were, owing to technical difficulties, unavailable.

It seems fair to conclude that education at Santa Clara tended to bring values into conformity with the norms of the church, and that this was more a process of broadening than of narrowing students' outlooks. The ethics course in the senior year played a more influential role in this regard than in producing critical thinking capacities. In general, however, the amount of change in any direction was hardly spectacular.

CONCLUSIONS AND SPECULATIONS

Practically all the changes revealed by this study are in the "desired" direction. It appears that education at the University of Santa Clara produced the kinds of effects that those in charge presumably desire. It also appears that these changes were mostly small in extent. Adequate comparative data were not available on some of the measures, and in these cases estimates of the magnitude of change can be impressionistic at best.

The standards for measuring the impact of college leave much to be desired. Some of Plant's findings, in particular, suggest that those who do not attend any college mature in much the same ways as those who do.[33] Possibly, then, experience in the "real world" of a full-time job and adult responsibilities can have as much impact on a high school graduate as college attendance. If this is so, a disturbing possibility is raised. Universities like Santa Clara — all male, largely residential, and in many ways sheltered from the stresses and variety of life — may even retard the social and political development of the individual. I have since been teaching at a state college, and in retrospect the students at Santa Clara seem to have possessed a certain happy and naïve irresponsibility. Occasional campus disturbances recalled the eccentricities of the twenties, rather than the demonstrations at Berkeley, Chicago, and CUNY in the sixties. Cheating was fairly widespread, and looked on by most as a relatively harmless and boyish game. Serious challenges to authority were virtually unknown. Strong social or political commitments or involvements were rare; pious religious conformity was common. Perhaps no institution can produce maturity until it is ready to discard paternalism.

A further conclusion, to which one's attention is called by measure after measure used in the present study, is that experience at Santa Clara produced diminishing returns. The change in freshmen was slight but consistent across

[33] Plant, *Personality Changes and College Ed.*

many dimensions. The following two years were less effective, and in the senior year many presumably desirable trends were halted or even reversed.

One implication of this appears to be that the senior-year course in ethics, which should be most relevant to many of the measures we employed, is not in fact effective. In making such judgments, of course, one must bear in mind that those involved in teaching such courses might formulate their goals in terms irrelevant to our measures. This possibility is also evident with respect to courses in theology. Our measure of "deviation" may easily be criticized as superficial, legalistic, and unimaginative. Yet it appeared to us that it was appropriate to the kinds of material that were being presented to the students by the theology department.

The over-all conclusion of the study might be that Catholic higher education in the form encountered here is not having any extensive and measurable impact. If the church is to proceed with this expensive enterprise, there may be reason to shift its focus to junior college operation, to the years when impact is greatest. Before such revolutionary proposals can be properly supported, much more data would be needed. It may be that there are or could be reasons that would reveal a significant impact by institutions like Santa Clara. It could be that no college experience produces much that we could have measured. It may be that Catholics who attend state institutions change in ways that are regressive by church standards. There is much we need to know.

THE UNIVERSITY OF SANTA CLARA: A POSTSCRIPT

This study is now five years old. A look at changes in the interim may be of interest. When one undertakes a study of the impact of an institution, he naturally hopes that the findings will have some bearing on future policies. In this instance, such hopes were hardly fulfilled. The university authorities originally approved application for the grant that made the research possible, but it seemed that this was done without great consideration of all the relevant issues. When the Department of Health, Education, and Welfare indicated their intention to grant funds, a hasty meeting of the trustees was called, to decide whether the university should accept the fairly substantial sum involved. It was decided to go ahead, on condition that the research group accept the addition of a senior member of the Jesuit faculty, who could keep watch on the operation. The emissary from Washington was received rather coolly. The present writer, a non-Catholic, encountered diminished enthusiasm for renewing his contract and left the institution shortly before completion of the final report. During the period of the study, no member of the administration ever expressed more than polite interest in our progress. Some of those charged with the running of the university have no doubt read the final report, and on occasion make reference to it, but there is little sign that it has had any particular impact on the institution's policies. If this is correct, some of the responsibility may lie with the research team, none of whom has, until now, provided a concise summary aimed at the general reader.[34]

Can the application of social science techniques tell more about the impact of an institution than the long experience of teachers and administrators in it? This seemed to be the issue as it presented itself to the administration, and their answer was generally in the negative. Behavioral science techniques seem to be alien to most of those trained in the traditional manner of the Jesuits. Philosophy can, they assert, provide important information about man's nature, and something called "philosophical psychology," which would horrify most professionals in either field, provides a link between the deductive and inductive methods. A thoroughgoing empiricism is impossible in such a framework, and Thomistic philosophy blurs rather than clarifies the distinction, crucial for an understanding of social science, between description and evaluation.

Perhaps the style of Santa Clara University is best displayed in its Honors Program, which was launched at the time this study was ending. The leadership in setting up the program was taken by an energetic Jesuit theologian, and although the new curriculum was supposedly focused on the liberal arts, no social scientist participated in its design. The "great books" approach was chosen, following a chronological scheme, a style of education in itself inimical to social science or to any discipline that places stress on rigorous methodology. In choosing a director for the new enterprise, the university avoided the dangers of an innovator, picking a political scientist emeritus from a distinguished institution. A man with a considerable reputation in traditional political theory, the director was wont to cast a certain blight over his followers by remarking that he had "retired" to Santa Clara. An unexpected consequence of his appointment was that younger political scientists were imported en masse to teach in a program that contained virtually no contemporary social science.

This departure, for which high hopes were held, suffered from some crucial weaknesses. It ignored the development of the new disciplines of social science, which are producing much that is intellectually exciting. It was firmly traditional in concept, stressing the kind of knowledge that in most universities is being relegated to a smaller and smaller corner of the curriculum. It took no account of professional specialization and limitation, since it involved a separate faculty who were assigned to teach all subjects in the program. The result was the production of students who were unprepared in any particular discipline, ungrounded in any methodology, who were

---

[34] The social scientist is again referred to Foster *et al.* for more detailed treatment.

handicapped in applying to most graduate schools and who, although well equipped to hold their own in conversation, were not really well educated in anything. The Honors Program ran into some fairly predictable difficulties and has now been abandoned.[35]

Concepts such as "educating the whole man" lend themselves to "reforms" that are reactionary rather than progressive. Academia is plainly moving toward greater specialization, and if the new knowledge is to be integrated at all, this surely must be done in new and imaginative ways, rather than by an attempt to return to the days when the liberally educated man was considered able to handle every field with distinction. Santa Clara is now experimenting with tutorials for the better students, taught within the various majors by professional, qualified faculty. Perhaps this will prove a more fruitful innovation.

Traditional slogans can also mask the need for the university to be a place where diversity flourishes. The Crosscurrents Club, which used to invite controversial speakers to the campus, is now defunct. A faculty discussion group, which became on occasion a lively and even bitter forum for the clarification of contrasting positions, has also fallen into decay. An AAUP chapter has been formed, but has yet to make its influence felt. Faculty government, started during the period of our study — I was the first president of the Academic Senate — has not yet become forceful or effective.

Certain changes have taken place. There has been considerable building. The introduction of girls into the student body has had a socializing effect, although the change was made for financial reasons. The Dean of Students is now a layman, and more companionable, less authoritarian than his predecessor. The ecumenical movement has made itself felt, with interfaith programs and interfaith services in the Mission Church. Students are more involved than they once were in community affairs, working actively in poverty programs; some participated in the march of the grape strikers to Sacramento in the spring of 1966. There are many more Negro students than there were; special scholarships exist to encourage this trend.

The University of Santa Clara is facing the crisis of identity common among Catholic colleges.[36] It can either move toward becoming a more professional, secular university, in which case the Jesuits may find themselves yielding increasing control over their own institution to faculty and to external scholarly influences, with the specifically Catholic character and purpose of the university becoming more and more obscure and diffuse.[37] Or it can retain its Catholicism intact, and try to make itself effectively Catholic,

[35] A similar program at Notre Dame has achieved better success, but appears to be less popular among the best students than a decade ago. — Ed.

[36] Edward Wakin, "How Catholic is the Catholic College?" *Saturday Review*, 59 (April 16, 1966), 92–105.

[37] This chapter was written before the changes at St. Louis and other Jesuit universities were announced in early 1967.—Ed.

developing programs that can somehow stand against the best that secular education has to offer. Six years ago, many thought that the first alternative was being followed, but subsequent events suggest that this was appearance rather than reality; a few people who have now left the campus may have been responsible for much of what seemed to constitute a trend. The second alternative, which combines the maintenance of clerical authority with a striving for excellence comparable to that of the great secular colleges, seems now to be the one chosen. Whether such a combination is feasible is the crucial question. Perhaps the next few years may show whether, as many critics (including myself) believe, this goal of Catholic academic excellence includes within itself inescapable and fatal contradictions.

Controversy on the
Catholic Campus

VII. SOME PROBLEM AREAS IN CATHOLIC HIGHER EDUCATION

A. THE FACULTY

John Leo

If Catholic higher education is a "time bomb," as has been alleged, the ticking became louder — if not faster — on December 15, 1965, when St. John's University in Queens and Brooklyn, New York — the largest Catholic institution of higher learning — dismissed thirty-one faculty members, both lay and clerical. This chapter is a brief history of the controversy.

St. John's main campus occupies a rolling hill in the midst of New York City's congested borough of Queens. The site was formerly a golf course, but the trees are gone. In their place are several stark, squat, and isolated buildings that suggest the most for the money with no nonsense about esthetics. There is plenty of grass, but the students may not walk on it. Even with students milling around, the campus has a way of seeming unoccupied. It is cold, almost brutal — a setting by Di Chirico. Physically, it suggests utility, order, homogeneity, and power; but little of community, diversity, or vitality.

The hill, along with a smaller, older campus in Brooklyn, serves 13,000 students, more than any other Catholic college in America. It has been noted chiefly for its size, its basketball team, and now for the academic uprising that catapulted it into headlines from coast to coast.

The first faculty complaints, which go back a number of years, dealt with isolated matters, large and small, and might have been made with some justification on many a Catholic campus: the policy on visiting lecturers was restrictive, the pension plan inadequate, and parking places for faculty (as compared to those for, say, maintenance men) decidedly inferior; paternalistic rhetoric in minor marching orders from the Vincentian administrators to professors was demeaning (teachers must "prowl the room" during exams, supervise student dress or be held accountable themselves, etc.); tenure regulations contained an escape clause that enabled the Vincentians to fire any teacher; even a switch from one textbook to another could get a professor in trouble with the administration.

John Leo is a former editor of the Davenport *Catholic Messenger* and is presently associate editor of *Commonweal* and a columnist for *The National Catholic Reporter*.

The caution of the administration in approving outside speakers provided a readily grasped issue with wide appeal. At various times and for various reasons, the administration had vetoed projected talks on campus by Earl Browder, Madam Nhu, Kenneth Keating, Bishop Sheen, Sargent Shriver, and John F. Kennedy. Socially aware and outspoken students have never been the ideal at St. John's, but some of the less docile began to complain of regimentation and an attitude that they were childlike wards of the administration. Student publications were censored and the editors chosen by the administration, usually for the virtues that produce unreadable journals.

The unrest first began to take the form of a movement in the fall of 1963, when a few faculty members founded a chapter of the American Association of University Professors (AAUP). Since the administration had for years refused permission for such a step, this time the professors did not approach the Vincentians, except to inform them that a chapter had already been formed. The administration, aghast at the impudence of the act, refused to acknowledge the AAUP, or even to reply to its letters. In this instance, as in many others that followed, the administration failed to perceive the depth of the unrest and lagged badly behind events. (A year later, after repeated buffeting from the administration, faculty militancy spilled over into the formation of a local of the United Federation of College Teachers [UFCT] of the AFL-CIO, which could have been prevented at any time by the simple expedient of recognizing the AAUP.)

The first practical issue for the AAUP was the faculty pension plan, which yielded a maximum retirement benefit of $100 a month, and which the faculty discovered was set up to cost the university even less money than had been supposed. The administration, in successive stages, refused to discuss the issue, changed over to a plan the faculty didn't want, promised to introduce an option for the plan the faculty wanted, and then declared a year's moratorium on the whole discussion — which the faculty furiously denounced as reneging on the promised option. At each stage the membership in the AAUP jumped, and seeds were planted for the formation of the union. Here also a set of attitudes emerged that were to become familiar and harden into a framework for events of the next two years: the administration, although willing to present new plans, was unwilling to *discuss* any of them with the faculty; a number of teachers began to lose confidence in the credibility of the administration. Each side began to envision changes on a radically different schedule — for the Vincentians, change was thought of as a careful and painstaking process, perhaps stretched over a ten- or twenty-year period; for the insurgents, who had done a bit of reading about the Vatican Council, the time for change was now.

Exasperation built during the spring and fall terms of 1964, with hopes dwindling that the administration would meet the growing array of faculty complaints — or for that matter, even meet the faculty. When a proposed agenda was drawn up by the AAUP for a meeting with the administration's executive committee, the committee refused to discuss the key item: a structure for regular dialogue between the AAUP and the committee. The other items—pay raises, administrative restructuring, reorganization of the Vincentian-dominated university senate, and an endowment fund for academic improvement — were all ignored. A white paper prepared by the faculty commented: "The executive committee had kept its barriers up, its authority intact. There was to be no meeting of peers." The committee went further and cut itself off entirely from the faculty by insisting that any future faculty recommendations be channeled through Father Munday, the academic vice-president.

With the help of its national headquarters, the AAUP tried a different tack and got an ad hoc committee made up of Vincentians and faculty. But the gain proved illusory. Pay raises were not to be discussed; other faculty proposals were shunted over to existing Vincentian-dominated committees. By this time the faculty was at the end of its tether. At an administration-called faculty meeting on March 6, 1965, the head of the AAUP, Dr. Andrew Robinson, accused the administration of bad faith and called a mass walkout on the part of the faculty. More than two hundred professors left.

The torches were now lit, and the administration moved to avert general conflagration by announcing a three-week study by an outside consultant. The consultant turned out to be Father Joseph Tinnelly, head of a Vincentian house in Brooklyn and a former dean of the St. John's law school. The faculty pointed out that this was hardly very far "outside," since the priest is a Vincentian, subject to the same provincial the administration is serving. In addition, they could see little use for more study, and for inserting a man between the faculty and Father Munday, just as Father Munday had been inserted between the faculty and the executive committee. (At the end of the three-week study, one more man was to be inserted for one more study, but with no more power to bargain with the faculty than Father Tinnelly.)

Still, Father Tinnelly was a respected man and he listened to everyone who would talk. On April 9, when the faculty assembled to hear the Tinnelly recommendations, the hopeful word was that his report would satisfy everyone and bring peace to the campus. This was not to be the case. A movement in protest against unilateral actions was not to be answered by unilateral action.

The Tinnelly "package" included pay raises for faculty ranging from $150 to $300, an improved pension plan, major medical protection, and a promise of more influence for the faculty in university affairs. For the students, he announced an easing of restrictions on publications and guest lecturers, and a lifting of the ban on campus political organizations. The "surprise" in the package, which the faculty had learned about the previous day in the *New York Times*, was the appointment of another outside consultant, Dr.

John J. Meng, president of Hunter College, sometime critic of Catholic education, for a six-month study of the problems at St. John's.

Andrew Robinson, head of the AAUP, termed the Tinnelly report entirely inadequate. A UFCT-called meeting of the faculty voted overwhelmingly to denounce it as totally unacceptable. "The result of Father Tinnelly's three-week study is that we should have a six-month study," said Father Peter O'Reilly, head of the union chapter. "It seems if you follow the logic of this, we will have a five-year study by some third party who knows even less about it than Father Tinnelly or Dr. Meng."

The faculty noted that the Tinnelly report said nothing at all about the demands for meaningful tenure regulations and an academic senate. The particular fear of the union was that the administration was playing for time and insulating itself with layer upon layer of nonmediating mediators with no delegated power. At the union meeting, about eighty of the hundred faculty members present offered to go along with the tentative AAUP plan to withhold contracts until the administration came to terms.

Most of the faculty rage over the Tinnelly report centered on financial matters. Both the AAUP and the union had demanded 25 per cent salary increases. The Tinnelly offer was in the area of 2 per cent. Father Tinnelly had carefully detailed St. John's expenses for the coming year but had omitted any reference to income. "Just as a housewife," said one teacher at the union meeting, "I am insulted by the report. I know very well I can't judge how much to spend until I know how much I have on hand."

Before the Tinnelly report, the AAUP's Robinson had suggested one reason why the administration provided no accurate financial information: it had projected such a large profit for the current academic year — two-and-one-half million dollars — that faculty would not be very well disposed to accept token pay raises if they knew about it. Father Tinnelly said only that "some estimates concerning the relationship between the University's income and expenses [are] entirely misleading," and failed to take into account the total operating expenses and the nature of "restricted funds" that could not go for salaries. What he did not know at the time was that the faculty had managed to get its hands on a secret report from the university to the New York State Department of Education. Excerpts from the report, released to the *New York Times* but never printed, proved very embarrassing to the Tinnelly interpretation. It indicated a budget, signed on November 1, 1964, by the treasurer of St. John's, Father Louis A. Fey, showing a 1964–65 income of $14,014,275 and an outgo of $11,511,600 — a budgetary surplus of $2,502,675. It also showed that St. John's, despite its four new buildings, is completely debt free. Robinson claimed that St. John's had $8 million on hand, and in addition to the $2½ million profit that year, could expect to push its annual profit over the $4 million mark the following year through an announced tuition increase.

The faculty's reaction to the disclosure was understandable. One instructor, who said she was earning $6,000, asked why she should be content with a $150 raise ("which will just pay the increase in the state sales tax") when St. John's would be clearing $4 million. Just what the average faculty member was then earning was open to some dispute. The administration released no figures. But an AAUP poll, reaching 60 per cent of the faculty, established the average at $7,500, nearly $2,000 lower than Fordham's, and equivalent to the starting salary at New York's City College. This would put St. John's into the "D" category — the lowest — on the AAUP salary scale.

In mid-April 1965, after a quick visit to the campus by national AAUP investigators, the administration, Father Tinnelly, and Dr. Meng committed themselves to faculty participation in hiring, promotion, tenure, budgetary matters, and the selection of department chairmen. They also announced a Faculty Planning Council, which would be elected by the faculty to meet during the summer and to work out forms of faculty participation.

The history of the Faculty Planning Council is filled with tales of bickering and more mutual charges of bad faith. In one key episode, Father Joseph T. Cahill, who had just been named as the new president of St. John's, unilaterally selected a temporary chairman of the philosophy department, which many teachers furiously denounced as a departure from the announced principle of faculty participation in such selection. Father Cahill, who was guilty at least of a bad tactical error, replied that the department needed a chairman immediately and that under existing statutes, he was still to be chosen directly by the Vincentians. The teachers considered control of the philosophy department crucial and apparently did not believe the appointment would be temporary at all.

The council tried to censure Father Cahill for the appointment but was prevented by a parliamentary maneuver on the part of Dr. Meng, who was chairing the session. At the next meeting, with Father Tinnelly in the chair, they tried to censure Meng for preventing censure of Father Cahill. With tempers more frayed than ever, the council, in disgust, adjourned sine die. (This was another tactical error: when the council tried to meet again in the fall, the administration took the position that it had voted itself out of existence and could play no further role on faculty planning.)

As a result of the summer by-play, the dissidents regrouped in the fall totally convinced that the Vincentians were going through an enormous charade and never intended to make substantial changes. The UFCT and the AAUP called for picketing of the university, but abandoned it after the administration agreed to a timetable for promulgation of the summer reports. In October, 1965, Father Tinnelly said the forthcoming document on academic freedom would be based on the standard AAUP statement of 1940 on the topic, but would be "subject to certain specific reservations or modifications which may be necessary by reason of the nature of St. John's as a

Catholic university confided to the direction of the Vincentian Fathers."
The faculty had previously been told that there would have to be some reservations on academic freedom in theology and philosophy; now these reservations would apply to all departments.

Restriction of the philosophy department was a particularly sore point, and Father Tinnelly had shut out any hope for an open department — or one in theology — by quoting canon law: "the study of Philosophy and Theology and the teaching of these sciences to their students must be accurately carried out by professors according to the arguments, doctrine and principles of St. Thomas, which they are inviolately to hold." (This section in the Code of Canon Law, it should be clear, applied to seminaries, not colleges.)

The AAUP commented: "We have arrived, after six months of planning, at a philosophy of education that is medieval in spirit." It denounced a fresh salary increase (which the Vincentians claimed would bring the total raises promised in the past year up to the million-dollar mark) as "an anesthetic for the pain that was to follow."

Dr. Meng, who had not proved to be the strong personality necessary to bring order out of the summertime chaos, was denounced for his "ambiguous" role, and for accepting only those faculty ideas that he already held on his own. Nor was there any sympathy for Father Tinnelly's promise that the trustees would consider the academic freedom plan within three-and-one-half months. "This obvious tactic of delay," said the AAUP statement, "bears dramatic witness to the deceit and bad faith that have characterized this entire endeavor."

The faculty dissenters now claimed that the administration, after a year of promises, was reneging on each key point: reservations on academic freedom, no discussions with the philosophy and theology departments, as promised; a diluted and carefully hedged version of a faculty senate (more than a third of which would be made up of administrators); and equivocation on the promised rules for tenure (the Vincentians offered no automatic tenure after seven years and no tenure at all for non-Vincentian priests). Believing that the administration did not intend to move at all, the AAUP called for a faculty-administration forum, but facilities were denied. An attempt to reconvene the Faculty Planning Council was prevented by the administration, which sent university security policemen to bar the doors. It met elsewhere, but the Board of Trustees officially disbanded the group to prevent another session. In the "cafeteria incident," two students invited professors to take their case to the student body by means of a lunchtime rally. A Vincentian appeared and pulled the plug on the public address system. The two students were suspended.

The blow-up of December, 1965, came when the fortunes of the dissidents had reached the nadir. An ad placed in several Catholic publications by seventeen St. John's philosophy teachers in search of other employment was both a provocative act and an act of despair. Most of the hard core had given up on St. John's and were willing to drift away to greener pastures. The mass firing of December 15 gave them a new lease on life.

Thirty-one teachers were originally dismissed, including about ten "normal" dismissals for less than glittering classroom performance or insufficient progress toward an advanced degree. The rest of the group, which includes some of the best teachers at the university, were casualties of the continuing faculty-administration discord. Most were members of the union — the United Federation of College Teachers. Some were not even allowed to finish teaching the September-January school term. None was given cause or a hearing.

The case for the administration went something like this: the dissident teachers had stepped up their guerrilla warfare against the university in the public press, in the cafeteria, and in the classroom, thus interfering with the educational process and bringing the university to the point of disruption. If hearings had been granted prior to dismissal, total disruption would have been certain: public furor would have mounted during the weeks — perhaps months — of hearings; it would have produced the spectacle of the Vincentian administrators putting other priests on public trial. In addition, St. John's was about to introduce strong regulations on tenure, and if it delayed past December 15, 1965, the dissidents would have been untouchable and the guerrilla warfare would have become permanent.

Nevertheless, the summary dismissal of a large group of teachers without hearings clearly violated the academic code, as well as the university's own statutes. Since most of the dismissed were UFCT members, the union called a strike for the beginning of classes in January. As the strike began, about one hundred fifty teachers walked out in support of the dismissed thirty-one. Wide sympathy for the strike came from the press, unions, student and teacher groups in other colleges, and a number of AAUP chapters. (Ironically, the only AAUP chapter known to have come out on the administration's side is the one at St. John's. At the time the strike began, no Vincentian was a member in good standing of the chapter; but in the month that followed, more than thirty Vincentian priests joined and all voted against a motion to censure the Vincentian administration. The motion to censure failed by one vote.)

A number of offers to mediate the dispute — from politicians, labor leaders, and ecclesiastics — were all rejected by the administration on the ground that there was nothing to discuss or mediate. By mid-April, 1966, it was clear that the Vincentians did not intend to come to terms with the strikers, despite deep antipathy to the university in the nationwide academic community and the risk of a censure from the National AAUP and possible loss of accreditation from the Middle States Association. The immediate crisis — that of filling scores of teaching jobs for the remainder of the term —

was met by cutting back on several courses, combining others, and importing a number of Vincentians and other teachers, some with dubious qualifications. Student dissatisfaction — on which the strikers had pinned many of their hopes — fizzled quickly, partly, it is said, out of fear that the selective service would overtake a student who joined the strike. As the term drew to a close, the number of strikers dwindled to about fifty. The AAUP, as expected, delivered its official censure. The Middle States Association, although refusing to revoke St. John's accreditation, delivered a stern warning and condemned the firings as "reprehensible."

The strike had obviously failed, in the sense that none of the dismissed teachers won his job back. Yet the administration had also lost. Some of St. John's best teachers were among the dismissed. Others announced an intention to leave as soon as possible, and the AAUP censure will militate against the recruitment of comparable replacements. For better teachers and students, St. John's has been branded as a college to be avoided at all costs. Only 1,600 freshmen were expected in 1966, down from 2,400 in 1965, and 2,600 in 1964.

Why did it happen at St. John's? It is hard to produce a ready answer. Most of the conditions that brought open conflict to Jamaica probably exist at many a sleepy Catholic college that has yet to hear a discouraging word — at least in public. The dramatic expansion of St. John's, not matched by comparable developments in university structures, left all authority for a 13,000-man university in the hands of about fifty Vincentians. The desire of lay teachers, and a few non-Vincentian priests, for some say in academic matters reinforced, by way of reaction, the traditional paternalistic notions of the administration. Further, the fact that St. John's is located in New York City should not be overlooked. Lured by the cultural attractions of the city, a number of outspoken and independent teachers — perhaps a larger number than the reputation of the university would warrant — were drawn to the campus during the expansion. They brought with them expectations of intellectual life apparently not shared by the St. John's Vincentians, almost all of whom did their college work at a Vincentian seminary and tended to take seminary structures and obedience as models for St. John's.

Yet it is not true to say that the administration flatly opposed reform. It recognized the AAUP, raised salaries three times, accepted the 1940 AAUP statement on academic freedom, agreed in principle to share some authority with teachers, lifted the more odious restrictions on student activities, and introduced reforms on censure and academic freedom. But in each case, the initial suggestion was curtly rejected, only to be accepted many months later when the issues were broader and deeper. (The tenure and freedom reforms were not released until *after* the mass firing.) The insurgent faculty became convinced that each promised reform would disappear through a technical loophole as soon as teacher opposition relaxed. A refusal to deal evenhandedly with the teachers as peers cost the Vincentians heavily and deepened suspicions. The protection of the dignity of authority and the constant appeal to Roman juridicism infuriated teachers who had had enough of the pre-Council exercise of authority and *Romanita*. The university's lack of openness and constant critical surveillance in small details of classroom procedure finally struck many teachers as something that need not be, even at a Catholic college.

This idea dawned slowly, for the faculty at St. John's had long been known for its conservatism. The fact that a major revolt could rise from such a faculty is the fullest measure of the Vincentian failure. At many junctures along the way, openness on the part of the administration could have brought out the faculty's inherent conservatism and generated an acceptable settlement. Even after censure, with the UFCT emerging as the fighting champion of professors' rights, there was precious little support on campus for the idea of a teachers' union.

With the clear risk of oversimplification, it can be suggested that what emerged from the upheaval at St. John's was confrontation between pre-Council and post-Council views of the church. The Vincentians perceived their function as one of stewardship and protection of students from undesirable influences. Wisdom is something received by St. John's Vincentians from above and handed on, intact if possible, to a docile new generation. The insurgents, like their counterparts on secular campuses, conceived of education as a quest, as an analysis of received wisdom preparatory to forming a personal world view. In this the Vincentians thought they detected seeds for the destruction of St. John's as a Catholic institution. If all ideas were to be sifted and analyzed impartially, they argued, what would distinguish a Catholic college from a secular one?

The major impact of St. John's, no doubt, has been on other Catholic colleges. Many of them are running scared and have hastened, for various reasons, to head off similar outbursts from their teachers. But the root question posed by the St. John's disaster is that posed by Msgr. John Clancy, one of the fired teachers: "Is a Catholic college engaged on a spiritual quest or in a search for a rule of safety?" Or to put it another way, are Catholic colleges going to gear their efforts to keeping students in the church, or will they promote the intellectual freedom that involves a measure of risk? The administration's pyrrhic victory over the strikers was won, in part, because the students, trained to docility and safety, played their traditional role. The quest for safety is still viable for a college apparently willing to risk total discreditation throughout the academic world. Aside from that, its time has come.

Robert J. McNamara, S.J.

Father John Courtney Murray once remarked, in the course of a conference for some soon-to-be-ordained seminarians, that shortly all of us would hear ourselves called "Father" by nearly everyone. He added that, no matter how idiotic some of the things we might then say, the standard reply would be: "Yes, Father."

Fortunately, the emerging layman tends to be less meek these days when confronted with clerical idiocy. He stands less apart from the priest than he did then, nor is he so subject to paternalistic authority. Nevertheless, in a certain sense, the priest must always stand apart from the layman. The paradox of the priest's position is that he stands apart from people in some ways to be closer to them in others. But how far apart? And in what ways? The priest who can find the answers to these questions, and live his answers, has solved the riddle of his priesthood.

The reflective, reasoned answers to those two questions should be at the basis of the policy determining the education and the religious formation of future priests. But I am very much afraid that they are not. I am afraid that the seminary exists too often in a cultural vacuum, isolated within a tradition that now has much less meaning than it may once have had. The active policy determining the foundation and administration of today's seminary is based too frequently on an unimaginative imitation of the past and on a somewhat inflexible interpretation of Canon Law. Then, too, one wonders if the planners appreciate what a college education could mean in the development of the priest.[1]

Robert J. McNamara, S.J. received his bachelor's and master's degrees from Saint Louis University and his Ph.D. from Cornell in 1963. From 1962 to 1966, Father McNamara was instructor and assistant professor of sociology at Fordham University; he is presently a research director of the National Opinion Research Center in Chicago. His contributions have appeared in *Social Order*, *Sociological Analysis*, *America*, and in several compendiums similar to this volume.

[1] I shall say nothing here of the high school education of seminarians. It is highly dubious that "minor seminaries" serve any solid purpose in the United States. Cf. James Michael Lee's admirable "Overview of Educational Problems

What a college education ought to mean in the life of any human being has been discussed ever since — and well before — the college evolved into its present form in American society. But one absolute requisite to the discussion cannot be forgotten: the American college exists in American society. It is not in Russia where, supposedly, the Establishment demands a "hard" scientific and technological orientation because of the way in which the Establishment conceives of Russian society. Nor is the American college located in some Latin country where the university may be a citadel of anticlericalism with an arsenal of absolute secular humanism. The American college exists in a society where, in the best of senses, egalitarianism is the generally accepted myth; where the college plays the somewhat contradictory roles of questioning the myth as well as of getting people to accept it, of preparing people to take business and professional positions while at the same time urging them to liberate themselves from values that mindlessly glorify these positions. Further, more and more people are going to these colleges: nearly half the nation's high school graduates now enroll in college; and colleges occupy a crucially important position in an educational system that differs structurally from any other educational system in the world.

In the few years I have spent as a professor of sociology, one of them in a seminary, I have come to one firm opinion about the college education of the American seminarian: whatever be the kind and degree of "apartness" that is good for the priest, the sort of general social isolation fostered by a seminary separated spatially and educationally from the rest of American colleges is bad for the future priest. College education is part of the process of becoming an educated American. The isolated seminary is not in the mainstream of American college education, and thus it can throw unnecessary roadblocks in the seminarian's path as he tries to become a mature priest in American society.

This opinion I would like to develop along the following lines: first, how college education is related to the separation of priest from people — the separation that, I must insist, helps keep the priest closer to the people he is ordained to serve; second, what the ideal college situation for the seminarian is; third, in what circumstances the seminarian's postgraduate, professional training should be undertaken.

AN EDUCATION APART?

The "close the seminaries" apologists take the stand that it is silly for the Catholic church to run separate undergraduate institutions for young men

in Seminaries," in *Seminary Education in a Time of Change*, eds. J. M. Lee and L. J. Putz, C.S.C. (Notre Dame, Ind.: Fides Press, Inc., 1965). I am heavily indebted to Lee's four articles, which appeared in this volume. Rather than cite him with dreary regularity, I shall state the general debt here and now.

who want to become priests. Formidable arguments support this stand. Maintaining such institutions is unwise because, in the great majority of American seminaries, there can never be enough seminarians to pay the cost of a first-class educational operation. Consequently, the operation is either wildly uneconomical or not first class. (The large number of seminaries existing without educational accreditation suggests that the latter is more often the case.)[2]

Secondly, the apologists for the immediate closing of the isolated seminary would say— and they are backed by sound intuition and some empirical evidence — the "total institution"[3] type of seminary separates the young man from the rest of mankind at too early a stage in his development. He needs to rub shoulders with people who do not see the rest of the world as he does, whose life goals are different from his own. As he rubs shoulders, he is forced to articulate and deepen his own goals or lose them. If he loses them, the argument goes, there is no real loss, for either he would have lost them anyway or he would have been somewhat less than effectual as a priest. And if he retains and deepens them, he will win other college students over to his cause. Thus the church would not lose in total numbers of priestly vocations, and it would actually gain in the strength of the average vocation. Perhaps.

This type of talk makes it clear that there are two pivotal points in the discussion: the quality of the seminarians' college education and their growth into mature priests. Whether, if all future priests went to college before they enrolled in a seminary, the number of vocations would increase or decrease, and whether they would be better or worse, is anyone's guess.

For the future priest, however, there is a "halfway house" between life in a total-institution seminary and life as an ordinary student on a college campus. Not only does the halfway house suggest itself as a practical solution to the educational problems of seminaries, but it gives the future priest some human support during his college years. It could demolish the supposed dichotomy of "apartness" and "togetherness" that has split — and thus stunted — the thinking about education of seminarians in the American church. This halfway house is nothing more nor less than residences, for the young men whose goal is the priesthood, created on or near the campuses of decently accredited colleges or universities. The college or university could do what it does for other young Americans: provide the seminarians with a college education. The residence seminary could provide the seminarians with apostolic formation and the opportunity to share ideals and ideas with each other: their own internal community.

---

[2] *Ibid.*, pp. 101–5.

[3] The phrase "total institution" is sociological shorthand for an institution that serves all the needs of all its members — e.g., a monastery, jail, or sanatorium.

The halfway-house concept will come up again in the next section of this essay. What I have glossed over is the all-important question: Why should a priest, or future priest, be "apart" in any sense? And how does his separation help him to be closer to the people he is ordained to serve?

First of all, the priest must be apart from the rest of mankind because he plays not only a specific, but even a unique, role among men. The specifics of his role include the familiar triad of "prophet, priest and king" — meaning that he must preach by word and deed, must offer Mass and administer the sacraments, and assist in governing the Christian community. But its uniqueness stems from the fact that, in these and all the other activities of his life that have a more than purely private relevance, he is the official witness of the church to something of value.[4]

This "something of value" is the redemptive will of God. The priest's whole public life must be an official proclamation that God has indeed redeemed mankind. Further, the proclamation must be made in — ideally — all areas of human life where that message is unknown, seriously questioned for a time, or needs constant reiteration: thus we have the mission priest, the "worker priest," and the parish priest. And just as the message needs constant reiteration in the parish, so it does in the fields of literature, the arts, and the sciences. This is not to twist the art or the science into an apologetic: each must be genuine, as must the priest who is the authentic artist or scientist. He speaks the redemptive word in an area of high human value, combining in himself the official witness of the church and the human utterance of man. In this way the church is present in these most vital areas of human life, proclaiming them both good and redeemed. It is the priest's unique role as "official witness," more than the prophet-priest-king triad, that makes him apart from the rest of men.

To those who are not members of that particular Christian community known as the Roman Catholic church, this type of thinking may seem a bit precious. But the church does define its priests in this way, and the candidates for its priesthood must fit the definition — and *desire* to be such men. If they do, they are apart from other men. Yet their efforts to bring redemptive love to men and women will make them, as priests, closer to all human beings. To help each become fully human, and thus redeemed, is the overriding concern of the priest.

To answer my own question — how is college education related to the separation of priest from people? — I would say that the experience of the college years must both link them and separate them. It must link them

---

[4] The basic insight concerning the priest as "official witness" is drawn from Matthew J. O'Connell's superbly reflective article, "The Priest in Education: Apostolate or Anomaly?" *Theological Studies*, 26 (1965), 65–85. I cannot, however, hold Fr. O'Connell responsible for the way in which I have applied his insight to the residence seminary.

because the future priest should share, as closely as possible, the common experience of young people maturing in American society. If the seminarian will one day be the official witness, he must have a sure sense of the feelings and the aspirations of those to whom his whole life speaks. Then too, he must be an adult in American society, one who has gone through the peculiarly American experience of the college years with their periods of self-doubt and protest, with their sharpening moments of intellectual and moral autonomy and responsibility, as well as their fun and games. Finally, it seems most unwise to segregate the future priest during his college years from the people he wants to serve. Daily contact with them gives him ever fresh evidence of just how much they need him.

The man who has decided to become a priest when he enters college or who makes the decision during the college years is normally helped by living on close terms with likeminded men. Here his separation from the rest of mankind, based on the unique role of official witness that will be his as a priest, can be given practical expression in the residence seminary. All men and women need community, and the seminarian is no exception. Sharing his ideas and ideals, his doubts and his confidence, his successes and failures with men who, like himself, desire to be the church's official witnesses, gives him this personal community. He also needs the advice of older men who are priests, just as any student needs the advice and the help of faculty members. And, since his future role in society is, to say the least, unusual, he should be able to see around him men who are successful human beings and priests. The residence seminary can give him all this. Thus, in providing for his educational and apostolic formation, the residence seminary on the college campus can stand as a sign of what the priest must be: apart from men but close to all of them.

COLLEGE AND THE SEMINARIAN: THE IDEAL

The proposal to bring the seminarians to the college campus is not radical, nor is it even new. In the Diocese of Pittsburgh, the seminarians attend college classes at Duquesne University and live in a residence not far from the campus. For the last two years, the Jesuits' New England Province has sent its seminarians to Boston College, half an hour away from where they live in what once was their total-institution seminary. The New York Province Jesuits want to locate their seminarians on the campus of Fordham University in 1968. And the Missouri Province Jesuits have educated their seminarians on the campus of St. Louis University for many years.

Seminarians belonging to religious communities or orders like the Jesuits do have one particular difficulty. They have already taken vows that make them members of the order. Diocesan seminarians are under no such vows. In the actual situation, however, this difference is not so important, for the members of each group need both some type of community life and a good college education. The internal community problems can best be solved by each group working within its own tradition, not that the problems can or will be solved easily — but their solution is not the task of this essay.

Again, as we move to the discussion of the ideal college situation for the seminarian, the two focal points are: his college education and his growth into a mature priest. As for all other college students, the quality of the education he gets depends on the quality of his teachers, his courses, his reading, his discussion, and his own effort. First, then, the college attended by the seminarian should be a good one. If it is a Catholic college, his residence seminary will not have to provide undergraduate theology — an important point that could determine the choice of the college. And the college should be larger, preferably part of a university, rather than smaller, lest the seminary overwhelm the college.

The number of elective courses within a field, as well as the number of possible fields in which course concentration is possible, is far larger in almost any good-sized college than it is in the typical seminary. At how many total-institution seminaries can a student major in physics, or sociology, or psychology? Yet all these fields are possible major areas of study in good-sized colleges. And the variety of courses, for example, in English literature and modern languages is far richer at the colleges than it can possibly be in the total-institution seminary. Not infrequently the seminarian takes all his courses in his field of undergraduate concentration from one professor. No matter how good the professor, neither he nor his students should be caught in such an academically intolerable situation.

As for reading and discussion, most seminaries have relatively meager libraries, and not a few prohibit seminarians from being in each others' rooms. ("Discipline" is so well kept that way, some administrators think.) The result, however unintended, is that seminarians may have too few good books to read and talk about, and no place to talk anyway. Yet college education is somehow supposed to take place.

The college campus and library, plus a more enlightened definition of discipline in the residence seminary, provide the opportunity for discussion and reading that the total-institution seminary too often lacks. A good college, by definition, has a good library as well as facilities for discussion groups, formal or informal. Thus the seminarian can be given the opportunity of participating in the vital part of college education that takes place outside the classroom.

What I have said so far seems so patently obvious — how I wish it were to everyone. Less obvious, and more problematic in its relationship to the seminarian's life, is the whole question of extra- or co-curricular activities and the social life of the ordinary college student. Few would claim that such activities are unrelated to the education of the college student, and no one denies that they are part of the maturing process that goes on during the college years. But should the resident seminarian be involved in them? And if so, how?

Just as we do not expect the seminarian whose future life is pledged to celibacy to "go steady" during the college years, we do not expect him to be involved in the dances and dating patterns of college students who are looking forward to marriage. The seminarian has already made his choice. On the other hand, it would be most unfortunate if he could not be involved in the usual campus clubs and activities just because the latter are open to coeds. And the thought of a section of the college cafeteria "Reserved for Seminarians" or of a rule prohibiting seminarians from having lunch with coeds makes one wince. Relationships with women do not have to be sexual, nor does friendship between men and women necessarily lead to marriage. But the uneasiness of some priests in the presence of women makes one wonder what women mean to them. Artificial barriers in the seminarians' formative years possibly fostering such uneasiness should be demolished with all deliberate speed.

In my opinion, the only clubs and activities from which the resident seminarians should be barred or in which their numbers should be restricted are those that take too much time or those that would run the risk of being overwhelmed by seminarians. Varsity sports probably fall into the first category, although intramurals do not. Campus religious and apostolic organizations, as well as Student Government, probably fall into the latter category. The religious organizations exist for the college student and can too easily be defined by students as a kind of seminarians' preserve, thereby scaring away possible members. Nor should key positions in student government be filled by seminarians in a Catholic college. Too many students would see rampant clericalism in such a situation; and, as a matter of fact, the seminarians are much more vulnerable to administration pressure than are the ordinary college students.

Only one further question can be asked here: How should the resident seminarians dress on the college campus? It is by no means a trivial one. To avoid situations that could be embarrassing to himself or others, and because he is a person aspiring to play a unique role in society, his dress should be distinctive, but not deceitful. He is not a priest and so should not dress like one. Roman collar or cassock ought not to be his regular campus attire. But a dark jacket, possibly with some small emblem on pocket or lapel, would define him as a citizen of two worlds and let him exist in both.

POSTGRADUATE TRAINING

An outstanding Protestant theology professor and ordained minister once remarked to me, rather wistfully, that the training given to his divinity students was inadequate in one respect: unlike the seminarians in Catholic theologates, they receive no "Church apprenticeship." He meant that, in the Catholic theologates, the seminarians lived in a community that prepared them for the patterns of parish life, and that they spent time helping out in parishes before and after ordination. His divinity students lived just like other graduate students and found it difficult to make the subsequent adjustment to parish life. In short, he considered their theological training excellent but their professional training deficient. (He was talking, of course, about a particular divinity school.)

Balance between professional and theological training — and those terms overlap somewhat — must be maintained in a theologate. A priest's career combines the roles of theologian and pastor, whether the priest be in the parish or at the university, college, high school, or anywhere else, no matter what he teaches or does. Obviously, there will be different emphases, but he will always be expected to have theological knowledge and pastoral concern.

The tremendous interest in questions theological, plus the increasing theological sophistication of today's young adults, make it imperative that the priest's grasp of theology be fairly profound and extensive. At the very least, it should be comparable in the United States to the control that a Master of Arts or Science has over his field when he takes his degree at an American university. To this must be added a professional knowledge of liturgy, moral theology, and canon law.

Again, the residence seminary on or near a university campus is the most sensible way of giving the seminarian his theological and professional training. A good graduate department of theology can take the responsibility for this theological training, and the residence seminary, perhaps in concert with the university in some instances, can provide the professional side of his formation. St. Louis University has undertaken to provide a center of theological learning on the residence seminary model. Different religious groups will maintain their residences at St. Louis while sharing the theological center and a common faculty. As these words are being written, Woodstock College, one of the most venerable of American theologates, is contemplating a move to a large university campus. Doubtless, this is the pattern for the future, and the future cannot come too soon.

Apart from the increasing need for excellence in theological training — which is far easier to provide in a university center than in many, small theologates — the city and the university provide more opportunities for pastoral training than do institutions located in lovely and remote rural areas. Just as the United States is spending more and more of its resources to fight the war on poverty, so must the churches turn their attention to solving the inner-city problems, especially the problems of faith and hope. They are beginning to do so, but their success may well be measured by the extent to which working in the context of these problems is made part of the formation of their priests and ministers. And the university itself is a far more likely spot for "ecumenical dialogue" — just to mention the other great movement of our day — than is the isolated seminary. Why postpone this development in the life of the priest until after his ordination? It could go on in the classroom itself, provided, of course, that the seminarian does not scant his own tradition.

CONCLUSION

The second Vatican Council, in its "Decree on Priestly Formation," explicitly avoided making specific rules for seminaries. It contented itself with general rules, requesting each nation to draw up its own particular "Program of Priestly Formation" so that "priestly formation will always answer the pastoral needs of the area in which the ministry is to be exercised."[5]

The general guidelines of the conciliar decree, insofar as they touch the present topic, can be summed up readily. The decree states flatly that "Major seminaries are necessary for priestly formation" and that they must help the young men to model themselves on Christ (III,4). The decree goes on to state that the "directors and professors should be chosen from among the best" (III,5); that "there should also be developed in seminarians a due degree of human maturity" (IV,11); that the courses in philosophy should help them understand their own "perennially valid" heritage and also "contemporary philosophical investigations" so that they "will be properly prepared for dialogue with the men of their own day" (V,15); that "theology should be taught in such a way that students will accurately draw Catholic doctrine from divine revelation" and that scriptural studies "ought to be the soul of theology" (V,16); that the seminarians "should be led to a more adequate understanding of the Churches and ecclesial Communities separated from the Roman, Apostolic See" so that they can "contribute to the restoration of unity among all Christians . . ." (V,16). The decree's sixth chapter concludes with the statement that

> Seminarians need to learn the art of exercising the apostolate not only in theory but also in practice. They have to be able to pursue their assignments both on their own initiative and in concert with others.

[5] *The Documents of Vatican II*, ed. Walter M. Abbott, S.J. (New York: America Press, 1966), p. 438. Further citations from the Decree on Priestly Formation are included in the text: roman numerals refer to the chapter of the decree and arabic numbers refer to the chapter sections.

Hence, even during their course of studies, and also during holidays, they should be introduced into pastoral practice by appropriate undertakings. (VI, 21.)

These wise directives must find expression in American — not Roman, Latin, or Russian — society. Separate — and, I am afraid, unequal — education has been the lot of many American seminarians for too long a time. The American college experience is on the campus and in the cities. It is hoped that the day of the residence seminary is dawning.

C. THE STUDENT

Robert Hassenger
and Gerald Rauch

The ferment of the nation's college campuses is obvious to even the most casual observer. Higher educational institutions that have drifted along peaceably for years find themselves suddenly engulfed by a rising tide of student discontent. In the postwar years and into the late 1950's, when Americans were in the midst of a national identity crisis, President Butterfield of Wesleyan labeled the vast majority of college students a "dutiful generation." Seeming to reinforce his judgment was Philip Jacob's widely quoted book, *Changing Values in College*.[1] After reviewing the available research on the value-outcomes of a college education, Jacob concluded that the various institutions of higher learning had been largely "ineffective in tingling the nerve centers of students' values." Contrary to widespread opinion, Jacob asserted, a process of liberalization did not accompany the college experience. Students remained, for the most part, "gloriously contented" both with a present "unabashed self-centeredness" and with their prospects for the future. Anticipating no die-hard struggle for survival, they "cheerfully expected to conform to the economic status quo and to receive ample rewards" in their private lives, content to leave to others any concern with larger issues of the sociopolitical order.

Students in the 1960's are different. Although there have always been critics of what has been termed our "waist-high" culture,[2] the depth of student disaffection reached new proportions by the time of its most visible manifestation at Berkeley in 1964. Other less publicized incidents have occurred elsewhere. Student protests are no longer simply occasions for letting off steam. The vacation exodus of some of the playlands of the nation

Gerald Rauch is a senior in the College of Arts and Letters, University of Notre Dame.

[1] Philip E. Jacob, *Changing Values in College* (New York: Harper Bros., 1957).

[2] Thomas Griffith, *The Waist-High Culture* (New York: Grosset and Dunlap, 1959).

213

still occurs, but the panty raids of past years have given way to more serious campus demonstrations.

Revolution on the campus cannot, of course, be divorced from the adolescent rebelliousness occurring in all parts of the world. Parents are baffled with their children's desire to disaffiliate from the societies that have apparently been so beneficent to them. Middle-aged, middle-class adults see on their television sets students in five cities around the world demanding of three prominent American statesmen that they justify the presence of the United States in Southeast Asia and in Latin America, and they wonder if these youngsters are not tools of a worldwide Communist conspiracy.[3] Why else would they act so?

Perhaps the escalation in discussion of the adolescent "identity crisis" has generated a certain antipathy on the part of the members of the "dutiful" and "silent" generations of the 1940's and 1950's. Or maybe they no longer really listen. As one angry young man recently put it, describing his school's faculty and administration, and by implication his parents and their friends as well:

> The trouble is that they take [education] as seriously as the rest of the piety we get about law and morality and the intellectual purpose of our existence. The most ironic thing on this campus is that they believe in their own hypocrisy. . . . One of the reasons that administration and much of the faculty alike draw grotesque pictures of students is that they probably have never talked with one, not that they'd listen if they did. For years the same situations occur, the same opinions are given, the same pleas are voiced, and the same nothing happens.[4]

The crux of students' discontent is the demand for a voice in their own education. During the 1950's, the college degree was sought as a passport to suburbia. By 1964, a concern with putting ideas to work had become predominant. Colleges that are what Riesman calls "human relocation projects" did not answer the demands for "meaningfulness" and "relatedness" among the young adults who have known affluence and gracious living and found it wanting.

The more zealous of the revolutionaries have lost faith even with the optimistic credo of liberalism. In light of the conditions about which they grieve, traditional liberal beliefs and sentiments seem irresponsible, having as little real relevance for those bereft of comfort and justice as novenas made to counteract the Black Plague. Ideas, they feel, should issue in social

[3] Personal correspondence from Charles Collingwood, CBS News, describing the criticism received from Americans with regard to his "Town Meeting of the World," October, 1965.

[4] Quoted by J. Glenn Gray, "Salvation on the Campus," *Harpers*, 230 (May, 1965), 53–59.

action. What is more, there is a deep-seated disaffection with American society. As Irving Kristol wrote in a highly sensitive discussion of what "bugs" the students:

> *They are bored.* They see their lives laid out neatly before them; they see themselves moving ahead sedately and more or less inexorably in their professional careers; they know that with a college degree even "failure" in their careers will represent no harsh punishment; they know "it's all laid on" — and they react against this bourgeois utopia their parents so ardently strove for.[5]

This attempted disaffiliation is not the only factor. A classical American commitment to pragmatism is, of course, at work. The Kennedy administration no doubt crystallized youthful idealism. More immediate causes include the increasing role of faculty research, with its corresponding reduction of contacts with undergraduates; pressures on first-rate students to gain admission to selective schools, and on less able ones to get in any "good" college; earlier specialization and implicit professionalization; the impersonality of the mushrooming state universities; the flabbiness supposedly encouraged by a beneficent society; all such factors are important. There are others.

The real difficulty lies not, however, in suggesting "explanations" for the new student mood; it is ascertaining how much is thereby understood. Although perceptive observers agree that undergraduates today differ from their counterparts in the 1950's, little research has been done on the student population. A number of investigations now underway will improve the situation, but our knowledge in this area remains only fragmentary, particularly with regard to the collegian's personal commitments. Despite some accumulation of data on student attitudes and values, there has been little investigation of religion on the campus, as either an independent or dependent variable. Most research on campuses and their various cultures has been designed to include students of all religions, even those without definite religious commitments. Virtually nothing is known of the meanings any particular religions have for the college population. Attention has been directed more toward the study of social and political attitudes, a trend undoubtedly influenced considerably by World War II, its aftermath, the McCarthy period, and the national identity crisis of the 1950's.

One of the recurring charges leveled at American higher education is that colleges have little real effect on their students. Other than providing visas to affluence, the critics suggest, the colleges and universities exert minimal influence on students' lives; their values, attitudes, and behavior are scarcely different from those of nonattenders. Jacob concluded that colleges appeared to have little effect on students preoccupied with their own con-

[5] Irving Kristol, "What's Bugging the Students," *Atlantic*, 216 (November, 1965), 108–11.

cerns; posted like gatekeepers to the greener pastures their clients envisioned, higher educational institutions were primarily — in Riesman's apt phrase — "watchdogs of the upper middle class." [6]

Although the American colonial college was intended to influence moral formation,[7] some will undoubtedly raise the question of the extent to which colleges *should* have an impact on the values of their students, as such critics as Jacob, Riesman, and Sanford would insist. Certain schools, however, are avowedly "value-oriented" institutions, and might be expected to have certain measurable effects. As Hassenger has elsewhere suggested,[8] the Catholic colleges and universities are of this type and should produce distinctive educational results, if their separate existence is to be justified. We shall not push this argument here. Nor is this brief contribution meant to be an "explanation" of the religious discontent becoming more widespread on the Catholic campus. It is too easy to provide facile "answers." We prefer to wait until more data are available.

This section of chapter 7 is meant only to furnish the reader with the responses of a few students to a challenge hurled at Catholic higher education, and specifically at Notre Dame. On December 1, 1965, a Notre Dame graduate of 1964, who was awarded a Woodrow Wilson Fellowship to study philosophy at Princeton, wrote the university president, Theodore M. Hesburgh, C.S.C., that Notre Dame suffered from a "pastoral gap" preventing the discovery of what it meant to be a "real Christian." Stating that he and many of his fellows had grown "farther and farther away from Christianity" during their Notre Dame years, the writer tended to blame those "who were thriving on the new Notre Dame, on academic excellence . . . on the university part of Christian university." The answer for Notre Dame and the Catholic schools would be, he stated, to place the greater emphasis on the other term, to become Christian communities.

Father Hesburgh turned over the letter and responses written by himself and two other Notre Dame priests to *Ave Maria* magazine, published at Notre Dame. The editors in turn solicited replies from the presidents of seven other leading Catholic colleges and universities, and printed the entire collection on April 16, 1966.

Following this issue, the junior author, a Notre Dame student, sought

[6] More recent investigations have shown that student change *does* occur on some campuses, however, and in distinctive student subcultures. The pertinent research is summarized in T. M. Newcomb and Kenneth Feldman, *The Impact of College*, in preparation.

[7] This is well documented in Frederick Rudolph, *The American College and University: A History* (New York: Alfred A. Knopf, 1962).

[8] R. Hassenger, "The Catholic Campus: A 'Christian Community'?" in E. Manier and J. Houck (eds.), *Academic Freedom and the Catholic University* (Notre Dame, Ind.: Fides Press, Inc. 1967), and more directly in "A Rationale for Changing Student Values," *Educational Record*, 48 (Winter, 1967), 61–67.

reactions from eight undergraduates. Respondents are identified by class year (in 1966) and area of major concentration.

A senior mathematics major said:

> Of course there's a pastoral vacuum! I don't see why people should be so surprised by this. It's silly to be upset by it. All this business about relating Christ to different courses — I can't see it. I really can't. Except maybe in a history of religion course — but not in a political science course. Christianity doesn't have a damn thing to do with politics. The idea of a Catholic university just doesn't apply anymore.
>
> I don't think this university should try to produce Catholic leaders. I don't think it will last if they are trying to do that. This place might have the avowed intention of putting out good Catholic leaders. I don't think it should. The purpose of this place should be the purpose of any university.
>
> I don't think you have much to fear from people who are honest. And whether they're honest in a Christian or in a non-Christian sense, well, who can judge? So somebody tells you, "Well I don't go to Mass, I don't go to Church. I don't care for the sacraments. I think that the Catholic church is full of bull. I don't believe that Christ was God. I don't even believe he existed." To my mind that person could still be just as decent and Christian a human being as any Christian.
>
> And you can't tell how many Christians there are by counting communions. Christianity is not made up entirely of devotion and prayer. I'm not saying that religious ceremonies are nothing. I am saying that they aren't everything.

A senior history major noted:

> The important thing to look at is what the priests are doing right now. Why are they burdened down administering a hall? Outside Notre Dame a priest in a parish offers pastoral services. The hall should be like a parish. It shouldn't be a place where the priest has to be the local government, a policeman. Priests are also tied down being disciplinarians, scholars, maintenance men for the halls.
>
> I am disappointed in Notre Dame and mostly disappointed in its priesthood. We seek academic excellence but that could be a Harvard or a Yale. What is supposed to be unique about Notre Dame is that the priest is supposed to be always open. But they are very busy pursuing their advances in the administrative hierarchy or becoming scholars or running their own feudal fiefs in the halls. But they aren't particularly concerned about the student. They are closed to the students. Maybe I was wrong in expecting priests always to be ready to help you. I don't find them here.
>
> The courses at Notre Dame can help you lose your childhood faith.

It becomes fashionable to lose it in, say, Fr. ————'s class. Or in Lyons Hall it becomes fashionable to become an agnostic. Notre Dame can speed you along in that process. But the only choice you have is to either be a Catholic or a non-Catholic. There is no opportunity to learn about other religions. The only other thing open to you is some form of humanism. Most become secular humanists.

At Notre Dame you can become the institutional church-going Catholic Notre Dame has prided itself on producing for several generations. And/or you can become the more apostolic Catholic. But you can't turn to priests to learn this second alternative. You turn to students. There are a small number here that offer a practical witness to what Catholicism should be. You do not get this witness from priests and that is the pastoral vacuum. The students I know who are Christian Catholics try to witness what they believe and this is where the priests fail. They do not witness. They are too tied down with administrative tasks.

Theology here doesn't rise above the level of an intellectual game. I think about Christianity but who can I turn to to witness to me how to live it? Certain priests can teach me to lose my childhood faith but there is very limited witness to the life that you live after you pass through this stage. Notre Dame offers a large quantity of religious services. It is the super welfare state for Christian consumers. But running through the rituals is not sufficient. We want quality. A depth of meaning. Intellectual quality is coming. But the quality of pastoral work is very low. I see priests doing all sorts of things but not what is expected of them as priests.

A junior philosophy major put it this way:

Fr. ———— talks as if everyone is searching and everyone is reading up on the subject though they may not be going to Mass. Few people are interested. People don't get to the finding, to the Christianity. I have a feeling it's a lack of concern, they have a casual interest. People who read existentialist things with religious concerns are few. And of those that see what Christianity is I wonder how many would have the courage to take it up. Christianity begins to look like an "elite-ist" religion. How many find out, even at Notre Dame, what Christianity is about? A tremendously small number come upon Christianity and few take it up. The number of Christians here is infinitesimal.

This pastoral vacuum means there aren't enough priests like Fr. ———— around. Priests that are just here as priests. People that accept students. Fr. ———— sees great hope in students. This is something you have to have. It will give you courage to go further. There must be priests available and able to do this.

Witness is paramount. Theology classes and theological talk don't help. There has to be witness. The priest has to be Christian manifestly. He has to have willingness to give of himself. Of the chaplains in the halls how many do the students even feel are approachable? The priest would have to go out to the students.

I don't think Fr. ———— senses the real problem. It's much greater than he thinks. There are fewer Christians than he thinks here. Mass attendance is just accidental. There are few students who are really Christian. I know very few. Certainly not more than twenty. I can't help thinking that Christianity is not just seeking. I can't help thinking that there is an act of faith to be made, a commitment to Christ, a giving of yourself. Few people see that you have to do this.

Intellectual life seems non-essential to Christian life. The only one I know who ties the two together well is Fr. ————. Intellectual life is an extra hindrance. It offers many more escapes. It allows many many chances to deviate from looking at Christianity. Coming to Christianity is not essentially intellectual. Very few people can sustain an intellectual approach to Christianity and live it at the same time.

A junior aeroengineer made this statement:

I think the person who is deeply interested in finding a way to guide his Christian life at Notre Dame does have somebody to turn to. I'm not necessarily talking about the priests.

The fact that most students are graduating agnostic is not peculiar to Notre Dame but it is a universal fact. Surely academic excellence is part of the Christian life. But there is also personal development, personality, theological development, development of ideals. Prayer is also part of Christianity. They afford the opportunity here to develop this in the facilities for Mass, Confession, and retreats. As far as teaching you, I don't know if they do.

Another senior mathematics major:

This moving away from Christianity as one grows academically, I am sure it happens at Notre Dame. I see it in myself and I see it in the students around me. I'm not really sure why it happens. As adolescents we pictured the Church as authoritarian, dogma with no choice. Of course this is anti-intellectual.

It would be unfair to say the priests are not concerned with the spiritual welfare of the students. There are a few good young ones. But the students don't think they can gain anything from seeing a priest, and in a lot of cases that is well-founded. I would not care to have too much contact with my rector, for example. I wouldn't go to him for counselling. There is nothing that I feel that I could gain by going to a priest.

The reaction of a senior history major was the following:

> We get to college and see that our old formulations were absurd. Just because a person stops going to Mass doesn't mean he is not a Christian. In the past the Church has been anti-intellectual. Because of this it seems to the student that he has to make a choice, and the freedom of the intellectual life seems much more reasonable than the dogma of the Church. You seem to have a choice: either hold to this absurd faith or take the academic life.
>
> As for hyphenated priests, in a university it's all right. Father ———— is good in philosophy, let him teach philosophy. If a person wants to see a priest around here, they are available. The thing is that a person decides he can't learn from a priest. Personally rather than go to Mass I would like to get together with a group of students in a room and let a priest come along if he wants and just discuss a play like *Waiting for Godot* because this is how our religious problems are being formulated today, in literature and plays. They are not being formulated from the pulpit or from things priests have to say.
>
> The teacher should not worry about relating his class to Christianity. To ask for answers in class is getting back to the Baltimore Catechism. If he has solved the problem of Christianity for himself that's fine. That's what all of us are trying to do. We're in this quandary because we haven't made this decision and we don't know how to make it or what it means. But you should not be worried about the problem.

The seventh respondent was a senior English major:

> The most creative, most intelligent students are not coming out Catholics, but I don't see any problem in that at all. Catholicism and Christianity are personal. The pastoral plan is impossible. I would go to a man whom I intellectually respected, but not because he was a priest.
>
> The academic discipline is the best place for the priest to be. Other students might respect a chaplain because he has some sports-oriented ideals. That's okay too. A priest in an academic discipline is setting an example I'd like to follow because I'd like to do something like that.
>
> In this looking for new forms in the change from daily Mass and Grotto visits, I think they overlook the classroom form. It can be just as sacramental as Benediction. I would like to see the percentages of people going to the sacraments dip down as far as they can go. You can't measure things in those terms.

Finally, a junior sociology major said:

> I think the situation here at Notre Dame did a lot more for him than he probably realizes. If only that it gave him a chance to break away and let his faith mature into something real. It might be only that it

drove him to look at this place and to find out why Christianity is lacking here and what Christianity could do and why it should be more
important here. But the pastoral plan he recommends seems like a
patterned Christianity.

I see a value in Fr. ————'s notion of seeking because I don't think
that Christianity is the only way for man to achieve salvation. But if
Fr. ———— says that a person is inside the Church even though he is
seeking, that doesn't sound very kosher. It sounds as though Fr. ————
is maybe trying to make everyone feel better or make the problem
sound not as severe as it may be. If someone is seeking so completely,
let him be considered as outside the Church for a while. I don't see any
need for him to seek from within the Church.

We shall leave it at this, defining our present role simply as middlemen
passing on student thought and feeling to the reader. This cannot be enough,
of course. Much study and reflection is needed, and careful research must
be done. But the starting point must be an "inside view" of the student, advocated by Havens and Keniston.[9] We have tried to make a start here.

[9] Joseph Havens, "The Changing Climate of Research on the College Student
and His Religion," *Journal for the Scientific Study of Religion*, 3 (1963), 52–69;
J. Havens, "A Study of Religious Conflict in College Students," *Journal of Social
Psychology*, 64 (1964), 77–87; Kenneth Keniston, *The Uncommitted* (New
York: Harcourt, Brace, and World, 1965), and "The Sources of Dissent," *Journal
of Social Issues*, forthcoming.

VIII. SOCIAL CONSCIOUSNESS AND ACADEMIC FREEDOM IN CATHOLIC HIGHER EDUCATION

Francis E. Kearns

The 1964–65 American academic year may someday come to be known as the year of the protest march. From Yale to Berkeley, university students manned the picket lines in connection with issues ranging from the publish-or-perish policy in the universities to civil rights and Viet Nam. More important than the specific causes involved, however, was the new activist orientation of the students: their desire to cast off the traditional notion of college as "the best years of our lives" and to make of college life something more than a four-year lark preceding one's initiation into the adult world and its concerns with money and social status. Admittedly, much of the new activism and agitation is silly, and a generation of adults not far removed from Jack Oakie racoon-coat college movies or from the Notre Dame-Army subway series may be tempted to dwell on such items as Berkeley's Sexual Freedom League and to denounce the new campus climate as the work of outside agitators and "beatniks." But a considerable part of the unrest reflects the students' desire to make their education more relevant to contemporary social and political problems. Not since the days of the G. I. Bill has there been such seriousness — one might even say such high moral purpose, were the word "moral" not suspect to the new breed of activists — on the college campus.

Given the new activism and seriousness in American student life, it is surprising to find such general quiescence among students at Catholic colleges. Even St. John's students have remained in large measure uninterested in the revolution taking place on their campus, except when their own courses and degrees are endangered.

Of course, editorial laments over the alleged failure of Catholic schools to excite a concern for social action in their students may have been overdone in recent years; such editorials, appearing at a time of new openness to criti-

Francis E. Kearns attended New York University and the University of Chicago and received his Ph.D. from the University of North Carolina in 1961. Articles by Mr. Kearns have appeared in *America, Carolina Quarterly, Chicago Review, Commonweal, Emerson Society Quarterly, Journal of the History of Ideas,* and *Ramparts*. This contribution was written while he was on a Fulbright Lectureship in Norway.

223

cism and self-scrutiny in the post-conciliar church, might tend to exaggerate the shortcomings of our Catholic schools. But even if the Catholic colleges were no less involved in concern for social justice than their secular counterparts, this fact in itself would be tragic. For, given the social encyclicals, to say nothing of the moral purpose that commencement addresses and course catalogs attribute to the Catholic colleges, these schools must be measured in terms of the extent to which they have shown leadership in fostering concern for social relevance in the academic community.

But what are the causes of this apparent general quiescence of Catholic university students in the face of the pressing social issues of the day? One cause, clearly, is the traditionally pragmatic orientation of their schools. Aside from protecting ghetto interests, another important practical function of the nineteenth-century Catholic college was to promote vocations to the religious life.[1] Throughout the twentieth century, at least until the time of President Kennedy, Catholic universities have played another important practical role in demonstrating to a not entirely unskeptical white Protestant majority the patriotism and loyalty of Catholics. The resulting emphasis on conformity and prudence in Catholic education led to the acceptance of Catholics as safe and dependable lower- and middle-rank workers in government and industry, particularly during the several periods in this century in which America experienced "red scares." Indeed, during the McCarthy era, a period in which, according to the research of Lazarsfeld and Thielens in *The Academic Mind*,[2] the faculty at denominational colleges showed a remarkably lower level of toleration for dissent than their counterparts at secular schools, a certain premium was attached in government circles to the possession of a degree from a "reliable" Catholic university. Thus it comes as no surprise that one of the first American universities to make a mass protestation of its loyalty on the Viet Nam issue was Fairfield, a Jesuit institution.[3]

But of more profound importance than this social inheritance are three interrelated factors arising out of the nature of religious life and its relationship to higher education. The first is confusion over the definition of Catholic higher education and its aims; the second, distrust of the intellectual life; and the third, the problem of adapting concepts of obedience appropriate for life in a religious community to life in an academic community.

The confusion over definition manifests itself in a variety of ways: in the debate over whether the institution is to be an intellectual center or a college-seminary dedicated to the formation of students' character; in the conflict over just how Catholic the Catholic school is to be. As a result of such

---

[1] Philip Gleason discussed these problems in chapter 2.

[2] Paul Lazarsfeld and Wagner Thielens, Jr., *The Academic Mind* (Glencoe, Ill.: The Free Press, 1958).

[3] As late as April 15, 1966, this institution advertised its graduates as "hardly ever effete" and "dependable" (*Commonweal*, 84). — Ed.

conflicts, the Catholic university sometimes appears to be presenting two different faces to the world. To parents, to diocesan authorities, and to the local Catholic newspaper, it sometimes offers itself as a religious institution preserving its students from the secular-agnostic influences of the competing nonsectarian schools. To the professional education associations and the foundations, it sometimes offers itself as a modern research center with only secondary and minor sectarian concerns.

In large part, this apparent facility in changing to fit the demands of circumstance rises out of sincere disagreement among administrators as to what course the Catholic university should follow; but, at the same time, confusion over definition is not without economic advantages for the administration. Low salaries and heavy teaching loads can be justified by appealing to religious loyalty, by citing the heavy financial burdens borne by Catholic schools in their task of keeping religious education available at a time of increasing competition from the state- and foundation-supported nonsectarian institutions, or by reminding the lay professor of the great sacrifices made by his clerical colleagues because of their vows of poverty. But one also finds that such questionable practices as rapid turnover in faculty without tenure (with the result that promotions and consequent salary raises are kept to a minimum) and the various deprivations suffered by faculty members who have not published, or who do not have the Ph.D., or who are no longer "marketable" because of age, may be rationalized as policies necessitated by what is alleged to be the rigorous professional requirements of an institution of high academic stature.

One could also point to the economic aspects involved in the maintenance of antiquated and excessively severe rules of student conduct at Catholic schools. The emphasis on discipline is, after all, a traditional selling point for Catholic education,[4] and every professor on a Catholic campus is familiar with the students whose parents chose a religiously affiliated school to save him from contamination by association with "pinkoes" and "beatniks" at the state university. Whether or not neo-Victorian student regulations are liberalized at a particular Catholic campus, then, may sometimes be largely a matter of economics, depending on where the school authorities believe the course of financial prudence lies — in retaining the loyalty of old boy alumni and traditionalists or in cultivating the school's image with the foundations by moving closer to the greater personal autonomy for students and faculty that characterizes the major nonsectarian schools.

But in dwelling on these economic aspects of the identity crisis faced by Catholic colleges and universities, I am in danger of giving a too deliberate, or even cabalistic, appearance to what is often not even a conscious policy.

---

[4] As serious discussions regarding the abolition of curfews for upperclassmen at Notre Dame were entered in 1966, more resistance was forthcoming from parents than from the Notre Dame administration. Many do not want their sons left entirely on their own. — Ed.

I suspect that, in the majority of cases, the presentation to the world of two contradictory faces by a Catholic university is the result of no willed hypocrisy but is, rather, an indication of the penchant of the religious order for neurotic drifting, for patchwork compromise and uneasy truce at a time of considerable internal unrest. The religious society can hardly be expected to carry out direct and coherent programs in the university under its administration when the society itself is torn over such questions as the nature of religious obedience and the relationship of the priestly vocation to contemporary social problems. While young priests struggle for a wider interpretation of obedience that would permit them to engage in open criticism of the order's policies and to take a more active part in civil rights demonstrations and in other social justice work, older members of the order sometimes fight a desperate holding action. While young priests discuss the possibility of turning the university over to lay control or of the order's wholesale withdrawal from the field of university education, some older clerics resist such talk with all the terror of veteran union workers facing the specter of technological unemployment.

This internal conflict within the religious order was deeply impressed upon me during my five years as a lay professor at Georgetown, the nation's oldest Catholic university. In 1963, when the Georgetown campus was the scene of student protest demonstrations that eventually resulted in the burning of an unused classroom building and in the calling out of police dogs, older Jesuits wrung their hands in bewilderment and considered various forms of reprisal, whereas a few young Jesuit prefects, according to students with whom I discussed the incident, actively encouraged student participation in the demonstrations and even helped to distribute mimeographed lists of student grievances. Later the Student Council invited several faculty members to form a Student-Faculty Grievance Committee with the purpose of hearing student protests, to avoid future riots. The Jesuit rector's initial opposition to the committee was overcome and, with the provision that the word "grievance" be dropped from its title, the committee was duly established. As a member of the committee, I was impressed by the students who appeared before it. Anticipating nothing more than the usual complaints about cafeteria food and dormitory curfews, I was surprised to encounter the students' carefully prepared arguments about such matters as the mediocrity of their theology courses, the absence of a vital Catholic intellectual life on the campus, and the secrecy surrounding the manner in which their high tuition fees were appropriated.

The committee might have served as an important communications link between students and administration but, unfortunately, it seems to have been regarded by the school's clerical officials as little more than a placebo. Its recommendations and summaries of hearings were received without administrative comment or action and were "filed for future reference," with the result that the committee soon died of atrophy. It had encountered two serious obstacles: the clerical administration's unwillingness to take decisive action at a time when such action might cause further friction within the school's religious staff, and the traditional dependence of clerical administrators on delay as an instrument of policy (given sufficient time, student rebels graduate and fractious faculty members will be mellowed or disposed of by the tenure system and by their dependence on authority for such professorial perquisites as research grants and sabbatical leave).

The conflict within the religious order over the identity of the university it controls was underscored by another incident at Georgetown. In 1963 I had written an article for *Commonweal* discussing the difficulties involved in implementing the social encyclicals at Catholic schools and describing the reactions of fear, timidity, and hostility with which faculty, administrators, and students had greeted a sit-in demonstration conducted by a group of Georgetown students at a segregated restaurant near their campus. At Georgetown, the article resulted in cries of outrage from administrative quarters, and within a year I felt retaliation in the form of a suspended pay raise and a dismissal decision. At the same time, however, the article resulted in an invitation, by vote of the Jesuit student body, to appear at Woodstock, perhaps the nation's leading Jesuit seminary,[5] and to address the future priests on problems of the lay professor. It would be hard for a writer of fiction to create two more opposite worlds than those of Woodstock and Georgetown. At Woodstock I was participating in a conference on "The Reassessment of Lay Ecclesiology" in which all the speakers were laymen, the idea behind the conference being that the laity were in the best position to lecture future servants of the servants of God on problems faced by the laity within the church and its institutions. At Georgetown, on the other hand, there were no faculty senate, no grievance committee, no elected rank and tenure committee, no elected departmental chairmen, and no faculty employment contracts. In short, aside from the rector's advice that "My door is always open," there was little evidence at Georgetown of an administrative interest in faculty opinion.

This conflict over identity was revealed at Georgetown in still another way — in the problem of just how Catholic the school would be. At a 1963 AAUP-sponsored [6] faculty meeting held shortly before the opening of the university's 175th anniversary fund-raising and public relations conference, a university official was queried about the establishment of a faculty senate.

---

[5] Allan O. Pfnister did a study for the Association of American Colleges (*A Report on the Baccalaureate Origins of College Faculties*, 1961) which indicated that Woodstock ranked first among the private liberal arts colleges in contributions to the ranks of college teachers. — Ed.

[6] Here, and throughout the volume, AAUP refers to the American Association of University Professors. — Ed.

This official countered with a question of his own: "Suppose such a senate voted to end the school's religious affiliation?" The argument that a greater lay voice in administrative decisions would be a threat to the religious identification of a Catholic school is a familiar one, and a few years ago it was fashionable to defend it in terms of what the Jesuit editors of *America* called "the apostolic mandate" of the order — as if Scripture had enjoined religious societies to go forth in the world founding universities which bar lay participation in their governments.[7] Nevertheless, at the conclusion of the anniversary year, the administration sounded a different note in regard to its religious identification. In a booklet mailed out to community business leaders that directly solicited their financial support, it was argued that the university "is not restricted to any religious belief," that over a third of the faculty and student body are non-Catholics, and that the President and Board of Directors are "counselled and advised by dedicated business and professional men and women from many walks of life, various faiths. . . ."

Such turmoil over the definition and direction of a religious order and of the schools it administers is by no means an undesirable situation. On the whole, it indicates vitality and promise in the life of the order. The situation becomes intolerable for the lay faculty and students, however, when they are required to wait silently for the outcome of the order's internal struggle, to demonstrate "loyalty" by publishing no comments or criticisms which would bear on the struggle, and to maintain for public consumption the appearance of that one big happy family so central in the rhetoric of clerical administrators.

Another major problem at Catholic schools is the difficulty they often experience in separating that concept of obedience appropriate for the religious life of the priests who administer the school from that personal autonomy necessary in the intellectual life of students and faculty. The effect of applying a religious sense of obedience to rules of student conduct is particularly tragic, since it occurs at a time when the impetus toward greater personal liberty in the church set in motion by Pope John and the Vatican Council will more and more require Catholics to depend on their own prudential judgment in areas, such as family planning, where formerly their conduct was determined primarily by ecclesiastical authority. The obedience problem also affects the students' intellectual development. It is thoroughly confusing for a Georgetown student, for example, to attend a conference on academic excellence where he is told by a Jesuit, "When you enter those gates you do so with an open catalog, and you accept on faith whatever the University does," and then go to a class in literature or the social sciences where he is berated by the professor for waiting to be told what to think and for not exercising his own critical faculties.

The obedience problem also creates a particularly distressing role conflict

---

[7] Further comments on this problem can be found in the final chapter. — Ed.

for the lay professor. In his academic field, he is expected to be an enquiring and skeptical professional, exercising an authoritative voice in the conventions and journals of his discipline, while, on his own campus, he is expected to play the role of silent hired hand, to leave policy decisions to the Fathers, and to abandon his traditional skepticism when considering administrative pronouncements about the university as one big happy family or as a "partner with the business community in service to the nation."

An instructive example of the transgression of "authority" into the realm of professional competence occurred at Georgetown with my dismissal. After publishing articles in *Commonweal* and *Ramparts* that discussed the failure of Catholic higher education to exercise moral leadership in the fields of racial justice and academic freedom, while at the same time examining particular abuses in these areas at Georgetown, I was informed that the next year's salary increase for which I had been recommended was now canceled. The department chairman had forwarded a list of proposed salary increases through regular channels and the list had come back with all the raises approved, but with my name removed. When I questioned the chairman about the matter he contended that the raise had been removed by a committee the name or membership of which he did not know. Ignoring the incongruity of his statement, he added that he had exchanged notes about the removal with the phantom committee; but, in answer to my enquiries about the contents of the notes, he explained that they were "confidential." Never having had a particular affinity for Kafka, I went to see the University's executive vice-president and explained to him, as I had to the chairman, that the only recourse I had was to place the matter before the American Association of University Professors. Two weeks later I received a letter announcing the restoration of the raise and explaining that it had originally been removed only through a "clerical error." [8] Three months later I received a letter announcing I was fired because of "the future needs of the Department."

At this point the members of my department got up a petition to the administration arguing that

> the dismissal of Dr. Kearns cannot be defended on any normal academic grounds . . . a realistic view of "the future needs of the Department" would call for a promotion of Dr. Kearns — not a dismissal . . . his dismissal will be interpreted — and we feel rightly so — as an attack on his controversial character as an articulate and outspoken liberal Catholic . . . [the dismissal] is an infringement on his academic freedom and therefore on ours.

The administration countered with arguments about overstaffing in my field but these were, in turn, rejected by the faculty, since the senior man in my

[8] Others have remarked on the marvelous double meaning of this phrase. — Ed.

field had just retired. Experienced members of the University's AAUP chapter warned me that, as the members of my department successively pointed out the fallacies in each defensive argument put forth by the administration, the administration would be forced to the wall and be left with only the "poor teacher ploy." This observation proved an acute one, for the school's three top Jesuit officials, the rector, the executive vice-president, and the academic vice-president, finally rested their case on the newly introduced argument that I was being fired because I was "competent but not outstandingly so." Ironically, a few weeks before this allegation was made, a representative of the department had conferred on this very point of competence with the Jesuit dean in whose school I taught. The dean admitted he had cast his vote for dismissal because of my critical articles and even added that he had been quite impressed with my teaching. After considerable discussion, the dean was convinced of the unreasonableness of his position and agreed to write a letter withdrawing his vote for dismissal and indicating his high estimate of my teaching. Yet, as the Washington *Post* reported, when the dean was later asked for the letter to counter the newly introduced competence argument of his superiors — none of whom had ever heard me lecture — he said he could not write it, and he would give no reasons for his refusal.

Nevertheless, the senior members of my department requested that they be empowered to form a committee, consisting of all the tenured men of the department, to weigh the question of my competence. This proposal was accepted and after several weeks of consideration the committee issued a report strongly endorsing my professional competence and urging my reinstatement. The recommendation was then rejected by the administration in a letter which thanked the committee for its services but offered no reasons for the rejection. At the same time a special committee set up by the Student Council to review the question of competence had, after interviewing faculty members and students, presented a favorable report to the Jesuit academic vice-president, but the priest refused to read it. (The whole question of competence was further complicated when it was announced, after the administration introduced the competence argument, that I had been awarded a Fulbright Lectureship at a European university and had been selected by the Student Council for the annual Edward Douglas White Award for faculty excellence.) Meanwhile, the American Civil Liberties Union examined the case and recommended my reinstatement on the grounds that a professor's professional peers ought to be the chief judges of his competence. The ACLU appeal to the rector went without even a letter of reply, although a few days later a Jesuit regent at Georgetown employed the odd circumstance of a lay professor's funeral mass in the university chapel for a counterattack. In his sermon, which was later mimeographed and distributed from various university offices, the Jesuit pointed to the late professor's special affinity for college athletes ("hard-hitting champions of the playing field") and praised his many years of loyal service. He added:

> Certainly, in all that time he grew aware of many weaknesses within the University — a human organization, after all. But so great was this gentleman's pride of family that he never descended to point out those spots for the world at large to see. Rather we all gratefully recall how he sought to remedy defects by quietly working the harder in his own sector of the vineyard. Cheap ambition and vulgar display were alien to this teacher's character. He never sought headlines as a controversial figure or a bone of contention. Among moral qualities there is no substitute for the quiet loyalty with which this lay teacher served the religious body, the Society of Jesus, which he loved so cordially.

The rhetoric of this sermon is particularly significant since it reveals the conception of the lay professor held by at least one type of clerical administrator. The lay faculty member "serves" the school's religious order rather than working with it as a partner, and his chief virtue involves not intellectual competence but the ability to serve with "quiet loyalty." [9] The identification of the university as a "family," moreover, is probably the single most familiar platitude still favored by older clerical administrators and may also be the most harmful. It is this familial conception of the academic community that is largely responsible for that narrow intramural concern some observers have seen as characteristic of Catholic higher education. Thus David Riesman has noted the frequency with which one encounters "Catholic professors whose identifications were with the Church or their order or even diocese rather than with their intellectual discipline or with the academic fraternity at large." Moreover, John Donovan's *Academic Man in the Catholic College* [10] finds that cordiality of personal relationships is one of the chief attractions of teaching at a Catholic school that offsets the lay professor's bitter complaints about second-class citizenship. And Lazarsfeld and Thielens [11] report that faculty at denominational colleges tend to stress "close social ties, belief in authority, and distrust of change" as opposed to the stress placed by professors at private and state colleges on "personal success and achievement and on intellectual values."

One consequence of this view of the university as family, then, is an emphasis on personal relations at the expense of intellectual standards, with the result that the ability to wait cautiously for the promptings of clerical au-

---

[9] A similar view can be found in the position of the administration of the San Diego College for Women (Catholic), which cited a "master-servant" relationship in the California labor code as a partial basis for its justification in dismissing two lay instructors (*National Catholic Reporter*, May 11, 1966). — Ed.

[10] (New York: Sheed and Ward, 1964.)

[11] Lazarsfeld and Thielens, *The Academic Mind.*

thority (seen from an administrative point of view as "prudence") may be more important for the lay faculty in the achievement of promotion and other rewards than any professional or intellectual attainments. The danger is that officials can sometimes forget the public function of a university. That is, they can forget the university's role as something more than a storehouse and dissemination point for knowledge. They can fail to see the university also as guardian of free inquiry and free speech, as critic of its time, its society, and itself, and, most importantly, as defender of the right of its professors to profess.[12]

I have here written at some length about the manner in which the attempt to apply a religious sense of obedience to the life of lay faculty and students at the Catholic university can result in curtailment of intellectual development and personal freedom. But there are a variety of other ways in which, at such schools, notions appropriate for the conduct of religious life impinge upon the intellectual activities of the lay personnel. There is, for example, the vexing problem for the clerical administration of the Catholic professor who becomes divorced. Frequently, the result of divorce is dismissal or, at best, a clouded future career for the lay professor involved. It is difficult to see how any religious principle can justify the firing of a professor because of divorce or other personal or religious problems. One can hardly defend such action on grounds of fear of "scandal" to the student body in an age when divorce is a fact of everyday life widely accepted by the secularized society in which the student lives and when, indeed, a large number of students on the Catholic campus may be non-Catholics who find no serious evil in divorce. Dismissal action as a result of divorce becomes all the more serious, though, when the clerical administration, for fear of losing status in the secular intellectual world, attempts to disguise its action as one based on academic grounds. The nominal Catholic on the lay faculty who gets a divorce or marries outside the church, discovers that his employment has been terminated because of "future needs of the department," and then becomes a bitterly anti-Catholic spokesman in his better paying job at the state university, is not an entirely unfamiliar figure in academic life.

But encroachment of standards of religious conduct into one's professional conduct can also be a problem for the convinced Catholic. For many lay professors the availability of the sacraments, the faculty retreats, and the Lenten lecture series may be among the chief rewards of teaching on a Catholic campus. Others, no less devout, may regard it as a matter of integrity to *separate* personal religious life from professional life; that is, they may be fearful about the possibility of connection between career advancement and their public participation in religious services conducted by their employer at their place of employment. Given the "family" approach to university life

---

[12] The reader may be interested in the cover story on professing professors, in *Time*, 87 (May 6, 1966). — Ed.

favored by some clerical officials, though, the latter professor may occasionally find himself at a certain disadvantage in competing for administration-dispersed perquisites, particularly when his competitor is another professor who, through no conscious design, may have come to be regarded by his employers as "a wholesome Catholic influence."

Related to the "obedience problem" is a certain lingering intellectual mediocrity that many observers have seen as characteristic of Catholic colleges. The Catholic administrator with a scholarly reputation is an extraordinarily rare commodity; and it is no surprise to find a priest academic vice-president with no earned doctorate, no publications, and no recent teaching experience exercising final authority over all appointments, promotions, and research grants on the Catholic campus.

An encouraging development, however, has been the growing tendency of religious orders in recent years to place Ph.D.-holding priests in positions of authority at their colleges and universities, a policy that has resulted in closer cooperation between administration and faculty. Too often, however, the appointment of a priest-Ph.D. to an administrative post is a matter of concern for tone or image rather than being an indication of the order's attempt to enrich the intellectual life of its school. Sometimes the clerical official with a doctorate will not have arrived at his administrative position as a result of scholarly attainments reached after his graduate studies but, on the contrary, will have first been selected for administrative rank and then sent to graduate school to earn a Ph.D. Thus it is not uncommon to see a priest appointed dean or president at a Catholic university within a year or two of his receipt of the doctorate. For example, in 1960 when I completed Ph.D. work at a state university, there were about six priests completing doctoral work on the same campus. Today, while most of my lay classmates are at the assistant professor level, my six priest-classmates include two presidents, two deans, and one departmental chairman. That the clerical official with Ph.D. will not be characterized by a scholarly reputation is further made likely by the fact that, having spent so many years in preparation for ordination, he will be ten to fifteen years behind in professional experience as compared to the lay Ph.D. of the same age in his field.

Another noteworthy aspect of the trend toward more priest-Ph.D.'s in administrative posts is the difficulty such priests, feeling a dual loyalty to both the order and the professional academic world, will encounter in dealing with the rigidly order-centered older clerics who staff their boards of directors. With the transition from the older, non-academic priest-president to the new, more scholarly priest-president there often comes not only a change in administrative style but also a certain blurring of the lines of administrative authority. For example, recently at one large Jesuit university a new priest-president with an Ivy League doctorate was selected to replace an old guard president who had served for twice the maximum length of tenure allotted for such an office under the Society's regulations. The faculty looked forward eagerly to long-awaited administrative reforms, but it was soon discovered that the former president, considerably more adept at order politics than his scholarly replacement, was to assume the newly created office of chancellor. With the creation of this new post and with the continued influence of the ex-president-now-become-chancellor on the order's higher officials, the extent of the new president's authority has become a question mark. The lines of command have become thoroughly confused at the school, and, instead of anticipated reform, the school is now witnessing a cautious regrouping of coalitions.

Nevertheless, the growing complexity of university administration in the age of Xerox and IBM may in the future cause universities to give more consideration to executive capacity than to scholarly reputation in choosing their top officials. Indeed, one already hears of graduate schools offering doctorates in university administration. Such a future trend would bode no particular ills for the nation's leading secular schools; at most of these there are democratic institutions guaranteeing wide-scale faculty participation in administrative decisions. But at Catholic schools, fundamentally administration-centered and generally deficient in machinery for faculty participation in policy decisions, the advent of the computerized, nonacademic administrative official might have disastrous effects on the school's intellectual life.

Aside from the complex question of the academic background of its administrators, another serious problem contributing to the stunted intellectual growth of American Catholic universities is the whole question of academic honesty. In my own teaching experience, at a state university and at a Jesuit university, I found considerably more cheating at the Catholic school, although it would, of course, be unfair to speak about Catholic schools in general on the basis of this limited experience.[13] Yet many of my friends who have taught at both Catholic and secular schools have had the same experience. Indeed, one friend who left a state university to take up a departmental chairmanship in a Catholic school was shocked during the first final exam period at the new school to discover that students had actually entered his home and searched for examination questions. At another Catholic university, where a large proportion of the student enrollment is religious, many of the anecdotes of alumni folklore have to do with the way in which nuns' habits can be employed to conceal crib sheets and other illicit exam aids.

But I am not arguing that the student at the Catholic school is personally less ethical in this matter than his counterpart at the state campus. What we are actually dealing with are two different philosophic outlooks on the whole question of academic honesty. At the southern state university where I taught

[13] The alert reader may recall the results of Robert McNamara's research, which would support Mr. Kearns' suggestion for two additional (and leading) Catholic universities (chap. 5). — Ed.

the enrollment was largely Baptist and Methodist and many students brought profoundly Calvinist consciences to the question of cheating. Moreover, the fact that the school had an effective student-controlled honor council, before which all cases of cheating were brought, caused the cheater to be regarded with disfavor by his classmates. On the other hand, at the Catholic school where I taught, cheating was generally regarded as a trivial concern, a matter of "venial sin," and although the school authorities maintained rigorous regulations concerning such matters as student dress and dormitory curfews, one could find almost nothing in the school catalog and student handbook about academic honesty. Moreover, given the existence of many detested rules of student conduct, such as those requiring attendance at daily mass and dormitory curfew with bed check by the prefect, cheating was often regarded as a means of getting back at the establishment (in the same spirit, many students would attend the required mid-week masses, at which attendance was taken, but would not go to Mass on Sunday).

Closely related to the problem of student cheating are certain practices in the intellectual lives of the religious orders themselves that tend to narrow the concept of intellectual integrity found on the Catholic campus. There is, for example, the "piety Ph.D.," the granting of an advanced degree to a member of a religious order without requiring those standards of academic achievement usually associated with the degree. For example, a few years ago while carrying out research on my doctoral thesis, I had occasion to read a thesis on a similar subject for which a nun had been granted a Ph.D. in English at one of the nation's largest Catholic universities. Not much longer than a term paper, the thesis consisted of little more than a paraphrase and summary of selected passages from the major biographies of the figure with which it dealt, and it abounded in historical inaccuracies, spelling errors, and tortured grammatical constructions. Although good enough to earn a Ph.D. in English for a religious at a Catholic university, the thesis might well have been rejected as an exercise in Freshman English at other institutions. Certainly it would be terribly unfair to indict the legitimate graduate work done by thousands of religious at Catholic schools on the basis of this one incident, but the fact that we may not yet have fully escaped the era of the piety Ph.D. was indicated this year when a young economics instructor at another Catholic university appealed for aid to the AAUP in a case resulting from a charge of plagiarism. According to his statement, the instructor discovered that the thesis submitted to his department by a member of the order administering the university was plagiarized, and when he brought the fact to the attention of school officials his objections were overruled and he was threatened with economic retaliation.

Yet, as I have suggested, such incidents are no doubt infrequent. Perhaps a more widespread misuse of the university's intellectual function occurs with "the order's luminary," with the careful promotion of the career of a priest-scholar who has already published and has some academic reputation, not for the purpose of advancing knowledge through the priest's scholarly work, but for the purpose of advancing the order's public image. Thus at a school that has a standard teaching load of nine to twelve hours and where research assistants are unknown, the order's luminary may have abundant research and clerical assistance and a considerably reduced teaching load. Not only freed by his religious vows from his lay colleagues' constant concern over mortgage payments and medical bills, he may also find in the order's treasury a perpetual ACLS-Fulbright annuity which enables extensive travel and research during those summer months when the lay professor must engage in extra teaching to repair the deficiencies of his substandard salary.

Now it may be argued that the criticisms of intellectual life at Catholic universities offered in the preceding paragraphs are too pessimistic and fail to take into account the sanguine view many commentators have derived from Father Greeley's recent National Opinion Research Center studies. Of course there may be grounds for cheer in the evidence that more Catholics are likely to go to graduate school or choose an academic career, that, in other words, Catholics are becoming fully integrated in the nation's academic establishment. I wonder, though, to what extent this rapprochement between academe and the new graduates of Catholic colleges can be interpreted as an enrichment of American Catholic intellectual life. The rapprochement comes about at a time when various social commentators have noticed the emergence of a "new professor," a highly specialized professor with deep technical expertise in a narrow field of scholarly endeavor but with only a tenuous relation to the intellectual life in general. Thus, although a greater number of Catholics may today be going to graduate school and entering academic life, one hesitates to predict that this trend will result, for example, in wider influence and financial stability for *Cross Currents, Continuum*, and other organs of American Catholic intellectual discussion. One might also point to the paradox in the fact that many Catholics are congratulating themselves on their rapprochement with professional academic life at precisely the time when many secular scholars are showing a deepening distrust of the moral basis of professional academic life — a distrust manifested in such recent occurrences as an *AAUP Bulletin* article on "The Moral Professor in the Immoral University" and a report by ten University of California professors on the recent unrest at their school which criticizes administrative immorality, faculty materialism, and the university's general failure to respond to "the moral revolution of the young." According to this report, "A cynic might say that while students are becoming more idealistic, professors are becoming more success-oriented." But perhaps the academic professionalism at which Catholics are now showing a growing talent was best summed up some years earlier in a mural painted by Orozco for Dartmouth College, a mural described by one art critic as showing "skeletons in academic robes surrounding another skeleton giving birth to a stillborn infant wearing a mortarboard."

Another significant factor militating against the intellectual growth of American Catholic universities is the burgeoning image industry on their campuses. Certainly the former newspaperman now occupying the post of "Director of Development and Public Relations" is today a familiar figure at every kind of university, but, in view of that peculiar obsession of many clerical minds with public relations, an obsession that J. F. Powers is fond of satirizing, it would seem that the image-makers may be more active on the Catholic campus than on others. Perhaps it is significant that, when two laymen were elevated to vice-presidencies at Georgetown — apparently the first laymen ever to occupy positions of such eminence in the university's structure — they were chosen not from the academic world, but from the fields of public relations and fund-raising. Further evidence of the university's obsession with public relations is the great deal of time and money spent in promoting its anniversary year project. As one student publication put it, "During the 175th Anniversary celebration, the Anniversary House brought distinguished leaders to the campus, not primarily to produce an intellectual dialogue with the students, but to produce an image."

Obviously such attention to image- and fund-raising is necessary, particularly at a time when so many Catholic schools have their backs to the wall as a result of competition from the tax-supported universities. But the chief danger of such image consciousness is that it gets in the way of the real function of a university — it substitutes an empty Orwellian "newspeak" for the vocabulary of honest debate, it places a premium on appearance at the expense of substance. During the Georgetown anniversary year, for example, professors were exhorted to attend a special anniversary concert to uphold the university's "cultural image"; a Poverty Conference that brought Gunnar Myrdal and Michael Harrington to the campus was held at the same time that the university's largely Negro housekeeping staff was being paid $1.05 to $1.15 an hour; and a "Freedom and Man Conference," featuring John Courtney Murray and Hans Kung, was held during the same semester that faculty members were protesting the dismissal of a colleague who, they believed, had been fired for publishing criticism of university policies.

Perhaps the most injurious effect of this image consciousness at Catholic universities, however, is the way in which it stifles open debate. Madison Avenue long ago learned that controversy does not sell bars of soap or automobiles. Thus since 1962 Georgetown has witnessed: an administration-issued threat of dismissal against Young Democrats who wished to picket in protest against the appearance of Madame Nhu on campus; the refusal to allow Young Republicans to hold a Goldwater rally on campus; the suppression of an anti-civil rights rally held by student conservatives; and the refusal to allow students from outside the sponsoring club to attend a campus lecture by a representative from the Soviet Embassy. One wonders how these limitations on controversy and social action can be squared with the words of Pope John in *Mater et Magistra*:

> No Christian education can be considered complete unless it covers every kind of obligation. It must therefore aim at implanting and fostering among the faithful an awareness of their duty to carry on their economic and social activities in a Christian manner . . . formal instruction, to be successful, must be supplemented by the students' active cooperation in their own training. They must gain an experimental knowledge of the subject, and that by their own positive action. . . . Knowledge acquired in this way does not remain merely abstract, but is seen as something that must be translated into action.

Nevertheless, in commenting on these instances of repression of the students' instinct toward social involvement, I do not wish to obscure the vast improvements recently made in this area at Georgetown. Between 1963 and 1965, the University Community Action Program, a type of city-wide Peace Corps, made tremendous accomplishments, enlisting over 600 students in a variety of programs ranging from settlement house work to tutoring for high school students in underprivileged neighborhoods. But here again fear of controversy is involved, for although UCAP has engaged in extensive good works, it had been rather wary of participation in more activist civil rights work, such as picket lines, sit-ins, and similar forms of protest. In other words, the emphasis has been on works of charity rather than works of justice. Moreover, it is clear that the work of UCAP is to be aimed strictly at off-campus projects. When, at the original organizational meetings for the group, it was suggested that the organization might also be concerned with problems on campus, with the wage scale paid the university's predominantly Negro laboring staff, with the holding of the annual faculty picnic at a segregated beach, or with complaints by CORE members about the number of residencies available at the university hospital for Negro doctors, the group's Jesuit advisor objected that this was an essentially "negative" approach.

Combined with the public relations mentality as a barrier to open discussion is the underlying assumption of many administrators that public criticisms amount to a traitorous "going outside the family," even though one often finds that Catholic schools lack faculty senates, grievance committees, employment contracts, and other machinery that would enable professors to air their criticisms inside "the family" without fear of retaliation. Underlying the state of affairs is the assumption that the university's functions are essentially private and the professor's responsibilities end with a reasonable competence in his own specialized field. Ironically, though, the same administrators who talk about the university as a family and who see the professor's chief moral virtue as "quiet loyalty" are often most outspoken in regard to the university's right to financial support from both government and business community because of the "public service" the university performs.

Another factor inhibiting clear vision by the priest-administrator is the very structure of the school he administers. The absence of democratic machinery through which honest dissent may be heard will sometimes result in a courtier system under which the administrator will be told only what hangers-on and favor-seekers believe he wants to be told. Insulated from contact with reality, the priest-administrator may develop a certain defensive aloofness, a "siege mentality" under which all criticism is viewed as a challenge to authority. As a result, minor complaints that might have been settled amicably through open discussion have a way of mushrooming into major grievances. Recently, when Georgetown officials announced a new tuition increase, many students were angered not so much by the increase itself as by the abrupt manner of the decision and by the administration's unwillingness to engage in preliminary discussions of the need for an increase. What might have been an opportunity for candid dialogue on the university's financial problems with future alumni contributors became instead an occasion for the exchange of bitter criticisms. Items in the student newspaper speculated on the possibility that tuition funds might be siphoned off for Jesuit activities outside the university, and the College Student Council requested that the university's business structure be publicly examined by a business efficiency agency. Replying to a student newspaper editorial supporting this proposal, one lay dean spoke a profound truth when he claimed: "I regard your editorial as an attack on the Jesuits . . . if I were not happy with the Jesuits, I would not be here."

But if the siege mentality exists, a large part of the responsibility for its existence lies with the lay members of the campus community. Too often the lay professor can settle into a general cynicism toward all administrative actions. He may prefer the safety of private backbiting and subterranean hostility to the risk of public criticism and debate. In such an environment the clerical administrator may become the object of unfair and sometimes outrageous criticisms. For example, some of the folklore of faculty-lounge gossip at one Catholic university concerns: a student who was forced to submit to lie detector tests when he was suspected of destroying university property during a protest demonstration held on campus; the wife of a young faculty member who committed suicide during a lengthy faculty-versus-administration battle over her husband's dismissal; the priest-administrator who was committed to a mental institution after an attempted rape of a student, while his would-be victim was driven to a mental breakdown as a result of threats from other clerical administrators concerning the retaliation that would follow should she ever make the story public. That such brutal slanders can be gleefully exchanged and often believed demonstrates that failure of communication on the Catholic campus is not entirely the responsibility of the administration. And the fact that grievance against the administration can sometimes find such vicious outlet explains why the administration will have difficulty in distinguishing legitimate complaints from unfounded ones, why, indeed, it may look upon any criticism as part of a continuous guerilla warfare carried out by the faculty against the administration.

But if underground lay criticism on the Catholic campus is sometimes spiteful or unfair, it is clear that such irresponsibility is only encouraged by the fact that some clerical administrations will accept no public criticism, whether responsible or irresponsible. The difficulties to be encountered in bringing about in Catholic academic life a general acceptance of the right of the professor to public criticism of his institution and its policies may be gauged from a recent public statement by Pedro Arrupe, S.J., Superior General of the Jesuits and director of one of the world's largest teaching orders:

> I am strictly opposed to any criticism of the Church. If reform should be made, this will be done by the duly constituted hierarchy. . . . It is intolerable that any defect of the Church, however real, should be broached publicly by individuals or groups, regardless of the good will they might have. . . . If the person who is critical is intelligent, he will be understanding and see that the best solution will be either to keep silent and wait . . . or meekly bring the defects to the knowledge of the proper authority.
>
> Cheap coffeehouse criticism accomplishes nothing. The Church will provide in the manner and at the time it deems proper. One should never undertake criticism on one's own. The only thing that can result from criticizing is the creation of a climate of confusion, and the obstruction, if not paralysis, of the work of the Church in behalf of all.

Thus one of the most disturbing aspects of my case at Georgetown was the fact that the administration consistently refused to reply to appeals ranging from student petitions to a public letter by a lay assistant dean, calling upon it to acknowledge the right of faculty members to public criticism of university policy. Of course, the president and executive vice-president insisted that my critical articles had nothing to do with the dismissal. On the other hand, the dean admitted to a departmental representative, as reported in the Washington *Post*, that he had voted for dismissal because of the articles; the assistant to the president contended in a letter to *Commonweal* that the dismissal was justified because my articles created an inaccurate impression of conditions at Georgetown and the Jesuit Regent delivered a sermon in the university chapel attacking those lay professors who, through publicly criticizing conditions within the university, go outside the family and thus violate their first moral duty of quiet loyalty.

Related to this unwillingness to acknowledge the right of criticism is a certain "credibility gap" — as in the resort to rhetorical evasion and buck-passing — surrounding the whole administration response to the case. Thus my dismissal notice was not issued in the middle of the academic year, as prescribed by the *Faculty Handbook*, but was sent by the academic vice-president only after the close of the academic year, when students and faculty had dispersed and the chances of campus outcry would be minimized.

Further, the academic vice-president complained that I had been "uncooperative" in not coming to see him for a discussion *after* I had received his dismissal letter. The rector contended that in appealing to the ACLU I had gone outside the university family, even though the appeal was made after the dismissal letter had turned me out of "the family." Although the case dragged on for over eight months from initial "clerical error" in salary to administration rejection of the tenured faculty's appeal for reinstatement, a few weeks after the rejection the executive vice-president delivered a Law Day sermon on the theme that justice delayed is no justice. When the rector's letter rejecting the recommendation of the committee of tenured men finally came, it arrived a few days before the convening of an anniversary year conference on "Freedom and Man." Far from noticing any irony in the conjunction of the two events, University officials accused me and my departmental colleagues of further "disloyalty" in not withholding public comment until after the conference.

Despite the extraordinary strain on credulity sometimes involved in the arguments set forth in defense of administrative policy at Catholic schools, particularly in disputes over academic freedom, I would hesitate to suggest that we are dealing here with willed mendacity or duplicity. Rather, what is involved is a lamentable inability on the part of some order members to see clear-cut moral issues, much less become involved in them, where "loyalty" and internal harmony of the order are at stake. In large part, this clerical myopia may result from a don't-rock-the-boat philosophy that, according to Michael Novak, is inculcated as early as the seminary training period:

> One of the chief characteristics of seminary life is the almost indiscernible but ever-present threat which places immense psychological power in the hand of the superior. He can refuse to ordain, and the seminarians know that. Consequently, many early begin a lifelong habit of "biding their time." They will become reformers when they get into a position of authority; meanwhile, they will keep their noses clean. They make themselves as untroublesome as possible in the eyes of authority. Thus psychological rewards go to the docile, the reliable, the orderly. "The perfect seminarian" can be a cipher, with talent, an affable manner, and an inoffensive piety.[14]

[14] Michael Novak, "Post-Seminary Thoughts," *Commonweal*, 83 (October 8, 1965), 10.

But, regardless of its causes, this clerical myopia, the resort to rhetorical evasions, general lack of candor, and sometimes even deceitful stratagems, is clearly one of the most corrosive factors at work in Catholic higher education. Who can resolve the paradox of deceit as an instrument of authority at an institution avowedly dedicated to the service of Christ? Who can measure the effect of such policies on the minds of lay faculty and students?

I see in re-reading the earlier sections of this essay that I have presented a rather pessimistic, perhaps captious, view of Catholic education. No doubt a considerable part of this picture is colored by my recent experiences at Georgetown, experiences not necessarily characteristic of Catholic higher education in general. I am aware that, although a clerical knee in the groin may provide one with a unique experience, the experiencer is not in the most balanced of positions from which to make observations. I realize, too, that criticisms of Catholic education written from the relative sanctuary of a secular campus can not be expected to carry the same conviction as criticism written from the highly vulnerable position of one holding a job at a Catholic school.

Moreover, it would certainly be unfair to stress the questionable conduct of a handful of frightened Georgetown administrators without acknowledging the support shown by so many students and faculty members. There were, for example, the general petition by the English department faculty, the resolution by the committee of tenured English faculty, the resignations in the department, the letters to the editor from professors in other departments, the editorials and letters in various student publications, the 1,200-signature student petition, the Student Council's unanimous vote of censure against the administration, and the vote by the same council to give me a special award. Perhaps more significant was the support shown by many Jesuits: the invitation to speak to Woodstock (although issued some time before the dismissal), the wide distribution of the critical articles on the Georgetown campus by a Jesuit who paid for reprints out of his own pocket, the action of one Jesuit who helped gather signatures for the student petition, the willingness of a few Jesuits to sign protest petitions, and the many apologies for the dismissal received from Jesuits at Georgetown and other schools. In considering any criticism I have made of Georgetown, then, one will have to remember that the indignation shown by students and faculty at that university over an infringement of academic freedom probably far exceeded the indignation one might anticipate in response to a similar case on many secular campuses.

Although Georgetown has still not adopted administrative procedures in regard to nonrenewal cases and in other areas that would be commensurate with standards of academic freedom as generally defined by the AAUP, the Jesuit administrators at the university must be congratulated for the progress toward reform they have recently made. Many of the abuses I pointed out in earlier critical essays have since been corrected. Today faculty members are given a few months' advance notice of their next academic year's salary, whereas in the past they had to wait for their first paycheck in October to learn what income their families would have to live on for the next nine months. Written employment contracts are now issued to the faculty, and although no general consultation of the faculty was involved in drawing up the contracts and although they failed to provide for grievance machinery or to meet AAUP requirements on notification of nonrenewal, they are a beginning. The problem of segregated facilities for the annual faculty picnic was resolved by federal and state civil rights legislation, but it was clear that the university was already moving toward the use of unsegregated facilities. Most significant of all, however, is the fact that a committee has been set up to study plans for creating a faculty senate. It is clear, then, that although public criticisms of administration policy by the faculty are not tolerated, such criticisms, if they result in sufficient outside pressure, can effect reform.

It is clear, too, that other general changes in Catholic college and university life are now being brought about by current economic trends in the academic profession. Today the Catholic university finds itself in a tight economic squeeze resulting from the growing affluence of the tax-supported schools with their expanding physical plants and increasing faculty salaries. In some respects, this financial pinch will cause problems of academic freedom. The clerical administration desperately seeking alumni contributions is not likely to take a kind view of the "disloyal" lay professor or student editorialist who criticizes official policies during an anniversary year fundraising drive, and the lay fund-raisers and public relations men and their computers brought in to advise the administrative "family" at a time of financial crisis will not always be the most sensitive guardians of academic free speech. On the whole, though, I believe the financial strain will result in more benefits than problems for the lay professor. The Catholic college competing with better-endowed state and private schools as prospective employers of the young Ph.D. will be less able to afford the luxury of administrative policies that alienate prospective lay faculty members by relegating them to second-class citizenship. And this trend will be further accentuated by increases in the already large ratio of lay faculty to clerical faculty at the Catholic school — a ratio which already is as high as thirty to one in some departments.

Yet there are still many factors, such as the nature of the rank and tenure committee at the Catholic school, that will work against progress. In *The Community of Scholars*, Paul Goodman has noted that the whole tenure system at American universities is designed to reward conformity and caution.[15] If this condition holds true for American universities in general, then

[15] Paul Goodman, *The Community of Scholars* (New York: Random House, 1964).

the reactionary effects of the tenure system are likely to be even more emphasized at the Catholic university, since, when tenure is not directly controlled by the clerical administration, it is usually placed in the hands of an administration-appointed committee. Rarely does the faculty on the Catholic campus have a voice in selecting the tenure committee.

Aside from the tendency of the tenure committee to perpetuate its conservative mentality in the faculty by preferring cautious or "prudent" professors for permanent positions, a further factor inhibiting reform on the Catholic campus will be the wary attitude toward change held by many older lay professors. It is only in recent years that the Catholic college has begun to emerge from under the cloud of the ghetto complex and to pursue genuine intellectual excellence. Thus some older lay professors may represent a lingering Holy Name Society mentality in the faculty: they may resent the tendency of younger faculty members to feel a higher loyalty to their academic discipline than to the religious order which writes their paychecks. Without doctorates or publications, they may manifest an opposition to change which arises partly from a realization of their own limited marketability. Indeed, the older lay faculty will sometimes be more conservative than the clerical administration. For example, the vigorous young Jesuit academic vice-president at one midwestern university complains that the faculty senate he helped establish has not gone far enough or fast enough in effecting reform because a serious mistake was made in limiting its membership to full professors. What is really in question here, however, is not whether reforms will come to the Catholic campus, but just how soon these reforms will come.

In a variety of other directions one sees evidence that reform is coming, and coming fairly soon. The emerging religiously affiliated university seems to be high in the priority of concerns of the AAUP, perhaps second only to the southern university with its racial and political problems. Recently the association established a special committee to consider the peculiar problems of denominational institutions, whereas another association committee designed to deal with the unique situation at St. John's University is already at work.[16] It is a sad commentary on the state of the church in America, however, that the AAUP has in the past generally concerned itself with denominational schools in terms of how normal concepts of academic freedom might be limited at these institutions in order not to conflict with their religious regulations. Nevertheless, today the problems of the "family" have become concerns of the wider academic world.

But should the coming reforms in Catholic higher education be brought about mainly through outside pressure from professional educational associations and through inexorable economic developments within the academic

[16] Mr. Kearns wrote this chapter prior to the Report of the Committee in the *AAUP Bulletin*, Spring, 1966, and the vote of censure at the national AAUP Meeting in Atlanta in late April, 1966. — Ed.

life, then we will face another tragic loss of opportunity in the American Catholic church. Given the fundamental concern of the gospels with freedom, the wide-ranging norms of social justice established by the encyclicals, and the new spirit of relevance set in motion by the Vatican Council, there is no reason why American Catholic universities should not only reform themselves but also assume a role of leadership in securing civil liberties and economic justice for the academic community.

Shortly after being fired by Georgetown, I took up duties as a Fulbright Lecturer at a Scandinavian university. Ironically, although Scandinavia is often grotesquely characterized in American Sunday supplements as the land of suicide, sexual license, and general godlessness, the guarantees of human dignity for professor and student seem to be light years in advance of those on the American Catholic campus. Here, for example, there is an academic senate in which the lower-ranking faculty has proportional representation. The rector, the highest-ranking university authority, is elected by the faculty from the faculty. Moreover, a detailed budget for the university is published, just as are faculty salary rates, and tenure generally is automatically attached to an appointment without the six years' waiting period of the American school. Furthermore, appointments and promotions to higher rank are decided by a board of scholars representing several Scandinavian universities. This democracy extends to student life too, since students are represented in individual departments by their elected *tillitsmann*, a type of "grievance man" with responsibilities similar to those shared by the *Ombudsman* in Scandinavian parliaments or the Parliamentary Commissioner for Administration in Britain's government. Similarly, the student union owns and operates dormitories, bookstores, and a variety of other services, thus freeing the university from the *in loco parentis* problem that plagues the American school.

But if Catholic universities are someday to play a leading role in securing and guaranteeing academic freedom and economic justice in American academic circles, then we will have to give close attention to the strategy through which this position of leadership is to be achieved. In recent years there has been a drift toward the secular in discussions of what to do about the Catholic universities. At first, one heard demands for a voice for the lay faculty in administrative decisions, then one heard talk of lay control of the university, and today one hears considerable discussion of the secularization of Catholic colleges and universities. It would seem that the more vigorous the rear guard action put up by the clerical administration, the more far-reaching grow the reforms proposed by the critics. Perhaps, though, this last explanation, "secularization," provides the most sensible answer. It was only after they abandoned their sectarian identification that universities such as Harvard, Yale, and Princeton achieved intellectual greatness. Whether we like the fact or not, in America the denominational identification of a university has generally meant intellectual mediocrity. Further, secularization of the American Catholic colleges and universities would not be without benefit for the church at large. Such a move would free thousands of religious for missionary work or for work in houses of study on secular campuses at a time of decreasing religious vocations. It would also make available vast sums of money for this work. Indeed, the many men and women who joined religious orders because they felt a vocation to the religious life, although they did not necessarily have a concomitant vocation to the academic life, might find an enrichment of their spiritual lives through work more closely associated with gospel injunctions. A further, and not inconsiderable, benefit would be the fact that the church would be disburdened of the scandal of intellectual mediocrity, academic intolerance, and economic injustice frequently associated with Catholic schools.

But "secularization" of the schools would mean a great deal more than merely adding up the financial costs or weighing the benefits against the disadvantages. It would mean a severe testing of the maturity of American Catholicism. It would mean that the religious orders would have to overcome pride of tradition and establishment. More than that, it would mean facing up to questions about the directions and relevance of the order in the modern world, questions frequently left in abeyance because of the great deal of time and labor required in just keeping the order's inherited educational establishment functioning. In *Protestant-Catholic-Jew*, Will Herberg argued that Catholicism is today a full-fledged member of America's triune religious establishment and that it is time for Catholics to abandon the justifiably defensive and selfish posture associated with ghetto status.[17] The willingness of Catholics to emulate many of their Protestant countrymen by voluntarily continuing economic support of denominational-schools-turned-nonsectarian would mean a willingness to make a return to the nation for the great benefits Catholics have received from American society. It would mean, in short, a willingness to help underwrite the cost of the nation's broad educational establishment without motives of sectarian benefit.

The "secularization" of the nation's Catholic schools does not, of course, mean that these schools would have to abandon religion. They could display a greater tolerance than the country's state universities by making courses in theology and religious culture important parts of the curriculum — while making sure that these courses remain strictly noncompulsory. Indeed, the formerly Catholic nonsectarian schools might encourage religious culture by establishing chairs for representatives of Protestantism, Judaism, atheism, and a variety of other beliefs. In the end the formerly Catholic campus might even become a haven of tolerance — for communists, homosexuals, and other professorial refugees from academic middle-class respectability — de-

[17] Will Herberg, *Protestant-Catholic-Jew* (New York: Doubleday Anchor Books, 1959).

manding of its faculty only professional competence and respect for the rights of other members of the academic community.

Although the primary concern of such schools would not be religion, they would not make the mistake of state and private universities which exclude religion from the curriculum. Indeed, it is quite conceivable that, by becoming noncompulsory, religion courses might have a more significant impact on the student. At present, in many of today's Catholic universities, required religion courses are regarded as "Mickey Mouse" or "gut" courses, the intellectual equal of required basic R.O.T.C. courses. Ironically, however, the Newman Clubs at some secular universities sometimes offer opportunity for religious discussion that is considerably more profound than that made available in the religion course on the Catholic campus.[18] As a further benefit, the variety of religious groups on the nonsectarian campus provides an opportunity for cross fertilization between denominations that is not available at Catholic colleges. While I was at North Carolina, the YMCA brought to campus a variety of Catholic speakers, including John Cogley, Michael Harrington, James Finn, and William Clancy. (Yet the YMCA's generosity was met by a letter from the area's Catholic bishop, read in the local Catholic church, which reminded Catholics that the Y was essentially a Protestant organization and warned them of the dangers involved in associating with such groups. The bishop was apparently miffed by the fact that the lay Catholic speakers had not sought his approval before speaking in his diocese.)

More important for religion than the intercommunication of denominations on the nonsectarian campus, however, may be the contact with the secular made available for religion on that type of campus. In reading *Generation of the Third Eye*, Daniel Callahan's collection of essays by "younger Catholic intellectuals" dealing with their personal problems in the modern church,[19] one is struck time and again with the desperate quest by the contributors for honesty in the church, with their admiration for the honesty and relevance in the lives of such agnostics as Camus. Perhaps through its experience on the secular campus, religion will gain a more mature understanding of the idiom required in addressing the modern world. Moreover, Harvey Cox, in a recent essay on the much discussed German theologian, Bonhoeffer, notes that:

> In his early writings he [Bonhoeffer] makes a good deal out of the fact that Peter's confession, the founding of the church, took place not in or around the temple, but at Caesarea Phillipi, that is, on the border of apostasy and paganism. The church always comes into existence, Bonhoeffer believed, where Christ is confessed on the borders of unbelief,

[18] See the contribution of John Whitney Evans in chapter 10.

[19] Daniel Callahan (ed.), *Generation of the Third Eye* (New York: Sheed and Ward, 1965).

doubt and heresy. The church is not at its purest and best in the inner keep of its own spirituality. Its very essence is its engagement with the world.[20]

But secularization, if it comes at all to the Catholic university, will most likely come only after lengthy and bitter debate. An area of deficiency that could be remedied in the more proximate future is the area of economic policy and labor-management relations. One of the profoundest paradoxes of life at the modern Catholic university is the school's growing adoption of twentieth-century managerial techniques in regard to finances (as in the use of IBM office equipment and the hiring of professional public relations and fund-raising personnel), but its continued dependence on paternalistic, mid-nineteenth-century managerial techniques in regard to employee relations. Thus it comes as no surprise that colleges using the most "mod" advertisements in the fall education issues of *America* and *Commonweal* sometimes have the most paternalistic of administrations and react with indignation to the suggestion by a faculty senate of meaningful employment contracts, while at the same time they continue to offer the lowest wages and poorest retirement plans in the profession. Such policies are all the more paradoxical since they conflict so markedly with the whole spirit of economic justice and the principle of subsidiarity laid down in the social encyclicals. The questions of economic justice and the dignity of the employee are also of particular importance to the Catholic schools in that it is clear that, if such schools are ever to play a role of intellectual leadership, they will have to attract professorial talent by offering good working conditions. It is significant that Notre Dame, generally recognized as the nation's leading Catholic university, offers a higher average compensation than any other Catholic school in the country and is one of only three Catholic universities represented in the AAUP's 1964–65 list of approximately 200 American institutions offering average compensations of over $10,000 a year.[21]

Traditionally, the attitude toward change displayed by the Catholic schools has been one of cautious waiting upon developments in the prestigious non-sectarian schools, at least in regard to questions of academic standards and organizational procedures. The young priest or lay professor urging new procedures soon learns that his most potent argument with the administration is the citation of a precedent at an Ivy League university. Paradoxically, this timid waiting for opinion outside the Catholic campus often goes hand in hand with an independence from — one might even say arrogance toward — the opinions of students and lay faculty inside the campus. Yet, given their freedom from pressure by the state legislature, their lack of wide-scale sup-

[20] Harvey Cox, "Beyond Bonhoeffer," *Commonweal*, 82 (1965) 653–57.

[21] Honesty compels the editor to point out that Fordham and St. John's have recently announced new pay schedules that, if effected, would place both institutions above Notre Dame.

port by (and pressure from) business or the foundations, and their general independence toward lay opinion, Catholic schools ought to be in a unique position to tolerate controversy, to try the new and the experimental, and to overcome the pressures toward respectability and conformity generally exerted upon American universities. Ironically, where Catholic schools have manifested independence from outside opinion, it has often been in academic freedom cases, with the clerical administration showing contempt for generally held standards of civil liberties in the academic profession. If only, for example, the cold disdain shown by the order in charge of Mercy College of Detroit toward AAUP censure for their having fired a professor who wrote unwholesome novels could be broadened into an aloofness from the opinion of bluestocking alumni and the local business community.[22]

Having raised this possibility, let me conclude with a few more "if only's." If only those Catholic schools that give awards to J. Edgar Hoover could also give awards to James Baldwin or Paul Goodman. If only Catholic university officials taking public stands against federal funds for birth control programs would also take public stands against social intolerance in the Los Angeles diocese or against government pressures exerted on demonstrators opposed to the administration's Viet Nam policy. If only, in the end, some Fordham or Notre Dame would bring together John Cogley, Harvey Cox, David Riesman, Paul Goodman, and representatives from the AAUP and the AFL-CIO Teachers Union, and ask them to work out plans for a university structure that would be a model of freedom, relevance, and intellectual stature to the world.

[22] See the *AAUP Journal*, 49 (1963), 245–52. — Ed.

The Future of Catholic Higher Education

IX: THE CATHOLIC COLLEGE: SOME BUILT-IN TENSIONS

Paul J. Reiss

What the Catholic college ought to be in the ideal order is a very challenging question. It might generally be agreed that the Catholic institution should have the characteristics of a good college but that this is not enough; it should have some characteristics that make it a Catholic college. Although it is difficult indeed to specify what ideally should be the characteristics of the Catholic college, it can be assumed that there should be some identifiable purposes that distinguish the Catholic college from other colleges and presumably a distinctive organization appropriate to those purposes.

Our concern in this chapter, however, is not with the ideal but rather with the actual characteristics of the Catholic college. As the sociologist is so fond of pointing out, the real usually diverges from the ideal at many points, and often the magnitude of this divergence is considerable. The ideal, however, is relevant as a source of important hypotheses about the real which can be subject to investigation.

The actual organization and operation of the Catholic college has eluded the careful scrutiny of the sociologist and student of higher education. There is some research on the structure of the Catholic college, but the full picture is not available; it is mainly with bits of scattered evidence, impressions, and personal experiences that we must paint our sociological portrait of the Catholic college. It is the intention here to sketch at least the main outlines of the present structure of the Catholic college, emphasizing those critical areas in its organization and functioning that might distinguish it from other schools. Of necessity, this effort will be directed toward pointing out important issues in the organization of the Catholic college, leaving to future research the necessary testing of the hypotheses that shall be proposed.

The college I shall be discussing does not exist. There is no institution that, even in theoretical terms, could be thought of as typical of the nearly three hundred Catholic colleges in the country. Every college will deviate from

Paul J. Reiss was graduated from Holy Cross in 1952, and took his Ph.D. from Harvard in 1960. After serving as a teaching fellow and an assistant senior fellow at Harvard, he became assistant professor, then chairman of the department of sociology, at Marquette University. In 1963, Mr. Reiss became an associate professor at Fordham, where he is now department chairman and editor of *Sociological Analysis*. His articles have appeared in several professional journals.

that which I describe in important respects. Most of all, the small colleges (those with enrollments below 500 students) and those designed primarily for the education of members of religious orders will not be within the main focus of our analysis.[1]

The Catholic college is a social organization as are General Motors, the supermarket, local and national governmental units, a diocese, and the U. S. Army. Social organizations all have certain problems of functioning simply because they are social organizations. These problems are (a) the attainment of the goals of the organization; (b) the necessary adaptation of the organization to its external environment; (c) the internal integration of the organization; and (d) the continuance of the organization's cultural patterns.[2] An analysis of the Catholic college according to the manner in which it deals with these problems should lead us to the main issues in the organizational dynamics of the Catholic college.

It is the main thesis of this chapter that the distinctive manner in which these four organizational problems are handled by the Catholic as contrasted with other colleges is owing mainly to the effort on the part of the church's schools to maintain an integration of education and religion in its purposes and organization.[3] This integration in some form becomes the rationale for a Catholic college. In other words, the Catholic college exists in the United States presumably because it is believed that there should be an integration or at least a relationship between Catholicism and higher education. In the attempt to maintain or develop this integration the Catholic college has established a social organization that distinguishes it from non-church-related colleges.

DIFFERENTIATION IN MODERN SOCIETY

There are a number of particular historical circumstances such as immigration and the proliferation of religious orders that have shaped Catholic colleges in this country. Philip Gleason has discussed such matters in chapter 2. For a complete sociological perspective, it would also be necessary to

[1] This chapter focuses on the Catholic college, rather than on the university. The undergraduate colleges within a Catholic university are, however, considered to be within the scope of our analysis.

[2] The conceptions of organizational problems are similar to the four functional imperatives of a social system of Talcott Parsons; the reader is referred to Parsons' "An Outline of the Social System," in *Theories of Society*, eds. Talcott Parsons *et al.* (Glencoe, Ill.: The Free Press, 1961), pp. 30–79.

[3] The distinction made here between religion and education is an analytic one that is not invalidated by the fact that in the concrete, education and religion as functions may overlap, as is the case in religious education. In this chapter, the educational or academic function shall mean education in secular knowledge. On the concept of differentiation in modern societies see Talcott Parsons, "Differentiation and Variation in Social Structures," in *Theories of Society*, pp. 239–64.

consider Catholic colleges in the context of the increasing differentiation of social organizations from each other, in modern society, and an increasing specialization within each organization.

The history of higher education in the United States clearly demonstrates the progressive differentiation between religion and education. The pluralistic society has demanded this in its public institutions of higher learning, and even in private institutions the trend toward differentiation of the two is the basis of the oft-noted secularization of higher education. Viewing this secularization as a process of differentiation brings into focus both aspects of the process, i.e., while institutions of higher learning became less explicitly religious institutions, as many were at their founding, so also did religious institutions become less involved in conducting higher education; both have become more specialized.

This process of differentiation between religion and education has proceeded to varying degrees for different colleges and different churches. At the present time the variety of forms that the relation between religious organizations and colleges may take is seemingly infinite; it becomes virtually impossible to define the church-related college. This diversity indicates that full differentiation has not taken place, and Catholic colleges are notable in their attempt to resist the differentiation trends, to maintain the integration of religion and education long abandoned by other private colleges. Compared to the diversity of relationships between religious organizations and private colleges, the Catholic college, whether a diocesan one directly under the authority of the bishop, or one operated by a religious order which is also subject to the authority of the hierarchy, is closely integrated with the organization of the church. Catholic colleges do not exist that are only nominally or partially Catholic colleges; there are no colleges operated by Catholics in which the church has only that authority which it would have over a publishing house or another business operated by Catholics.

Despite this formal integration, the process of differentiation is also at work. Many Catholic colleges in fact operate rather independently of the local bishops and religious orders. As a practical matter, many of those in authority in the church realize that they do not possess specialized competence in higher education, nor the time and energy needed to become directly involved in the operation of colleges within their jurisdictions. The typical pressures toward specialization in large organizations have permitted the development of an actual operating independence of the Catholic college from the dioceses and religious orders that own them. The tensions and conflicts — actual and potential — in this area are high, however, as the degree of independence is often a consequence of practical considerations rather than the product of a consensus on principles. Some of these tensions will now be discussed, with reference to the functional problems of the Catholic college as a social organization.

THE ATTAINMENT OF
ORGANIZATIONAL GOALS

A problem for all social organizations is the mobilization and allocation of resources to move toward the attainment of their goals. Since social organizations typically have more than one goal, an initial issue involves the determination of some hierarchy of goals. This issue of priority among a complex of goals is particularly acute for the Catholic college since it is in a state of partial differentiation between secular educational goals and religious ones. One manifestation of the existence of this problem is the effort to solve it through an assent to a principle that denies its existence. Thus the belief that true learning can only take place within a religious context, or that being Catholic simply makes a college a better college, denies in principle that there can be any problem of goal priority or even a valid differentiation between educational and religious goals. Our concern, however, is with the practical order and here the organizational problem remains despite the effort at ideological solution.

The problem of goal priority is further complicated by the fact that an educational or religious orientation each in itself contains a complex of goals. It is important to examine these goal complexes, as well as to analyze the manner in which decisions are made relative to them.

There are a number of separate religious goals that the Catholic college may seek and among which priority problems are clearly manifested. These religious goals include: (a) the maintenance and development of religious practices such as attendance at Mass and at the sacraments on the part of the students; (b) the inculcation of moral principles and ethical behavior patterns; (c) the attainment of an intellectual understanding of religious beliefs; and (d) the development of a commitment to the church and its mission.[4] Although these goals are certainly related to each other, they are also independent and not always simultaneously achieved. An intellectual understanding of religious truth need not be accompanied by approved moral behavior, nor does frequent reception of the sacraments necessarily mean that the student is actively committed to the work of the church.

There appears to be substantial evidence to support a hypothesis that Catholic colleges, during the past decade at least, have shifted the priority of their goals: religious practices and moral training have been given a relatively lower priority, with intellectual understanding and religious commitment receiving higher priority. The greater concern in earlier years with

---

[4] Each of these goals is focused upon the student and thus is involved in the religious education aspect of the college. A college may also seek to be a center for the development of Catholic thought rather than simply an institution for its transmission. This goal, however, pertains more to the Catholic university with an emphasis upon research, writing, and graduate education than to the undergraduate college.

religious practices was reflected in the requirements for compulsory attendance at Mass, retreats, or other religious services. The emphasis on moral education was clear in the content of theology and philosophy courses that stressed ethics and moral guidance. These concerns are still present in varying degrees today, but they are no longer primary. College administrators have relaxed the requirements for religious practice, owing in some measure to student protests that the enforcement of religious practice is not a legitimate goal of the college. Philosophy and theology faculty have also insisted that moral training should not be their main concern. On the other hand, there has been a noticeable effort to provide a more intellectual orientation to the faith. The attempt to give theology courses solid academic standing is part of this trend.

At the same time, there is also an increased emphasis given to religious commitment. This is probably most clearly expressed in the interests of student organizations and the orientations of their moderators. The social apostolate has become influential on the Catholic campus, whether expressed in joining the Peace Corps, the Papal Volunteers, work in a neighborhood settlement house, or more traditionally Catholic organizations such as the Confraternity of Christian Doctrine. These changes in the priorities of religious goals are consistent with changes occurring both in the society and in the church. An emphasis upon intellectual understanding of religion is consistent with recent attempts to achieve academic quality: the rediscovered lay apostolate finds its counterpart in the college. There may also be a growing realization that the goals of moral education and the development of religious practices are more effectively sought at the secondary school level, that colleges cannot hope to achieve much in these areas.[5]

Similar problems of priority among the goals of secular education are found. Here the Catholic college faces the same question as do other schools in assigning relative priorities to education in the liberal arts and sciences and to education that is more career or pre-professionally oriented. Although the goals are not in opposition to each other, the relative attention given to each is at issue. On this matter the Catholic college is subject to conflicting pressures. The long-term commitment of Catholic colleges to classical liberal education is reflected in the curriculum, with more required courses in literature, history, and philosophy and considerably more attention given to the classics than is normally found in other liberal arts colleges.[6] On the other hand, the Catholic students, typically the children or grandchildren of

[5] No attempt will be made here to evaluate the extent to which these goals have been achieved. See Peter H. Rossi and Andrew M. Greeley, "The Impact of the Roman Catholic Denominational School," *School Review*, 72 (1964), 34–51; and A. M. Greeley and P. H. Rossi, *The Education of Catholic Americans* (Chicago: Aldine Publishing Co., 1966).

[6] As Philip Gleason pointed out, this is a reflection of Jesuit influence in Catholic higher education. — Ed.

immigrants, and their parents, have desired an education for a career or profession that will lead to middle-class status. Career education, not humanistic education, is perceived as the avenue to higher social status. While other colleges drawing upon a middle-class population, with students often the children of college graduates, receive support for a liberal arts orientation, the Catholic population until recently has not provided the parents and students who would tend to support much a "non-practical" education. This was well illustrated in the profiles of Catholic universities in the chapter by Father Weiss and in Robert Hassenger's portrait of "Mary College." The reaction of the Catholic college to these conflicting pressures has been to develop professional and pre-professional programs that are probably in themselves more career-oriented than those in other colleges, while retaining in the required liberal arts courses and in the "arts" program a classical humanistic education. Changes in the status of the Catholic population may well leave the Catholic college with this problem in a form little different from that in other colleges.[7]

In addition to questions concerning the relative priorities among religious goals and among the goals of secular education, there is the basic issue of the relative priority of religious vis-a-vis educational goals. We might phrase this issue as the extent to which the organization is a college that is Catholic or a Catholic organization that is a college; it will be listed in the *Official Catholic Directory* among the institutions of the diocese and in the publications of the Office of Education among the colleges of the state. This is the most basic issue reflecting the partially differentiated state of the Catholic college: what is its identity as an organization? Typically the Catholic college does not come to any firm resolution of this problem — perhaps none is possible — but the issue is relevant to almost any important policy decision in the college.

The priority of religious or secular educational goals becomes relevant to such questions as these, for example: should the college join non-Catholic colleges in various endeavors or be related mainly to other Catholic colleges and educational organizations; who should be on the board of trustees, a Protestant business man, a Catholic, or even a bishop; shall the theology requirement be increased or decreased; shall the college seek to match grants for laboratories in the natural sciences or use resources in greater measure for the humanities; is a Catholic faculty appointee to be preferred? At times it appears that a schizophrenia develops over this dilemma, with the college anxious to polish up its secular image when it comes to seeking government

[7] The extent to which the intellectual goals of Catholic colleges are attained is related to the general discussion of the Catholic intellectual life. Cf. John Tracy Ellis, "American Catholics and the Intellectual Life," *Thought*, Vol. 30 (Autumn, 1955); Thomas O'Dea, *American Catholic Dilemma* (New York: Sheed and Ward, 1958); and Andrew M. Greeley, *Religion and Career* (New York: Sheed and Ward, 1963).

or foundation grants or support from the general community. At such times recognition is duly made of the fact that there are non-Catholics on the faculty; that the college accepts students of all faiths; that the whole range of secular subjects is taught; that large numbers of professional and business men have been educated for the nation and the community; that the board of lay trustees includes many prominent citizens, including non-Catholics, and so on. (The reader will recall the examples cited by Mr. Kearns.) At other times, however — as for example, when recruiting students — the Catholic character of the college is played up, emphasizing that the college provides a "Catholic education," that the religious needs of the students are fully met with Mass offered daily on the campus, sodalities flourishing, a good moral education provided, and a social life that provides for the association of the students with girls (or boys) from other Catholic colleges. This Catholic angle is particularly effective in recruiting the girl for the Catholic college that promises a safe environment for turning out the ideal "Catholic lady."

As would normally be expected in such an organization, there is no explicitly established priority between religious and educational goals; each decision that raises the issue is solved on an ad hoc basis. While the issue has been present for years and will undoubtedly remain with the Catholic college for some time, it has become more obvious of late.

In some Catholic colleges the pursuit of academic excellence has meant that the secular academic goals have become dominant. The major criterion for selecting students is not religious but academic promise (although few but Catholics apply); faculty are sought who bring the prestige of degrees from secular universities; resources are directed to the development of science laboratories and libraries; the curriculum is designed to emphasize the competence in a major that leads to fellowships at the better secular graduate schools. All these efforts are directed toward creating an excellent college on the secular model. In fact, secular colleges are often explicitly the model used for particular developments. A question may be raised in this situation about whether religious goals have become secondary. No Catholic college has, in terms of formal organization, "gone secular," as have many formerly Protestant colleges subject to the same forces, but it is clear that in operating policies the secular educational goals have become the important ones.[8] The stance of Catholic colleges of previous decades — that while they may not be excellent academically, they were very Catholic — has become untenable for most today. Postures of academic excellence with secondary attention to religion are in vogue.

The process by which goals are given priority and resources allocated to the attainment of these goals is the organizational decision-making process.

[8] Students react in different ways to this phenomenon. See the contribution of Hassenger and Rauch to this volume.

In the Catholic college, operated by a religious order or a diocese, the style of decision-making has been basically authoritarian rather than democratic. The board of trustees, whether a board with legal authority or a lay advisory board, has not been the focus of power. This has resided in the president appointed by the order or diocese. It is in the power to appoint or relieve the president that the ultimate control of the college lies. The president, in turn, makes all other major appointments, with authority being essentially delegated authority. Because of the concern for adequate control by Catholic college administrators, there has been only the minimum delegation or decentralization of authority required for organizational functioning. Decisions are made in the typically bureaucratic manner according to the appropriate bureaucratic level. (For recent examples, the reader is referred to the Kearns, Leo, and Foster contributions.)

Such a decision-making process does not preclude a wide variety of advisory bodies on every level. Senior faculty may act as the advisors to the department chairmen, and a board of lay trustees as advisors to the president. Catholic colleges have developed these advisory mechanisms to a considerable extent, in recent years, partly as a result of pressure on the part of faculty (and some students) to be heard, but also partly owing to an increased awareness of administrators of the need for informed advice.

There has been considerable discussion of the organization of the Catholic college that, taking the model of the community of scholars, has looked to the possibility of authority resting in the faculty. This has been implemented in the lower levels such as in departments where the faculty is given the authority to devise curricula or to pass on faculty appointments. On the college-wide basis such democratic measures, even when attempted in the form of a faculty senate, meet great difficulty in implementation. As a complex social organization, a college necessarily develops a bureaucratic structure to handle the decision-making process, which cannot be efficiently handled on a collective basis in the college, any more than it can at General Motors or in the Department of Agriculture. Some administrators apparently believe that the greatest usefulness of a faculty senate is that it may serve the important social-psychological needs of faculty to be consulted. Administrators may have to pay more attention to the interests and views of the faculty when there is a mechanism through which they can collectively be expressed, but the appointed administrators may still insist on making all decisions. It does seem, however, that there is presently in the Catholic college more delegation of authority and the use of advisory bodies than in the past, perhaps largely in response to the exigencies of bureaucratic efficiency. If this is so, then the decision-making process at the Catholic college will be little different from that at other colleges, except that most major administrators will continue to be chosen from among the members of a religious order or diocesan clergy.

ADAPTATION

Like other social organizations, the Catholic college faces the problem of adaptation to its external environment. The main focus of this problem is the exchange relationships with the environment through which the college acquires the material and personnel resources necessary for its operation. One exchange relationship involves compensation by the college for services to its operation. The principal aspect of the latter is compensation for faculty, since this represents the major part of the college's budget, but it also includes other expenditures for goods and services.

Compensation to a college comes from a variety of sources: student tuition, contributions of alumni, and foundation and government grants. As this support is actually an exchange for a service being performed by the college, the goals which the college seeks help determine the potential sources of support. In the fulfillment of its educational goals the Catholic college produces for the country and the local community educated people who have an increased potential for contributing to the community.[9] On this basis, support is sought from the general community, whether it be a government-facilities grant for a new library, tuition from parents primarily interested in seeing that their son becomes a physician, or contributions from local business and industrial leaders.

But Catholic schools can also seek support on the basis of their contribution as religiously affiliated colleges. Students and their parents may choose to pay tuition to the college because it will provide a Catholic education, and coreligionists can be appealed to on this basis. There is, in this connection, the claim of some colleges that their graduates are numerous among the members of the hierarchy of the church, the local clergy, or in religious orders. In addition, it may be pointed out that a large proportion of the Catholic lay leaders were educated at a given college. Thus the college may seek support from the Catholic community for services directly to it.

The undifferentiated state of the Catholic college gives a particular cast to this problem of adaptation. In the first place, its religious goals may well be a hindrance to its search for support from the general community and even from foundations and the government. Fortunately for the Catholic colleges, church-related institutions have not been clearly distinguished from other colleges for the purposes of governmental and foundation support and some grants from these sources have been made;[10] occasionally there is

[9] Community in this section does not mean the local geographical community but the people and organizations that represent the college's public, whether local, regional, or national. It is the community toward which the college would direct its public relations.

[10] The recent decision of the Maryland Court of Appeals that state appropriations for St. Joseph and Notre Dame Colleges in Maryland were unconstitutional

also a substantial gift from a non-Catholic. On the whole, however, the Catholic college has had to rely on the Catholic community for its support, whether it be from student tuition or contributions, since non-Catholics are no more inclined to support a Catholic college than are Catholics to support a Lutheran or Baptist one.

Catholics have not, however, provided their colleges with adequate support; they do not even provide the financial backing that Protestant religious bodies provide for the colleges they own.[11] With a few significant exceptions, the Catholic college does not receive organized support from the diocese, nor, with the exception of The Catholic University of America, from the national Catholic community. Nor have Catholic college alumni been notably generous to their alma maters. The main compensation the Catholic community provides for the college in exchange for its services is a desire by parents to send their children to a Catholic college and therefore to pay the higher tuition. For this source of support the Catholic colleges are in active competition with each other for the same students, a competition that becomes deleterious in some localities where the potential students are distributed among a number of colleges, none being able to obtain enough qualified students.[12]

One consequence of the adaptation problems of the Catholic college and the heavy reliance on tuition for support is the steady rise in tuition fees. Since the Catholic college also lacks the endowment necessary to provide numerous scholarships to offset the higher tuition, the result has been that the students at Catholic colleges have begun to come from families of a higher socioeconomic status than previously and higher than that of Catholic students at secular colleges where the less well-to-do Catholics must send their children.[13] The adaptation problem, then, has forced the Catholic college to provide a Catholic education more exclusively for students of middle-class backgrounds. This has in the past been particularly noticeable among many of the Catholic residential women's colleges and in what were formerly commuter colleges that are now becoming increasingly residential. For example, it might well occur at institutions like "Mary College," if residence facilities are expanded.

Another exchange relationship is involved in the problem of adaptation, viz., compensation, especially of faculty, in exchange for their services to the college. Compensation to faculty includes a number of elements in addi-

(June 2, 1966) may throw new light on this problem. The case will be taken to the Supreme Court. — Ed.

[11] Manning M. Pattillo, Jr. and Donald M. Mackenzie. *Eight Hundred Colleges Face the Future: A Preliminary Report of the Danforth Commission on Church Colleges and Universities* (St. Louis: The Danforth Foundation, 1965).

[12] This is discussed at greater length in the final chapter. — Ed.

[13] See Rossi and Greeley, "Impact of the Catholic School," and Greeley and Rossi, *Ed. of Catholic Americans.*

tion to salary and fringe benefits. Faculty may be compensated by the prestige of being on the faculty of a certain college, by prestige or authority of rank within the college, by security of status, or by a satisfaction in contributing to the cause of Catholic higher education (presuming a dedication and commitment to this cause). Every college offers a broad package of compensation with each element given a certain weight by a faculty member or potential member. Catholic colleges of the past, both because of their economic problems and because of their undifferentiated status, have tended to give relatively greater stress in the package to dedication, loyalty, and security, to make up for the lack of economic reward and prestige of the institution. As a consequence, many colleges can point to a number of long-term, underpaid faculty who have demonstrated their loyalty and who are given the security of a status free from competition in their particular disciplines.[14] They may be underpaid, but they are not faced by the competitive, publish-or-perish situation that they might find at other colleges. Higher rank or prestige within the college may also be used as compensation in lieu of professional status and recognition in a professional field.

A more recent tendency, however, has been for faculty to be oriented more toward their fields and their professions than toward the institutions at which they are located. The high mobility of faculty today is an indication of their orientation to their disciplines and research rather than to teaching and institutional involvement. This was seen in the institutional profiles of Kearns and Foster, and even to some extent at Hassenger's "Mary College." The undifferentiated state of the Catholic college presents certain problems in dealing with this situation. As potential faculty who are Catholic and who may have received their graduate degrees from secular universities become more discipline-oriented, they are attracted to the Catholic college only if it measures up to other colleges in terms of salary, teaching situation, research possibilities, and institutional prestige. They may make some adjustment out of a feeling of dedication to the religious goals of the Catholic college, but usually not a great one. The religious goals of the Catholic college are today of reduced value in recruiting the Catholic faculty member, while remaining no less a deterrent to the recruitment of the non-Catholic faculty member. Most Catholic colleges would be more than willing to appoint qualified non-Catholics to faculty positions, but the non-Catholic is rarely attracted to the Catholic college. Thus the Catholic college is increasingly in the position of having to compete with non-Catholic colleges for the Catholic faculty member and of not being able to compete on an equal basis for the non-Catholic faculty member.

[14] This is often the case even when no official tenure is given; as the president of a West Coast women's college put it, in the midst of a dispute over the lack of a policy on tenure at her institution: "Those who have tenure know it." This was apparently sufficient in her view. — Ed.

It should also be pointed out that, in this situation, Catholic colleges are in severe competition with each other for the services of those Catholic scholars who remain, for one reason or another, interested in an appointment at a Catholic institution. The Jesuit institutions, for example, have worked out a gentlemen's agreement, aimed at reducing some of the competition among themselves for the same faculty, but this competition has bid up the price of those faculty willing to accept an appointment at a Catholic college, leading to radical adjustments in salaries and other faculty policies to remain competitive. As a result, the younger faculty are often adequately compensated, whereas the older faculty may be expected to get by on dedication.

Another major adaptive problem of a college is the provision of administrators. It is in this area that the Catholic college is only beginning to realize that there is a competitive adaptive problem involved. Since the major administrative positions have traditionally been filled with members of the religious order controlling the college, there has been no problem of providing compensation by the college sufficient to attract and hold capable administrators. Until recently it has been deemed essential that such positions be filled by religious. In the Catholic universities the need first became apparent for capable lay deans of professional schools. Colleges first perceived the need for technically competent administrators in such positions as registrar, business officer, librarian, director of development, and so on, with the presidency, academic vice-presidency, and academic deanships remaining reserved exclusively for members of the religious order. Qualified and interested personnel for the latter offices have not been numerous, and the compensation required to recruit lay occupants would be considerable. More important, such a move would be perceived as lessening the control by the religious order or diocese over the college. It is apparent that this is beginning to change, however, as dioceses and religious orders realize that they do not have within their own ranks those best qualified to hold these positions, and that to provide the academic leadership needed to allow the college to compete and meet its adaptive problems, it will have to recruit and compensate competitively on the open — or at least on the "Catholic" — market for administrators.

ORGANIZATIONAL INTEGRATION

The attainment of goals and the adaptation of the organization to its environment refer primarily to the external relationships of the organization; the problems of integration and the maintenance of its cultural patterns refer to the internal requisites of the organization. The problem of integration is that of the interrelationships between people and groups within the organization. As a social organization a college develops a set of rules, written and unwritten, that regulate the internal relationships of the organization. These include the delimitation of the authority of various administrators; the rights and responsibilities of faculty, including questions of rank and tenure; student regulations and organizations; and the relationships among faculty, students, and administrators. Those rules that have a formal character may be found in various handbooks and directives, but many more of an informal type exist.

All colleges have problems of internal integration, but the undifferentiated character of the Catholic college gives it some distinctive problems. One is the problem of the integration of the religious order and its members into the total faculty. At times in the past when a large majority of the faculty were members of the religious order, the only problem of integration was that of fitting in the lay faculty who were essentially appendages to the main religious faculty. At the present time the picture is quite different. Religious comprise only about thirty per cent of Catholic college faculties, a decrease of about ten per cent in ten years; they constitute only seventeen per cent of the faculties at colleges for men.[15] Thus the issue may now be more accurately phrased as the relationship of the religious faculty to the total faculty. A college may handle this by having a separate set of norms for religious faculty. The clerical status of a faculty member is taken into consideration in such matters as appointment to administrative office and initial appointment or retention on the faculty. Administrators, whether lay or religious, do not have the same freedom of action with respect to religious faculty that they have with the lay faculty member. With respect to course assignment, promotion, and other matters, however, the tendency appears to be to treat religious faculty officially like other faculty.[16]

The religious faculty, since they normally constitute a residential community in addition to their faculty roles, form an informal subgroup who have closer contact with each other, and who also have greater contact with the principal administrators who are part of the same residential community. Thus while officially religious faculty are not distinguished from other faculty, there is an informal association of religious faculty and administrators that functions as an "in-group." It is for this reason that lay faculty, although in the majority, can still think of themselves as part of the "out-group."[17] They are brought into full consultation on a particular policy question as members of committees or as administrators, but they may often find that an issue has

[15] *Summary of Catholic Education* (Washington, D.C.: National Catholic Welfare Conference, Department of Education, 1962).

[16] Indeed, some orders do not give their teaching members contracts, so they may have *fewer* rights than lay faculty. — Ed.

[17] On the other hand, lay faculty are less susceptible to organized attempts to "get" promising young men who become "too visible" from the point of view of older members of religious orders. The editor knows of several cases where young men destined for high position within their orders were ambushed by less talented older members, usually with techniques putting Machiavelli to shame. — Ed.

already been extensively discussed and shaped by the "in-group." The operation of the "in-group" thus creates certain problems of integration, although it clearly presents certain advantages in the operation of a college not to be found at the non-Catholic college.

The problem of integration is also reflected in the role of faculty members on the Catholic campus. Since the college is attempting to integrate both educational and religious goals, the faculty member is faced with this issue in his own role. The goals of the Catholic college have certainly provided a basis for a role commitment on the part of faculty to both religious and educational goals. The demands of role specialization, however, have hindered the integration of the two for most faculty. The requirements of specialization have led most faculty in the Catholic college, as in the non-Catholic college, to concentrate on their own fields, to offer instruction in those fields and to leave to the theology or philosophy departments — or even more to those directly concerned with student religious life — the pursuit of the religious goals of the college. It is relatively easy for this decision to be reached by the lay faculty member who is likely to view his role on the faculty of the Catholic college as being no different from what it would be at a secular institution. This is not to say that he has no interest in the religious welfare of his students, but his concern is expressed in a way little different from that of a concerned faculty member on a secular campus.[18]

For the religious faculty member the problem is more severe; the potential role conflict is considerable. It is not that his religious and faculty roles are in direct opposition, but rather that competing demands are made upon his time, energy, and interests. For some, the problem is resolved by developing as primary the role of professor-scholar, with their clerical roles perceived as quite unrelated and perhaps even secondary to academic pursuits. For those whose clerical role is kept primary, it is quite likely that academic performance, especially in research and publication, will suffer; one cannot be writing an article in physics while hearing confessions, counseling students, or providing religious instruction in a parish. To overcome the problem of role conflict for the clerical faculty member, role specialization has often been the solution. As a result, there are at the Catholic college the religious religious and the academic religious. Integration of the clerical role with that of a professor without reducing the quality of performance in either is certainly difficult if not impossible to achieve.[19]

Specialization, with its concomitant differentiation of religion from other

[18] It may be that there are latent functions to this, considering the characteristics of today's undergraduates. See R. Hassenger, "Competence, the 'Pro,' and the Catholic Student," *National Catholic Guidance Conference Journal*, 10 (1966), 233–34.

[19] John Donovan, *The Academic Man in the Catholic College* (New York: Sheed and Ward, 1964), refers to this dilemma — which shows up clearly in his data — as "parish or publish."

academic concerns, has also had consequences for the issue of academic freedom, an issue that can be seen as one of the integration of roles. In an ideal order of integration every Catholic college professor in his teaching and research might be integrating religious perspectives with those of his particular discipline. If this was the situation on the Catholic campus, practical problems of academic freedom would be more frequent and severe. As a result, however, of the partial differentiation of religion and education in the Catholic college, religious perspectives do not become frequently involved in instruction in areas other than theology and perhaps philosophy. The Catholic orientation of the college does not usually come into conflict with teaching and research in literature, social science, and the natural sciences. Most professors have no need in their disciplines to raise religious issues except perhaps with respect to some restricted point. A professor can be the same economist, for example, that he would be at another college; the issue of academic freedom does not arise. Even if he were to criticize the papal encyclicals purely on economic grounds, he would probably encounter little, if any, difficulty. On the other hand, if he, as an economist, were to criticize the *religious* perspectives of the encyclicals and indicate that he had no sympathy with the social teachings of the church, then the issue of academic freedom might be raised. The reason why such an issue has not frequently been raised is simply that most economists and other professors do not find it to be within their interests or competence to deal with the question in that manner, and those who do and have an orientation incompatible with a Catholic position do not choose to become faculty members at a Catholic college in the first place. In other words, the mutual selection of faculty and college has insured that almost all those who have joined the faculty do not raise or encounter problems of academic freedom because of the Catholic orientation of the college; the issue simply does not arise as they pursue their particular disciplines in their accustomed manner.[20]

One mechanism through which integration is maintained or disrupted is the allotment of prestige, recognition, and resources to those in different roles. In any college a balance must be maintained among the various departments and interests. The distinctive problem for the Catholic college is that of the relative prestige granted to religious roles as compared to academic roles. The stress on academic improvement has provided greater recognition within the college for academic roles, whether it be for a dean whose students are winning more fellowships, a clerical faculty member who publishes a new book in mathematics, or a student who has attained the Dean's List. In each

[20] In April, 1966, a symposium on "Academic Freedom and the Catholic University" was held at Notre Dame. Rev. John L. McKenzie, S.J., addressed himself to the issue of academic freedom and the priest-teacher. These proceedings will be published by Fides Press, most likely about the same time as the present volume appears. See also P. Gleason, "Academic Freedom," *America*, 115 (July 16, 1966), 60–63.

case academic achievement is recognized and often rewarded financially. It is in this context that recognition for religious roles and activities may be needed to retain an equilibrium. The status of the theology department may be upgraded or a college chaplain or staff appointed or given greater status. When, on the other hand, a dean announces that theology is the "queen of the sciences" and should hold that status at the college, it serves to give greater attention to the religious goals of the college but is not so well received by the biologist or historian who begins to feel that his field has a second-rate status it would not have at other colleges. Thus the process of seeking an equilibrium continues. Although ideally it can be postulated that all secular activity has religious meaning and vice versa, the necessity of giving adequate recognition to each is still a practical problem of integration for the Catholic college.

THE MAINTENANCE OF ORGANIZATIONAL PATTERNS

Every social organization faces the problem of providing for the continuation of its cultural or behavioral patterns. For an organization to continue to exist, it must deal with the question of how the organization, with its particular values and goals, is to be continued. This does not mean that all change must be resisted but that changes and modifications in the organization will be within the same general values and goals. The principal mechanism for the continuation of patterns is the recruitment, retention, and motivation of personnel who are committed to the values and goals of the organization.

With respect to its academic goals, the college must continually recruit administrators and faculty who have the competence and interest to maintain and increase the academic stature of the college if that be its goal, or to increase enrollments, for example, if that be the goal. Since it is quite easy for students to develop among themselves an anti-intellectual culture that is in opposition to the goals of the college and faculty,[21] the college must be successful in turning out students who exemplify the attainment of its academic goals. Such factors as social class background may be of crucial importance here; the vocational orientations of students from first-educational generation families are reflected in the college profiles found for the large, coeducational universities by Robert Weiss.

The Catholic colleges have been about as successful as other colleges in encouraging and improving the intellectual orientations of Catholic college students and faculty; although deficient in the past, they are probably little different today from those of the range of secular colleges.[22] There are as

[21] See Hassenger's summary of the effects of college subcultures in chapter 5.
[22] See *ibid.* for a summary of Greeley's work in this area, and his more recent

great differences in academic orientation among the Catholic institutions as among the non-Catholic colleges, but the general range is undoubtedly very similar.[23]

With reference to the religious culture of the Catholic college, the problem is more complex. The question here is the manner in which the Catholic college continues in some sense to be Catholic. The mechanisms through which this is accomplished must also be primarily the recruitment of administrators, faculty, and students committed to the Catholic values of the college. In the past the Catholic college solved this problem largely through the connection of the college with a religious order that supplied all the major administrators as well as a large proportion of the faculty. With the pressures toward differentiation and the advent of lay faculty and administrators, the problem today is more acute.

Catholic colleges are faced with the problem of recruiting qualified administrators and faculty who are committed to the religious goals of the college as well as to its academic goals, and with the problem of providing continual motivation for them to seek these goals, however they be defined. The question here is not that of considering how many non-Catholic administrators and faculty a college can have and still be Catholic (although it is often phrased in these terms). We can assume that all the faculty do not have to be Catholic for the Catholic orientation to continue, but it would seem necessary for a major portion of the faculty to be Catholic, including those in some crucial areas. Of course, the fact of being a Catholic does not preclude role specialization to the point where a person's religion becomes quite unrelated to his role on the faculty or administration. The real issue is the motivation and interest of the administrators and faculty, whether Catholic or not, in determining and furthering the distinctively Catholic goals and values of the college. Such persons are not easy to find and such motivation is not easy to maintain in the face of the pressures toward specialization in academic roles.

The problem of the maintenance of the Catholic orientation of the college can perhaps best be seen in its relationship to the curriculum and to instruction in the college, which, after all, is the focus of its operation. The integration of Catholicism into the curriculum of the Catholic college has been effected in several ways. All Catholic colleges maintain the requirements that each student must have a certain number of courses in theology and philosophy. The increased importance of the major field as a preparation for graduate and

article with Seymour Warkov, "Parochial School Origins and Educational Achievement," *American Sociological Review*, 31 (1966), 406–14.

[28] This can be seen in R. Hassenger and R. Weiss, S.J., "The Climate of the Catholic College" (Paper read at the 1966 Meetings of the American Catholic Sociological Society, Miami, and appearing in slightly different form in *School Review*, 47 [Winter, 1966], 419–45).

professional study, and the requirements for general education in other areas have created pressures, however, to reduce the number of required courses in theology and philosophy. They generally have a secondary importance in the total program of the student (and, to generalize from the Foster study, little real effect). Theology has been considered of little intellectual value and of minor academic importance by students and faculty alike. The poor quality of the instruction in these fields and the failure in most instances to present material in a manner that convinces the students of their importance for his life and work has not contributed to the integration of Catholicism in the curriculum.

A second mechanism for the integration of Catholicism and education has been the infusion of religious values and perspectives into instruction in other subjects. Through the direct efforts of the professors and through the use of "Catholic" textbooks, an integration of Catholicism and secular knowledge was often attempted. In the natural sciences, however, it long ago became clear that there is little place for the introduction of religious perspectives; there is no great demand for Catholic textbooks in physics, mathematics, or biology, for example, and little concern on religious grounds over the manner in which the professor approached his subject. The presumption was that the instruction in these courses is not different than that at non-Catholic institutions.

In many, if not most, Catholic colleges, the instruction and the books used in the social sciences today are also little different from those in non-Catholic schools. In sociology, for example, aside from the minimizing of examples and illustrations that might be antagonistic to Catholics, and perhaps a greater use of illustrations that have meaning for Catholics, the instruction in many Catholic colleges varies little from that in non-Catholic institutions and the textbooks used are the same. Instructors point out that there is no Catholic sociology. In some Catholic colleges the secularization is not so complete; sociology courses emphasize normative and ethical issues with considerable attention given to the social teachings of the church. In such situations, however, the program is usually deficient from the scientific sociological point of view. The point has now been reached where many faculty members in the humanities and even in philosophy do not see that there is a particular approach that they should take to their subject because it is part of Catholic education.[24] Even when this is not accepted in principle, it is in practice. Not only does the faculty member often not see any necessity to integrate Catholicism with instruction in his field, but specialization has often made it difficult for him to do so. The physical scientist, social scientist, and even the philosopher, then, may not in his own mind have integrated

---

[24] Conflicts between philosophers of "Scholastic" and either analytic or phenomenological persuasion have split many departments, the most notable recent case being at Duquesne, in Pittsburgh. — Ed.

Catholicism with his discipline in any meaningful way. It is unlikely that he will have the ability or interest in doing so in the classroom. He may be more concerned that he not compromise his academic orientation by an attempt to introduce religious perspectives in a way that has been rejected as invalid in the past.[25]

The consequence of this situation is that the integration of religion and knowledge in the various disciplines generally does not exist within the minds of many, if not most, of the faculty, and does not appear in the courses of instruction offered by the individual departments. In the more complete form of this differentiation process (which is being approached in an increasing number of colleges), the student receives an education almost identical to that received in secular colleges, with some required courses in theology, unrelated to his other courses, added to his program.[26] The integration of Catholicism and education that is to represent Catholic education does not really exist in the instructional program and therefore can hardly be expected to occur in the mind of the student.

One pertinent example of the problem is the status of the social teachings of the church in the curriculum of the Catholic college. Owing to the orientation of the faculty and the programs in the various disciplines, neither the sociology, theology, philosophy, or any other department believes that instruction in this area is part of its discipline. To a considerable extent each is correct. The consequence, however, is that Catholic education may very well not include any opportunity for the study of the social teachings of the church. Here one suspects that the demands of education in a differentiated society have created patterns in the Catholic colleges which render it unlikely that the integration proposed in the goal of providing a Catholic education is actually achieved.

The Catholic orientation of the college may also be sought in the extra-curricular lives of the students. We see here that the student culture also exhibits the effects of differentiation. It is clear that for many students the differentiation between their education in various fields and their religion is rather complete. Catholicism can easily be something for Sunday plus the required theology course; their education, however "safe," is greatly secularized. Probably only for a very small minority does a religious perspective pervade the academic life. The same may be said for the organized spiritual life on the campus, where only the committed few are really involved and where the sodality, for example, may take on the role and patterns of

---

[25] Analogous questions have faced the Catholic learned and professional societies. The reason for the existence apart from the general learned societies of a Catholic historical, sociological or philosophical society has not been established firmly in the minds of their members.

[26] Most colleges have or are in the process of reducing required courses in philosophy and theology. This trend will undoubtedly continue. — Ed.

a Newman Center on a secular campus. It is possible that recent liturgical renewals in the Catholic colleges may involve more of the students and faculty and further the religious orientation of the college; but whether more than a minority will be involved remains to be seen.[27]

Our analysis of the cultural patterns of the Catholic college indicates that there is no firm support for the integration of Catholicism and education in either the orientation of the faculty, the courses of instruction, or in the student culture. It may be that the Catholic orientation of the college is continued mainly by the fact that most of the faculty and students are Catholic, even if the orientation of their academic life does not differ greatly from the orientation found in non-Catholic colleges.[28]

CONCLUSION

We have seen that the Catholic college as a social organization is faced with the problems of goal attainment, adaptation, integration, and maintenance of organizational patterns, and that the distinctive ways in which these problems are presented and handled by the Catholic college are related to the attempt to integrate Catholicism and education. This integration has been opposed and often prevented by the tendency in modern society to bring about increasing differentiation between religion and education, a differentiation that is associated with a secularization of higher education. Our analysis indicates that secularization has progressed in the Catholic college to a considerable extent, even though the colleges are still formally controlled by the church through diocese and religious orders and have faculties and student bodies that are almost completely Catholic. Many of these colleges are succeeding as colleges — and this is to be admired and encouraged —

[27] See Andrew M. Greeley, "The Place of Religion," *Commonweal*, 84 (1966), 104–10, and Robert Hassenger, "The Catholic Campus: A 'Christian Community'?" in E. Manier and J. Houck, *Academic Freedom and the Catholic University* (Notre Dame: Fides Press, 1967, 145–61).

[28] One consequence of having an almost completely Catholic student body is the impetus it gives to intra-faith marriages. An opportunity for Catholics to meet Catholics is present on the coed campus and without much additional difficulty it is achieved through formal and informal associations between the students of Catholic men's and women's colleges. This promotion of Catholic marriages as a by-product of the Catholic college is particularly important for the continuation of Catholicism as a distinctive subgroup in the society. It appears that a significant number of Catholics are involved with the Catholic educational institutions for generation after generation, with the same ones sending their children to Catholic grade schools, high schools, and colleges where they often meet and marry other Catholics, send their children to Catholic schools, and so on through the next generation. David Riesman, who read the draft of this chapter, has pointed out that a university such as Brigham Young has a tightly integrated curriculum and extracurriculum, with the result that B.Y.U. students are "overflowing with the spirit of the Latter Day Saints." But difficulties are met when these individuals come out of this environment into the secular world.

but the extent to which they continue to be Catholic is open to serious question. From a long-term point of view, the Catholic college may be seen as moving along the same paths toward secular status which were followed by many church-related colleges before them. In this process the Catholic college may remain or become an excellent college academically and this is certainly good. For it to remain a Catholic college, however, a more solid rationale will have to be developed, and this rationale will have to be implemented with no sacrifice of academic goals.

X. CATHOLIC HIGHER EDUCATION ON THE SECULAR CAMPUS

John Whitney Evans

> The ruling of the society of tomorrow lies principally in the minds and hearts of the university students of today. — PIUS XI[1]

Perhaps nothing has so alerted the American church to the necessity of a new definition for the phrase "Catholic higher education" as the statistics on Catholics in college.[2] A recent study, for example, indicated that, in the fall of 1963, for each of the 366,000 students who entered Catholic colleges and universities, two Catholics enrolled at other institutions of higher learning. This report predicted that by 1985 the present trend would increase the ratio by as much as eight or nine to one. Viewing higher education as it may exist in the United States twenty-five years from now, the observers estimated that only one out of twenty-five students would have any vital contact with the heritage preserved on the Catholic campus.[3]

The American hierarchy have commissioned the Newman Apostolate to carry out the work of the church in the secular campus community.[4] Although the program involves faculty members, alumni, and laymen who serve in consultative capacities, this essay will focus on the students who attend secu-

John Whitney Evans was ordained in 1957 for the Diocese of Duluth. After receiving an M.A. in Church History from The Catholic University of America, he completed his doctoral work at the University of Minnesota. Father Evans has served as a Newman chaplain at Duluth and Ann Arbor, and has written widely on educational history and philosophy.

[1] Pius XI, "Discourse to the University Catholic Action of Italy, December 22, 1935," cited in *Catholic University of America Bulletin*, 31 (October, 1963), 9.

[2] See Richard J. Clifford, S.J. and William R. Callahan, S.J., "Catholics in Higher Education," *America*, 111 (September 9, 1964), 288–91.

[3] *Ibid.*

[4] The term "secular" will be used in this essay in a descriptive, not a pejorative, sense. It is employed as shorthand for "independent and/or non-church-related colleges and universities." Although these institutions generally claim to be "non-oriented as to values," I know that the possibility of and the propriety of this assumption are questionable. I have "taken sides" on the question, but hope that my use of the word does not reflect this "prejudice." Perhaps the pejorative form of the word would be "secularistic." Harvey Cox makes such a distinction.

lar institutions of higher learning and the priests who serve them.[5] It will attempt to describe the magnitude of the educational task that confronts the church in non-Catholic colleges and universities; to point out current developments on the campuses and within the church that are leading Newman in new directions; and to assay certain consequences for Catholic higher education — and, indeed, for the American church generally — implied in these developments.[6] I regret that the reader cannot be offered the findings of extensive, carefully conducted surveys into the situation of Catholics on the secular campus and their relationship to the church through the Newman Apostolate; these do not yet exist. Therefore, I base my presentation and analysis upon my own experience with students in large and small non-Catholic institutions, as well as upon the impressions and interpretations offered by dozens of chaplains and hundreds of students I have visited on campuses from New England to California and Minnesota to Texas.

In the winter of 1966, when the number of Catholics on the secular campuses had already grown to over 900,000, the Newman Chaplains Association detailed the response of the church to these developments. A survey of 1,272 non-Catholic colleges and universities showed that 272 had full-time chaplains and 876 had priests dividing their time between the campus and other duties. Ninety of these campuses were served from fully equipped Newman centers; that is, those comprising chapels, classrooms, offices for administrative and counseling work, libraries, and provisions for seminars and large gatherings. Another 113 universities were supplied with "makeshift" houses. The rest had no facilities of any kind. Compared with conditions in 1955, these figures represented a gain in excess of 100 per cent. During the same interval the Catholic population of the secular campuses rose by 300 per cent.[7]

Statistics, however, cannot adequately suggest the complexity found within the student populations the American church is attempting to influence on non-Catholic campuses. To gain some insight here, one must try to under-

[5] The National Newman Apostolate embraces the following cooperative branches: National Newman Foundation; National Newman Chaplains Association; National Newman Students Federation; John Henry Cardinal Newman Honorary Society; National Newman Alumni Association; National Newman Association of Faculty and Staff. The National Director has offices at the National Catholic Welfare Conference, 1312 Massachusetts Ave., NW, Washington, D.C.

[6] In trying to isolate what most influenced the hierarchy to promote work on the secular campus, a bishop told the writer: "After the war, all of a sudden the large number of Catholics going to secular colleges stood up and hit us between the eyes."

[7] National Newman Chaplains Association, "The Pastoral Role of the Newman Apostolate: A Report to the Bishops of America, 1965," *Newman Apostolate Newsletter*, 2 (Winter, 1966), n.p. (Both available from the National Director, Washington, D.C.)

stand the attitudes these students manifest, first, toward the life of the institutions they are attending and, second, toward Catholicism.

Students presently exhibit three general orientations to the campus and the society it prepares for, and we can classify these as "commercial," "academic," and "alienated."[8] Among the commercial students, the vocationally oriented generally come from the lower-middle and middle classes, whereas those intent upon a professional career come from the middle and upper-middle classes. All are chiefly interested by courses that will prepare them for post-college employment. Some also use their college years to hold jobs or to cultivate business connections through membership in fraternities. The broader social life on the big residential campuses and the recreational advantages of urban settings appeal to them, especially those seeking mates; but increasing numbers of earnest students are entering junior and community colleges where pressures for achievement are sometimes stronger.[9] These collegians do not regard the campus as an intellectual community. The commercially oriented, both because of their background and because of the pressures of the Diploma Society, often regard college primarily as a convenience.

The academically oriented students differ from this group in the importance they attach to the life of the campus itself as a cultural and intellectual experience. Many of them set the acquisition of employable skills on a par with knowledge. Yet this group also includes those who are basically concerned with intellectual affairs. As one might expect, this group is smaller in numbers than the first. But both types of student know in a general way why they have come to college and expect eventually to find some kind of rewarding role in life.

The alienated students comprise, perhaps, ten per cent of college populations and represent several divergent tendencies. The majority are "activists" who scorn both the "greed" of the commercials and the "luxury" of the academics. They want to change the power structures justifying the existence of both, whether found on the campus, in the community, or across the nation. Most of these students seem to come from prosperous, business-dominated families, although a significant number are children of the "Old Left" that was active in the thirties. They avidly read and discuss Mao, scoff at Marx, and revere C. Wright Mills. Although they have participated in headline-spawning demonstrations, an important minority prefer quiet dialogues

[8] Parts of the analysis that follows are based upon Martin Trow and Burton R. Clark, "Determinants of College Student Subculture" in *College Peer Groups*, ed. T. M. Newcomb and E. K. Wilson (Chicago: Aldine Publishing Co., 1966), 17–70; and Ralph Underhill, "Values and Post-College Career Change," *American Journal of Sociology*, 72 (September, 1966), 163–72.

[9] See George K. Malone, "Commuter Campus: Newman Challenge," *U. S. Catholic*, 31 (March, 1966), 26.

and play zealous but unpretentious roles in campus, civil rights, and inner city movements. The "beatniks" are the second type of alienated student. Their nonconformity is based on apathy rather than concern. Although the popular imagination has fixed upon the "woolly ones" as symbolic of the entire category under discussion, the activist students often show a high disdain for the futility of the beatnik posture, but at the same time they accept it as a concomitant of individual freedom. All the alienated appear to be fascinated by something they call "community," however, and though rebellion against the impersonalization of the establishment provides an occasion to achieve a temporary sense of belonging and purpose, the apathetic seem to dabble in euphoria while the activists pursue utopia.[10]

We can summarize this typology of college students by saying that the commercial exploit the campus to enter society; the academic enjoy the campus on their way to society; and the alienated either endure or reject both the campus and society as they presently operate.

Present in each of these classifications, college students who are Catholic exhibit three types of orientation toward their religion. The largest group make up the "quiet." Some of these have simply "had it" as far as the church goes, and "take a faith-leave" for a few years "to give the other side a chance." Others, who have not made so bold a declaration of autonomy, are "regular" practitioners in the sense that they show up at Mass on prescribed days and approach the sacraments when the effort is convenient or necessary. But their relationship to the Newman Center, the chaplain, or the neighboring parish is extremely tenuous — if it exists at all.

A smaller group of Catholic students can be classified as "committed." They live well within the moral and ritualistic limits of Catholicism and show a concern for its intellectual, cultural, liturgical, and apostolic demands. They express their allegiance to the church on the campus in ways that range from regular attendance at social and educational events sponsored by the Newman Center to deep involvement in personal or communal religious and action programs. This group provides most of the student leadership of the Newman Apostolate.

[10] Many articles have appeared on "The New Left." The reader is referred to Michael V. Miller and Susan Gilmore (eds.), *Revolution at Berkeley* (New York: Dell Publishing Company, 1965); Gerald Rosenfield, "Generational Revolt and the Free Speech Movement," *Liberation*, 10 (December, 1965 and January, 1966), 13–17 and 15–21, 23; articles appearing in *Issues*, 3 (Spring, 1965), 1–47 (published by the Publications Commission of the University Church Council, Berkeley); articles under the general heading "Thoughts of the Young Radicals," appearing in *The New Republic*, 153 (December 18, 1965 to March 19, 1966); Samuel Lubell's survey of thirty-six campuses appearing in the *South Bend Tribune*, April 25–30, 1966 and in many major newspapers in April, 1966; and Kenneth Keniston's *The Uncommitted* (New York: Harcourt Brace and World, 1965), are also valuable. So is Tom Kahn, "The Problem of the New Left," *Commentary*, 42 (September, 1966), 30–38.

A third segment of Catholic students might be called the "questing." They prefer to term themselves "Christians," not "Catholics." They reject definitions of sin remembered from catechism days; but they are deeply moved at the sight of personal and social evil. They shun traditional ritual and doctrinal forms; but they long for a union with God and his people. They slight the intellectual achievements of a Teilhard or a Rahner and seem to ignore the statements of the Second Vatican Council, not only because all this seems to be unrelated to their personal predicament, but also, and more precisely, because these statements have about them the aura of "high authority" and represent "establishment thinking."[11]

It would be interesting to know how the commercial, academic, and alienated attitudes present on the campus today relate to this threefold orientation of Catholics to the practice of their beliefs. Some chaplains seem to feel that being a "quiet" Catholic corresponds generally with the "materialism" involved in being "commercial." Others argue that the "committed" Catholics come chiefly from the ranks of the "academic." Some might maintain that the "questing" Catholic is, in reality, an "alienated" student. Yet a moment's reflection shows that many "academic" students are also indifferent to their faith; that a "quiet" Catholic may not have shed his faith but is experiencing a crisis of belief; that where the majority of the "alienated" students denigrate all western religion, the "questing" Catholics seek a new Catholicism; that often the "committed" and the "questing" share common concerns over personal values, updating of the church, and service to humanity; and that some of those "quiet" in a ritualistic sense engage generously in humanitarian enterprises.

Other considerations complicate attempts at analysis. What are Catholic students at secular campuses quiet, committed, and questing about? Presumably, their relationship to the Newman Apostolate constitutes their relationship to Catholicism. Yet the reference points are neither stable nor univocal. Take, for example, the current changeover from clubs with part-time priest-moderators to centers with full-time chaplains. The clubs were largely social,

---

[11] For example, the following statements might well "turn off" this type of student: "Sometimes we prefer to the term of Catholic that of Christian, almost forgetting that, in concept and in reality, the first is intended to encompass all of the second and not always vice versa." See Paul VI, "The Church Must be Catholic" (Address of May 17, 1964), in which the Pope announced the establishment of the Secretariat for Non-Christians. The Holy Father here seems to be speaking, not of a "Romanized Catholicism," but, rather, of an acceptance of all that is human, which includes not only the actual grandeur of mankind and its achievements, but also the recognition of what he terms "a terrible penury, a narrowness" which only an openness to God as He has revealed Himself and communicates Himself through a church, both earthbound and transcendent, can transform. The complete text can be found in Titus Cranny (ed.), *Pope Paul and Christian Unity* (Garrison, N. Y.: Chair of Unity Apostolate, 1965), pp. 91–96.

defensive, and seldom reached anyone who did not join. The Newman Center, on the other hand, ideally attempts to offer a full program of worship and education, to foster an apostolic and ecumenical spirit, and to reach a greater number of Catholics and non-Catholics as well. While some students remain attached to the idea of a club and to the whole system of student-directed provincial and national hierarchies that this entails, most prefer the center and are willing to replace the club with a more generalized type of local board for coordinating a variety of student clubs and programs. (Some break entirely with Newman to form student parishes. — Ed.)

Yet the emergence of the full-time chaplaincy has created a new problem of identification. In the first place, not all chaplains are alike. Some are keenly interested in the intellectual life; others are strongly oriented toward liturgy or social action or ecumenism; a few appear to be frankly "sin-obsessed" or "anti-university." Places that have had a succession of chaplains of differing temperaments and styles have attracted students with similar inclinations — always a minority of the Catholic student population. In another respect, the consolidation of the Newman Apostolate around the Newman Center and its programs has intensified the perennial rivalry between the generations and given it a curious twist. It is not merely a case of some students feeling that the diocese has denigrated the importance of the student organization by setting up and perhaps financing a center. Some students argue that the *Newman Apostolate* is not the same thing as the *lay apostolate* and cite the Second Vatican Council in support of their position.[12] A few feel that they are being good Catholics, and perhaps more apostolic than the "grown-up rah rah's" who push Newman events, by carrying on their own student-to-student campaigns . . . even when this means only "giving a good, quiet example."[13]

Another emergent issue, the "structure *vs.* community" polarity, also leads to a confusion of perspectives and a dissipation of energies. Some students as well as some chaplains think that the Newman Apostolate is "hung up" on formalism. They will argue that anything smacking of *Roman* Catholicism and the juridical system its mention implies cannot create a sense of community among students and scholars. Those who reflect these attitudes

[12] See *Decree on the Apostolate of the Laity*, paragraphs 2, 3, 12, 14, and 33. All these documents are collected in Walter M. Abbott (ed.), *The Documents of Vatican II* (New York: America Press, 1966). Since several different editions and translations of these documents are available, I have chosen to cite paragraph numbers rather than pages, since the latter do not lead the investigator to the same sections of documents if he is using different editions. In most cases, however, the paragraph numbering of the original Latin texts is observed.

[13] Although the Vatican Council recognizes the worth of the "testimony" presented by "Christian life and good works done in a supernatural spirit," it also adds: "a true apostle looks for opportunities to announce Christ by words." See *ibid.*, paragraphs 6 and 13.

sometimes argue that any formalized effort to carry on "an apostolate" will inevitably lead to something "too Catholic," confiscate personal values, and substitute organizational techniques for the substance of interpersonal communications. On the other hand, in an age that has witnessed the "end of ideology," other students find in Newman programs, which they often plan and carry out entirely by themselves, a happy combination of principles and activities that gives meaning to their college years and satisfies their desire to share the good news of salvation with others.

These reflections indicate that the work of the church in the secular campus community involves more than merely "reaching" 900,000 Catholics on hundreds of campuses. Rather, Catholicism must make itself an influential presence among three roughly discernible groups of Catholics, both in undergraduate and graduate ranks, found in mixtures that differ according to the nature of each institution. Furthermore, through these students, the church must somehow touch, shape, and, in some instances, even transform, the personal lives, the collegiate subcultures, and the academic structures of the secular campus.[14]

THE NEWMAN APOSTOLATE

Since its beginnings in the nineteenth century among Catholic clubs at non-Catholic colleges, the Newman Apostolate has regarded itself as an educational movement dedicated to the purposes alluded to above. Traditionally, its undertakings embraced religious, educational, and social activities. When, in 1962, the American bishops commissioned priests, faculty members, and students to make renewed efforts to involve the church in the life of the secular campus, their mandate placed "the religious education of Catholics on the secular campus" second only to the salvation of souls.[15] In a certain way, the triple program of the first clubs found its fulfillment in the idea of "religious education."[16]

Religious education makes religion, in John Henry Newman's phrase, a

[14] Michael Novak has argued that the "next step for the Newman movement" is "to humanize the university." See *National Catholic Reporter*, March 30, 1966. Novak says the Newman movement has been "named for a 19th century dream" without clarifying what he means; he also uses the term "apostolate" in a questionable way. While several chaplains have commented that his view of the Newman Apostolate seems highly colored by his personal experiences and that his suggestions cannot be carried out in many situations, others feel that his insights have considerable validity.

[15] See "Minutes, Newman Apostolate Meeting" (Ann Arbor, Michigan, June 22–24, 1962), p. 3. In Archives, National Newman Apostolate, NCWC, Washington, D.C.

[16] See Sr. M. Alexander Grey, "Development of the Newman Club Movement, 1893–1961," *Records of the American Catholic Historical Society of Philadelphia*, 74 (June, 1963), 75.

"condition of general knowledge" in two ways.[17] In its first sense, the term signifies the scientific, objective, systematic study of religious phenomena of all kinds: creeds, codes, cults, history, experiences. It advances theological literacy or religious learning. Accordingly, religious education falls within the purview of the university: we regard the "university function" as the discovery, preservation, and promulgation of all knowledge. Furthermore, since the American university exists also to serve the people, the citizens of a religiously pluralistic society have a right to the betterment in human relations and the advancement of social and international harmony and understanding that theological literacy facilitates.

Religious education has a second meaning. Here the term refers not to the dissemination of theological learning but to the development of theocentric living. Its aim is conversion or formation, its goal is personal commitment and apostolic development. The church-related college or university performs this function. It does not do so, however, because it is a center of academic pursuit, but because it is founded by a religious body to serve a religiously homogeneous group. The independent or public institution, on the other hand, cannot impose theocentric living, although it may indirectly facilitate it and often does through counseling services, dormitory programs, boards of religious advisors, and the personal example of its administrators, faculty, and staff. These can be called "collegial functions."

The Newman Apostolate undertakes the university function only by default, either because the university does not promote theological understanding or because it does so in a prejudicial or incompetent manner necessitating complementary or supplementary efforts from the chaplain or those who help him. Accordingly, we can find at Newman centers formal courses in biblical, doctrinal, moral, philosophical, and ecumenical studies ranging in quality and scope from inquiry classes that convene weekly to carefully structured courses that meet several times each week. Under various "transfer-of-credit" arrangements, courses in Catholic studies offered in thirteen Newman centers receive university recognition and are applicable toward undergraduate degree requirements.[18]

Because the apostolate is primarily dedicated to spiritual welfare, however, it is more basically concerned with the collegial function of religious education. The Newman Center attempts to intensify the religious lives of students through liturgical programs, pastoral counseling, and informal educational activities such as occasional lectures, study clubs, and various sorts

[17] See John Henry Newman, *The Idea of a University* (New York: Doubleday Image Books, 1959), p. 103.
[18] See *Newman Apostolate News Letter*, 2 (Winter, 1966), n.p. For a summary of times, places, and ways in which religion has been taught in tax-supported institutions see Milton D. McLean and Harry H. Kimber, *The Teaching of Religion in State Universities* (Ann Arbor: University of Michigan Press, 1960).

of apostolic groups, as well as social affairs, which sometimes lead the less interested students to enroll in these programs.

In most places, unfortunately, the various phases of religious education offered by Newman Centers do not reach a majority of Catholic students.[19] The quiet, as we suggested, are indifferent or temporarily alienated. The committed are already quite busy with heavy class schedules — dedication to the intellectual life is a prime element in "Newman Spirituality" — and those who can leave the campus to engage in "extra-curricular" learning at the "unincorporated universities" sponsored by a center are proportionately few. The questing seem to find the offerings too bland or traditional, both in what they offer and how they are conducted, although lectures on "Catholic Existentialism" draw them. In most of these cases, however, programs at the various centers suffer from neglect, not because students cannot be interested, but because the chaplain is too busy as a business man, maintenance engineer, and therapist to be an effective teacher or full-time pastor.

DEVELOPMENTS

Changes currently taking place within the American church and the American university indicate new orientations that the Newman Apostolate can take and that, in some instances, it is already taking. In general, these involve a movement of personnel from Catholic colleges to Newman centers, a movement of the Newman Apostolate from the periphery of campus life to a deeper engagement in its affairs, and a movement toward more student initiative.

At present, nearly 1,000 diocesan priests and about 200 priests belonging to religious orders are working among Catholics on secular campuses. Some observers suggest a transfer of more men and women in religious life to the secular campuses.[20] Less than four per cent of the present manpower of the six largest religious orders of men could supply the desired ratio of one chaplain for every 300 to 500 Catholics. Two religious women could take up residence at each secular campus and tap the national reserves of the sisterhoods by less than two per cent.[21]

The idea of redeploying religious personnel of the Catholic church in the United States to strengthen programs of religious education at the secular

[19] One experienced chaplain placed the figure at ten per cent or less: Anthony P. Wagener, quoted in "The World Parish" (A monthly service bulletin for priests published by the Maryknoll Fathers, Maryknoll, New York, February, 1965).

[20] A Jesuit told the writer: "We could get many religious orders involved in the campus work if the American hierarchy, *as a group*, would make this desire known to religious superiors."

[21] See Clifford and Callahan, "Catholics in Higher Ed.," p. 290.

campuses is attractive for several reasons. The university itself provides the first. In accordance with their commitment to the discovery and dissemination of all learning, the faculties of secular universities have invited a number of priests teaching at Catholic institutions to accept part-time appointments. These arrangements have distinguished the scholars, the schools they represent, and the disciplines they teach.[22] Experiences at Newman centers offer other incentives. Priests from teaching orders have taken over the formal educational programs at a few centers, freeing the chaplain for administrative and pastoral work. Approximately two dozen sisters are also working in administrative and counseling capacities at some centers. Students report that often they find it easier to approach a sister with their problems, either to formulate them with her or to assure themselves that "father will understand"; many students simply like to visit with the sisters, or find that their presence and advice makes visits to the chaplain unnecessary. Where a center has been able to provide adequate spiritual counseling, the universal mission of the church has benefited through increased applications for membership in religious orders.[23] Sisters' contacts with faculty members and religious workers of other faiths have expanded the mutually enlightening dialogue of the church with the world and with Christian and Jewish communities.

The movement of personnel from Catholic colleges to Newman centers has several drawbacks, however. Arrangements concerning the placement of theological specialists from Catholic institutions temporarily on the faculties of secular universities must be made between the administrations of the respective schools. Newman chaplains encourage such transactions; but be-

[22] Prominent examples are offered by Fathers Ernan McMullin (Minnesota), William Lynch (Carleton), Joseph Fichter (Harvard), Robert McNally (Brown), John McKenzie (Chicago), Roland Murphy (Yale), and John Tracy Ellis (Brown). For reflections by some of these participants, see "Catholic Professors on the Secular Campus: A Symposium," *America*, 115 (September 24, 1966), 318–21. Western Michigan University created what some observers called "a stir in academic circles" in employing Father John Hardon in July, 1962. The termination of his contract, effective December, 1966, has occasioned additional comment. "Proselytism" was not a factor in the dismissal. But issues involving "personalities," "value teaching," and "academic freedom," both for the instructor and the student interested in exploring dominant American religious traditions, have been mentioned. One WMU professor told the writer that "semantics" lay at the bottom of the disagreements between Jesuit Hardon and his colleagues. For a summary of events and statements by Father Hardon and Dr. Cornelius Loew, Chairman of the Department of Religion, see *National Catholic Reporter*, August 3, 1966, and *The Detroit News*, July 17, 1966.

[23] For example, in the five years between 1951 and 1956, twenty-five students associated with the Newman Center at the University of Illinois entered seminaries and thirty-one at UCLA entered the convent. See "Religious Vocation Survey Report" (National Newman Chaplains Association, Apostolate Archives, Washington, D.C.). See also John Ahlhauser, "Nun in Newman — Sister Judine," *The Sign*, 45 (July, 1966), 9–12.

yond trying to help their university to satisfy its desire for theological enlightenment by appealing to Catholic faculties, and serving, perhaps, as advisors or coordinators, there seems to be little else they can do. They realize, of course, that the priests, brothers, and sisters best fitted by temperament and training for work in the Newman Apostolate are often those most needed by the Catholic colleges. Helpless as chaplains often feel in their own situations, they do not want to weaken the work of the church in other places or to impede current efforts in Catholic schools to attain higher standards of excellence. Bitter experience has taught some chaplains that no help is often better than assistance from those who are unfit in one way or another for working in the secular campus community. The responsibility of religious orders and Catholic colleges for Catholic students on the non-Catholic campus has yet to be fully examined and discharged.

While a redistribution of ecclesiastical personnel is slowly getting underway, the Newman Apostolate has already begun to follow a course that leads it from the Newman center into the various academic and social sub-communities of the campus. Several things account for this development.

The constitutions and decrees issued by Vatican II provide the most basic reasons for the new ferment within the Newman Apostolate. These teachings have confirmed and commanded a pastoral orientation that has always been present within the Apostolate. They have also underscored for the chaplain his haunting awareness that he is not, in most cases, a professionally trained educator, philosopher, or theologian. He is a teacher of the faith, and he teaches best, not by expounding the doctrines of the church, but by relating Christianity to life by his liturgical and pastoral work. This does not mean that formal education in such things as "Christian Marriage" will vanish from Newman centers: not so long as students continue to affirm that these courses are more meaningful for them than most of the accredited university offerings.[24] But it does mean that chaplains and students are giving greater emphasis to the Mass and the sacraments, preaching Bible vigils, discussions of biblical subjects, and the discovery through small-group activities of how the life of scholarship and social action flows from authentic participation in divine worship. As we have suggested above, the Newman center is a place of collegial, not university-type, religious education. Students are formed where they are. They are to be found both around the altar and in every corner of the campus. Newman, taking new inspiration from the altar refurbished by Vatican II, is following them.

[24] Students report that the priests, doctors, and married couples who jointly conduct courses in "Christian Marriage" at Newman centers deal more frankly with sex and talk more meaningfully about love and religion in marriage. Faculty members have also commented upon the value of these courses. Furthermore, because of difficulties involved in conducting liturgical and pastoral programs among their fluid populations, commuter campuses seem to be best served by strictly intellectual programs. See Malone, "Commuter Campus," p. 25.

At the same time, the university is calling the chaplain to itself. In some schools, Newman chaplains have been invited to fill chairs of religion in newly formed departments of religious studies. Administrators are also beginning to provide chaplains with office space, inviting them to attend meetings of student personnel workers and faculty groups, and calling upon them in other ways to "get into things." Such overtures are spurring the development of "multi-faith" centers on or near campuses in which ministers of various co-operating religions share a chapel, classroom, and office space, and, as one state university president put it, "have a home on the campus where they can be available to students."

Students are also calling upon Newman to take a more prominent place in their lives. Characteristically, dormitories have always buzzed with religious discussion, debate, and dialogue, and union lounges have often resembled the Areopagus with its clusters of citizens arguing about the Un-known God. Today, students are manifesting a heightened interest in religious knowledge and meaning. At some schools, teach-ins on "Death of God" theology have outdrawn those on foreign policy. One prominent professor recently noted an "apocalyptic mood" among students, and many chaplains, visiting with faculty members in the coffee-bar or campus "ven-den" hear frank admissions about the student desire — and the faculty desire — to have religion play a greater role in the classroom and on the campus. The dean of a large midwestern state university has written that "the present intellectual climate provides few bearings for young people seeking to find meaning and direction for their lives." He asserted that while critical thinking, openness to new ideas, and the free exchange of opinions — what we have called the "university function" — must remain at the heart of the process of higher education, he added that "the purely intellectual commitment seems sterile" to many students.[25] From such encounters with professors and students, the chaplain learns that many of the quiet as well as the questing are open to religious or philosophical conversations, exchanges ordered not only to inquiry and analysis, but to values and commitment.

In some instances, the students are not merely calling the apostolate to themselves; they wish to take it unto themselves. They have found that many religious discussions can get under way only when no professional representative of religion is about. Attuned to the personalist and activist mode of the times, they also know that many religious confrontations occur best, not in structured educational or social situations, but in the heat of crusading activity. To offer a single example: students driving to Selma for the march on the capitol analyzed their deepest motivations and bared their most dis-

[25] See Robert Michaelson, "The Study of Religion: A Quiet Revolution in American Universities," *Journal of Higher Education*, XXXVII (April, 1966), 181–86, and Paul A. Varg, "Intellectual Climate and Student Unrest," *ibid.*, (February, 1966), 76–79.

turbing doubts. After returning from the land of Southern Baptism, one of them confided: "I cannot live on Civil Rights all my life." Through similar encounters students on the secular campus explore the human situation and "pre-evangelize" each other. In a way, as one faculty member put it, they are participating in "a theology in the making all around them." Such experiences demonstrate how the questing and the committed can lead some of the quiet to reappraise their complacency and to develop a social awareness based upon religious convictions or upon the search for religious meaning.

Students on denominationally administered campuses show similar concern for autonomy and relevance in their religious lives. A study of Protestant colleges recently disclosed what some of the most effective forms of religious education are: extracurricular discussions of biblical and theological topics; cultural programs designed to relate religion to technology and the arts; service projects in social, political, and international spheres of action; overt protest against institutional and bureaucratic forms that stifle the prophetic voice of the churches.[26] Campus leaders of the extracurricular National Federation of Catholic College Clubs (NFCCC) have found inspiration in similar enterprises. These experiences have encouraged Catholic students on both the secular and Catholic campuses to set up joint apostolic and social projects. As one of them put it, this seems to be the only way to build an effective apostolate among Catholic students "out of two mediocre groups," namely, the National Newman Student Federation and the NFCCC.[27]

CONSEQUENCES

So far we have been looking at the situation among Catholic students on the secular campus and trends within the Newman Apostolate. It is now appropriate, if risky, to anticipate some consequences of what is going on. Some of these will take place within the mission of the American church to higher education. Others will be felt throughout the church itself.

The projection of an apostolate fully controlled by students has both negative and positive aspects. On the negative side, one discovers considerable immaturity in the proclamations of nonidentity and in the denunciations of "clericalism," ecclesiastical "indifference," and "structure hang-up" many of these students voice. The more perceptive among them are beginning to realize that their attempts to develop forms of Christian initiative free of "bureaucrato-sclerosis" eventually call for an institutionalization of the anti-

[26] See Myron F. Wicke, *The Church-Related College* (New York: Center for Applied Research, 1964), pp. 79–81.

[27] The University Christian Movement has recently been formed out of the NFCCC, the NNSF, and the Protestant National Student Christian Federation. It is expected that this amalgamation of the major Protestant and Catholic student groups will embrace more than 40,000 collegians in 1967. — Ed.

institutional.[28] Ten years from now many of *them* may be the establishment another college set assaults.

The evanescent quality of radicalism, however, is more fundamental to our discussion. All campus radical and liberal movements suffer from attrition as their members pass on to adult responsibilities. One observer of the Berkeley happening has remarked: "The plaint of the leftist campus agitator that today's picket will be tomorrow's staid suburban commuter is probably the single most rational thought to float above chanted slogans and bobbing placards."[29] The current enterprises may undergo a heightened attenuation of allegiance because the nonconformity of their adherents often seems to be related more to confusion than to conviction. A friend of the New Left has, perhaps, provided us with some insight here. Four years ago, he writes, Michael Harrington and Bayard Rustin were held in near-messianic esteem by many activist students. Today, he goes on, they "are now frequent targets of attack by the New Left." And although a Tom Hayden-Staughton Lynd axis has emerged in the meanwhile, its influence also seems to be on the wane.[30] But if activist students appear to substitute heroes almost as rapidly as the consuming public switches brands, we need not conclude that this situation makes the cause of the young radicals either comical or hopeless. We must remember that our college students were infants during the status-conscious years of postwar adjustment and passed through adolescence during the static era of cold war certitudes. Now they are coming to intellectual maturity in times that are very different. The traumas of young adulthood are probably even more acute in the case of Catholics. They spent their emotionally formative years in the last decade of the post-Reformation era; now they find themselves in a church that has opened doors on the world and replaced a policy of stability with a mandate of reform, renewal, and relevance. The fifties denied youth a commitment to process and progress; the sixties demand that they learn flexibility and adaptation. Hence, in some respects it is not quite accurate to refer to our college students as the "New Breed" or the "New Radicals." Rather, they seem to be the "Last Generation." The really "New Generation" is today passing through childhood and early adolescence. It is growing up in a milieu permeated with tranformation and inspired by developing ideologies and moralities in international, domes-

[28] See Thomas Herron, "Fragmentation, Duplication and Waste in U.S. Catholic Student Movements," *World Campus*, 9 (April, 1966), 1–2. (This valuable "round-up" of events and issues of interest to contemporary collegians is published by the Maryknoll Fathers, Maryknoll, New York.)

[29] John F. Ohls, "Berkeleyitis: A Second Look," *School and Society*, 94 (February 5, 1966), 66. For another "second look" at the Berkeley situation, see Lewis S. Feuer, "The Decline of Freedom at Berkeley," *Atlantic*, 218 (September, 1966), 78–87, and "Comments and Criticisms," *ibid.*, (October, 1966), 105–11.

[30] See Kahn, "Problem of the New Left," pp. 32–33.

tic, and ecclesiastical spheres. It is hoped that their identity problems will fester less acutely within them and their nonconformity will be less shrill and more enduring.[31]

But these speculations do not negate the hope that the Last Generation holds for church and nation. Rebellion is the first movement of generosity. The society that created a teen culture to pamper and to exploit affluent youth must also be prepared to honor the corporate idealism latent in this culture, and today we are experiencing a renewal of society motivated primarily by spiritual, even religious, concerns. If the Last Generation's commitment to the essence of service, as represented in the Peace Corps, VISTA, Civil Rights work, and other movements, remains intact, their mature years may find them a part of a swelling and creative political force. The presence of Catholics, be they committed or questing, in such a situation can have crucial significance for the future shape of American life and the relevance of the church to it.

The Newman Apostolate will also feel the impact of academic developments on the campus. A generation ago, less than ten per cent of state universities offered religion courses; today ninety per cent of them do. Two decades ago a dozen state universities had full-fledged programs in the study of religious truth; today more than twenty per cent of them have separate religion departments. Students enroll in these courses by the thousands, are described as "more serious than casual." At some schools, professors view these developments with "excitement," and what was once a pioneering venture has become an easily discernible educational trend.[32] As American higher education continues to assume its responsibilities toward the advancement of theological literacy, formal education programs at Newman centers may suffer from increased neglect. We would expect Catholics who can study religion in a university-sponsored sequence to have even less inclination to attend unaccredited courses. Yet religious interest and religious doubt will be whetted, and this augurs well for the general religious consciousness and atmosphere of the campus. Religious studies offered in the spirit of university inquiry and presumably in a milieu of neutralism toward ultimate values could conceivably occasion a need for more formally Catholic education at Newman centers.[33] Should this happen, the Newman Aposto-

---

[31] A student who read this essay while it was in manuscript form commented upon this section: "I find this analysis very hopeful. I hope *they* will not have to go through what we are."

[32] See *Christian Science Monitor* (November 30 and December 2, 1965); *Time*, 87 (February 4, 1966), 72–73; Robert Michaelson, "The Study of Religion."

[33] Research by C. Robert Pace and Lawrence G. Thomas, for example, suggests that even the professor who is "value-free" in presenting his material is, as a matter of fact, inculcating values. See their essays in *Higher Education in California: Its Responsibilities for Values in American Life* (1962), available

late would depend all the more upon help from nearby Catholic schools. Some observers feel that these can make two long-range contributions here. They may prepare professional theologians to accept positions on secular university faculties; at present most of these chairs are being filled by graduates of non-Catholic divinity schools and programs such as that offered by the University of Iowa. Catholic colleges may also prepare and inspire some of their graduates and teaching fellows to become full or part-time administrators, counselors, program directors, instructors, and volunteer workers at Newman centers.[34] Both responses will increase the religious literacy and promote the religious life of Catholic students on the secular campuses. This help will also free chaplains for their specific liturgical and pastoral work on the campus, and assist them in adapting this work to the cultural, ecumenical, and apostolic imperatives of their situation.

from the California Teachers' Association. A professor in a state university told the writer that "I used to begin my course [anthropology] with the avowal that we would approach it with scientific objectivity. Now I tell them that the name of this course is 'Learn to Believe Like I Do' and give them a target." In such discussions, one is reminded of A. N. Whitehead's remark that "the real dogmatist is not the man with ultimate convictions, but the one who has them in a covert form and who resists any attempt to bring them out into the clear light of day." See John E. Smith, *Value Convictions and Higher Education* (New Haven: The Edward W. Hazen Foundation, 1958), p. 5. Clyde Holbrook in *Religion as a Humanistic Field* (Englewood Cliffs, N. J.: Prentice-Hall, 1963), pp. 177–84, has argued quite cogently that the university ought not attempt to "represent" dominant religious traditions in its theological offerings for several reasons: the impossibility of adequately presenting the teachings of all variants of religious thought present in American society, to say nothing of the wide range of religious heritages found in other cultures and civilizations; the impropriety of social conditions determining the university function; and the thought that such an attempt might constitute a religious test for employment. His conclusion that academic competence assures "fair treatment" of religious heritages follows quite convincingly. Indeed, Catholics, who have always maintained that Truth is one and that honest, competent investigation hold no threat to their faith must agree, in the opinion of the writer, with Holbrook. Yet the writer also discerns several limiting factors. Even in considering the university function, Holbrook, in treating "indoctrination," admits that certain broad sociological conditions must be taken into consideration (See *ibid.*, pp. 88 ff. and 101 ff.). Nor does he consider the collegial role of higher education as we have described it. At the same time, the spirit of openness, trust, and dedication to the search for and transmission of religious truth which Holbrook exhibits ought to serve as an example for administrators, faculty committees, and representatives of religion as they carry on the current work of bringing the American university to age intellectually.

[34] See John F. Bradley, "Jesuits and Higher Education," *Woodstock Letters,* 94 (Summer, 1965), 245–52. Circulated privately among American Jesuits, *Woodstock Letters* is published at Woodstock College, Woodstock, Maryland. This entire issue is devoted to a discussion of Jesuit responsibilities in the higher education of American Catholics.

In the long view, however, not merely the Newman Apostolate, but the entire American church seems likely to feel with growing intensity what is taking place on the campuses today. One can look at this prospect solely from the point of view of numbers. Henceforth the vast majority of educated parishioners will hold degrees from non-Catholic institutions of higher learning. These men and women will be relatively prosperous and influential in their communities. Some of them will hold important positions in middle management, communications, and the professions. They will rear the children going to college in the last quarter of this century, when over fifty per cent of all youths will enjoy the advantages of American higher education. To the extent that these future parishioner-parents will be uninformed theologically and unformed spiritually, parochial schools, vocations to the religious life, missionary activity, parish loyalty, home atmosphere, and the vitality itself of American Catholicism will suffer. These graduates may well constitute a postgraduate version of the quiet.

Yet it seems likely that the church will face a different kind of challenge, one not of too much lethargy but of too much life. By the very act of going there, Catholics on the secular campus signify that they belong to a divergent strain within the American Catholic subculture. The developments on the campus and within Newman that we have summarized will accentuate intellectual, cultural, and spiritual differences between Catholics graduating from secular schools and those from other institutions. These disparities may be especially sharp if centers for the training of priests, sisters, and brothers fail to up-date themselves. In some ways, the threat of losing a sizeable portion of the educated class was never greater for the church in this country than it is today.

But the problem does not baffle solution. The American church has already learned how to cope with problems of cultural pluralism. It once faced the enigma of assimilating ethnic groups and found an answer in the establishment of national parishes and societies; in many instances, the "American" church did not initiate these developments: the "immigrant" church itself demanded them. But the experiment maintained a balance between autonomy in the local congregation and essential unity with the faith and discipline required by the church. Today ecclesiastical authorities face the emergence of a different type of subculture, one generated by intellectual and social pressures on its students who attend secular universities. By permitting a similarly appropriate pluralism of thought and action on the secular campuses of the country, the American church can maintain a vital contact with these students and, hopefully, assist them to attain a spiritually productive adulthood.

The choice, then, does not seem to lie between graduates who are either religiously quiet or alienated. The secular university may already be producing its share of the first group; its rising involvement in theological matters may hasten the arrival of the second. The choice would appear to be between permitting the Newman Apostolate to be merely a denominational custodian or an instrument vigorously creating at each secular campus an indigenous Catholic culture that will be authentic, convincing, and therefore effective in forming out of its Catholic and non-Catholic population those committed to the fullness of an updated Catholicism.

But if the American church decides consciously to strive for the production of "an indigenous Catholic culture" on secular campuses, will this not imperil the future of its own colleges and universities? We must not minimize present and possible problems here. But at the same time, local loyalties, broadening bases of financial support, increased numbers of alumni, the zeal that has always driven those connected with the colleges to maintain and to develop them, various cooperative plans, and continuing pressures on youths to get a college degree, will assure the continuation of the Catholic college.

As never before, state systems of higher education are counting upon private and church-related schools to help in the educational task. And the quality of religious education in Catholic institutions will very likely be transformed, making them all the more attractive. Within a decade we can expect to find substantially improved sequences in philosophy and theology, at least at the better schools.

The factor of size must, however, be considered. Even today, some observers accuse the larger Catholic universities of being "impersonal" and "un-pastoral." [35] Their bulging enrollments, their growing cleavages between faculty preoccupations and student life, the restlessness among students under such conditions, all seem to call for a renewed emphasis on the role of the chaplain in the Catholic college. In addition, other observers note that curricular developments, the increasing employment of non-Catholic professors, and the admission of rising numbers of non-Catholic students are "secularizing" the Catholic university.[36] And the trend seems to be toward more of the same.

Hence, we may expect that eventually the Newman Apostolate will be doing the work of the church, not only on the historically "secular" campus,

---

[35] Ralph Martin, "Letter From a Catholic College Graduate to the President," *Ave Maria*, 103 (April 16, 1966), 7–9, and the replies of several presidents on the following pages. See also chapter 7 C of this volume.

[36] The reader is referred to the discussion at the end of chapter 2. See also Phillip E. Hammond, "Secularization, Incorporation, and Social Relations," *American Journal of Psychology*, 72 (September, 1966), 188–94, and the exchange between the author and this volume's editor: Robert Hassenger, "Competence, the 'Pro,' and the Catholic Student," *National Catholic Guidance Conference Journal*, 10 (Spring, 1966), 233–34; and John Whitney Evans, "A Note to Catholic Counselors from a Newman Chaplain," *ibid.* (Summer, 1966), 280–85.

but at the Catholic "multiversity" as well. Such an outcome has long been an ingroup joke among Newman chaplains. One even hears that some chaplains in Catholic colleges want to attend special workshops or training sessions similar to the "Newman Chaplains' Schools" which the National Newman Foundation has been sponsoring, with increasing success, for the last five summers. Such a development may seem absurd. But Newman chaplains have found that the line separating absurdity from providential opportunity is often quite thin. "One thing alone I know," said the patron of the Newman Apostolate as he greeted a second spring, "according to your need, so will be your strength. . . . Who is to stop you. . . ?" [37]

[37] Charles Frederick Harrold (ed.), "The Second Spring," *A Newman Treasury. Selections from the Prose Works of John Henry Newman* (London: Routledge and Kegan Paul, 1943), p. 221.

XI. THE FUTURE SHAPE OF CATHOLIC HIGHER EDUCATION

Robert Hassenger

The reader might recall our warning in the Preface that this is not the definitive book on Catholic higher education. By now he may heartily concur. Throughout the volume, a diversity of stances and styles has been represented; we approached our tasks differently. Some have been more detached than others — or at least made greater efforts to approach objectivity — but none of us has defined his role as that of expert or seer. We have, of course, pointed to some past and present practices that seem dispensable, and suggested reforms appearing clearly necessary. This volume is concerned with the *shape* of Catholic higher education, not with whether it "ought" to exist, a question outside the competence of the editor and his colleagues. But there are two questions about Catholic higher education that must at least be considered in this final chapter: (1) how viable are the American Catholic colleges and universities; and, (2) what ought they look like, i.e., how will these institutions differ from their secular counterparts?

We begin with the hard facts. In the fall of 1966, on a schedule as inexorable as that of the sun, the largest freshman class in history appeared at campus gates. The nearly six million college students in 1966 represented an increase of two-and-a-quarter million over the number enrolled in 1960 and was nearly ten per cent above the preceding year. But the college crush has not been unpredictable: educators have long seen it coming.

Immediately after the return of U. S. servicemen at the close of World War II, the birth rate jumped considerably; from 2.8 million births in the twelve months ending June 30, 1946, there was a sharp increase to almost 4 million births in the next year. And the rate stayed up during the postwar boom. The result: 12,090,000 young Americans between 18 and 21 in 1965, with a projected 15,768,000 in this age bracket by 1975. These potential undergraduates are *already born.*

At the same time, the percentage of young adults intent on embellishing themselves with what Irving Howe has called the great American tattoo of a college degree has steadily increased. From the fourteen per cent of college-age Americans going on for higher education in 1940, through the twenty-nine per cent in 1955, to the approximately forty per cent in 1965,[1] the trend

[1] The 1965 figure usually cited was 43%, but Robert Havighurst pointed out to

has been ever upward. It is estimated that almost half of the college-age young adults will be enrolled by 1970, and sixty per cent by 1980. So the peculiar kind of multiplier effect sending increased percentages of an ever larger pool of potential students to college is expected to result in ten or eleven million attempting to elbow into the classroom by 1980, little more than a decade hence.

And yet the scramble for places may never be so frantic as in the mid-1960's. Colleges themselves have been striving mightily for tattoos of a slightly different sort, usually bearing some variation of the inscription "excellence." Classrooms and laboratories, dormitories and cafeterias have been thought less likely than nuclear particle accelerators and social science facilities to lead to this state of academic blessedness. But as college edifice complexes get resolved, and as the Higher Education Acts of the Kennedy-Johnson administration begin to take hold, some of the overdriven quality of the present quest for institutional status may diminish.

The escalation of higher education to a larger-scale enterprise, however, will continue. In the autumn of 1965, nearly 108,000 full-time students were enrolled in the State University of New York, with an additional 98,000 and 76,000 in the California state colleges and university, respectively. There were 9,614 *freshmen* at the University of Minnesota, more than the combined freshman enrollment (9,240) of eight Ivy League schools: Harvard, Yale, Princeton, Brown, Dartmouth, Cornell, Columbia, and Pennsylvania. Freshman classes across the country were at an all-time high. What does this mean for Catholic higher education?

It seems clear from numerous studies that Catholics are now attending college in proportion to their numbers in the American population.[2] But, according to Clifford and Callahan,[3] only 366,000 of approximately 1,070,-000 Catholic college students in 1963–64 were enrolled in Catholic institutions.[4] Two out of every three were found on secular campuses. They estimate that, even if the Catholic proportion of the population remains at its present

the writer that this included *all* students enrolled, even those in the fifth year of five-year programs. A more accurate figure can be obtained, notes Havighurst, by dividing the number of first-time students by the number of eighteen-year-olds, for a result of about 37% in 1965. It might be noted that Havighurst believes that this figure represents something of a plateau for *first-time* students that has not changed appreciably for three or four years, as this is written. President James Perkins of Cornell also suggests that a plateau may be reached, around 50%, if not sooner (*The University in Transition* (Princeton, N.J.: Princeton University Press, 1966).

[2] David Riesman has pointed out to me after reading the draft of this chapter that, if one thinks of the urban white population — which is a more appropriate comparison group, for Catholics — this may not be entirely true.

[3] R. J. Clifford, S.J., and W. R. Callahan, S.J., "Catholics in Higher Education," *America*, 111 (1964), 288–91.

[4] Roughly 400,000 are in Catholic colleges in 1966–67.

level (23 to 25 per cent),[5] there will be nearly three million Catholics in college by 1985. Clifford and Callahan predict that eighty per cent of these students will be educated on secular campuses. In 1960 Catholic institutions enrolled one student in twelve, but only one in twenty-five will attend Catholic schools in 1985. By that time, about one-fifth of the enrollment at secular institutions will be Catholic students. The implications are obvious: if any provision is to be made for the vast majority of these young adults, the concept of "Catholic higher education" must be greatly expanded. John Whitney Evans has addressed himself to this problem in chapter 10.[6] The present chapter is confined to Catholic higher education in the more limited sense: institutions run by American Catholics. Another way of phrasing this is: we shall concentrate on the distinctively Catholic (or, more broadly, "committed") quality of the colleges and universities, leaving to such eminently qualified educators as President Perkins the discussion of such matters as maintaining a balance among the research, education, and public service missions of the university, and the need for each mission to be integrally related to the others.[7]

There are, of course, a number of critics who suggest that the church ought to withdraw from higher education — or at least, that religious orders and dioceses abandon the venture. The assertions of some that academic freedom is an impossibility at Catholic colleges and universities will be considered later in this chapter. For the present, it will simply be suggested that it is highly unlikely that men and women with a considerable investment — both financial and emotional — in an enterprise will withdraw entirely from their institutions (although it may in the long run be more realistic for religious orders to think of "presence," and not necessarily "ownership" or "patrimony.").[8] The first part of this concluding chapter proceeds on the assump-

---

[5] Although this proportion has been steadily increasing, B. J. Wattenberg and R. M. Scammon (*This U.S.A.* [New York: Doubleday, 1965]) report that by 1960 Baptist families had more children than Catholics, with the latter only a negligible fraction above the "total Protestant" group (including such diverse denominations as Episcopalians and Congregationalists — which have traditionally had lower rates — and The Disciples of Christ). According to the 1966 *Official Catholic Directory* (New York: P. J. Kenedy and Sons, 1966), there were 46,245,175 U. S. Catholics, but figures differ.

[6] Archbishop Paul Hallinan has told the National Catholic Educational Association (1963): "We should redefine Catholic education as the education of Catholics, wherever they may be." For a rather alarmist discussion of this matter, see Richard Butler, O.P., *God on the Secular Campus* (New York: Doubleday, 1963).

[7] Perkins, *University in Transition*. In fact, the writer would ask the reader to digest President Perkins' fine little book and to *assume* its content in the present discussion, which is not to say I entirely *agree* with it.

[8] It should be clear, however, as Neil J. McCluskey, S.J. pointed out at the 1966 Meetings of the National Catholic Educational Association, that the operative concept is not control, but *influence*. The religious founders of Catholic

tion that the Catholic colleges will remain part of the higher educational land-scape for the foreseeable future. They face, however, some real problems; a few of the more salient of these will be discussed here.

It is perhaps not too dramatic to suggest that one of the most pressing concerns facing many Catholic colleges is the matter of sheer survival. The dangers of proliferation have been alluded to in some of the preceding chapters. It appears curious to many that, at a time when some Catholic schools are turning to the state to bail them out,[9] small Catholic colleges continue to be founded, often with enrollments under 200. Jencks and Riesman note that there are six four-year Catholic colleges and two junior colleges in Iowa,

colleges were not necessarily committed to keeping the "patrimony," but were concerned that a job get done. If new controlling bodies (such as laymen) share the same commitments, Father McCluskey suggested, no real problems are faced (April 13, 1966). (Since the above was written, several Catholic schools — most notably, St. Louis and Notre Dame — have announced plans which would radically reduce the control of religious orders over the institutions. Webster College in St. Louis is being entirely turned over to an independent board of lay trustees.)

[9] Facing a "low-enrollment crisis," the presidents of Catholic Detroit University and Marygrove College (along with those of Protestant Hope and Calvin Colleges) met with Michigan's Governor Romney in late 1965 to request direct tuition grants of up to $500 per student, and about $3.2 million for capital outlay. These educators claimed that the aid would result in long-range savings for the state and noted that the direct-tuition plan was in effect in New York and Wisconsin (*South Bend Tribune*, December 16, 1965). In late summer, 1966, a bill was passed, providing grants ranging from $50 to $250 a semester, depending on family income. In the fall of 1966, between seven and eight thousand freshmen were expected to benefit from the measure. It was planned that a college class would be added in each of the succeeding three years, until all four undergraduate years were covered.

But all may be changed by three recent developments. On June 2, 1966, the Maryland Court of Appeals ruled four-to-three that state matching fund grants to Western Maryland College, a Methodist institution, and to St. Joseph's and Notre Dame Colleges, both Catholic schools, were unconstitutional. The money, provided by the Maryland General Assembly in 1962, was the continuation of a policy of aiding private colleges which dates from 1784. Also in the summer of 1966, the New York State Supreme Court struck down a law which would have gone into effect September 1, 1966, requiring public schools to lend textbooks to parochial schools. And on July 29th, the U. S. Senate passed and sent the House a bill that would authorize legal suits against federal aid to church-related schools and other institutions under the Elementary and Secondary Education Act, the National Defense Education Act, the Higher Education Facilities Act, the Higher Education Act of 1965, the Economic Opportunity Act, the Public Health Service Act (Title VII), the Mental Retardation Facilities Act and the Community Mental Health Centers Construction Act. Perhaps the tangled issues will be unraveled when the Maryland case is taken to the U.S. Supreme Court, possibly in 1967.

enrolling less than 6,000 students among them.[10] The city of Milwaukee has three Catholic colleges for women, in addition to coeducational Marquette. A similar situation can be found in Erie, Pennsylvania. One far western city has seen established a college for women only two blocks from a large Jesuit university, with concentration in precisely the two departments that have been the strongest for years at the Jesuit school. As late as the mid-1960's, Mundelein and Loyola in Chicago existed cheek by jowl without so much as a cross-referenced library system (indeed, one was on the Dewey Decimal, the other on the Library of Congress, system). Often such institutions compete with each other not only for students and faculty, but for funds to build duplicated facilities. It is difficult to disagree with Msgr. John Tracy Ellis:

> This sort of thing comes perilously close to a scandal in my judgment, and I can see no remedy except for one of two things to happen: a) institutions will be faced by bankruptcy and then begin to cry for help; b) public exposure of the scandalous duplication will arouse the bishops under whose jurisdiction in a general way those schools operate, or the laity whose money is being squandered in this fashion.[11]

Part of the difficulty for many Catholic schools is their reluctance to raise tuition, both because of a sense of "mission" to the less affluent among the Catholic population, and probably also because of a fear that more wealthy Catholics would be little interested in paying "Ivy League rates" for an education in less posh settings. Perhaps the Higher Education Act of 1965 will provide the means to solve this particular problem; Christopher Jencks makes a cogent argument that the right kind of federal scholarship program could be a great benefit to colleges and students alike, allowing the former to raise

---

[10] In chapter 7 of the draft of *The Academic Revolution*, forthcoming. Professor Riesman points out in correspondence (April 7, 1966), however, that he has since learned St. Ambrose College is moving to combine classes both with the neighboring women's college, and the Lutheran college across the river in Illinois.

[11] Personal correspondence, February 3, 1966. As early as 1917, Rev. William J. Bergin of St. Viator College, Illinois, deplored the existence of fourteen Catholic colleges in his state, at a time when, he said, there were not enough Illinois Catholics for more than two fair-sized colleges. (St. Viator College is an interesting phenomenon, little studied in Catholic educational history. Among its alumni are Bishop Fulton J. Sheen and Msgr. Ellis, but the college was forced to close its doors for financial reasons in 1939, and was never revived.)

At the 1964 Meetings of the National Catholic Educational Association, President Paul C. Reinert, S.J., of St. Louis University, noted that there were 61 Catholic colleges for religious and lay students with student bodies of less than 100. The average size of these schools was 58 students, 16 faculty (a ratio of slightly more than 3 to 1); three-fourths of these did not meet the minimal standards of their regional accrediting organizations.

their tuition and the latter to have a real choice about the college they attend.[12] The effects such a program would have on the Catholic (and other church-related) colleges are difficult to predict. While the increased tuition might provide a more secure economic base, the opportunity for less affluent collegians to attend other than commuter colleges might reduce the pool of potential clientele, particularly for the large urban institutions. But the multiplier effect described at the beginning of this chapter would more than likely allow such schools to retain at least their present enrollments, and the higher tuition would provide funds to make their offerings more attractive.[13] (Catholic college administrators will still be faced with the necessity of marshalling resources in the most effective possible ways; Anthony Seidl addresses himself to this problem in Appendix A.)

Even radical federal or state intervention will not solve the problem of what Msgr. Ellis terms the "scandalous duplication of facilities." Several cooperative relationships are concerned with this situation. Four institutions in St. Paul began cooperating in a modest way in 1953; Methodist Hamline, independent Macalester, and Catholic St. Thomas and St. Catherine began to share area-studies courses sponsored by the Hill Foundation. The two Catholic schools undertook the exchange of men (St. Thomas) and women (St. Catherine) in 1957. St. John's University of Collegeville and the College of Saint Benedict have had a similar arrangement for several years, and have begun a Tri-College Program with Saint Cloud State College, to enable the colleges to get better acquainted and to share faculty and students. The Central States College Association is a recent attempt at an even broader exchange of teachers, students, and programs among private church-related colleges in several mid-western states.[14] Among the more interesting ventures is the Consortium of Universities in the Washington Metropolitan Area, with five participating institutions: American University, Catholic University, Georgetown, George Washington, and Howard University. Cooperation at the graduate level will work for the upgrading of programs without unneces-

---

[12] In *The New Republic*, 153 (October 16, 1965), 21–23.

[13] The real danger of the commuter college, however, is that students do not make the psychological break from home that may be necessary for developmental change. Those at such institutions, David Riesman suggests, "drift on as shoppers or passive customers, half in and half out, half at college and half at home, dropping in and dropping out" ("College Subcultures and College Outcomes," in *Selection and Educational Differentiation*, ed. T. R. McConnell [Berkeley: Center for the Study of Higher Education, 1960], p. 10).

[14] This and other cooperative programs are described in William E. Cadbury, Jr., "Cooperative Relations Involving the Liberal Arts Colleges," *School and Society*, 94 (1966), 213–17. The entire issue of *School and Society* for April 16–30, 1966 (double issue), is devoted to cooperative relations in higher education. See also Sr. M. Dolores Salerno, D.M., "Patterns of Inter-institutional Cooperation in American Catholic Higher Education," *NCEA Bulletin*, 62 (No. 4), (May, 1966) 1–31.

sary new facilities, the elimination of duplication so that each school may specialize in greater depth, and the over-all improvement of graduate study and research. Notre Dame and St. Mary's now cross-list a number of their courses, and will modify class times to facilitate interchange. In the spring of 1966, nearly 150 Notre Dame students were enrolled in 188 courses "across the road," with about half that many belles of St. Mary's attending classes under the Golden Dome; in the fall of 1966, more than 120 St. Mary's girls attended 202 Notre Dame courses. There are those in South Bend who would like to see additional women's colleges built to expand the interchange, particularly for the leavening effect on the students at each of the sex-segregated institutions, many of whom have not attended classes with their opposite numbers since grade school.[15] Whether such changes will occur — and if so, whether they will evoke the wrath of past legions of Notre Dame men, as did the recent reforms at Yale — remains to be seen. Other variations are possible. Fordham's Thomas More College — with a lay woman dean, the first in Fordham's history — is intended to enroll high-caliber women on the Bronx campus, although the remainder of the Fordham undergraduate student body remains entirely male. Perhaps similar experiments will be tried at Holy Cross, Georgetown, and Boston College, all of which remain male only in the undergraduate college, allowing women on the campus in graduate and professional school. One of the most daring of the innovations is the impending affiliation of Immaculate Heart College of Los Angeles with the Associated Claremont Colleges.[16] Whatever changes are made will necessarily be tailored to institutional differences; there seems little doubt that such schools will survive, although they may be largely unrecognizable to old boy alumni.[17]

[15] As late as 1929, Pius XI wrote, in his encyclical on "The Christian Education of Youth," that "there is not in nature itself . . . anything to suggest that there can or ought to be promiscuity, and much less equality of the two sexes." He declared it "False . . . and harmful to Christian education," that "the so-called method of 'coeducation' " was propagated.

[16] Such "cluster colleges" as are found at Claremont will become a more common phenomenon in the years immediately ahead. (Clark Kerr came out strongly for these at the convocation "The University in America," sponsored by Santa Barbara's Center for the Study of Democratic Institutions in early May, 1966. Ex-President Kerr expects these more intimate settings to solve some of the problems associated with undergraduates' perceived loss of "identity.") Some express concern that Immaculate Heart, presently (1966) characterized by a distinctive Christian climate, will be absorbed by the high-powered Claremont atmosphere, but this is by no means certain. See Andrew M. Greeley, "Academic Growth in Catholic Colleges," forthcoming. Another experimental college on the drawing boards, Surmonté, may be established by a group from Loretto Heights College in Denver.

[17] For an illustration of how threatening such changes can be, see "Alumni Profile," by R. Hassenger, Notre Dame *Alumnus*, 28 (September–October, 1966), 10–13. And yet, it is a well-known fact in South Bend that Notre Dame has been more favorably disposed toward increased coordination than St. Mary's.

For one thing, many of the best Catholic colleges are following the careers of their secular counterparts to emphasize graduate education. While there are overtones of status-seeking about this, at least some Catholic educators seem inspired by a sense of mission. One spokesman asserted that

> a university is incomplete without a theology department, and . . . only in a true university which encompasses the complete spectrum of scholarly pursuits can an embryonic scholar absorb the proper view of his own subject and its place in the totality of man's knowledge. Perhaps only in Catholic graduate schools can the competent, committed Catholic scholar and future teacher be trained.[18]

Possibly reflecting my own recent four years in one of the nation's top secular graduate schools, I would take serious issue with the above statement. Higher degrees in the subject areas of the mid-twentieth century take a great deal of concentrated preparation. Any synthesizing that is to be done can only be accomplished after a thorough grasp of the subtleties of a given field, and this takes rather complete immersion for all but the most gifted. The social sciences, especially, have so recently fought loose from the past encroachments of philosophy and theology that there would seem to be real disadvantages accruing to any attempts at a premature synthesis. The individual scholar who is so inclined can carry out his own synthesizing within a Catholic framework after getting the best possible preparation in top graduate schools. And these are not — with rare exceptions for particular programs in certain schools — likely to be Catholic institutions. There would appear to be a case for throwing out the doctoral sequences at most Catholic universities, to concentrate on top-flight undergraduate education, as do the best of the nation's colleges.[19] But this proposal is probably impractical, for at least four hard-nosed reasons.

[18] J. F. Mulligan, S.J., "The Catholic Campus Today," *Commonweal*, 83 (1966), 499. The reader may be interested in contrasting this attitude with Fr. Mulligan's predecessor at Fordham, George Bull, S.J., whose position regarding graduate work and research was cited by Philip Gleason, pp. 48–49.

[19] By most criteria, schools such as Amherst, Antioch, Bennington, Oberlin, Reed, Sarah Lawrence, Shimer, and Swarthmore (cf. George G. Stern, "Characteristics of the Intellectual Climate in College Environments," *Harvard Educational Review*, 33 [1963], 5–41). These colleges are almost all small, non-urban, residential, high-tuition institutions with great student autonomy (including participation in college decision-making), advanced placement, low student-faculty ratios, and an absence of fraternities and sororities. Although there is little difference in faculty salaries at these and other well-known institutions, the low student-faculty ratios mean proportionately more professors (faculty ranks are usually not found in these schools), and the large number of scholarships also means a heavy drain on institutional resources. The trustees and administrators at these colleges apparently believe that graduate education is out of the question if undergraduate excellence is to be preserved.

First, whatever "excellence" is, it seems to be currently denoted by foundation grants and research projects, which go to institutions with the men who prefer to concentrate on training graduate students. There are a lot of indications that this situation is at least partly dysfunctional for the over-all educational picture, as the Berkeley rebels would be the first to insist. Nevertheless, it *is* the name of the game, as presently played, and it would be naïve in the extreme to expect those Catholic university presidents who have this kind of "excellence" within their grasp to pull out of the race now.

Second, there is the argument of some educators that

> (c)olleges which confine their efforts to undergraduates will find themselves relegated, by the end of this century, to the position occupied today by the good preparatory schools. In fact, they will not be in as good a position, for unlike first-rate preparatory schools today, they will not get the best students. The best students will go to universities.[20]

We may be in a better position to judge the merits of this argument when the extensive study of twelve quite different liberal arts colleges by the Carnegie Corporation is completed.[21] For the present, one can only admit that the argument has cogency, given the recent trends within higher education and American society generally.

Third, it is difficult to disagree with the case made by Nevitt Sanford that the participation of graduate students in undergraduate affairs is one of the most striking features of the contemporary educational scene.[22] As graduate departments have grown increasingly larger and more depersonalized, and graduate students do the same meaningless work that characterizes so much of undergraduate and high school education, they have begun to involve themselves in the "causes" of the undergraduates, who in turn look to them both as "older" and as successful survivors of the selection hurdles of the educational establishment. Most graduate students are under thirty — the age after which one cannot be trusted, according to the leaders of the New Left. As this group begins to "change sides" from the "management" (administration and faculty) to the "workers," [23] the alliance results in new personal identities for undergraduates and graduates alike, as they seek to attain social justice and community with other people. Perhaps this is reason enough to have graduate departments.

Finally, there is the eminently pragmatic consideration of the need to staff

[20] W. Allen Wallis, "The Plight of the Small College," *Atlantic*, 216 (November, 1965), 126.

[21] Administered through Antioch College, under the direction of Morris Keeton.

[22] In "Causes of the Student Revolution," *Saturday Review*, 48 (December 18, 1965), 64–66, 76–77.

[23] These are Sanford's terms.

the myriad of second-rate Catholic colleges and universities. This is strong language, but it is difficult to judge so many schools otherwise. However attractive the designs of the educational planners, the bulk of these "colleges" will simply not amalgamate, coordinate, or disappear.[24] They will have to be supplied with faculty, and the vast majority will continue to come from the Catholic graduate schools.[25]

We hope it is not too much to urge that at least the various universities offering doctoral sequences cease trying to provide programs in every conceivable area, that they map out some kind of strategy whereby the best men in an area — say American Catholic history, or higher religious studies, or the sociology of social change — concentrate in one institution, avoiding needless duplication and the spreading thin of resources.[26] (It should be

[24] Although they could perhaps be more profitably (and honestly) run as junior colleges. Joseph Kauffman ("The Student in Higher Education," in *The College and the Student*, eds. L. E. Dennis and J. F. Kauffman [Washington, D.C.: American Council on Education, 1966], pp. 141–62) reports that Edmund J. Gleazer, Jr., who is the executive director of the American Association of Junior Colleges, estimates that approximately one million students will attend junior colleges in the mid-1960's, and that half of the beginning college students in 1970 will be found in public junior colleges. As the junior college "movement" takes hold, perhaps it is time to convert many of the Catholic "colleges" into two-year institutions, maybe as "cluster colleges" near a parent institution, Catholic or secular.

[25] There is no real reason why these instructors need have the research-based Ph.D., however; it may be that many of the Catholic graduate schools should concentrate on programs for college teachers in the various subjects, who would obtain a degree between the master's and the Ph.D. Some refer to this as a doctor of arts, others as a master of philosophy, degree.

[26] In Cartter's survey of 29 doctoral programs at 106 institutions, the duplication of effort in present Catholic graduate programs is readily seen (Allan M. Cartter, *An Assessment of Quality in Graduate Education* [Washington, D.C.: American Council on Education, 1966]). Cartter's research group sent questionnaires to the graduate deans and weighted (by the number of degrees their departments had granted between 1953 and 1962, with only those schools granting an average of at least ten doctorates a year included) samples of junior and senior professors at all 106 universities. Seven Catholic institutions were included: Catholic University, Fordham, Georgetown, Loyola of Chicago, Notre Dame, St. John's, and St. Louis. Only five of these appear in the tabulated results, in which graduate departments are rated "distinguished," "strong," "good," and "adequate plus," on the quality of their faculty; and "extremely attractive," "attractive," or "acceptable plus," on the overall effectiveness of their graduate programs.

Twenty departments in Catholic graduate schools are rated at least "adequate plus" on faculty quality, with three of these (Spanish at Catholic University, biochemistry at St. Louis, and chemistry at Notre Dame) meriting the "good" rating. Only ten of these appear at all in the rating of general program effectiveness.

Two departments made the "top 20" lists in their respective areas: Classics at Catholic University, and Astronomy at Georgetown; neither was rated "good,"

clear, however, that such duplication is no monopoly of Catholic education.) This is not to suggest that an institution be held to one or two fields, but simply that the same sequences ought not be duplicated on several campuses. In the case of the field I know best, sociology, it would seem obvious that no single Catholic university can pretend to offer expert concentration in every area within this mushrooming discipline. Fordham, Notre Dame, St. Louis, Boston College, Loyola, Catholic University, and the other schools seriously pursuing doctoral sequences in sociology should concentrate their efforts and resources on two or three broad areas, with other departments doing so in other subfields. If Catholic graduate schools continue to exist — and they undoubtedly will, although probably not for the reasons Mulligan suggests — they ought to define their objectives carefully, so that excellence of an at least limited kind remains available to them.

The foregoing caution, some would say pessimism, will not be matched in the brief comment about undergraduate education here. For, unlike my hesitation with regard to Catholic graduate schools, I would go all-out in advocating support of Catholic colleges.[27] Although the data summarized in chapter 5 did not present an entirely positive picture of the Catholic college student, the more recent research indicated that changes may be underway. As late as 1963, Wakin wrote that Catholic undergraduates "seem to reflect the worst qualities of their secular counterparts."[28] While such statements may have a ring of truth about them, they are largely uninteresting to the

however. Notre Dame led the list of Catholic schools in total departments listed, with six (chemistry, English, history, mathematics, philosophy, and physics); St. Louis was next, with five (bacteriology-microbiology, biochemistry, English, philosophy, and physiology). Four departments were ranked at Fordham (Classics, English, French, and philosophy); there were three at Catholic University (Classics, French, and Spanish), and two at Georgetown (astronomy and pharmacology). No other Catholic graduate departments were considered strong enough to be awarding Ph.D. degrees.

It is interesting to note the overlapping of strong departments at two or more Catholic schools, with the humanities especially strong. Not a single graduate department in the social sciences at a Catholic university was ranked.

David Riesman has suggested that the development of the Interstate Compact for Education should have valuable lessons for Catholic educators. As relative latecomers to higher education, the Catholic schools should be able to avoid some of the decisions which have proven unfortunate in American colleges and universities. But situations such as the one faced by St. Louis, with three of its five ranked departments in the Medical School, which drains a vast sum from other programs, may make it difficult to determine what lines of action are to be followed.

[27] Particularly in the original sense of *collegium* — the gathering of students in a common life (see pp. 331–34).

[28] In *The Catholic Campus* (New York: Macmillan, 1963). Mr. Wakin's comments are no more positive in Edward Wakin and Joseph Scheuer, *The De-Romanization of the American Catholic Church* (New York: Macmillan, 1966).

demanding educational consumer, who will likely want evidence of a more sophisticated kind.

With virtually every aspect of Catholic higher education, however, college climates have been scarcely researched. There have been a number of "self-studies," which are typically little more than white papers,[29] and a few rather frothy journalistic accounts, attempting a kind of pop sociology.[30] These are of minimal use to the tough-minded. Robert Weiss has sketched some portraits of Catholic college "climates" in chapter 3, and we shall not attempt to improve on his work here. The "instrumental," vocational emphasis in the Jesuit schools, and their comparative rigidity and control may surprise some, although the existing research on institutions tends to corroborate these results.[31] Perhaps large, urban, streetcar colleges cannot be expected to rate high in the dimensions of awareness and scholarship, both

[29] For examples of self-studies that are not white papers, see Norbert J. Hruby, "The Mundelein Self-Study: An Experiment in Reorientation," *North Central News Bulletin*, 22 (March, 1963), 2–10 and "Truth and Consequences: Mundelein College Emerges from Analysis," *ibid.*, 24 (March, 1965), 2–23; and Gordon DiRenzo, "Student Imagery at Fairfield University, 1963–64" (Department of Sociology, Fairfield University, 1965, mimeographed). DiRenzo found that students at this Jesuit university held a "minimally positive image of their institution." Most critical of the college were students who were most liberal and non-dogmatic, and those with the highest academic averages, majoring in the behavioral sciences, and from higher income families. Students at Fairfield felt that moral-spiritual growth was emphasized at the expense of academic stimulation; only 60% would attend the college if they "had it to do all over again," and barely half would encourage their sons to matriculate there.

Two things should be noted before the first stone is cast. Perhaps other Catholic colleges would not fare even this well, were they to encourage honest self-evaluation, and Fairfield University is to be commended for their courage in this regard. Secondly, results are not strikingly different from those of Greeley's "Criticism of Undergraduate Faculty by the Graduates of Catholic Colleges," *Review of Religious Research*, 6 (1965), 96–106, which was discussed in chapter 5.

[30] Probably the best known of these (aside from the plethora of volumes dealing with Knute Rockne, the Four Horsemen, the Seven Blocks of Granite at Fordham, the basketball fortunes of St. John's, and other athletic lore apparently of great importance for the Catholic minority) is Edward Wakin's book, *The Catholic Campus*. For a similar, but more perceptive, volume, considering a number of non-sectarian colleges, see the late David Boroff's *Campus, U.S.A.* (New York: Harper Bros., 1961). More sophisticated, however, are the college "ethnographies" of David Riesman and Christopher Jencks ("The Viability of the American College," in *The American College*, ed. N. Sanford [New York: John Wiley & Sons, Inc., 1962], 74–192).

[31] As Greeley ("Academic Growth") points out, the data on graduate school attendance, coupled with the Weiss data on the rather uninspiring climates, indicates a desire to enter the academic life *despite* the college experience. In this connection, see James A. Davis, "The Campus as a Frog Pond," *American Journal of Sociology*, 72 (1966), 17–31.

indicators of an intellectual campus climate.[32] An emphasis on the pragmatic at the expense of the aesthetic can be found at virtually all of the large, urban coeducational Catholic universities in the sample of Robert Weiss.[33] These are precisely the types of orientation lamented by the more vociferous of the Catholic self-critics. As a number of observers have pointed out, however, such a syndrome is not surprising, given the backgrounds of their clientele. The athleticism of the past may be dying, as Catholic minority groups make it in the larger society, and are less in need of killing, maiming, and dismembering — to mention only the printable verbs — their opponents on the gridiron and the court. But a largely vocational orientation remains. Although Catholic colleges and universities still lag in National Merit Scholars attracted [34] and national fellowship winners turned out, the record for the years since the early 1950's is impressive at some schools. Notre Dame probably has the biggest haul of national fellowship winners,[35] but St. Louis, Catholic University, Fordham, Gonzaga, Trinity, Manhattanville, Clarke, and others also do well.[36] While there is the danger of totaling such awards like touchdowns, and the ever present temptation to assert that "we're Number One," it is clear that the Catholic higher educational institutions are not all cut from the same cloth.

This is important in any discussion of the viability of Catholic higher education and its "success." Notre Dame, for example, has been particularly adept at capitalizing on a glamorous image to attract bright but largely unin-

[32] Jencks and Riesman provide more insightful comments on the problems faced by such colleges in *The Academic Revolution*, forthcoming, chapter 7.

[33] Students at more affluent Catholic colleges probably have different orientations. For example, the freshmen entering Notre Dame in September, 1965, were given the *College Student Questionnaire* of the Educational Testing Service. In checking one of four "philosophies" of education, over half (59 per cent) picked the "collegiate" as the most accurate statement of their "philosophy," with only 21 per cent choosing the "academic," and 16 per cent the "vocational" orientations. To what extent this is influenced by the football atmosphere during autumn at Notre Dame remains unknown.

[34] Less than half of the Catholic students winning National Merit Scholarships in the years 1956–59 chose to attend Catholic colleges, and those who did so were found to be less intellectual and more authoritarian than the Merit scholars choosing other colleges and universities (E. D. Farwell and J. R. Warren, "Student Personality Characteristics Associated with Types of Colleges and Fields of Study," mimeographed at the Center for the Study of Higher Education, Berkeley, 1959). Yet, in 1965, Notre Dame was 17th in choice by high ability students (Robert C. Nichols, "College Preferences of Eleventh Grade Students," National Merit Scholarship Corporation Research Reports, vol. 2, #9 [mimeo.], p. 12).

[35] Between 1952 and 1966, Notre Dame students were awarded 122 Woodrow Wilsons, 39 Fulbrights, 23 Danforths, 9 Root-Tilden Fellowships, and 6 Rhodes Scholarships.

[36] For the most part, however, Catholic parents and prospective students are unaware of the vast differences among schools.

tellectual students, then turning a fair number of them into serious scholars.[37] Not all Catholic schools have had the good fortune to be blessed with the glamour of Notre Dame,[38] but several — particularly a few women's colleges — have moved a long way from their early identifications as "convent-schools" emphasizing manners, morals, and motherhood.[39]

To what extent the Catholic colleges will be changed as students in the 1970's and 'eighties come with different backgrounds and expectations remains to be seen. One of the most interesting patterns may be the increased preponderance of the more recently arrived Catholic ethnic groups — primarily Italians and Poles. Not only are students generally more rebellious today, even on the Catholic campuses;[40] a case might also be made that the greater proportion of students from Italian families will lead to a less-inhibited and docile campus climate than prevailed in the largely Irish-dominated Cath-

[37] It is interesting, however, that although 65% of the 1965 Notre Dame graduates (with those receiving commissions in the armed forces excluded) intended to enroll in graduate and professional school (*The Notre Dame President's Newsletter*, October, 1965; Vol. 8, No. 1), there is some consternation at Notre Dame that the number of Woodrow Wilsons has declined from a peak of 21 in 1959 to a level of about 10 annually since 1962. There may be a number of reasons for this. Among them are the possibilities that (1) there was something of a novelty in awarding Wilsons to Catholic college seniors in the heady, pre-ecumenical days of the late 1950's, which has since worn off; (2) someone on the regional board, who was partial to Notre Dame or to Catholic colleges, is no longer present; (3) Notre Dame is no longer getting as many first-rate men as in the late 'fifties, perhaps because they are today more likely to attend the Ivy League colleges, Stanford, or Berkeley; (4) women are competing more favorably with men now; (5) the "market" is more flooded, especially by applicants from the small midwestern liberal arts colleges sending comparatively high percentages of their graduates into college teaching, which is the intent of the Wilson grants (this is the suggestion of Dean Charles E. Sheedy, C.S.C., of the Notre Dame College of Arts and Letters).

[38] The importance of image should not be underestimated. Realizing this, the Carnegie Corporation has given The Center for Research and Development in Higher Education at Berkeley a grant to study the causes and effects of institutional image.

[39] It will be recalled that, whether one attends to research on college climates or to that on students' traits, values and attitudes, Catholic women appear more interested in intellectual pursuits, as well as being less rigid and constrictive than Catholic men (chapter 3, pp. 68–76; chapter 5, pp. 136–37).

[40] E. G. Williamson and J. L. Cowan report that seventy per cent of the Catholic college presidents in their study stated that their students were becoming increasingly more demonstrative ("The Role of the President in the Desirable Enactment of Academic Freedom for Students," *Educational Record*, 46 [1965], 351–72, also reprinted in Dennis and Kauffman, *College and the Student*). Suicides also occur on Catholic campuses today, which can be expected as more critical and sensitive students are recruited, and as counseling programs remain grossly inadequate.

olic colleges in the past.[41] Whereas the Irish mother tends to dominate, the Italian father is traditionally boss in his family. It is tempting to speculate that Italian males will be more likely to rebel against the institutional authorities, particularly if they are "fathers." Polish students remain an unknown quantity, although the high independence of the "Mary College" Polish girls was a consistent pattern in chapter 4.[42]

It might also happen that, were something like the Jencks scholarship plan described above put into practice, the Catholic schools — particularly the large urban universities and commuter colleges — would attract greater numbers of minority group collegians. A survey of Catholic institutions in 1965 found very few Negroes enrolled;[43] some of the schools are making concerted efforts to attract Negro students, but a dearth of qualified candidates exists — as Ivy League recruiters have also found.[44] It is difficult to disagree with those who insist that the white, middle-class student is in some ways more culturally deprived than the slum-dwellers to whom this description is usually applied. But this is, of course, a reflection of long-standing injustices in American society, only recently beginning to change.[45] The education acts of the Kennedy-Johnson administration may help to rectify the situation, but it will probably be some time before there are noticeable effects in higher education.[46] It is difficult to predict the influence of these

[41] See Nathan Glazer and Daniel P. Moynihan, *Beyond the Melting Pot* (Cambridge, Mass.: Harvard University Press, 1964).

[42] John Whitney Evans suggests that, having been socialized in large numbers by the public schools, Poles will more likely move into state college and university systems. The situation cited in note 9, in an area with a substantial Polish population (Michigan), may well support this interpretation.

[43] J. M. McLinden and J. M. Doyle, "Negro Students and Faculty on Catholic College Campuses," *NCEA Bulletin*, 62 (1966), 1–49. Chris and Mary Weber ("Discrimination on Catholic Campuses," *Ave Maria*, 103 [January 15, 1966], 12–18) found that Marquette and Detroit, both with about 11,000 students, had approximately twenty Negroes each; six of the 900 New Rochelle women were Negroes, and Webster College had five Negroes in a student body of about 700. At the same time, however, a survey ordered by Chancellor Roger Heyns showed only 231 American Negroes enrolled among the 26,063 students on the Berkeley campus (*South Bend Tribune*, April 20, 1966).

[44] David Riesman told the writer that President Paul Reinert, S.J., has noted that several of the eight or ten St. Louis Negroes he had recruited for St. Louis University one year had turned down the awards for full scholarships to Harvard.

[45] The deplorable effects of inequality are documented in Daniel P. Moynihan, *The Negro Family* (Washington, D.C.: U.S. Department of Labor, 1965), although some indications of slow but steady improvement in the situation are found in Wattenberg and Scammon, *This U.S.A.*

[46] Robert Havighurst states that the Higher Education Act of 1965 provided scholarships to only 5% of the college-age population, which is "a drop in the bucket." He further suggests that about 4 of these 5 out of 100 would have gone to college anyway, although they might have had to work their way through and

programs on the Catholic colleges and universities. Urban institutions are most likely to be first affected, although many of these are attempting to move away from their "streetcar college" images to attract increasing numbers of resident students.[47] The particular problems of the small Catholic college have been recently considered by Louis Vaccaro; we shall not elaborate this discussion here.[48]

In addition to their steady academic upgrading, the most likely immediate changes within Catholic higher education will undoubtedly be in the areas of longstanding weakness, such as student freedom and faculty autonomy. A few of the factors associated with the maximization of undergraduate student growth have been discussed in some detail elsewhere.[49] With an increasing diversity of student populations, greater opportunities for individual development will become available. Catholic college administrators have been moving away from the overprotective paternalism of the past, although vestiges remain, particularly with regard to the expression of unconventional beliefs and sentiments. Lazarsfeld and Thielens[50] found Catholic college professors to be much less tolerant of Communist teachers, student Socialist Leagues and the like. Many still fear "controversy." For example, the recent survey by Williamson and Cowan[51] showed that only seven per cent of the Catholic university presidents they polled would have offered a platform to Malcolm X, compared with 68 per cent of the presidents of private universities, 61 per cent at the large public universities, 56 per cent at the private liberal arts colleges, and 21 per cent at the Protestant liberal arts colleges. Others still distrust free inquiry. In this study, one of the Catholic presidents articulated his stance on such matters in a statement with which many of

would perhaps have attended less excellent schools. Havighurst sees motivation as still the key factor in college attendance, and notes that the real difficulty is finding and motivating the large numbers of qualified students who have never considered college (Personal conversation, Winter, 1966).

[47] The account of such an evolution at Boston College can be found in Riesman and Jencks, "Viability of the Amer. College."

[48] In "Three Ways Out for Small Catholic Colleges," *America*, 113 (1965) 580–82. An illustration of how Mr. Vaccaro's suggestions might be applied to a specific location can be found in Appendix B.

[49] In the writer's contribution to *Academic Freedom and the Catholic University*, eds. Edward Manier and John Houck (Notre Dame, Ind.: Fides Press, 1967). See also "A Rationale for Changing Student Values," *Educational Record*, 48 (Winter, 1967), 61–67.

[50] Paul F. Lazarsfeld and Wagner Thielens, Jr., *The Academic Mind: Social Scientists in a Time of Crisis* (Glencoe, Ill.: The Free Press, 1958).

[51] Williamson and Cowan, "The President and Academic Freedom." Charles Y. Glock and Rodney Stark (*Religion and Society in Tension* [Chicago: Rand McNally, 1965]) also cite some data indicating that faculty members in both Catholic and Protestant colleges were "much less favorable towards free speech and civil liberties in general, as well as more opposed to several varieties of dissent, than were their colleagues in secular schools" (p. 273).

his compeers would undoubtedly agree: ". . . as a Catholic college there are fundamental concepts of natural law, dogma, and morals which would prevent [a statement supporting freedom of inquiry and expression] from being accepted in an absolute manner. In some matters it would be permissive to 'express viewpoints,' but not to advocate them."[52] Although it is still possible for the consumer of Catholic publications to find references to the tiresome distinction between "freedom" and "license," such rodomontades are becoming fewer and farther between. There are a number of reasons for this, not the least of which is the changing climate of American Catholicism. In recent years there has been a considerable re-thinking of traditional positions on virtually every aspect of Roman Catholicism. If change has not occurred as quickly or to the extent that many would wish (e.g., the difficulties of the Vatican Council in passing the declaration on religious liberty), the church in the last third of the twentieth century will almost certainly be more relevant to the modern world than in its pre-Council representation. This has been and will be reflected in Catholic higher education.

The Sister Formation Movement has probably been most responsible for the changes occurring in the Catholic women's colleges (which perhaps had the most changing to do). The movement began in the early 1950's as an attempt to replace "blue-apron mysticism" — the judgment of religious zeal in terms of housework — with professional preparation in the sisters' various fields of endeavor.[53] Real efforts have been made, for example, to train the teaching sisters to the extent demanded by the state for those in the public schools. On the college level, this means sending more and more of the brightest young sisters on for their doctorates, often to first-rate secular

---

[52] Williamson and Cowan, "The President and Academic Freedom," p. 356. In his preliminary report of the Carnegie-backed research on "growth" in American Catholic colleges and universities ("Academic Growth"), Andrew Greeley stated that the most useful predictor of institutional advancement between 1952 and 1965 was the quality of administrative leadership, particularly the president himself. The top-flight president must be able, according to Greeley: (1) to symbolize in his own person the goals of the institution, and to radiate confidence that these are being achieved; (2) to bring about consensus among the various factions; (3) to understand what an educational institution is, and to be an ambassador of its mission to the world outside the campus; (4) to play the key role in picking and replacing under-administrators, and to be able to delegate authority; and (5) to be the primary representative of the school to contributors, government agencies, foundations, civic and national leaders, and the like. But, Greeley noted, his research team found far more "safe," fort-holding Catholic college presidents than charismatic leaders such as he describes.

[53] The *Sister Formation Bulletin* is published quarterly and is devoted to aspects of this movement. The first four volumes, containing a number of comments on the movement, were published in a bound volume by the Marquette University Press, 1959; see also Sr. Ritamary, *Sister Formation Conference* (New York: Fordham University Press, 1957).

universities. It may mean living away from the convent, such as at The International House of the University of Chicago, as do sisters from several orders.

Perhaps the most significant changes have been the more subtle ones of general atmosphere. There seems to be more emphasis on rational authority, rather than blind obedience.[54] The personality of the individual sister is today more likely to be taken into account in determining what work she will do. For one thing, she is usually allowed to pursue her areas of academic interest, rather than to study subjects in which the community is lacking teachers, as was often the case not too many years ago. At the same time, there appears to be more long-range planning, with a lessened likelihood of facing emergency decisions. These changes and others have been reflected in the schools the orders staff; as Robert Weiss showed in chapter 3, the Catholic institutions highest on intellectuality and social concern are the women's colleges. Reforms in seminary education have been slower in coming; the reader is referred to Lee and Putz,[55] and the excellent treatment of this problem by Robert McNamara, S.J. in chapter 7 (B). (Some of the changes McNamara predicted are already happening as this book goes to press.)

The other change that will be briefly discussed here is the new role of the Catholic layman and its implications for higher education. Lay faculty are coming to dominate in all but the small Catholic women's colleges. Where, in 1940, lay men and women constituted only about half of the faculty in Catholic institutions, by 1965 they out-numbered priests and religious better

[54] Two incidents can perhaps illustrate this and may be portents of things to come. In one far western archdiocese known for the opposition of its prelate to "liberal" Catholics, an attempt was made to prevent the appearance of a speaker at one of the better Catholic women's colleges. The superior called the archbishop and discreetly expressed some doubt that all of the numerous grade and high schools run by the order administering the college would be adequately staffed for the next year, and wondered whether some of these might not have to be closed. Although the sister did not directly respond to the prelate's demand to know if she were "threatening him," the opposition to the college's guest speaker suddenly dissolved (not, one might suggest, without considerable weeping and gnashing of teeth).

The other incident was at a midwestern women's college. In early 1966, when a key faculty member leaked to the press the notice of the sister-president that a widely heralded symposium would have to be cancelled because of the archbishop's opposition, the chancery office relented, stating its position had not been accurately represented. Although the role of the sister in this confrontation was perhaps less dramatic — she seemed at first to prefer avoidance of a showdown — the absence of episcopal sanction may embolden her and other sister-presidents in the future. (Indeed, a curious disparity in the visibility of some nationally known priests and sisters and the rather unglamorous bishops within whose diocese their home bases are located may lead to some interesting patterns of confrontation in the future.)

[55] James M. Lee and Louis Putz, C.S.C. (eds.), *Seminary Education in A Time of Change* (Notre Dame, Ind.: Fides Press, 1965).

than two to one.[56] In addition, they hold an increasing number of department chairmanships,[57] and even some administrative posts, including the presidency of two diocesan colleges. Accompanying the change in laymen's status is a revolution in his relations with the clergy. Wakin noted that some Catholic campuses could be described as places "where priests tried to act like laymen and laymen tried to act like priests."[58] In many cases, of course, the lay teachers at Catholic colleges *were* seminary dropouts, who were teaching philosophy or kindred subjects they had picked up while preparing for the priesthood. The awareness of this fact, and the prevalent feeling that subjects other than theology were less than complete, exacerbated clerical feelings of superiority. But this is not now the case — or if so, only rarely. No longer is the clerical faculty member as wont to say, with the Anglican divine to the nonconformist minister, "We are both doing God's work; you in your way and I in His." Traces of paternalism still persist, of course, as Francis Kearns and John Leo clearly document. Proclamations to the contrary, some lay faculty — particularly at the less impressive schools — remain second-class citizens.[59] But as the independence accompanying first-rate doctorates, consulting assignments, and both federal and foundation grants begins to accrue to the layman teaching on a Catholic campus,[60] his rights — and obligations — will increase. Whether the evolution is due to principled reform or pragmatic adjustment is not the point; with increased "clout," the layman's services become more valued. There are of course dangers, particularly the possibility that research and consulting become more interesting than teaching,[61] or at least more time-consuming, adding to the depersonalization many

[56] In 1950, there were 61 Jesuits, two other priests and 105 lay professors on the liberal arts and science faculty at Fordham. By 1964, there were 99 Jesuits, 10 other priests, and 202 lay men and women. Only 119 of the 608 full-time professors at St. Louis were Jesuits in 1965, and Notre Dame's full-time faculty then consisted of 65 Fathers of the Holy Cross, who operate the university, 13 other priests, one sister, one laywoman, and the remainder laymen. (*Los Angeles Times*, February 21 and 23, 1966).

[57] More accurately, "headships," since they are still appointed by administrations, not elected by colleagues.

[58] Wakin, *The Catholic Campus*, p. 199.

[59] To use the overworked metaphor. In some senses, they are not really citizens of the academic community, since they neither hold office nor vote for representatives to do so. But much has happened since this was written. Some of the developments of late 1966 and early 1967 will be discussed in R. Hassenger, "American Catholic Higher Education," in *Catholics, U.S.A.: Perspectives from Behavioral Science*, eds. W. T. Liu and N. J. Pallone, in preparation.

[60] Only recently has federal research money begun to flow into a few Catholic institutions. Jencks and Riesman note that, in 1962, no Catholic university ranked among the top 75 recipients of government research grants (*The Academic Revolution*, chapter 7, forthcoming).

[61] Christopher Jencks has some marvelous suggestions for federal appropriations to innovating professors, which would give them the same freedom to plan

students already feel.[62] And some may, of course, find that the values they once looked for in an ivy-covered setting are unattainable in the world of grantsmanship. Perhaps their early dreams were illusory; and perhaps they have not been hoodwinked at all, but have actively sought (some would say whored after) the academic big-time.[63] Despite the dangers apparent here, the reader will probably not disagree that the increased number of options available to the scholar of the present *can* be used to maximize his freedom, as well as his responsibility.

Whatever the solution to such problems, there can be no doubt that the status of the lay faculty on the Catholic campus has changed, and in almost certainly permanent ways. It would serve little useful purpose here to recount academic atrocity stories featuring lay professors in the hero-victim roles. These there have been in abundance. Kearns and Leo have sketched some of the forms lay-cleric conflicts within Catholic academia can take; the firings at a number of Catholic colleges and universities have been alluded to in the chapters above.[64] The religious group that has come in for the greatest criticism for their treatment of the increasing numbers of laymen on their

and execute a program of instruction that they have in research ("A New Breed of BA's," *New Republic*, 153 [October 23, 1965], 17–21).

[62] Then-president John Gardner of The Carnegie Foundation for the Advancement of Teaching has discussed this possibility in "The Flight From Teaching" (New York: Carnegie Corporation, 1964). Not all would agree that "depersonalization" is wholly dangerous. Some, arguing as does Harvey Cox in *The Secular City* (New York: Macmillan, 1965), would suggest that the impersonal environment of many campuses is a healthy antidote to the spoonfeeding and coddling of a more "familial" college atmosphere.

[63] This may be the place to cite the limerick of Don K. Price, made more famous by Clark Kerr (in *The Uses of the University* [Cambridge, Mass: Harvard, 1963]):

> There was a young lady from Kent
> Who said that she knew what it meant
> When men took her to dine
> Gave her cocktails and wine
> She knew what it meant — but she went.

[64] At least two colleges have fired admittedly competent teachers in the few months preceding the writing of this chapter, for daring to suggest, in one case, that changes be made in the curriculum and academic standards (*National Catholic Reporter*, February 16, 1966), and for supporting this instructor (*National Catholic Reporter*, February 23, 1966); the men in question were not only given a hearing, but were ordered to stay off the campus. The order administering this college, which also staffs two of the best Catholic women's colleges in the country, handled faculty requests to know why they had been dismissed by stating the men had violated "long-standing policies of the college which were in process of being written" (*National Catholic Reporter*, April 13, 1966). Faculty were told by this administration, when asking for a clarification on tenure at this college: "Those who have tenure know it and those who do not have tenure know

campuses is the Jesuit order. "The position of the lay faculty member on a Jesuit campus is both intolerable and absurd," wrote a critic as late as 1963:

> The Jesuit administrator is ordinarily pleasant, charitable, well-meaning, almost avuncular. But he doesn't listen. The little jolt of anguish one often feels just after closing an interview with a Jesuit administrator is the knowledge that beneath the superficial kindness and the patience, the administrator simply didn't listen, that the words used by a professional lay person do not exist for him. The Jesuit doesn't wish to be uncooperative; rather he cannot see that anything outside his own Order is significant enough to make any ultimate difference in the career of the university or Catholic thought. Being outside the Order, it doesn't really signify.[65]

Not all who have worked with Jesuits would agree with the above sentiments; perhaps Mr. Kearns would even find them a bit strong, at least for *some* Jesuit administrators.[66] And others would prefer to substitute the name of another order of priests, sisters, or brothers in the statement. As this is being written, of course, many would substitute "Vincentian" for "Jesuit."

The tangle of issues in the academic revolution at St. John's is too complex to be unraveled here; John Leo has addressed himself to some of these

it, too" (*ibid.*). Perhaps this is why there were only six Ph.D.-holders among the sixty lay faculty at this school.

Curious circumstances also surrounded the dismissal by an Iowa Catholic men's college of a man who had been with the school for seven years, and had been commended several times in the past for his work. This man had openly supported the need for a public community college in the county, which caused the president to express to him his fears that such an enterprise would be harmful. Shortly afterwards the teacher was dismissed by this same man, while being told that "this action does not constitute any reflection on your teaching ability." He was unable to obtain from the president any reason for the dismissal.

The writer experienced a similar situation during his one year spent at a particular Catholic women's college. After the dean had solicited from him a verbal commitment in February that he would return in September, he was notified on May 4, 1962, that his services would not be needed in September. No reason was given. The college then stated that "a sister who had been finishing work on her degree was now available," but no such person turned up in September.

It is interesting that the same religious orders seem to be involved in such cases, while progressive groups like the California sisters of the Immaculate Heart of Mary, the Sisters of Charity, B.V.M., and the Sisters of Loretto, do not generate these conflicts.

[65] Robert O. Bowen, "The Lay Faculty on the Jesuit Campus," *Ramparts*, 3 (1963), 16.

[66] The institution recently announcing one of the most complete reorganizations, St. Louis, was a Jesuit university.

in chapter 7. Grievances may be partially resolved before this volume appears; new ones may have emerged, on Long Island or elsewhere. Several of the St. John's faculty view their struggle as a preview of things to come in Catholic higher education generally. Although there are most likely numerous skirmishes yet to be fought, it is not at all certain that these will escalate to the proportions of the St. John's showdown.

The battle being waged on Long Island has something of an overkill quality. The Vincentian administration seems clearly to have been more concerned with becoming the largest Catholic university in the country than with any real commitment to academic quality.[67] Their salary scale was wholly anachronistic; as Francis Canavan, S.J., reported, St. John's would have had to raise the salaries of full professors by 22.8 per cent, associate professors by 12.8 per cent, and assistant professors and instructors by 7.8 per cent and 8.4 per cent, respectively, to compare with ten other major Catholic universities (most of which are located in areas with lower living costs than the New York metropolitan area).[68] Tenure was meaningless, even if it were obtained, since a man could have his rank changed, and then be fired. Faculty members had no rights in negotiating salaries, choosing course materials, or planning curriculum. No grievance procedures existed, and the professors fired were not given a hearing (at least, as this is being written). They were not even allowed to finish the term in which they were teaching, a procedure unheard of in American higher education. Teachers were expected to prowl classrooms during tests, and to supervise students' dress, which is scarcely consistent with professionalism for the college teacher. Finally, the Vincentians "packed" the American Association of University Professors chapter with company men and were able to reverse the stand of that body.

On the other hand, the behavior of some of the faculty was less than professional. One can legitimately question the usefulness of advertising one's availability for a new position in large-circulation publications. Requests for proportional representation on faculty committees evolved into

[67] Full-time enrollment increased from about 6,000 in 1946 to about 12,000 in 1965 (from "Academic Freedom and Tenure: St. John's University," *Bulletin of the American Association of University Professors*, 52 [Spring, 1966], 12–19). The reader is referred to this report for an objective treatment of the St. John's controversy.

[68] Francis Canavan, S.J., "Academic Revolution at St. John's," *America*, 113 (1965), 136–40 and "St. John's University: The Issues," *America*, 114 (1966), 122–24. New salary scales were announced shortly before this was written, but they have not yet been put into effect. Fordham also indicated its intention to pay salaries that would move the university into the "A" (second highest) category in the AAUP classification. The very real possibility that St. John's might lose its standing in the Middle States Association may prompt the reforms that principle has not.

demands for participation in running the university.[69] This strikes many academics as rather curious, since they feel their precious time is already too filled with proliferating committee meetings and paper work. Most college professors who care about both their teaching and research cannot become too interested in the actual running of the university. It is possible, of course, that their legitimate academic freedoms were so infringed upon that only a massive overhaul appeared likely to rectify the situation. The historian of academic freedom, Richard Hofstadter, noted that the administration's arbitrariness resembled nothing in the twentieth century, and termed their approach "antediluvian."[70] But the leaders of the faculty revolutionaries made a number of tactical errors, and failed to allow the Vincentians a face-saving way out. The demand for collective bargaining is also difficult for some to understand, since they prefer to believe that they can better handle such matters on their own. Perhaps this really means that the academic deludes himself that he is "better" than his colleagues, and thus worth more; but the fact remains that the first-rate man receives any number of offers for positions and prefers to work independently of group bargaining.[71]

There have been some positive results from the St. John's brouhaha. Some of the students who had approached education on a cash and carry basis became involved for the first time with issues of legitimate protest. Further, the greater public scrutiny given to Catholic higher education and its many subspecies uncovered a few small but excitingly innovative colleges — such as Immaculate Heart, Webster, and Mundelein — and called attention to the fact that they had changed greatly since last people looked.[72] And the

[69] It is tempting to suggest a comparison with the similar escalation of demands at Berkeley. As students began — many for the first time in their lives — to have an effect on "the system," they could not stop with administration capitulation. With committees organizing and mimeograph machines humming, the "Free Speech" movement became the "dirty speech" campaign, and the issues became more global. Part of this *is* the "system's" fault, of course, for allowing American youth so little real control over their own lives. It is, as the rebels say, "all laid on."

[70] Quoted in *The National Catholic Reporter* of January 5, 1966. Hofstadter's belief may be an example of what David Riesman calls "New York provincial": the paternalism on Long Island is probably not, unhappily, a unique phenomenon in Catholic higher education (although it may be more accurate to label some varieties "maternalism").

[71] It may be uncharitable to note that the typical St. John's faculty member is in a less advantageous bargaining position than the professor with a more marketable degree. But this is one of the hard facts of academic life: few of the faculty at St. John's would be there, if they could do better; and when the young men get their degrees, many move on, as they do from all second-level Catholic (and other) schools. There is nothing specifically Catholic about this, of course; the same situation obtains throughout American higher education.

[72] David Riesman has lamented the paucity of "consumer research" on colleges and universities; the recent publication of College Board scores, and other data from institutional research, is an effort to help rectify this situation.

handful of top-rank Catholic institutions stand further out from the rest. The greatest single benefit, however, has been the renewed interest in the "nature" of Catholic higher education; it is to this question that we now turn.

At present, as the reader is undoubtedly well aware, the controversy as to whether religious organizations can rightly sponsor higher education rages on. Taking a leaf from Bernard Shaw, one of the leading opponents of the administration at St. John's stated:

> Churches and universities don't mix. The Catholic Church, or any other Church, ought not to operate a university. It is a natural thing for them to impose . . . doctrines on the students. . . . Disassociation will eventually come about. It has to. It has already been achieved at colleges affiliated with Protestant groups.[73]

There are at least two different problems implicit in this statement.

The first can be quickly dispatched. Are Catholic colleges contradictions in terms? Are they "impossible"? At the risk of seeming flippant, one is here tempted to invoke the rejoinder of Professor Skinner's alter-ego Frazier in *Walden Two*: when the philosopher Castle (a marvelous choice of name) insists that the program to raise children without anxiety, hostility, or jealousy is doomed to failure, Frazier replies: "That's an *experimental* question, Mr. Castle." Wait, that is to say, until the last man is out. Or the last Catholic university. Those who suggest withdrawal of the church from higher education because of the alleged incompatibility of religious commitment and a spirit of free inquiry might be urged to look around them: there are, in fact, *several* real colleges and universities sponsored by Catholic Americans. Nowhere near three hundred, to be sure. But even one institution where critical inquiry proceeds untrammeled would seem to disprove the purported contradiction. Such an argument may appear glib. It is advanced with the greatest seriousness.[74] Those who chart the demise of Catholic higher education from their armchairs often fail to grasp the incontrovertible fact: there *are* Catholic colleges where freedom prevails — at least no less freedom than is found in American higher education generally. We must begin with the phenomenon, not an abstraction. The same argument obtains in

[73] Dr. Rosemary Lauer, quoted in the *New York Times* of January 10, 1966. This was an extemporaneous statement in response to a question from the floor, during a symposium, but Dr. Lauer has supported the statement's substance in later communications (*The National Catholic Reporter*, February 9, 1966; and *America*, 115 [September 17, 1966], 285–86. Jacqueline Grennan of Webster College seems to agree.

[74] It is also useful to adduce here the response of A. Robert Caponigri when he was told that his *Modern Catholic Thinkers* (New York: Harper Bros., 1961) was meaninglessly entitled: no one could be simultaneously Catholic and thinker. "Look," advised Caponigri, "there they are," men who were quite obviously thinking, and identifying themselves as Catholics.

reverse. George N. Shuster told me that he had seen at least fifty plans for "the ideal Catholic university" during his long career, and yet all — particularly those drawn up a priori — would almost surely have been unworkable. They were in varying degrees divorced from reality. Had they got off the ground, they would undoubtedly have been modified by the hard exigencies of reality, much as the U.S. Constitution has been bent to a changing society. Catholic — and other church-related — colleges can exist, but the way to talk about them is to begin with those already thriving.

The second question is a much thornier one: what ought their character be? The bulletins of Roman Catholic colleges are given to rhetoric about "educating the whole man," and "integrating" all the students' educational experiences. The oldest Catholic institution of higher learning in the country issues a catalogue stating: "A special function of the Catholic college is to impart in a thousand ways, which defy formulation, the Catholic attitude toward life as a whole." In the abstract, one might well agree with, even applaud, this description. In practice, however, such promises have tended to lead — not only at Georgetown, to be sure — to a kind of "rescue project" approach to education, with a rather heavy dose of courses to "condition the will," that students may be made "more free." Jencks and Riesman have well caught the flavor of this position:

> There are priests and nuns who, faced with Father Cavanaugh's question, "Where are the Catholic Oppenheimers and Einsteins?" would reply that it didn't matter so long as the students kept the faith and were saved. Indeed, they would say, if Catholic Oppenheimers and Einsteins can only be bought by allowing Catholic orthodoxy to go the same way as Jewish orthodoxy, they are not worth the price.[75]

Some of the most exasperated criticism has been directed at the Jesuit institutions, often for quite diverse reasons. Harvard's Eliot took the Society to task for what he called their anachronistic curriculum,[76] and one of the Jesuits' contemporary critics admonishes them for an over-emphasis on science, engineering, business administration, law, and medicine.[77]

In 1937, Robert Hutchins accused Catholic educators of imitating the worst features of secular education, ignoring most of the good ones. But, as David Riesman noted twenty years later, Catholic schools move in much the

[75] In chapter 7 of the draft of Jencks and Riesman, *The Academic Revolution*, forthcoming.

[76] Cited in F. Rudolph, *The American College and University: A History* (New York: Alfred A. Knopf, 1962), p. 296.

[77] Edward Keating, "Jesuit Education: A Layman's View," *Ramparts*, 3 (1963), 6–9. Jencks and Riesman, *The Academic Revolution*, also note this tendency and add that the Catholics who become engineers mostly go to non-Catholic colleges, perhaps because of a reluctance of the Catholic schools to spend the money and make the changes the burgeoning field requires.

same circles as their secular counterparts: a few front-rank colleges and universities compare favorably with Wellesley and Northwestern, if not Radcliffe and Swarthmore, and those less luminous have direct counterparts as well, institutions which are, in Riesman's apt phrase, "colleges only by the grace of semantic generosity."[78] The best of the schools have made it. No longer is there a concentration — as one irreverent critic put it — on "Thomism and the split-T." Just as the few remaining Catholic football teams now imitate the formations of the professionals, so too do the Catholic intellectuals look to the "pros" of their respective disciplines. Department by department, the major Catholic universities begin to look more and more like comparable secular schools. Indeed, this may be the key problem for such institutions: in "making it," how many elements of their original identities remain?[79]

This is the real dilemma of at least those schools with basic academic respectability. What directions can their future growth take? Philip Gleason pointed out that many Catholic self-critics have appeared to assume that a commitment to "research" and "excellence" will solve all problems. But, of course, it will not and *has* not at the handful of institutions on the fringes of the elite. One of the outcomes especially feared by the St. John's Vincentians seemed to be the possibility that the university would pass from the control of the order, and that the character of the institution would thus be altered. Some of the dissident faculty certainly would welcome such a change, pointing to the parallels among the originally Protestant colleges. As any general history of American higher education will indicate, there has been a pattern of more strictly orthodox denominations becoming disenchanted with the increasingly secular colleges, establishing their own, and watching these become "worldly" in turn, making social and intellectual compromises with the larger society. It is not at all impossible that a parallel evolution will occur within Catholic higher education.[80] But it is fair to ask, as do many concerned educators, whether such schools would then be different from

[78] David Riesman, *Constraint and Variety in American Education* (New York: Doubleday Anchor Books, 1958), p. 62.

[79] It is tempting to suggest parallels with the American Negro here. Some far-sighted critics wonder if Negroes — finally able to pursue unfettered the chrome and tinsel of American gracious living — will really be "better off" than at present: is it all that great a bargain to trade ghetto community for exurban anonymity? The answer can only be yes: free of the subhuman identity foisted upon him by whites, Negroes of the future will at least be able to opt for alternatives to comfort and material security, once achieved.

[80] This was written before the recently announced changes in some universities. But many lay faculty members are less interested in actual participation in policy-making than they are in solving the problems arising from the lack of clarity in the relationship of religious communities to the schools they administer. Such individuals are more concerned that administrators be appointed for their competence and style than they are with whether or not such people wear roman

secular ones, and if not, what justification for their separate existence could be found.

The problem lies in determining what it means to be different. How different? Certainly not to the extent that the commonly observed principles and practices of American higher education can be scanted. As late as 1965, an official of the largest Catholic school in the country could insist that the governing body of his institution would be justified in imposing restrictions on the academic freedom of faculty members because "of the nature of St. John's as a Catholic university." He asserted that such restrictions could apply "not merely in the departments of theology and philosophy, but in other departments in which matters of faith or morals may be or may become pertinent to the curriculum."[81] What can this possibly mean? Such matters *may* become pertinent in *any* subject, including mathematics. Who decides such weighty questions? The St. John's chapter of the American Association of University Professors branded this statement as a "philosophy of education that is medieval in spirit."[82] Whether the reader would go this far back in history to find appropriate parallels is not important. Whatever the date, it is somewhere prior to Vatican II.

The most obvious shortcoming of such a point of view is that it is simply unrealistic for contemporary teachers and students, most of whom will live to see the twenty-first century. It just won't work. Perhaps many older faculty and administrators fail to see the depth of the changes that have occurred in students and young faculty. Whether "apostasy" among collegians is as widespread as it sometimes appears,[83] there can be little doubt for anyone who really listens to contemporary undergraduates that their disaffection with traditional religious forms is deep.[84] It is no longer ap-

collars. What they would avoid at all costs is the selection of college presidents and vice-presidents for the qualities which would make a good religious superior, rather than a professional educator. Few would chafe under Greeley's charismatic president (note 52), cleric or layman.

[81] Quoted in *The National Catholic Reporter*, November 3, 1965.

[82] *Ibid.* John Whitney Evans has insisted to me that this is a misrepresentation of the situation in the thirteenth century. "They did not realize that had St. John's been a truly medieval university, the New York Chancery, not the administration, would be saying those things" (Personal correspondence, March, 1966). This should not be taken to mean that Father Evans looks kindly on the situation at St. John's: he simply is opposed to cliches, particularly those that are less than accurate.

[83] The data of Andrew Greeley, cited in chapter 5, seem to indicate that it is not, at least for Catholic graduate students.

[84] Little can be explained to those who would answer, with the Notre Dame priest learning of a student's alleged immoral behavior, that "things like that just don't happen under The Golden Dome" (Quoted in the Notre Dame *Scholastic*, reporting a survey of the religious attitudes on campus, January 15, 1965). It is always saddening to find those who were at one time in the forefront of change

propriate to inform students that "if you don't like it here, you can always go somewhere else." This is to wholly miss the point. Nor is it relevant to chalk off student discontent to moral problems. There are undoubtedly some who stay away from religious activities because of guilt arising from personal conduct, primarily sexual behavior. But this is not the principal cause of most of the decrease in religious participation. One must look at what such behavior really means.

To forego Sunday religious services because one wishes to sleep late is not the same as to stay away because it seems the most honest thing to do, since attendance had been out of fear and guilt and was generative of anger and frustration.[85] We are no longer dealing with President Butterfield's "dutiful generation."[86] At a time when the most widely read book on many Catholic campuses is Harvey Cox's *The Secular City*,[87] when a number of theologians are proclaiming the "death of God" and asking whether it is possible to be a Christian without an awareness of the divine or a sense of the transcendent, it is naïve in the extreme to expect undergraduates to buy the formulas and rituals they feel obstruct real religious commitment. No longer in need of a deity who was primarily a "need filler" and "problem solver," they react against even the more exciting of the contemporary theologians.[88] This is in large part due, one might suggest, to the tendency of these students' past (and a few present) teachers to make acceptance of the entire "package" of Catholicism — including its pieces of folklore and gadgetry — a necessity. To rule out the possibility of legitimate questioning may well *cause* "apostasy," simply by operation of a self-fulfilling prophecy. Erikson

within the American church failing to comprehend the different nature of contemporary students' problems. The writer has recently seen two religious sisters, both years ahead of their compeers a decade ago, utterly baffled by the fact that some of the women at their respective Catholic schools were not sure that God exists. (This is part of the story of the Sister Formation Conference — and indeed the Civil Rights movement.)

[85] This is the story for virtually every Notre Dame student who expresses to the writer his great disenchantment, but his reluctance to give up the religious participation he has known all his life. It is always risky to estimate the extent of student discontent, but a *very* conservative estimate for the 1965–66 Notre Dame upperclassmen would be ten per cent with such mixed feelings. The comments of some of the more articulate of these are found in chapter 7 (C).

[86] Cited in chapter 1. And he knows it. President Butterfield retains his great insight into the lives of his students. See "Counter-Attack in Liberal Learning," *Liberal Education*, 52 (1965), 5–21.

[87] (New York: Macmillan, 1965). The reader is also referred to the Catholic Michael Novak's *Belief and Unbelief* (New York: Macmillan, 1965). (In early 1967, Joseph Fletcher's *Situation Ethics* [Philadelphia: Westminster, 1966] is also frequently seen.)

[88] For Catholics, men such as Bernard Lonergan, Hans Kung, Karl Rahner, Edward Schillebeeckx, Pierre Teilhard de Chardin, and Leslie Dewart.

and Friedenberg[89] have understood that one can live *down* to — as well as up to — expectations; since it is better to have a deviant role and a "negative identity" than none at all, those who rule out alternatives to the acceptance of the whole "package" may well force abandonment of religious commitment. If it is "apostasy" to stay away from religious observance — for whatever reasons — and this is opposed with punitive responses of megaton proportions, then priests, teachers, and parents may well confirm their honestly questing adolescents in their roles as "deviants" and effectively cut off any paths of return. The process is very similar to that whereby grade school boys are typed as "troublemakers" from their early school careers, with successive teachers informed of this "fact" and reacting to the child's quite innocent attempts to gain attention with behavior which confirms them in "delinquency." In most Catholic grade and high schools, and perhaps many Catholic colleges, a parallel sequence of events may well determine the future course of students' religious lives.[90]

But it is not the purpose of this concluding chapter to throw barbs at the Catholic educational system. More than a few are willing to serve in the capacity of critics. And the necessity of such criticism should not be minimized. As Greeley points out: "The problems Catholic schools face may well be not that they are being criticized but that they're not being criticized strongly enough, articulately enough, or by enough people."[91] Criticism must be directed at presently extant targets, however, not those of ten, or even five, years ago.[92] Radical changes have, after all, been taking place in Catholic education. Whatever one's personal feelings about the traditional place of theology and philosophy at the center of Catholic higher education,

[89] The work of Erikson has been cited in chapter 5. Friedenberg's *The Vanishing Adolescent* (Boston: Beacon Press, 1959) and *Coming of Age in America* (New York: Random House, 1965) are very perceptive treatments of the young American in the 1950's and 1960's. See also K. Keniston's *The Uncommitted* (New York: Harcourt, Brace and World, 1965).

[90] The conflicts of some of the present members of the younger adult generation are portrayed in Daniel Callahan (ed.), *Generation of the Third Eye* (New York: Sheed and Ward, 1964); and *The Newman Review* of 1964.

[91] Andrew M. Greeley, "Catholic Education," *America*, 112 (1965), 522–28.

[92] One of the most outrageous and completely misrepresentative of the critical pieces appeared in *Fact* for January–February, 1966. The great danger in such distorted accounts of Catholic education is that they allow some of those who most need to hear the many things wrong with Catholic higher education to lump the responsible and perceptive critics with the incompetents who cite figures that are completely outdated, infer from several examples of sexual or aggressive hang-up that Catholic colleges foster maladjustment, and generally distort virtually every "fact" they have at their disposal. Such "critics" need vocational guidance. For a debunking of Wakin and Scheuer's *The De-Romanization of the American Catholic Church*, see Philip Gleason, "De-Romanized Scholarship?" *Ave Maria*, 104, no. 11 (September 10, 1966), 18–21, 28.

and his reactions to the somewhat catechetical mission of these schools in the past, it is difficult to ignore the dynamic changes that have occurred.

Where many schools had relied on the same philosophy and theology courses since their founding — courses with dogmatic, defensive orientations and content — it has recently been realized that the seven-century emphasis on Thomism in philosophy, with rather abstract courses in logic, ethics, the philosophy of nature, metaphysics, and natural theology, is not likely to produce a cultivated familiarity with contemporary thought; nor is a defensive post-tridentine theology calculated to result in a Christian synthesis operative in the mid-twentieth century. Hegel, Darwin, Marx, and Freud have to be encountered, and on their own terms.

If philosophy is to integrate at least partially the other areas of knowledge,[93] it cannot exist in splendid isolation from contemporary thought. If truth is its object, there is nonetheless an obligation to be relevant to the practical order. "In a sense each man begins philosophy anew and brings to it not only his own character and background but the contributions of his own age."[94] Instead of imposing the Thomistic synthesis on twentieth century students, there is today in progressive Catholic philosophy departments more awareness that Thomism was but a moment in the history of philosophy; one may draw great inspiration from this perspective, but he cannot "pose only the same problems or in the same way (Aquinas) did, or answer in exactly the same way or especially the same language."[95] Philosophy sequences inaugurated in many colleges in the past few years reflect this new thinking. There are often several courses dealing with modern philosophers such as James, Whitehead, Dewey, and Santayana, and the phenomenologists, existentialists, and logical positivisits. Their orientation is to problems, with solutions always considered in historical context. The emphasis becomes one of question-asking, not of answer-giving, as in the past.

Students have also benefited from recent developments in theology. Where, in 1951, an investigator found the theology departments of forty-two Catholic women's colleges "drifting along satisfied," retaining a "negative approach in moral instruction [and] a tendency to inculcate an over-individualistic spirituality,"[96] progressive theology departments today place more emphasis

[93] H. R. Klocker, S.J., "The Nature and Function of Philosophy in Undergraduate Education," in *Christian Wisdom and Christian Formation*, eds. J. B. McGannon, S.J., G. Klubertanz, S.J., and B. J. Cooke, S.J. (New York: Sheed and Ward, 1964), pp. 202–12.

[94] *Ibid.*, p. 211.

[95] W. N. Clarke, S.J., "Current Views on the Intrinsic Nature of Philosophy," in *Christian Wisdom and Christian Formation*, p. 106.

[96] Sr. M. Gratia Maher, R.S.M., *The Organization of Instruction in Catholic Colleges for Women* (Washington, D.C.: The Catholic University of America Press, 1961), p. 138.

on social worship and action. John Courtney Murray, S.J. well described the theology of social commitment: "that intelligence of the faith, especially in its relation to human life and the good of mankind, which is required in order that the laity of the Church may be able effectively to collaborate with the hierarchy in accomplishing the renewal and reconstruction of the whole of modern social life."[97] Where Father Murray stood among the vanguard when this statement was written twenty years ago, American Catholicism has today caught up with such pioneers.[98]

In the educational realm, changes have occurred in the teaching of religion on the primary and secondary levels, and in the approaches to college theology. Emphasis today is on a return to the original spirit governing the Christian message, on "kerygmatic" theology. According to "kerygmatic theologians,"

> the fundamental reason for the sad state of Christianity today is found in our scholastic theology . . . too much set up within the circle of its own concepts and theses, too preoccupied with outdated controversies and with defense against adversaries long dead. It has hardened into a dry set of impeccable formulas in which nothing is missing except life. School-theology, moreover, fails to prepare anyone to teach and preach the Christian revelation as meaningful for Christian living.[99]

More attention is given to a psychological approach to the Christian Mystery, which means a change in methodology as well. No longer is there primarily an attempt to justify the church to non-believers, but rather to "discover more deeply its living reality and the challenges to which our commitment in the Church calls us."[100] This means a more scriptural-historical approach, examining Christ's "human involvement in the history of salvation."[101] There is much greater awareness of the historical development of dogma, a realization that only over time has the church arrived at the current conceptualization of her tradition. And of course the concern of younger Americans

[97] John Courtney Murray, S.J., "Towards a Theology for the Layman," *Theological Studies*, 5 (1944), 75.

[98] Some who attended the Conference on the Theological Issues of the Second Vatican Council at Notre Dame in March, 1966, might suggest that at least a few American Catholics have even passed up their mentors in this regard. But the Vatican Council has also created a backlash, so that a real polarization is found in 1966 Roman Catholicism, as can be seen in such developments as the Catholic Traditionalist Movement. Some of the polarities are described in Wakin and Scheuer, *The De-Romanization of the American Catholic Church*.

[99] G. Van Ackeran, "Current Approaches to Theology," in *Christian Wisdom and Christian Formation*, p. 84.

[100] *Ibid.*, p. 91.

[101] *Ibid.*, p. 88.

with problems of social injustice is also reflected in the new theology and in religiously based extra-curricular programs as well.[102] This is as it should be.

The Newman whom Catholic educators have been so fond of quoting about the place of theology in higher education also stated that the university "is not a convent, not a seminary; it is a place to fit men of the world for the world." The Constitution on the Church in the Modern World, of the Second Vatican Council, explicitly recognizes that secularity is the defining characteristic of lay men and women. The products of Catholic colleges and universities will best serve the church, not by making Catholicism an independent cultural, political, or social force, but by serving directly the needs of the world.[103] Harvey Cox has well described the "diakonic" (service or healing) and "koinoniac" (fraternal) — in addition to the "kerygmatic" — functions of the church.[104] The Church of the Secular City must speak of God as a sociological problem and as a political issue, as well as a theological question. More recently, Cox has written that "this new urban man displays a different personality from Bunyan's stolid Pilgrim, plodding single-mindedly toward the light above the gate."[105] The Puritan pilgrim cannot be the only model of Christian personality. An education attempting to train students to "resist the world" will be wholly inappropriate and seems to be based on a human condition conceived of as simply one damned thing after another, as Aldous Huxley once put it. Rather, the key word to describe the task of the Catholic college is the one once used by Theodore M. Hesburgh, C.S.C.: mediation.[106] But many of us feel more at home with a specifically secular mediation than the priestly connotations of traditionally Catholic usage. Harvey Cox illustrates this perspective:

[102] Many of the old guard still believe that religious issues can only be confronted in courses with "theology" in their title. The reaction to the 1966 NCEA talk by a Webster College sister, describing the curriculum revision requiring no theology at Webster, indicated considerable resistance and an apparent conviction that religious matters will not present themselves outside such courses.

[103] I have drawn from John Cogley in this formulation ("Changing Roles in the Church," *Commonweal*, 80 [1964], 5–7).

[104] "The Greek word *koinonia* is usually translated 'fellowship.' In our discussion it will designate that aspect of the church's responsibility in the city for a visible demonstration of what the church is saying in its kerygma and pointing to in its diakonia. It is 'hope made visible,' a kind of living picture of the character and composition of the true city of man for which the church strives" (Cox, *The Secular City*, p. 144).

[105] Harvey Cox, "Secularization and the Secular Mentality: A New Challenge to Christian Education," *Religious Education*, 61 (1966), 86. Christian education, says Cox, needs (1) education for change and innovation; (2) education for phantasy, the dreams of the visionary; (3) education for uncertainty and ceaseless readjustment (p. 87).

[106] In his address before the National Catholic Educational Association Convention, April, 1961, and appearing as "The Work of Mediation," *Commonweal*, 74 (1961), 33–35.

In the age of the secular city, the questions with which we concern ourselves tend to be mostly functional and operational. We wonder how
power can be controlled and used responsibly. We ask how a reasonable
international order can be fashioned out of the technological community
into which we have been hurried. We worry about how the wizardry of
medical science can be applied to the full without creating a world population constantly hovering on the brink of famine. These are pragmatic
questions, and we are pragmatic men whose interest in religion is at
best peripheral. . . . Secular man relies on himself and his colleagues
for answers. He does not ask the church, the priest, or God. This is not
because he has no respect for religion. He is probably not an anticleric.
He simply feels that the issues he is concerned with relate to a different
field. Like all contemporaries, he is a specialist, usually scrupulously
tolerant of those with a different specialty. So it is pointless and unfair
to try to force secular man into asking religious questions, consciously
or otherwise, before we can converse. We begin by accepting pragmatic
man as he is. . . .[107]

Some will not take kindly to suggestions such as the above, or to those of
men like H. Stuart Hughes, who thinks it quite possible that the church of
the future — at least for the educated — "will become so private, so personal,
so enmeshed in the vocabulary and concepts of the secular world as to be
almost unrecognizable as the Catholicism of the past."[108] But this appears
a distinct likelihood for many who consider themselves Catholic Christians,
if not for the church as an institution. And it is to secular man that the
Catholic colleges must speak.

Paul Goodman has lamented the lack of commitment on the part of
more than a handful of colleges and universities, stating he could not name
ten in America that strongly stand for anything peculiar to themselves; there
is great conformity to the national norm.[109] Mr. Goodman suggested a small
secession from established institutions, for those interested in a genuine
"community of scholars." It might well be that higher education could profit
from such a venture.[110] But this is not our concern here. John Gardner wrote

[107] Cox, *The Secular City*, pp. 80–81. It is not clear whether Cox's concept of
secularization is a descriptive term or a statement of desired outcomes. Fathers
Evans and Greeley have noted that "secular man" as Cox described him is hard
to find. But the contemporary collegian does prefer to describe himself in much
the same terms as Cox's pragmatic man. Perhaps John Kennedy best caught this
mood, when he termed himself "an idealist without illusions."

[108] In "Pope John's Revolution: Secular or Religious?" *Commonweal*, 82
(1965), 301–3.

[109] In *The Community of Scholars* (New York: Random House, 1962).

[110] The Students for a Democratic Society established in 1965 a few "Free
Universities"; whether these organizations can outlive their many similar prede-
cessors remains to be seen. The critics of the "Free University" at Ann Arbor

in 1961 that "each of the different kinds of institutions has its significant part to play in creating the total pattern, and . . . each should be allowed to play its role with honor and recognition."[111] Whatever "excellence" can mean for an institution, it must be in terms of its own objectives.

Educational goals are, of course, modified by changing circumstances. Formerly, Catholic higher education was often charged with being *too* Catholic; the "salvage operation" approach fought primarily a delaying action. One official theological and philosophical view was inculcated, not only in courses in these areas, but often in other subjects as well, through "organizing principles." This has greatly changed in most Catholic colleges. Whether by design or by the exigencies of their new situations, with increasing numbers of lay faculty and young clerics trained at the best secular universities, is unimportant: de facto "disestablishment" of a sort has occurred, at least with regard to secular subjects.[112]

Presently, the Catholic colleges confront another problem. No longer "too Catholic," some institutions are in a sense not Catholic enough. When largely cut off from the rest of higher education, the Catholic campus was isolated and self-centered. Having moved away from this posture, it now may face dangers of a different sort. For it would seem that there *are* particular studies for which Catholic schools are especially well suited. Experts in theology and philosophy should be naturally drawn to a Catholic college offering the pursuit of these subjects as legitimate university disciplines. Those who have specialized in matters that, for quite irreversible historical reasons, have a Catholic taste to them (e.g., Chaucer, Dante, medieval studies, Irish history, Latin American civilizations) might well prefer to work in settings where colleagues and research materials are more congenial, *for primarily professional reasons*. Yet most Catholic institutions are today little different from their secular counterparts. Their concern with providing courses of greater immediate relevance to members of immigrant groups on the make has led to a concentration in business, engineering, and pre-professional programs at the expense of the liberal and humane. It is a curious thing that a number of non-Catholic colleges and universities are presently establishing chairs or programs in Catholic studies, and many such endeavors bid fair to surpass the work done on Catholic campuses, either singularly or collectively. If this happens, it will be a bitter harvest for Catholic higher education. Previously pragmatic decisions to establish vocational sequences should not bind Catholic schools for the future. Their lack of dependence on state legis-

protest its dogmatically radical cast. The "cluster colleges" proposed by Clark Kerr and others (see note 16) may provide a partial solution to this problem.

[111] John Gardner, *Excellence* (New York: Harper Bros., 1961), p. 83.

[112] Parallel "disestablishments" of a sort can be found in the disaffiliations of many Catholic campuses with such specifically Catholic student organizations as the National Federation of Catholic College Students, as Catholic undergraduates prefer to become active in groups such as the National Student Association.

latures and popularly elected boards of regents *could* make such institutions more free for experimentation and innovation, particularly in light of the relative affluence of Catholics in the 1960's, who can better afford humanistic education.[113] It has been shown that the vast majority of Catholic students desiring business and engineering education now go to less expensive state schools. Many Catholic educators might well ask themselves if they are willing to continue concentration in areas such as engineering, which require increasing expenditures to remain up-to-date. The establishment of *new* sequences in these areas would seem in most cases folly.

If different programs are to be inaugurated, they should be ones that bring the value-commitments of Christianity to bear on the areas needing precisely this influence in the contemporary world: the family, education, urban studies, the economics of abundance, and the like. Here is where values have immediate relevance, and where the "committed" universities would appear to have distinctive contributions to make. Some of the more forward-looking educators have lately stated that the schools and colleges must involve themselves with values — even, Philip Phenix would insist, religious values.[114] The aim of teaching should be the moral application of knowledge, says Phenix; students should be taught to uphold "worth" in every area of their lives. Any teacher, religious or agnostic, makes some unspoken commitments. Those questions of relevance to his specialty, and the aspects of life his discipline affects, will naturally be matters of some involvement for him.[115] Few professors or institutions would want to proceed randomly; they have assumptions and points they want to make. Some instructors feel it is their obligation to disabuse students of all their beliefs and values, and this may have positive functions. But to pretend these beliefs and values are not replaced with others, however implicit, is to be grandly self-deceptive. Certainly the insistence on the meaninglessness of values is itself a commitment (and one not discovered in nature, but imposed upon it). It is not possible for either universities or complex societies to proceed in wholly neutral ways. "Doctrines" of one sort or another are always expounded. But there is no

[113] The case histories of the universities of California and Colorado attest to the difficulties with such systems of university control. It is interesting that Christopher Jencks has recently suggested that more competition with innovative private schools would do the public institutions great good ("Is the Public School Obsolete?" *The Public Interest*, 1, No. 2 (Winter, 1966), 18–27.

[114] In *Education and the Common Good* (New York: Harper Bros., 1961).

[115] Irving Kristol has urged intellectuals to take a role in defining the moral quality of our society, by concentrating on the implications of change in the areas where they have competence (but not to express opinions on a whole range of topics about which they really know little): "The Troublesome Intellectuals," *The Public Interest*, 1, no. 2 (Winter, 1966), 3–6. Walter Lippmann would go further, stating that the universities have replaced the churches and governments as sources, in the quest for "a good life in a good society" ("The University," *New Republic*, 154 [May 28, 1966], 17–20).

reason why value-influenced instruction cannot go on within a context, as Martin Marty put it, "of pluralism, of dialogue, of vigorous contention";[116] if religious bodies do not expound value-commitments, other ideologies and quasi-religions will. The danger, notes Marty, is sameness. A variety of viewpoints can be expressed, and a plethora of controlling assumptions brought to public view .

Catholic colleges must then be Catholic. Not in the triumphal, defensive ways of the past, but with the spirit of *aggiornamento* and dialogue. For the departments of theology, this means ecumenical faculties, giving first-rate instruction, and doing contemporary research in a variety of religious systems. It also means institutional structures for pursuing the relevance of theology to contemporary culture, to man in the secular city.[117] In other disciplines, guidelines are less clear. Some would state that learning can be done "in a Catholic form," even in subjects such as the social sciences; Father Leo Ward seems to hold that the believer will be better able to understand some things.[118] I would concede this possibility for some areas of philosophy, and perhaps for the understanding of works done in a specifically Christian milieu (e.g., those of Dante), but I am not at all sure what this might mean for subjects such as mathematics, sociology, nuclear physics, or cytobiology. The scholar in such disciplines will admittedly bring his assumptions and values to bear on the teaching and research he does, and will probably try with all seriousness to integrate his knowledge with his own belief system. No scholar can ignore many problems if he pursues his own discipline very far. It seems clear that the Catholic scholar will feel obliged to point out those matters that appear simultaneously to be verified by the methods of his own discipline, and at some odds with the teachings of Catholicism.[119] But it seems that he can do no more than fairly present the apparent contradictions, manifest genuine efforts to resolve them, and engage in

[116] In *The National Catholic Reporter*, January 26, 1966.

[117] The Center for the Study of Man in Contemporary Society at Notre Dame is inaugurating programs of this sort, with the establishment of institutes for the interdisciplinary study of religion, education, the family, population, delinquency, and other appropriate areas. Similar institutes have been established at Georgetown, Fordham and St. Louis; but, it should be noted, a group of Jesuits have moved their social science center from St. Louis University to Harvard, and no Catholic university had an American style Ph.D. program in theology until Fordham's and Marquette's in the 1960's.

[118] In "Is There a Christian Learning?" *Commonweal*, 59 (1953), and in *New Life in Catholic Schools* (St. Louis: B. Herder and Co., 1958). But Ward has never implied that education should be apologetics, and long stood fast against those who would have made Catholic education only indoctrination and moral training.

[119] The reader might refer to *The Catholic Educational Review*, 64 (March, 1966), 155, for the statement of Vatican II that the church "intends that by their very constitution individual subjects be pursued according to their own principles, method, and liberty of scientific inquiry, in such a way that an ever deeper under-

discussions with his colleagues who may help illuminate his understanding.[120] If a university really does approximate the community of scholars envisioned by Paul Goodman and others, it is precisely this kind of arrangement that should be most stimulating. Reciprocal exploration, discovery, and criticism should be of immeasurable benefit to theologians and other scholars alike. This, after all, is what the Constitution on the Church in the Modern World encourages.[121] Not only would theologians be basing their concepts on a realistic view of man as a behaving individual, compared to the rather abstract conception of "human nature" behind much of the theologizing of the past, but secular scholars should find such interchanges profitable for their own work, as well. It is difficult, however, to see how the specifically mathematical, sociological, or scientific work of secular scholars can be done in a "Catholic" — or even "Christian" — way.

This is not to suggest that the Catholic campus is simply a *place*, a locus for teaching and research. To the extent that scholars and researchers share bonds that transcend the merely intellectual, the campus — and their work — will be affected. As a *community*, that is to say, Catholic colleges and universities *will* be different. How? Andrew Greeley recently suggested that the Catholic campus "is a segment of the pilgrim people of God gathered together for a dialogue which is essentially intellectual." [122] At about the same time, John Courtney Murray, S.J., wrote that, now that the differentiation between the sacral and the secular has been effected in history, the Catholic university must "be the bearer of the new movement that will transcend the present dichotomy of sacral and secular," as the "artisan of their new unity." [123] This is not to say that such unity is a given; it is aimed at. The quest must take place in an open atmosphere of free inquiry. The Catholic college or university is *not*, Notre Dame's John Walsh, C.S.C., points out, the teaching arm of the Church; it is "a manifestation of the Church *learning*." In this learning process, all the data must be accessible:

> If Catholic scholars learn only with one another and from one another, can they be said to be honestly and genuinely engaged in learning; are they open to all possible sources of fact, knowledge, and understanding? One of the most basic laws of learning is that ideas are strengthened

standing of these fields will be obtained. . . ." I am grateful to Whitney Evans for calling my attention to this statement.

[120] I have drawn from J. R. Burke's letter to the editor, *America*, 114 (1966), 231, in this passage.

[121] The document states: "Let those who teach theology in seminaries and universities strive to collaborate with men versed in the other sciences through a sharing of their resources and points of view."

[122] Andrew M. Greeley, "The Place of Religion," *Commonweal*, 84 (1966), 104–10.

[123] John Courtney Murray, S.J., "The Declaration on Religious Freedom: Its Deeper Significance," *America*, 114 (1966), 593.

or destroyed by conflict, by challenge, by demands for proof and explanation. These would not be likely to be forthcoming even in a
scholarly community in which there was general agreement on all
fundamental issues.[124]

Another speaker at the Conference on Academic Freedom at Notre Dame
put it extremely well: "I conceive of the university as the institutional embodi-
ment of *fides quarens intellectum*, . . . The college is the locus of the
discursive examination of our commitments. The primary purpose of college
is inquiry, not instruction." [125]

In light of these lucid statements, I would want to modify Father Greeley's
statement to read: the Catholic campus *contains* a segment of the pilgrim people of God gathered together for dialogue that is essentially intellectual. I do
not think the Catholic campus can be a Christian community. The familial
models of the past will not work in the age of secular man. A Christian community should be *available*, of course, on the Catholic campus. But there
will be many outside it. Some cannot, at least at present, involve themselves
this way. Which does not mean they are not concerned; many would undoubtedly agree with Harvey Cox:

> Man is summoned to be concerned, first of all, for his neighbor. In the
> age of organization, he can only do this by getting into the fray, by
> losing a little skin from his own nose, perhaps even a spiritual value
> here and there, in the tough but epochal battle for the control of the

[124] John E. Walsh, C.S.C., "Academic Freedom and the Goals of a Catholic
University" (Paper read at the Conference on Academic Freedom in Catholic
Universities, Notre Dame, April 22–23, 1966), published in Manier and Houck,
Academic Freedom, forthcoming.

[125] Frederick Crosson, "Commitment as the Basis of Free Inquiry" (Paper
read at the Conference on Academic Freedom in Catholic Universities, Notre
Dame, April 22–23, 1966). Mr. Crosson elaborated: "Far from biasing the objectivity of the investigator, a commitment to the reality of a certain level of meaning
may well be the necessary condition for insight into the pattern of phenomena on
that level. Cantor's discovery of transfinite numbers in mathematics and Freud's
discovery of the unconscious meaning of human behavior are two examples of
insights which were hotly disputed by competent scholars for decades before they
were accepted. In both cases, a commitment to the reality of the field of investigation was a precondition of access to the data of the field. Religious faith appears
to share in the same cognitive structure: only a commitment, an affirming insight,
opens up the dimension of the sacred in human experience. Those who lack that
commitment literally cannot see the meaning affirmed by others." Mr. Crosson
concluded that academic freedom does not depend on a precondition of neutral-
ity, and a "committed" university may well have men around who concentrate
on the "discursive examination" of their commitments, in a manner they might
be unable to do elsewhere. But not all the scholars at such a university would be
so inclined. There are great advantages to even an absence of shared commitments. See Daniel Callahan, "Reforming the Catholic University," *The New
Church* (New York: Scribner's, 1966), pp. 124–44.

organization. But as he does leap in, perhaps at the risk of his own life, he may discover that, even in the age of organization, precisely he who loses his life gains it.[126]

Such students are those who have decided that they can work most effectively from within the power structure, that the effectiveness of sit-ins and picket-lines is limited at best. Because of their needs for immediate involvement, they often work away from the campus several hours a week in action-oriented tutoring projects, community organizing, and the like. But when on campus, they want to be free to pursue the studies that will make them more effective in the organizations they intend to infiltrate. They have read Cox. They agree that they must learn about the iniquities of the tax structure, the maneuvers of real estate boards, the machinations of zoning committees. These sophisticated students know they must hone their skills of analysis and communication, that they can grasp the reins of power more efficiently. They want not community, but the competence and cool detachment of the secular city. The men they admire seem to have little time for socializing, for conversation. Or even, often, for praying. They are on the move, doing the work of the world. There must be a place for these individuals on the Catholic campus. A Christian community should not be forced upon them. The influence it exerts will be indirect.

At the 1966 Meetings of the National Catholic Educational Association in Chicago, the Bishops' Commission for Ecumenical Affairs released a milestone document, "Educating for Ecumenism." A strong case was made against the poverty that the tragic separations of four hundred years have created for the Christian community: "We need each other. Our basic change of heart consists in a deep conviction that we are incomplete as long as division continues." The same thing might be said for the necessary plurality *within* the Catholic campus. Students of diverse orientation, too, need each other.

Perhaps what we are moving toward is the concept of a "public Catholic university," with a primary task of preparing students — the majority of whom are Catholics — for the pluralistic world in which they live. Whatever their own religious beliefs, the faculty and students at such an institution will share a commitment to the "cognitive accessibility" of the supernatural, as one of the dimensions of man's experience.[127] They will hold that there are spiritual realities, and important questions to be asked about them. Not all will do the asking, of course; many will prefer to concentrate on the secular city. But they will agree that such explorations should take place at the university.

The present absence of real Christian community on the Catholic campus is a scandal. But it would be foolhardy to attempt to cram such a community

[126] Cox, *The Secular City*, p. 181.
[127] The words in quotes are Crosson's, from whom I have drawn in this paragraph.

down the throats of every undergraduate at the Catholic colleges and universities. For the foreseeable future, a number of approaches will have to flourish side by side on such campuses, taking nourishment from each other. "The world," sang out John Kennedy in 1961, "is very different now." The diverse orientations of the students will undoubtedly generate a variety of subcultures as well. Like John Kennedy's world, the Catholic campus must be made "safe for diversity."

The future of Catholic higher education? No one really knows. But it will never be the same again. John Cogley said this well, at the closing session of the 1966 NCEA meetings:

> An era has ended; an historic period has passed. Like all historic periods, it was on balance a mixture of magnificence and mistake, of benevolence and mischief, of accomplishment and stupidity. We can praise it or denounce it, but we cannot prolong it. It is over. A new day has dawned for the Church and with it a new day for Catholic education.

Appendixes

APPENDIX A

PLANNING FOR THE FUTURE

Anthony E. Seidl

On occasion a bishop would save a college; but usually the bishop had neither money nor credit, and colleges overburdened with debt had no alternative but to close their doors when it became impossible for them to find their way through the maze of liabilities. . . . The main reason for the demise of these schools was insolvency . . . the most carefully guarded secret of the Catholic colleges was their financial status . . . when the colleges became embroiled in embarrassing liabilities they appealed to groups or individuals for help. The results of these appeals were frequently good, but likely less successful than they would have been had the colleges been more open about their situation. They were always willing to admit they needed money, but they were seldom willing to distribute a balance sheet. . . . Because of this condition, colleges were anxious to take and retain any students, regardless of aptitude and motivation for studies.[1]

Although Power wrote the above in discussing the Catholic colleges of the last century, it might well be that he has already written the history for many Catholic colleges in this century. As a consequence of their problems — largely financial — only one-fourth of the Catholic colleges opened before 1850 survive today, slightly less than thirty per cent of those opened between 1850 and 1899 are still in business, and only thirty-six per cent of those opened between 1900 and 1955 survive.[2] Of the 268 Catholic men's colleges founded in the United States up to the time that Power wrote his history, only 82 still existed, a loss of 186 institutions.[3] The first four-year

Anthony E. Seidl attended The University of Portland, Portland State College, Stanford University, and Notre Dame, where he received a Ph.D. in 1964. After a career in high school teaching and administration, Mr. Seidl has turned his attention to graduate instruction in educational administration and finance. He is now an assistant professor of education at the University of San Francisco, and a member of the Academy for Educational Development.

[1] Edward J. Power, *A History of Catholic Higher Education in the United States* (Milwaukee: Bruce Publishing Company, 1958), pp. 160–61.

[2] *Ibid.*, p. 47.

[3] *Ibid.*, pp. 333–39.

Catholic college for women was not established until 1896, and the mortality rate for them has been much lower.[4]

Philip Gleason, in discussing these statistics at greater length in chapter 2, points out that Catholic higher education has forced radical social adjustments in the past; but changes continue to occur, necessitating further social and economic adjustments. Today's fierce competition for survival — and survival funds — requires astuteness in management and planning. When individuals, businesses, foundations, and federal agencies are asked to support an educational enterprise, they quite rightly demand indications of managerial expertise. It would be ironic if the legal aspects of government support to Catholic education were solved — as they seem about to be, with changes in the patterns of control — only to have sophisticated agency heads frightened away by indications of haphazard management and planning. These are, not to put too fine a point on it, the tools of survival.

How healthy is Catholic higher education? How viable will it be in the years ahead? Will Catholic colleges continue to exist? Can they exist? The dangers of proliferation alluded to in some of the preceding chapters indicate that viability is one of the most pressing concerns facing many Catholic colleges today. Survival may well be primarily an economic question, for these schools must be fiscally sound to operate at even minimal levels of existence.

Although the economic question is frequently the conversation topic in corridors, at meetings, or at informal discussions, there seems to be a defensive attitude of silence that prevents frank and open discussion of this question in public meetings. Whatever the date and cause of such an attitude, it is a luxury that no longer can be afforded. The lack of understanding and paucity of data resulting from this attitude contribute to the fact that Catholic higher education is today at a crossroads with its future depending in no small part on how well Catholic educators understand and meet the economic question.

The 1959 *Summary of Catholic Education* reported that there were 231 Catholic colleges and universities in the United States, enrolling a total of 285,654 students. In addition, 46 diocesan teacher colleges, teacher-training colleges (junior college level), and normal training schools enrolled 5,506 students.[5] A total of 277 institutions of higher learning, then, enrolled 291,-160 students in 1959. It is estimated that by 1985 a maximum of 500,000 Catholic students will be enrolled in Catholic institutions of higher learning. Thus, approximately 2.4 million Catholic students will be on campuses of other than Catholic institutions.

Four factors have influenced the demand for more education: (1) the

[4] *Ibid.*, p. 183.
[5] *Summary of Catholic Education, 1959* (Washington, D.C.: National Catholic Welfare Conference, Department of Education), pp. 12–21.

great increase in birth rates following World War II; (2) the increased need, desire, and financial ability to obtain more education; (3) the social pressure that keeps young people in school longer; and (4) the effect of automation and mechanization in the reduction of jobs. The implications for Catholic colleges and universities are clear. Simple division indicates that in 1959 the average student population at the Catholic colleges and universities was 1,051 students, while by 1985, assuming that the present number of 295 institutions does not change significantly, the average student load will be approximately 1,695 students. Averages, however, can be misleading. One must remember that after the students enrolled at the large Catholic institutions (such as Fordham and St. John's in New York, St. Louis, Marquette in Milwaukee, Loyola in Chicago, and the University of San Francisco, to name a few) have been withdrawn from the totals, the average decreases so rapidly for the remaining Catholic institutions of higher learning that it becomes a question of whether or not there are enough students for the remaining Catholic colleges to conduct fiscally viable programs.

The objective here is not to discuss what the purposes of Catholic higher education are, nor to discuss whether other institutions are able to handle the situation better than Catholic institutions, thereby causing withdrawal of the church from such efforts.[6] We prefer to concentrate on the problems surrounding the continued operation of Catholic colleges and universities.

The changing numbers of students have caused, and will continue to cause, major financial problems for Catholic colleges unless plans are formulated to meet the situation. The problems, in turn, point to the necessity for long-range planning (which is, in essence, nothing more than long-term budgeting), and for prudent financial and business practices, so that maximum returns can be gained from the funds expended. Admittedly, decisions about whether the educational benefits are worth the cost must be made, but this must at least in part follow from an evaluation of management practices in terms of how well they contribute to the realization of the objectives of the school and how much they minimize waste in the utilization of financial and material resources in the educational program. More specifically, plans for students, buildings, faculty, curriculum, and non-teaching personnel must be detailed so they can be translated into the common denominator — the dollar — and financial transactions need to be accounted for so that administration has information necessary to decision-making.

Because the purpose of administration is the facilitation of instruction, costs have made management an important segment of the administrative process. It must be realized that, within the organizational structure, current university administration is definitely different from that of the past. Administration can no longer exclude policy formation and coordinated plan-

---

[6] The reader is referred to the discussion of the goals of Catholic Higher Education, pp. 318 ff.

ning. Resistance to reorganization and change is no longer a tenable position, nor are good intentions a valid reason for continued existence. Within this framework one must also be aware of the fact that in recent years the term "organization" has acquired different meanings. Characteristic of an organization, be it formal or informal, is that it has a specific goal or goals. We do not consider educational objectives here; suffice it to say that an astute administration will want to run a continual check on the possibility that the institution is more concerned with maintaining itself in existence than with achieving its proper objectives. After such determination, attention can be directed to the problems at hand, such things as the "costs and productivity measures, budgetary techniques and long-range fiscal planning, development programs and voluntary gifts, and a broad group of questions encompassed by the term 'economics of higher education'." [7]

Much of the available literature indicates that space utilization studies, projections of building need, and more extensive use of the school plant have evoked the greater interest in recent years.[8] Cost, always a sensitive subject in higher education, requires planned attention by Catholic institutions, both for the purposes of decision-making by administration and for providing information to donors attempting to decide where best to give their support.

Against a background of increasing numbers of students, mobility of population, suburban expansion, industrial development, scientific achievement, educational innovations, and increasing costs, the institution of higher learning that develops long-range plans will find itself in a feature role. "When it is a question of money," Voltaire once noted, "everybody is of the same religion." Those who support educational institutions are asking questions, for they are becoming increasingly concerned with where the money goes and whether it is being spent wisely. Prudent management, which necessarily becomes part of long-range planning, has become a watchword for successful colleges and universities. The logical approach to such planning is to consider it an integral part of the school's responsibility.

Like interacting individuals, institutions can be said not only to react to their environments, but in some measure to create them. The realization that it is possible to change conditions, or reshape an institution to meet changing conditions, seems seldom to be grasped, perhaps owing to the fear of change many people have. Basically, long-range planning points out what these conditions are and what must be done to meet them.

For years Catholic colleges and universities have received a steady income of praise and admiration for their performance; of late, however, they find themselves in financial environments where their performance becomes in-

---

[7] James I. Doi, "Organization and Administration, Finance and Facilities," *Review of Educational Research*, 35 (1965), 353–54.
[8] *Ibid.*, p. 354.

creasingly difficult. Only for those who have faith in their long-term viability, who realize that to give an institution meaning and long life such characteristics must be built into the institution, will there be dignity, meaning, and continued survival. Because long-range planning forces the asking of fundamental questions, it becomes the sine qua non for "building in" these characteristics.

Administration, as part of its leadership function, must involve its constituents to gain their support, their understanding, and their acceptance. Although administration will — if alert, positive leadership exists — recognize the problems, it must interpret these needs to the faculty and to those whose support is sought, while being willing to admit that opinions and judgments of others may be better than its own. Perhaps the most difficult area for such planning is the determination of the variety and quality of subject matter and the way in which it is to be taught. Despite such difficulties, the planning process that has involved both teachers and lay people has proved to be the most effective because it has fostered understanding and support at the same time that it has sought appropriate solutions to the problems.

The American Association of School Administrators recorded the following statement on planning in its Twenty-fourth Yearbook:

> It is no small task to discharge the responsibility for planning, to create an atmosphere in which creative planning can flourish, to cultivate public opinion to a point where it will accept such planning, and to set up machinery for collection of facts in an amount sufficient to insure the accuracy of interpretations. Yet no board of education will be able to find sufficient time actually to study the needs of the community without the knowledge and freedom growing out of such a procedure. Planning, when properly done, makes it possible for a school to do at least a few things with certainty. It helps to maintain the morale of the school employees, promotes the good will of the community, and contributes much to public understanding.[9]

Of great importance to all is the highest output of educational excellence from the input of resources for the greatest number of students. To further improve the use of material and human resources, to evaluate the present needs, and to provide a plan for future operations are the purposes of long-range planning or budgeting. As a vehicle for forcefully indicating the need for developing programs to meet the money shortage, long-range budgeting is indispensable; it has long been advocated by Sidney Tickton.[10] Assuming

[9] American Association of School Administrators, *School Boards in Action: Twenty-fourth Yearbook*, 1949.

[10] Sidney G. Tickton, *Needed: A Ten-Year College Budget* (New York: The Fund for the Advancement of Education, 1961). I am indebted to Mr. Tickton for permission to outline the specifics of this planning process.

that quality is recognizable and that there are ways to improve quality without necessarily increasing costs, Tickton writes:

> . . . the techniques of management and long-range planning are essentially the same regardless of whether an educational institution is one of the 450 colleges that have used our tables or one of the three or four dozen universities . . . that has been involved . . . the technique is quite similar to the technique used in planning and management by large business corporations and government agencies. The problems differ, the solutions differ, but our experience is that the methodology is essentially the same.[11]

Such a technique has become a useful tool at many educational institutions because management has begun to recognize the great need to prepare for the important years ahead. All of the indications point to an increasing market for education; a plethora of new educational techniques and activities will be needed as costs rise and as new patterns of educational efforts emerge.

> Long-range budget plans bring educational needs into focus. They provide a common denominator which can bring together such diverse items as tuition, scholarships, salary paid to teachers, space utilization, new construction, new teaching techniques, library acquisition and the hundred other factors that go into the running of an educational institution. . . . None of the steps . . . can be accomplished without a sound long-range budget plan. It must be workable and realistic, and it must be developed at the very same time the academic plan is worked out.[12]

Tickton's conclusion is simply that the problems of the educational institutions are going to multiply in the years ahead, even faster than the students will increase, and that the problems of nonpublic schools may well multiply faster than those of other educational institutions because, as a group, they cannot expect much government money, nor have they generally "excited the imagination of most of the large foundations." [13]

Administrators of tomorrow will be directing most of their attention to the financial capacity of willing parents and potential students, as well as to reluctant donors; these sources of funds will generally be willing to support only those institutions they consider to be of high quality both from an educational and from a managerial point of view. Further, because there are real pos-

---

[11] Sidney G. Tickton, "Every Independent School Needs a Long Range Financial Plan" (Telelecture read to the April 2, 1965, Seminar on Long-range Planning sponsored by the Council for Independent School Aid, Inc., at Cate School, Carpenteria, California), p. 5.

[12] *Ibid.*, pp. 16 and 20.

[13] *Ibid.*, p. 21.

sibilities of making funds go further at many colleges, there will be a need for administrators to utilize better their resources — people, buildings, time, and finances — with the realization that the schools of tomorrow may well bear only a faint resemblance to the schools of today.

Filling out tables such as Tickton recommends will graphically demonstrate the need for having competent people in charge of institutional financial and business management, the necessity of having an organizational structure that subordinates business administration to educational administration while maintaining a relationship that allows efficient and economic management of the institution; it will also show the vital necessity for translating the school's program into an operational and formal budget. The budget will, in turn, demonstrate the need for an accounting system that provides information on financial progress and performance and will indicate the necessity for periodic appraisals of the financial picture and of the management itself, as well as the necessity for reporting to higher authority and to those from whom support is sought. Making out the budget will focus attention on how clear procurement policies and practices will not only strengthen the organization but also realize vast savings in quality and dollars for the institution.

Trying to make a budget balance will, among other things, forcefully indicate to administrators the necessity for having plant and property management that will arrest misuse and deterioration, provide funds for maintaining a proper state of repairs by adequately trained and paid personnel, and demonstrate the necessity of having a complete personnel program for non-teaching employees and for giving attention to the conditions of their employment. By making out a budget, administrators will become aware of the magnitude of the institution's auxiliary enterprises, such as the bookstore, cafeteria, boarding facilities, and athletic program, realizing that these consititute, in effect, a large business that must be properly managed and can no longer be left to chance.

What does this mean for the Catholic college and university of tomorrow? The choice of much hard work and fund-raising as opposed to mediocrity and/or death. The planning determines the amount of financial help needed after the most useful part of this long-range planning has been accomplished, viz., the specific task of filling out the tables for such a budget. There is a very hopeful future for colleges and universities willing to perform this function. On the other hand, the changes that are taking place will not only threaten the existence of some institutions, but will also cause others to die prematurely if no preventative measures are taken. One need only to look at the history of the last century, or, if he so chooses, view more recent history, to note the names of good companies and schools that have fallen by the wayside during the greatest economic boom this country has ever had, simply because they failed to meet the competitive test. Such names as

Studebaker, Packard, and Colliers perhaps first come to mind; institutions of higher learning such as the University of Buffalo and the University of Pittsburgh are more recent examples of identity changes linked to economic factors. More meaningful to Catholic educators, perhaps, are the periodic summaries of Catholic education published by the National Catholic Welfare Conference. The 1959 summary, for example, lists sixteen Catholic colleges that changed their identity or were discontinued between 1955 and 1959.[14]

The threat posed by the importance and expansion of public junior colleges and university extension centers has already become a reality for a number of Catholic institutions. If the above indicators do not ring the fire bell, a comparison of the present public-private enrollments with the projections for 1985 should cause at least some apprehension. Private colleges and universities currently enroll approximately forty-one per cent of the students in higher education, but it is estimated that by 1985 they will enroll no more than twenty per cent.[15] After the enrollments of the large private institutions have been removed from this twenty per cent, the number of clients remaining for the myriad of other private institutions will be comparatively microscopic.

The success story of Parsons College of Iowa, on the other hand, provides evidence of what can be accomplished in a relatively short span of time by using a managerial approach to college problems. An almost bankrupt institution with 212 students eleven years ago, Parsons today enrolls 4,600 students and has "a faculty with salaries second only to Harvard and the University of Chicago, [and] a constantly growing physical plant. . . ."[16] Earlham College of Indiana and Knox College of Illinois give solid evidence of the benefits that can be derived from long-range budgeting, as do Bowdoin and Harvey Mudd at Claremont. In recent years the projection tables involved in such planning have been filled out by institutions varying in enrollments from 300 and 400 students to such large universities as Ohio State University and Pennsylvania State University.

Despite the fact that Catholic colleges and universities differ from other schools in some respects, they are subject to the same principles of good management, economics, and finance. These institutions will not be able to project into the future their images of the past; they will find, instead, the need for making dramatic changes in policies and programs to meet the demand for higher education *with the funds available*.

The actual working out of the tables for long-range budgeting will tell more eloquently than institutional white papers where present practices are

[14] *Summary of Catholic Education, 1959.*
[15] Tickton, *Ten-Year College Budget*, pp. 6–7.
[16] "How Parsons College Stays in the Black," *College Management*, 1 (May, 1966), 39.

leading. A long-term budget is a neutral medium of analysis; it need not advocate anything. A budget must balance, allowing various possibilities to be tried out on a theoretical basis and then either be discarded or utilized. Businessmen and institutional donors will understand it, since they live in a world of long-term projections and plans as protection for their future; faculty will understand it, if they work closely in the planning.

Some colleges and universities are finding that such planning has additional advantages when they computerize their program. Because of the ease in changing variables in the program and the ability to do in minutes what formerly would have taken days, the use of forecasting is considerably encouraged for the analysis of short-, intermediate-, or long-range effects of any of the wide variety of fiscal decisions. For example, what effect(s) will a change in tuition, or a change in interest rate, or a change in salaries or fringe benefits have on the total program? Whether or not a computer is available is not the main point, however, but rather, as Tickton points out, that

> the long-term budget can become a powerful persuader to a reconsideration of old policy decisions with respect to curriculum, academic calendar, etc., because it emphasizes the consequences of continuing to do business as usual. . . . It's risky to run a big business — and colleges and universities are big business these days — on the assumption that "God will provide." Miracles do happen but there haven't been many recently. And they can't always be counted on to happen in the year that the money is needed.[17]

The making of a long-term budget is a cooperative venture involving all those concerned with the institution; it will focus attention on the difficult, "hot," and sometimes explosive questions, each of which must be translated into dollars and sources of dollars. There will be a need to answer such questions as:

1. How big is the college going to be?
2. How much is the faculty going to be paid next year, the year after, and each year for the ten years ahead?
3. How much is it going to cost to run the plant?
4. How much is going to be spent for student services, development, campus activities, athletics, and the like?
5. How much should be set aside for scholarships?
6. How many new buildings are to be built?
7. How many faculty members are actually needed?
8. And then, finally, where is the money coming from? Which class of donors can reasonably be expected to make increased contributions?

[17] Tickton, *Ten-Year College Budget*, p. 14.

And how much can be expected from tuition increases and from other sources under the control of the college?[18]

Table 1 is a simplified example of what a ten-year budget might look like. Although the figures are illustrative only, they indicate that several preliminary steps must be taken to (1) fill out supporting schedules, or worksheets (indicated by column two); (2) assemble as much data on operations and activities of previous years as possible to provide a base from which the planning can begin; (3) make assumptions about the nation's economy in the years ahead; (4) make assumptions about the future of the particular institution in regard to purpose, program, enrollments, teaching methods and ratios, plant construction, and salaries, to list just a few of the items; and, (5) begin the unglamorous task of putting pencil to paper. This last step is undoubtedly the most important, for this is where the action starts — the differentiating factor between successful and unsuccessful administration.

For some Catholic college and university administrators the development of such a projection will be an interesting exercise; for others it may be a soul-searching experience. In either case, it will focus attention on the consequences of what must be done today to establish an effective educational institution in the years ahead. (Interestingly enough, in the preliminary report of the Danforth Commission study of church-affiliated colleges, the second of six recommendations outlined for improving and strengthening Catholic higher education is that these institutions make better provisions for planning to improve their efficiency, define their over-all educational goals, and have well-planned financial development programs to replace "spasmodic campaigns."[19]

Those Catholic institutions of higher education that are willing to take an honest look at the future will find themselves looking for change instead of waiting for change to come; this will be the action of the composer as compared to that of the fiddler, the fruit of tomorrow rather than the vintage of yesterday, the implanting of the taproot that will give sustaining life to those who utilize this tool of management. The progress of Catholic colleges and universities will, it is true, advance no faster than the curriculum of the classrooms, but it will distinguish those institutions that are third-rate from those that are communities of scholars concerned with the pursuit of truth. Paul Davis succinctly summarizes the situation:

> If a college, its faculty, administrators and board of trustees have not, first of all, settled the question of who they are and what purposes they intend to serve, they are likely to face increasingly difficult times in persuading donors to give adequate support in an era which calls for

[18] *Ibid.*, p. 15.
[19] "Catholic Colleges: A New Self-Consciousness," *Education U.S.A.*, National School Public Relations Association (April 21, 1966), 163.

TABLE 1
TEN-YEAR BUDGET SUMMARY FOR . . . COLLEGE

	Detail: Schedule	1966–67	1967–68	1968–69	1969–70	1970–71	1971–72	1972–73	1973–74	1974–75	1975–76
Income Items											
Tuition and fees	A	$540	$600	$650	$700	$750	$800	$850	$940	$990	$1,080
Endowments	A	30	60	75	90	100	120	140	170	190	205
Gifts and grants	A	40	0	0	0	0	0	0	0	0	0
Organized activities	A	10	10	11	11	11	12	12	12	12	12
Auxiliary enterprise	C	2	4	7	10	10	10	10	10	10	11
Miscellaneous	A	4	7	7	8	8	8	11	11	11	11
Total		$626	$681	$750	$819	$879	$950	$1,023	$1,143	$1,213	$1,319
Deficit		83	47	17	0	0	0	0	0	0	0
Expense Items											
Instruction	A	$320	$335	$350	$400	$450	$500	$550	$600	$650	$700
Administration	A	62	58	57	56	56	57	59	60	60	61
Student services	A	64	63	65	66	67	67	69	70	71	72
Library	D	31	32	35	36	36	38	42	44	47	47
Operation and maintenance		92	86	86	88	88	92	98	98	100	102
Contingency	A	0	10	20	40	40	45	50	10	10	60
Scholarship	B	19	20	26	32	38	41	46	48	50	50
Auxiliary enterprises	C	91	90	93	94	96	96	98	101	106	111
Plant construction	D	30	33	35	7	8	14	11	112	119	115
Total		$709	$728	$767	$819	$879	$950	$1,023	$1,143	$1,213	$1,319

vast expansion in the quantity and great improvement in the quality of higher education. And if one man, or a few men, are so egotistical, or fool-hardy, or unknowing that they think they must and can do the whole job, they are, sooner or later, in for grave disappointment. . . . Donors should not and will not contribute substantially to anything less than good organization and management.[20]

The moral obligations these institutions have incurred are beyond dispute; the practical problem is how these obligations can be realized.

[20] Paul H. Davis, *The Good Way of Life For Fund Raising in Colleges and Universities* (Washington, D.C.: Association of American Colleges, 1963), Foreword and p. 7.

APPENDIX B

THE CATHOLIC UNIVERSITY OF CHICAGO

Robert Hassenger

Mention was made in chapter 11 of the needless duplication of effort and facilities within Catholic higher education in America, and the numerous small schools which can be called colleges only — as David Riesman put it — "by the grace of semantic generosity." Louis Vaccaro has recently addressed himself to this problem.[1] After noting the appalling qualifications of many teaching in some of the newer Catholic colleges,[2] Vaccaro suggests that many of these schools could be more honestly (and perhaps more profitably) run as junior colleges. He further suggests, as have Catholic educators for at least a decade, that any future colleges be established adjacent to major secular universities, utilizing their library, laboratory, and physical education facilities. Only classrooms, dormitories, and a minimum of administrative apparatus would need to be constructed. Such an arrangement has usually involved a number of colleges around a larger university, such as at Waterloo, in Canada. And of course autonomous colleges within the university have characterized many British and European higher educational institutions. Probably the best-known arrangement involving a Catholic college is St. Michael's, within the University of Toronto. Perhaps Mr. Vaccaro makes clear in his longer contribution why he suggests such an arrangement on state university campuses.[3] It would seem to me that such a plan would meet less opposition at the first-rate private university (e.g., Harvard, Princeton, Johns Hopkins, Chicago, Stanford) than at a state university.[4] There is, in

[1] Louis Vaccaro, "Three Ways Out for Small Catholic Colleges," *America*, 113 (1965), 580–82.

[2] He states that a "recent research report completed by the NCEA shows that of a total of 787 full-time and part-time faculty members teaching in the newest colleges maintained by religious communities, 118 had only the Bachelor's degree and 90 had no college degree whatsoever" (*Ibid.*, p. 580).

[3] *Catholic Higher Education Examined: Issues and Answers* (Berkeley, Calif.: McCutchan Publishing Co.), forthcoming.

[4] The four-year employment of a Jesuit priest by Western Michigan University seemed to be something of a test case for some of the problems involved here, but the unfortunate outcome of this experiment may only have confused the issues.

fact, support available for such a venture, which would be run by laymen. The difficulties to date have involved either opposition by (a) the local bishop or archbishop, or by (b) the local Catholic colleges, which fear a drainage of both talented students and top-drawer faculty. All of the above five schools have expressed interest in such an arrangement, but the local ordinary was opposed in at least three of the above locations, and the Catholic university administrations in the only archdiocese where there was strong support from the archbishop.

More recent attention has been directed to the establishment of "cluster

TABLE 1
1963 ENROLLMENTS OF CHICAGO-AREA INSTITUTIONS (IN ROUND NUMBERS)

College	Undergraduate	Graduate
Barat	450	
DePaul (excluding professional schools)	7,050	1,300
Loyola (excluding professional schools)	7,760	1,930
Mundelein	1,200	
Rosary (including library school)	800	200
St. Xavier (including education master's program)	1,000	50
	18,260	3,480

TABLE 2
PROPOSED DISTRIBUTION: "CATHOLIC UNIVERSITY OF CHICAGO"

	Underclassmen
North Suburban (at present Barat)	500
North Side (at present Loyola, Lake Shore; and at Mundelein)	3,500
West Side (at present Rosary)	1,000
South Side (at present St. Xaxier)	1,000
Central (at present DePaul North)	4,000
	10,000

colleges," as ways are sought to preserve the advantages of the small college while allowing an institution to expand to a more practical size. Universities containing semi-autonomous colleges — sometimes each with its own specialty — are springing up. The Santa Cruz campus of the University of California is being constructed along these lines. The University of the Pacific at Stockton, California, contains: the liberal arts program, College of the Pacific; Covell College, with Spanish spoken in its entire curriculum; Raymond College, modeled after the tutorial system at Oxford; and the newly established Callison College, emphasizing history and the social sciences, with particular attention given to the non-Western civilizations.

But what Mr. Vaccaro envisions is less novel, and it is this that will be illustrated here, in the course of overhauling the Catholic higher educational system in a major city. Chicago has been chosen, primarily because I know it best; but similar plans could be worked out for any number of cities (St. Louis, Detroit, Milwaukee, San Francisco, and Erie, Pa., to name a few). The present construct of Catholic colleges and universities is shown in Table 1. With the concession that the following arrangement is hopelessly impractical, given the psychological investments of religious orders in "their" institutions, I can conceive of "The Catholic University of Chicago" having lower-division (freshmen and sophomore) courses at five locations, all around the city. The upper-division courses would be held at the present Loop campuses of DePaul and Loyola, with a total of 7,000 juniors and seniors. An additional 1,000 would be enrolled at an elite college on the campus of either Northwestern or The University of Chicago. The latter select group would be gleaned from the 10,000 freshmen and sophomores at the five lower-division locations. It will be noticed that only 8,000 of the original 10,000 would go on to upper-division work; the bottom twenty per cent would not qualify, and would either take a terminal Associate of Arts (A.A.) degree, or transfer to a less selective institution. The 1,000 "elite" students should not necessarily be the top ten per cent by academic standards, although many of course would be from the "talented tenth" (to paraphrase W. E. B. DuBois). We have so far accounted for 17,000 of the rightly 21,750 "places" available, using the 1963 figures (the 1,000 "elite" students would be using new facilities). The additional 4,750 "places" would probably be those of graduate students, although I have real reservations about this (see chapter 11).

SELECTED BIBLIOGRAPHY

Abbott, W. M. (ed.). *The Documents of Vatican II*. New York: America Press, 1966.

Adorno, T. W., Frenkel-Brunswik, Else, Levinson, D. J., and Sanford, R. N. *The Authoritarian Personality*. New York: Harper Bros., 1950. Reissued as Harper Torchbook, 1965.

Aherne, P. H. *The Catholic University of America, 1887–1896: The Rectorship of John J. Keane*. Washington, D.C.: Catholic University of America Press, 1948.

Allport, G. W., Gillespie, J. M., and Young, Jacqueline. "The Religion of the Post-War College Student," *Journal of Psychology*, 25 (1948), 3–33.

American Association of University Professors. "Academic Freedom and Tenure: Gonzaga University,"*AAUP Bulletin*, 51 (1965), 8–20.

―――. "Academic Freedom and Tenure: Mercy College," *AAUP Bulletin*, 49 (1963), 245–52.

―――. "Academic Freedom and Tenure: St. John's University (N.Y.)," *AAUP Bulletin*, 52 (1966), 12–19.

―――. "Statement on The Academic Freedom of Students," *AAUP Bulletin*, 21 (1965), 447–49.

Argyle, M. *Religious Behavior*. London: Routledge and Kegan Paul, 1958.

Arrowsmith, W. "The Shame of the Graduate Schools," *Harpers*, 232 (#3) (1966), 51–59.

Astin, A. "An Empirical Characterization of Higher Educational Institutions," *Journal of Educational Psychology*, 53 (1962), 224–35.

―――. "Further Validation of the Environmental Assessment Technique," *Journal of Educational Psychology*, 54 (1963), 217–26.

―――. "A Re-Examination of College Productivity," *Journal of Educational Psychology*, 52 (1961), 173–78.

―――. *Who Goes Where To College?* Chicago: Science Research Associates, 1965.

Astin, A. W. and Holland, J. L. "The Environmental Assessment Technique: A Way to Measure College Environments," *Journal of Educational Psychology*, 52 (1961), 308–16.

Augustine, D., F.S.C. "The Catholic College Man and the Negro," *American Catholic Sociological Review*, 8 (1947), 204–8.

Babin, P. *Crisis of Faith*. New York: Herder and Herder, 1963.

———. "Rethinking the Life of Faith," *Lumen Vitae*, 15 (1960), 233–46.

Bailyn, B. *Education in the Forming of American Society*. Chapel Hill, N.C.: University of North Carolina Press, 1960.

Baltzell, E. D. *The Protestant Establishment*. New York: Random House, 1965.

Barry, C. J., O.S.B. *The Catholic University of America, 1903–1909: The Rectorship of Denis J. O'Connell*. Washington, D.C.: Catholic University of America Press, 1950.

———. *Worship and Work: Saint John's Abbey and University*. Collegeville, Minn.: St. John's University Press, 1956.

Barton, A. H. *Studying the Effects of College Education*. New Haven, Conn.: The Edward W. Hazen Foundation, 1959.

Baskin, S. (ed.). *Higher Education: Some Newer Developments*. New York: McGraw-Hill, 1965.

Bay, C. "A Social Theory of Higher Education." In *The American College*, ed. N. Sanford, pp. 972–1005. New York: John Wiley & Sons, Inc., 1962.

Becker, H., Geer, Blanche, and Hughes, E. *Boys in White*. Chicago: University of Chicago Press, 1962.

Benne, K. D. (ed.). "The Social Responsibilities of the Behavioral Scientist," *Journal of Social Issues*, 21 (1965), entire issue.

Berelson, B. and Steiner, G. *Human Behavior*. New York: Harcourt, Brace and World, 1964.

Bidwell, C. E. and Vreeland, Rebecca S. "College Education and Moral Orientations: An Organizational Approach," *Administrative Science Quarterly*, 8 (1963), 166–91.

Bidwell, C. E., King, S. H., Finnie, B., and Scarr, H. A. "Undergraduate Careers: Alternatives and Determinants," *School Review*, 71 (1963), 299–316.

Bieri, J. and Lobeck, R. "Self-Concept Differences in Relation to Identification, Religion, and Social Class," *Journal of Abnormal and Social Psychology*, 62 (1961), 94–98.

Bloom, B. *Stability and Change in Human Characteristics*. New York: John Wiley & Sons, Inc., 1964.

Boroff, D. *Campus, U.S.A.* New York: Harper Bros., 1961.

Bowen, R. O. "The Lay Faculty on the Jesuit Campus." *Ramparts*, 1 (#5) (1963), 16–20.

Bowler, Sr. M. *A History of Catholic Colleges for Women in the United States of America*. Washington, D.C.: Catholic University of America Press, 1933.

Bressler, M. and Westoff, C. "Catholic Education, Economic Values, and Achievement," *American Journal of Sociology*, 69 (1963), 225–33.

Brim, O. Jr. *Sociology and the Field of Education*. New York: Russell Sage Foundation, 1958.

Brim, O., Jr. and Wheeler, S. *Socialization After Childhood*. New York: John Wiley & Sons, Inc., 1966.

Brown, D. "College and Value Conflict," *American Association of University Women Journal*, 55 (1962), 216–20.

————. "Personality, College Environment and Academic Productivity." In *The American College*, ed. N. Sanford, p. 536–62. New York: John Wiley & Sons, Inc., 1962.

Brown, D. and Bystryn, Denise. "College Environment, Personality and the Ideology of Three Ethnic Groups," *Journal of Social Psychology*, 44 (1956), 279–88.

Brown, D. G. and Lowe, W. L. "Religious Beliefs and Personality Characteristics of College Students," *Journal of Social Psychology*, 33 (1951), 103–6.

Brownson, O. "Catholic Schools and Education." In *Catholic Education in America*, ed. N. McCluskey, pp. 95–120. New York: Teachers College, Columbia University, 1964.

Bull, G., S.J. "The Function of the Catholic Graduate School," *Thought*, 13 (1938), 364–80.

Burchinal, L. G. "Some Social Status Criteria of Church Membership and Church Attendance," *Journal of Social Psychology*, 49 (1959), 53–64.

Burns, J. A., C.S.C. and Kohlbrenner, B. J. *A History of Catholic Education in the United States*. New York: Benziger, 1937.

Butler, R., O.P. *God on the Secular Campus*. New York: Doubleday, 1963.

Butz, O. *The Unsilent Generation*. New York: Rinehart, 1958.

Cadbury, W. E., Jr. "Cooperative Relations Involving the Liberal Arts Colleges," *School and Society*, 94 (1966), 213–17.

Callahan, D. "The Catholic University — The American Experience." In *Theology and the University*, ed. J. Coulson, pp. 66–77. Baltimore: Helicon Press, 1964.

———— (ed.) *Generation of the Third Eye*. New York: Sheed and Ward, 1965.

————. *The Mind of the Catholic Layman*. New York: Scribners, 1963.

————. *The New Church*. New York: Scribners, 1966.

————. "The Schools," *Commonweal*, 81 (1965), 473–76.

Callahan, D. and Callahan, Sidney. "Do Catholic Colleges Develop Initiative?" *The Catholic World*, 186 (1957), 180–85.

Callahan, Sidney. *The Illusion of Eve*. New York: Sheed and Ward, 1965.

Canavan, F., S.J. "Academic Revolution at St. John's," *America*, 113 (1965), 136–40.

————. "St. John's University: The Issues," *America*, 114 (1966), 122–24.

Carnegie Foundation for the Advancement of Teaching. "The Flight from

Teaching." In *The 1963–64 Annual Report of the Carnegie Foundation for the Advancement of Teaching*. New York: The Carnegie Foundation, 1964.

Cartter, A. M. *An Assessment of Quality in Graduate Education*. Washington, D.C.: American Council on Education, 1966.

Cassidy, F. P. *Catholic College Foundations and Development in the United States, 1677–1850*. Washington, D.C.: Catholic University of America Press, 1924.

Cavanaugh, J. J., C.S.C. "American Catholics and Leadership." In *American Catholicism and the Intellectual Ideal*. eds. F. Christ and G. Sherry, pp. 227–29. New York: Appleton-Century-Crofts, Inc., 1961.

————. "Survey of Fifteen Surveys," *Bulletin of the University of Notre Dame*, 34 (1939), 1–28.

Center for the Study of Higher Education. *Omnibus Personality Inventory Research Manual*. Berkeley, Calif.: Center for the Study of Higher Education, 1962.

Christ, F. and Sherry, G. (eds.). *American Catholicism and the Intellectual Ideal*. New York: Appleton-Century-Crofts, Inc., 1961.

Christie, R. and Jahoda, Marie (eds.). *Studies in the Scope and Method of "The Authoritarian Personality."* Glencoe, Ill.: The Free Press, 1954.

Clark, B. R. "The Sociology of Education." In *Handbook of Modern Sociology*, ed. R. E. L. Faris, pp. 734–69. Chicago: Rand McNally and Co., 1964.

Clark, W. H. "Religion as a Response to the Search for Meaning: Its Relation to Skepticism and Creativity," *Journal of Social Psychology*, 45 (1963), 127–37.

Clarke, W. N., S.J. "Current Views on the Intrinsic Nature of Philosophy." In *Christian Wisdom and Christian Formation*, eds. J. B. McGannon *et al.*, pp. 141–63. New York: Sheed and Ward, 1964.

Clifford, R. J., S.J. and Callahan, W. R., S.J. "Catholics in Higher Education," *America*, 111 (1964), 288–91.

Cogley, J. "Changing Roles in the Church," *Commonweal*, 80 (1964), 5–7.

Cohen, A. A. (ed.). *Humanistic Education and Western Civilization*. New York: Holt, Rinehart and Winston, 1964.

Cohen, J. W. (ed.). *The Superior Student in American Higher Education*. New York: McGraw-Hill, 1966.

Commager, H. S. "Is Ivy Necessary?" In *American Education Today*, eds. P. Woodring and J. Scanlon, pp. 167–77. New York: McGraw-Hill, 1963.

Cook, S. W. (ed.). "Research Plans in the Fields of Religion, Values and Morality and Their Bearing on Religious and Character Formation." Mimeographed. New York: The Religious Education Association, 1962.

Coulson, J. *Theology and the University*. Baltimore: Helicon Press, 1964.

Cox, H. "Beyond Bonhoeffer," *Commonweal*, 82 (1965), 653–57.

————. *The Secular City*. New York: Macmillan, 1965.

————. "Secularization and the Secular Mentality: A New Challenge to Christian Education," *Religious Education*, 61 (1966), 83–87.

Cross, R. D. *The Emergence of Liberal Catholicism in America*. Cambridge, Mass.: Harvard University Press, 1958.

Cunningham, W. F., C.S.C. *General Education and the Liberal College*. St. Louis: B. Herder Book Co., 1953.

Daley, J. M., S.J. *Georgetown University: Origin and Early Years*. Washington, D.C.: Georgetown University Press, 1957.

Dauw, D. C. and Pugh, R. C. "Creativity and Religious Preferences," *Religious Education*, 61 (1966), 30–35.

Dean, D. G. and Reeves, J. A. "Anomie: A Comparison of a Catholic and a Protestant Sample," *Sociometry*, 25 (1962), 209–12.

Deferrari, R. J. *Memoirs of The Catholic University of America, 1918–1960*. Boston: Daughters of St. Paul, 1962.

————. *Some Problems of Catholic Higher Education*. Boston: Daughters of St. Paul, 1963.

Demerath, N. J. *Social Class in American Protestantism*. Chicago: Rand McNally, 1965.

Dennis, L. E. and Kauffman, J. F. (eds.). *The College and the Student*. Washington, D.C.: American Council on Education, 1966.

DiRenzo, G. "Student Imagery at Fairfield University, 1963–1964." Mimeographed. Fairfield, Conn.: Fairfield University, Department of Sociology, 1965.

Doi, J. I. "Organization and Administration, Finance and Facilities," *Review of Educational Research*, 35 (1965), 353–54.

Donohue, J. W., S.J. *Jesuit Education*. New York: Fordham University Press, 1963.

Donovan, J. D. *The Academic Man in the Catholic College*. New York: Sheed and Ward, 1964.

————. "The American Catholic Hierarchy: A Social Profile," *American Catholic Sociological Review*, 19 (1958), 98–113.

————. "Creating Anti-Intellectuals?" *Commonweal*, 81 (1964), 37–39.

Dressel, P. L. and Mayhew, L. B. *General Education: Explorations in Evaluation*. Washington, D.C.: American Council on Education, 1954.

DuBay, W. H. *The Human Church*. New York: Doubleday, 1966.

Dukes, W. F. "Psychological Studies of Values," *Psychological Bulletin*, 52 (1955), 24–50.

Dunigan, D. R., S.J. *A History of Boston College*. Milwaukee: Bruce Publishing Co., 1947.

Dunkel, H. B. *General Education in the Humanities*. Washington, D.C.: American Council on Education, 1947.

Dunne, J., C.S.C. *City of the Gods*. New York: Macmillan, 1965.

Durkin, J. T., S.J. *Georgetown University: the Middle Years (1840–1900)*. Washington, D.C.: Georgetown University Press, 1963.

Eddy, E. D., Jr. *The College Influence on Student Character*. Washington, D.C.: American Council on Education, 1959.

Editorials on the "Speaker Ban" at Catholic University. *Commonweal*, 77 (1963), 608; 79 (1964), 4.

Educational Reviewer. "Survey of the Political Attitudes of American College Students," *National Review*, 15 (October 8, 1963), insert.

Educational Testing Service. "The Institutional Research Program for Higher Education." Princeton, N.J.: Educational Testing Service, 1965.

Ellis, J. T. *American Catholicism*. Chicago: University of Chicago Press, 1956.

———. *American Catholics and the Intellectual Life*. Chicago: The Heritage Foundation, 1956. Originally published in *Thought*, 30 (1955), 351–88.

———. *The Formative Years of the Catholic University of America*. Washington, D.C.: Catholic University of America Press, 1946.

———. *Perspectives in American Catholicism*. Baltimore: Helicon Press, 1963.

Erbacher, S. A., O.F.M. *Catholic Higher Education for Men in the United States, 1850–1866*. Washington, D.C.: Catholic University of America Press, 1931.

Erikson, E. H. *Childhood and Society*. New York: Norton, 1950.

———. "Inner and Outer Space," *Daedalus*, 93 (1964), 582–606.

———. "The Problem of Ego Identity," *Psychological Issues*, 1 (1959), 101–64.

———. (ed.). "Youth: Change and Challenge," *Daedalus*, 91, No. 1 (1962).

Etzioni, A. *A Comparative Analysis of Complex Organizations*. New York: The Free Press, 1961.

Evans, J. W. "Has the Catholic Intellectual a Future in America?" *Sociology of Education*, 38 (1965), 150–63.

Farrell, A. P., S.J. *The Jesuit Code of Liberal Education*. Milwaukee: Bruce Publishing Co., 1938.

Femminella, F. X. "The Impact of Italian Migration on American Catholicism," *American Catholic Sociological Review*, 22 (1961), 233–41.

Ferman, L. "Religious Change on a Campus," *Journal for College Student Personnel*, 1 (1960), 1–12.

Fichter, J. H., S.J., *Parochial School: A Sociological Study*. Notre Dame, Ind.: University of Notre Dame Press, 1954.

———. *Priest and People*. New York: Sheed and Ward, 1965.

———. "The Profile of Catholic Religious Life," *American Journal of Sociology*, 58 (1952), 145–49.

————. *Social Relations in the Urban Parish.* Chicago: University of Chicago Press, 1954.

Fitzpatrick, E. A. *The Catholic College in the World Today.* Milwaukee: Bruce Publishing Co., 1954.

Foster, J., Stanek, R., and Krassowski, W. "The Impact of a Value-Oriented University on Student Attitudes and Thinking." Mimeographed. Santa Clara, Calif.: University of Santa Clara, and Cooperative Research Project No. 729, Office of Education, Department of Health, Education, and Welfare, 1961.

Fox, J. J. "The Attitude of Male College Students Toward Their Church," *American Catholic Sociological Review,* 24 (1963), 127–131.

————. "Authoritarianism and the St. Ambrose College Student," *Religious Education,* 60 (1965), 272–276.

Freedman, M. "The Passage Through College." In "Personality Development During the College Years," ed. N. Sanford. *Journal of Social Issues,* 12, no. 4 (1956), 13–28.

Fuller, E. (ed.). *The Christian Idea of Education.* New Haven: Yale University Press, 1957.

Gamson, Zelda F. "Utilitarian and Normative Orientations Toward Education," *Sociology of Education,* 39 (1966), 46–73.

Gannon, R. I., S.J. *The Poor Old Liberal Arts.* New York: Farrar, Straus and Cudahy, 1961.

Ganss, G. E., S.J. *Saint Ignatius' Idea of a Jesuit University.* Milwaukee: Marquette University Press, 1954.

Gardner, J. W. *Excellence: Can We Be Equal and Excellent Too?* New York: Harper Bros., 1961.

Gilliland, A. R. "Religious Attitudes of College Students," *The Christian Student,* 39 (1938), entire issue.

Glazer, N. and Moynihan, D. *Beyond the Melting Pot.* Cambridge, Mass.: Harvard University Press and M.I.T. Press, 1963.

Gleason, P. "Academic Freedom," *America,* 115 (1966), 60–63.

————. "Catholic Intellectualism Again," *America,* 112 (1965), 112–19.

————. "Immigration and Catholic Intellectual Life," *Review of Politics,* 26 (1964), 147–73.

Glock, C. Y. "On the Study of Religious Commitment," *Religious Education,* 62 (1962), 98–118.

Glock, C. Y. and Stark, R. *By Their Fruits: Christian Belief and Anti-Semitism.* New York: Harper and Row, 1966.

————. *Religion and Society in Tension.* Chicago: Rand McNally, 1965.

Goldsen, Rose K., Rosenberg, M., Williams, R. M., and Suchman, E. A. *What College Students Think.* Princeton, N.J.: D. Van Nostrand, Inc., 1960.

Goodman, P. *The Community of Scholars*. New York: Random House, 1962.

Gottlieb, D. and Hodgkins, B. "College Student Sub-cultures," *School Review*, 71 (1963), 291–99.

Gray, J. G. "Salvation on the Campus: Why Existentialism is Capturing the Students," *Harpers*, 215, no. 5 (1965), 55–59.

Greeley, A. M. "Anti-Intellectualism in Catholic Colleges," *American Catholic Sociological Review*, 23 (1962), 350–68.

———. "Catholic Education," *America*, 112 (1965), 522–28.

———. "Criticism of Undergraduate Faculty by Graduates of Catholic Colleges," *Review of Religious Research*, 6 (1965), 97–106.

———. "Entering the Mainstream," *Commonweal*, 81 (1964), 33–37.

———. "The Place of Religion," *Commonweal*, 84 (1966), 104–10.

———. "The Protestant Ethic: Time for a Moratorium," *Sociological Analysis*, 25 (1964), 20–33.

———. "The Real Problems of American Catholicism," *America*, 113 (1965), 571–76.

———. *Religion and Career*. New York: Sheed and Ward, 1963.

———. "The Religious Behavior of Graduate Students," *Journal for the Scientific Study of Religion*, 5 (1965), 34–40.

———. "Some Information on the Present Situation of American Catholics," *Social Order*, 13, no. 4 (1963), 9–24.

———. "Temptations of the New Breed," *America*, 112 (1965), 750–52.

Greeley, A. M. and Rossi, P. *The Education of Catholic Americans*. Chicago: Aldine Publishing Co., 1966.

Gropper, G. L. and Fitzpatrick, P. *Who Goes to Graduate School?* Pittsburgh: American Institute for Research, 1959.

Gusfield, J. and Riesman, D. "Academic Standards and the 'Two Cultures' in the Context of a New State College," *School Review*, 74 (1966), 95–116.

Hadden, J. K. "An Analysis of Some Factors Associated with Religious and Political Affiliation in a College Population," *Journal for the Scientific Study of Religion*, 2 (1963), 209–16.

Hadden, J. K. and Evans, R. R. "Some Correlates of Religious Participation Among College Freshmen," *Religious Education*, 60 (1965), 277–85.

Hamilton, R. N., S.J., *The Story of Marquette University*. Milwaukee: Marquette University Press, 1953.

Hammond, P. E. *The Campus Clergyman*. New York: Basic Books, 1966.

Hansen, D. "The Responsibility of the Sociologist to Education," *Harvard Educational Review*, 33 (1963), 312–25.

Hassenger, R. L. "The Catholic Campus: A 'Christian Community'?" In *Academic Freedom and the Catholic University*, eds. E. Manier and J. Houck, pp. 145–61, Notre Dame, Ind.: Fides Publishers, 1967.

———. "Catholic College Impact on Religious Orientations," *Sociological Analysis*, 27 (Summer, 1966), 67–79.

————. "Religious Values and Personality Traits of Catholic College Women," *Insight*, 3, no. 2 (1964), 37–48.

————. "The Sociologist and the College Student Personnel Worker," *National Catholic Guidance Conference Journal*, 11 (1966), 5–21.

————. "A Rationale for Changing Student Values," *Educational Record*, 48 (1967), 61–67.

————. "Varieties of Religious Orientation," *Sociological Analysis*, 25 (1964), 189–99.

Havens, J. "The Changing Climate of Research on the College Student and His Religion," *Journal for the Scientific Study of Religion*, 3 (1963), 52–69.

————. "A Study of Religious Conflict in College Students," *Journal of Social Psychology*, 64 (1964), 77–87.

Hawes, G. "Civil Liberties for College Students," *Saturday Review*, 49, No. 25 (1966), 61–63, 77.

Heath, R. *The Reasonable Adventurer*. Pittsburgh: University of Pittsburgh Press, 1964.

Hellkamp, D. T. and Marr, J. N. "Dogmatism and Field Dependency," *Perceptual and Motor Skills*, 20 (1965), 1046–48.

Henle, R. J., S.J. "Objectives of the Catholic Liberal Arts College." In *Christian Wisdom and Christian Formation*, ed. J. B. McGannon *et al.*, pp. 14–37. New York: Sheed and Ward, 1964.

Herberg, W. *Protestant, Catholic, Jew*. Garden City, N.Y.: Doubleday, 1955.

————. "Religious Group Conflict in America." In *Religion and Social Conflict*, ed. R. Lee and M. E. Marty, pp. 143–58. New York: Oxford University Press, 1964.

Hesburgh, T. M., C.S.C. *Patterns of Educational Growth*. Notre Dame, Ind.: University of Notre Dame Press, 1958.

————. "The Work of Mediation," *Commonweal*, 74 (1961), 33–35.

Hildebrand, D., von. *The New Tower of Babel*. New York: P. J. Kenedy, 1953.

Hinrichs, G. "Faculty Participation in the Government of Catholic Colleges and Universities," *American Association of University Professors Bulletin*, 50 (1964), 336–41.

Hofstadter, R. and Metzger, W. P. *The Development of Academic Freedom in the United States*. New York: Columbia University Press, 1955.

Hogan, P. E., S.S.J. *The Catholic University of America, 1896–1903: The Rectorship of Thomas J. Conaty*. Washington, D.C.: Catholic University of America Press, 1949.

Hopwood, Kathryn. "Observations of Student Values at Hunter College," *Religious Education*, 60 (1960), 45–48.

Howe, I. "Beleaguered Professors," *Atlantic*, 216, no. 5 (1965), 115–18.

Hruby, N. J. "The Mundelein Self-Study: An Experiment in Reorientation," *North Central News Bulletin*, 22, no. 7 (1963), 2–10.

———. "Truth and Consequences: Mundelein College Emerges from Analysis," *North Central News Bulletin*, 24, no. 6 (1965), 2–23.

Hughes, H. S. "Pope John's Revolution: Secular or Religious?" *Commonweal*, 82 (1965), 301–3.

Hutchins, R. M. Paper read to the College and University Department of The National Catholic Educational Association, 1935. *College Newsletter of The National Catholic Educational Association* (May 1937), pp. 1 and 4.

Jacob, P. E. *Changing Values in College.* New York: Harper Bros., 1957.

Jencks, C. "Education: What Next?" *New Republic*, 153, no. 15 (1965), 21–23.

———. "Is the Public School Obsolete?" *The Public Interest*, 1, No. 2 (1966), 18–27.

———. "A New Breed of BA's," *New Republic*, 153, No. 16 (1965), 17–21.

Jencks, C. and Riesman, D. "Patterns of Residential Education." In *The American College*, ed. N. Sanford, pp. 731–73. New York: John Wiley & Sons, Inc., 1962.

Jones, H. M. "The Meaning of a University," *Atlantic*, 216, no. 5 (1965), 157–60.

Jones, V. "Attitudes of College Students and the Changes in Such Attitudes During Four Years in College," *Journal of Educational Psychology*, 29 (1938), 14–25.

Kane, J. "Anti-Semitism Among Catholic College Students," *American Catholic Sociological Review*, 8 (1947), 209–18.

———. "Social Structure of American Catholics," *American Catholic Sociological Review*, 16 (1955), 23–30.

Katz, D., Allport, F. H., and Jennes, M. B. *Students' Attitudes.* Syracuse, N.Y.: Craftsman Press, 1931.

Katz, J. and Sanford, N. "The Curriculum in the Perspective of the Theory of Personality Development." In *The American College*, ed. N. Sanford, pp. 418–44. New York: John Wiley & Sons, Inc., 1962.

Kearns, F. E. "A Case of Academic Freedom," *Commonweal*, 79 (1964), 430.

Keating, E. "Jesuit Education: A Layman's View," *Ramparts*, 1, no. 5 (1963), 6–9.

Kelly, W. D. "What is a Catholic College?" *Commonweal*, 83 (1966), 494–97.

Kelman, H. C. "Manipulation of Human Behavior: An Ethical Dilemma for the Social Scientist," *Journal of Social Issues*, 21 (1965), 31–46.

Keniston, K. *The Uncommitted.* New York: Harcourt, Brace and World, 1966.

Kerr, C. *The Uses of the University.* Cambridge, Mass.: Harvard University Press, 1963.

Klocker, H. R., S.J. "The Nature and Function of Philosophy in Undergraduate Education." In *Christian Wisdom and Christian Formation*, eds. J. B. McGannon *et al.*, pp. 202–12. New York: Sheed and Ward, 1964.

Knapp, R. H. and Goodrich, H. G. *Origins of American Scientists.* Chicago: University of Chicago Press, 1952.

Knapp, R. H. and Greenbaum, J. J. *The Younger American Scholar: His Collegiate Origins.* Chicago: University of Chicago Press, 1953.

Kolesnik, W. B. and Power, E. J. (eds.). *Catholic Education: A Book of Readings.* New York: McGraw-Hill, 1965.

Koob, C. A., O.Pr. (ed.). *What is Happening to Catholic Education?* Washington, D.C.: National Catholic Educational Association, 1966.

Kosa, J. L. "Religious Participation, Religious Knowledge and Scholastic Aptitude: An Empirical Study," *Journal for the Scientific Study of Religion*, 1 (1961), 88–97.

Kosa, J. L. and Rachiele, L. D. "The Spirit of Capitalism, Traditionalism, and Religiousness: A Re-Examination of Weber's Concepts," *Sociological Quarterly*, 4 (1963), 243–60.

Kosa, J. L., Rachiele, L., and Schommer, C. "Psychological Characteristics of Ethnic Groups in a College Population," *Journal of Psychology*, 46 (1958), 265–75.

Kosa, J. L. and Schommer, C. "Sex Differences in the Religious Attitudes of Catholic College Students," *Psychological Reports*, 10 (1962), 285–86.

Kristol, I. "The Troublesome Intellectuals," *The Public Interest*, 1, no. 2 (1966), 3–6.

———. "What's Bugging the Students," *Atlantic*, 216, no. 5 (1965), 108–11.

Kuhlen, R. G. and Arnold, M. "Age Differences in Religious Beliefs and Problems During Adolescence," *Journal of Genetic Psychology*, 65 (1944), 291–300.

Lane, R. E. "The Need to be Liked and the Anxious College Liberal," *The Annals*, 361 (1965), 71–80.

Lawler, J. G. *The Catholic Dimension in Higher Education.* Westminster, Md.: Newman Press, 1959.

Lazarsfeld, P. F. and Thielens, W., Jr. *The Academic Mind: Social Scientists in a Time of Crisis.* Glencoe: The Free Press, 1958.

Lee, J. M. (ed.). *Catholic Education in the Western World.* Notre Dame, Ind.: University of Notre Dame Press, 1967.

Lee, R. and Marty, M. E. (eds.). *Religion and Social Conflict.* New York: Oxford University Press, 1964.

Lee, J. M. and Putz, L. J., C.S.C. (eds.). *Seminary Education in a Time of Change.* Notre Dame, Ind.: Fides Press, 1965.

Lehmann, I. J. "Changes in Critical Thinking, Attitudes, and Values From Freshman to Senior Year," *Journal of Educational Psychology,* 54 (1963), 305–15.

Lehmann, I. J. and Ikenberry, S. *Critical Thinking, Attitudes and Values in Higher Education.* East Lansing: Michigan State University Press, 1959.

Lenski, G. *The Religious Factor.* New York: Doubleday, 1961.

Leo, J. "The Kearns Case," *Commonweal,* 81 (1965), 562–66.

Lipset, S. M. "Opinion Formation in a Crisis Situation." In *The Berkeley Student Revolt: Facts and Interpretations,* eds. S. M. Lipset and S. S. Wolin, pp. 464–93. New York: Doubleday Anchor Books, 1965.

————. "Religion and Politics in the American Past and Present." In eds. R. Lee and M. E. Marty, *Religion and Social Conflict,* pp. 69–126. New York: Oxford University Press, 1964.

Lipset, S. M. and Wolin, S. S. (eds.). *The Berkeley Student Revolt: Facts and Interpretations.* New York: Doubleday Anchor Books, 1965.

Long, Barbara. "Catholic-Protestant Differences in Acceptance of Others," *Sociology and Social Research,* 49 (1965), 166–72.

MacArthur, C. "Subculture and Personality During the College Years," *Journal of Educational Sociology,* 33 (1960), 260–68.

McAvoy, T. T., C.S.C. "The Catholic Minority in the United States, 1820–1860," *Review of Politics,* 10 (1948), 13–34.

———— (ed.). *Roman Catholicism and the American Way of Life.* Notre Dame, Ind.: University of Notre Dame Press, 1960.

McClintock, C. G. and Turner, H. A. "The Impact of College Upon Political Knowledge, Participation and Values," *Human Relations,* 15 (1962), 163–76.

McCluskey, N. G., S.J. "America and the Catholic School." In *Catholic Education in America: A Documentary History,* ed. N. G. McCluskey, pp. 1–44. New York: Teachers College, Columbia University, 1964.

————. (ed.). *Catholic Education in America: A Documentary History.* New York: Teachers College, Columbia University, 1964.

————. *The Catholic Viewpoint on Education,* rev. ed. New York: Doubleday Image Books, 1962.

McConnell, T. R. *A General Pattern for American Public Higher Education.* New York: McGraw-Hill, 1962.

———— (ed.). *Selection and Educational Differentiation.* Berkeley, Calif.: Center for the Study of Higher Education, 1960.

McCullers, J. C. and Plant, W. T. "Personality and Social Development: Cultural Influences," *Review of Educational Research,* 34 (1964), 599–610.

McGannon, J. B., S.J., Klubertanz, G., S.J., and Cooke, B. J., S.J. (eds.).

Christian Wisdom and Christian Formation. New York: Sheed and Ward, 1964.

McGucken, W. J., S.J. *The Catholic Way in Education.* Milwaukee: Bruce Publishing Co., 1934.

————. *The Jesuits and Education.* Milwaukee: Bruce Publishing Co., 1932.

McLean, M. D. and Kimber, H. H. *The Teaching of Religion in State Universities.* Ann Arbor: University of Michigan Press, 1960.

McLinden, J. M. and Doyle, J. M. "Negro Students and Faculty on Catholic College Campuses," *National Catholic Educational Association Bulletin,* 62, no. 3 (1966), 1–49.

McKenna, Sr. Helen Veronica, S.S.J. "Religious Attitudes and Personality Traits," *Journal of Social Psychology,* 54 (1961), 279–88.

McNally, R. E. *The Unreformed Church.* New York: Sheed and Ward, 1965.

McNamara, R. J., S.J. "Intellectual Values and Instrumental Religion," *Sociological Analysis,* 25 (1964), 99–107.

Mack, R. W., Murphy, R. J., and Yellin, S. "The Protestant Ethic, Level of Aspiration and Social Mobility," *American Sociological Review,* 21 (1956), 295–300.

Maher, Sr. M. Gratia, R.S.M. *The Organization of Religious Instruction in Catholic Colleges for Women.* Washington, D.C.: Catholic University of America Press, 1951.

Mahoney, J. "The American Catholic College and the Faith," *Thought,* 39 (1964), 238–52.

Manier, E. and Houck, J. (eds.). *Academic Freedom and the Catholic University.* Notre Dame, Ind: Fides Publishers, 1967.

Maritain, J. *Education at the Crossroads.* London: Oxford University Press, 1943.

Mayer, A. J. and Sharp, H. "Religious Preference and Worldly Success," *American Sociological Review,* 27 (1962), 218–27.

Mayhew, L. B. "Catholic Education and the Nature of the University," *Liberal Education,* 50 (1964), 476–80.

————. *The Smaller Liberal Arts College.* New York: Center for Applied Research in Education, Inc., 1962.

Medsker, L. L. *The Junior College: Problems and Prospect.* New York: McGraw-Hill, 1960.

Messick, J. and Ross, R. (eds.). *Measurement in Personality and Cognition.* New York: John Wiley & Sons, Inc., 1962.

Michael, D. *The Next Generation.* New York: Random House, 1965.

Michaelson, R. *The Study of Religion in American Universities.* New Haven, Conn.: Society for Religion in Higher Education, 1965.

————. "The Study of Religion: A Quiet Revolution in American Universities," *Journal of Higher Education,* 37 (1966), 181–86.

Miller, D. R. and Swanson, G. W. *The Changing American Parent*. New York: John Wiley & Sons, Inc., 1958.

Miller, M. V. and Gilmore, Susan (eds.). *Revolution at Berkeley*. New York: Dell Publishing Co., 1965.

Mooney, G. "College Theology and Liberal Education," *Thought*, 34 (1959), 325–46.

Morison, R. S. (ed.). *The Contemporary University: U.S.A*. Boston: Houghton Mifflin Co., 1966.

Morris, C. *Varieties of Human Value*. Chicago: University of Chicago Press, 1956.

Mulligan, J. F. "The Catholic Campus Today," *Commonweal*, 83 (1966), 497–99.

Murphy, Lois and Rauschenbush, Esther. *Achievement in the College Years*. New York: Harper Bros., 1960.

Murray, J. C., S.J. "The Declaration on Religious Freedom: Its Deeper Significance," *America*, 114 (1966), 592–93.

———. "On the Future of Humanistic Education." In *Humanistic Education and Western Civilization*, ed. A. A. Cohen, pp. 231–47. New York: Holt, Rinehart and Winston, 1964.

———. "Towards a Theology for the Layman," *Theological Studies*, 5 (1944), 43–75.

Neal, Sr. Marie Augusta, S.N.D. *Values and Interests in Social Change*. Englewood Cliffs, N.J.: Prentice-Hall, 1964.

Newcomb, T. M. *The Acquaintance Process*. New York: Holt, Rinehart and Winston, 1961.

———. *Personality and Social Change*. New York: Dryden Press, 1943.

———. "Student Peer-Group Influence." In *The American College*, ed. N. Sanford, pp. 469–88. New York: John Wiley & Sons, Inc., 1962.

Newcomb, T. M. and Wilson, E. K. (eds.). *College Peer Groups*. Chicago: Aldine Publishing Co., 1966.

Neuwien, R. A. (ed.). *Catholic Schools in Action: The Study of Catholic Education*. Notre Dame, Ind.: University of Notre Dame Press, 1966.

Newman, J. H. *The Idea of a University*. New York: Doubleday Image Books, 1959.

Novak, Michael. *Belief and Unbelief*. New York: Macmillan, 1965.

———. *A New Generation: American and Catholic*. New York: Herder and Herder, 1964.

———. *The Open Church*. New York: Macmillan, 1964.

———. "Post-Seminary Thoughts," *Commonweal*, 83 (1965), 9–12.

——— (ed.). *The Experience of Marriage*. New York: Macmillan, 1964.

O'Brien, J. A. (ed.). *Catholics and Scholarship*. Huntington, Ind.: Our Sunday Visitor Press, 1939.

O'Connell, M. J. "The Priest in Education: Apostolate or Anomaly?" *Theological Studies*, 26 (1965), 65–85.

O'Dea, T. F. *American Catholic Dilemma: An Inquiry Into the Intellectual Life.* New York: Sheed and Ward, 1958.

O'Donovan, T. R. and Sr. M. Keila, R.S.M. "Non-Academic Involvement of Students and Their Academic Achievement," *Catholic Educational Review*, 62 (1964), 217–30.

O'Donohue, J. "Reforming the Seminaries," *Commonweal*, 81 (1964), 194–96.

O'Flaherty, V. J., S.J. "The Place of Religious Activities on the Catholic College Campus." In *Christian Wisdom and Christian Formation*, ed. J. B. McGannon *et al.*, pp. 238–48. New York: Sheed and Ward, 1964.

Ong, W. J., S.J. *American Catholic Crossroads.* New York: Macmillan, 1959.

————. *Frontiers in American Catholicism.* New York: Macmillan, 1957.

O'Reilly, C. and O'Reilly, E. J. "Religious Beliefs of Catholic College Students and their Attitudes Toward Minorities," *Journal of Abnormal and Social Psychology*, 49 (1964), 378–80.

Pace, C. R. *College and University Environment Scales: Preliminary Technical Manual.* Princeton, N.J.: Educational Testing Service, 1963.

————. "Implications of Differences in Campus Atmosphere." In *Personality Factors on the College Campus*, ed. R. L. Sutherland *et al.* Austin, Texas: Hogg Foundation for Mental Health, 1962.

————. "When Students Judge Their College," *College Board Review*, 58 (1966), 26–28.

Pattillo, M. M., Jr. and Mackenzie, D. M. *Eight Hundred Colleges Face the Future: A Preliminary Report of the Danforth Commission on Church Colleges and Universities.* St. Louis: The Danforth Foundation, 1965. To be published in 1966 by the American Council on Education, under the title *Church-Sponsored Higher Education in the United States.*

Perkins, J. A. *The University in Transition.* Princeton, N.J.: Princeton University Press, 1966.

Pfnister, A. O. *A Report of the Baccalaureate Origins of College Faculties.* Washington, D.C.: Association of American Colleges, 1961.

Phenix, P. *Education and the Common Good.* New York: Harper Bros., 1961.

————. *Realms of Meaning.* New York: McGraw-Hill, 1964.

Photiadis, J. D. and Biggar, Jeanne. "Religiosity, Education and Ethnic Distance," *American Journal of Sociology*, 67 (1962), 666–73.

Pinner, F. "The Crisis of the State Universities: Analysis and Remedies." In *The American College*, ed. N. Sanford, pp. 940–71. New York: John Wiley & Sons, Inc., 1962.

Plant, W. T. "Changes in Ethnocentrism Associated with a Four-Year College Education," *Journal of Educational Psychology*, 49 (1958), 162–65.
———. "Changes in Ethnocentrism Associated with a Two-Year College Experience," *Journal of Genetic Psychology*, 92 (1958), 189–97.
———. *Personality Changes Associated with a College Education*. Washington, D.C.: Department of Health, Education, and Welfare, 1962.
Poole, S. *Seminary in Crisis*. New York: Herder and Herder, 1965.
Pope, L. "Religion and the Class Structure," *The Annals*, 256 (1948), 84–91.
Potter, G. *To the Golden Door*. New York: Little, Brown and Co., 1960.
Power, E. J. *A History of Catholic Higher Education in the United States*. Milwaukee: Bruce Publishing Co., 1958.
Putz, L., C.S.C. (ed.). *Catholic Church, U.S.A.* Chicago: Fides Press, 1958.
Rauschenbush, Esther. *The Student and His Studies*. Middletown, Conn.: Wesleyan University Press, 1964.
Riesman, D. *Abundance for What?* New York: Doubleday, 1964.
———. "College Subcultures and College Outcomes." In *Selection and Educational Differentiation*, ed. T. R. McConnell, pp. 1–14. Berkeley, Calif.: Center for the Study of Higher Education, 1960.
———. *Constraint and Variety in American Education*. New York: Doubleday Anchor Books, 1958.
———. "Foreword," *The Reasonable Adventurer*, by R. Heath. Pittsburgh: University of Pittsburgh Press, 1964.
———. "The Influence of Student Culture and Faculty Values in the American College." In *Varieties of Modern Social Theory*, ed. H. Ruitenbeek, pp. 319–40. New York: Dutton Paperbacks, 1963.
———. "Innovation and Reaction in Higher Education." In *Humanistic Education and Western Civilization*, ed. A. A. Cohen, pp. 182–205. New York: Holt, Rinehart and Winston, 1964.
Riesman, D. and Jencks, C. "The Viability of the American College." In *The American College*, ed. N. Sanford, pp. 74–192. New York: John Wiley & Sons, Inc., 1962.
Rokeach, M. *The Open and Closed Mind*. New York: Basic Books, 1960.
Rose, P. I. "The Myth of Unanimity: Student Opinions on Critical Issues," *Sociology of Education*, 37 (1960), 129–49.
Rosen, B. "Race, Ethnicity and the Achievement Syndrome," *American Sociological Review*, 24 (1959), 47–60.
Rosenberg, M. *Occupations and Values*. Glencoe, Ill.: The Free Press, 1957.
Rossi, Alice S. and Rossi, P. H. "Some Effects of Parochial School Education in America," *Daedalus*, 90 (1961), 300–23.
Rossi, P. H. and Greeley, A. M. "The Impact of the Roman Catholic Denominational School," *School Review*, 72 (1964), 34–51.
Rourke, F. E. and Brooks, G. E. *The Managerial Revolution in Higher Education*. Baltimore: Johns Hopkins Press, 1966.

Rudolph, F. *The American College and University: A History.* New York: Random House, 1962.

Rudy, W. *The Evolving Liberal Arts Curriculum.* New York: Columbia University Press, 1960.

Ryan, Mary P. *Are Parochial Schools the Answer?* New York: Holt, Rinehart and Winston, 1964.

Salerno, Sr. M. Dolores, D.M. "Patterns of Interinstitutional Cooperation in American Catholic Higher Education," *National Catholic Educational Association Bulletin,* 62, no. 4 (1966), 1–31.

Sanford, N. (ed.). *The American College.* New York: John Wiley & Sons, Inc., 1962.

————. "Causes of the Student Revolution," *Saturday Review,* 48, no. 51 (1965), 64–66.

———— (ed.). *College and Character: An Abridged Edition of "The American College."* New York: John Wiley & Sons, Inc., 1964.

————. "Developmental Status of the Entering Freshman." In *The American College,* ed. N. Sanford, pp. 253–80. New York: John Wiley & Sons, Inc., 1962.

————. "Ends and Means in Higher Education." In *Higher Education in an Age of Revolutions,* ed. G. K. Smith, pp. 10–20. Washington, D.C.: National Education Association, 1962.

————. "Higher Education as a Field of Study." In *The American College,* ed. N. Sanford, pp. 31–73. New York: John Wiley & Sons, Inc., 1962.

————. "Higher Education as a Social Problem." In *The American College,* ed. N. Sanford, pp. 10–30. New York: John Wiley & Sons, Inc., 1962.

————. (ed.). "Personality Development During the College Years," *Journal of Social Issues,* 12, no. 4 (1956), entire issue.

————. *Self and Society.* New York: Atherton Press, 1966.

————. "Research and Policy in Higher Education." In *The American College,* ed. N. Sanford, pp. 1009–33. New York: John Wiley & Sons, Inc., 1962.

Schmidt, G. F. *The Liberal Arts College.* New Brunswick, N.J.: Rutgers University Press, 1957.

Schommer, C. O., Kosa, J., and Rachiele, L. D. "Socio-Economic Background and Religious Attitudes of Catholic College Students," *American Catholic Sociological Review,* 21 (1960), 229–37.

Scott, W. A. *Values and Organizations.* Chicago: Rand McNally, 1965.

Segal, B. E. "Fraternities, Social Distance, and Anti-Semitism Among Jewish and Non-Jewish Undergraduates," *Sociology of Education,* 38 (1965), 251–64.

Selvin, H. "The Impact of University Experience on Occupational Plans," *School Review,* 71 (1963), 317–39.

Selvin, H. and Hagstrom, W. "Sources of Support for Civil Liberties," *British Journal of Sociology*, 11 (1960), 51–73.

Sheridan, M. P., S.J. "Student Rights in Higher Education," *America*, 114 (1966), 731–32.

Shuster, G. N. *The Catholic Spirit in America*. New York: Dial Press, 1927.

———. *Education and Moral Wisdom*. New York: Harper Bros., 1960.

Smith, G. K. *Higher Education in an Age of Revolutions*. Washington, D.C.: National Education Association, 1962.

Snavely, G. E. *The Church and the Four-Year College*. New York: Harper Brothers, 1955.

Spilka, B. and Reynolds, J. F. "Religion and Prejudice: A Factor-Analytic Study," *Review of Religious Research*, 6 (1965) 163–68.

Stark, R. J. "On the Incompatibility of Religion and Science: A Survey of American Graduate Students," *Journal for the Scientific Study of Religion*, 3 (1963), 3–20.

Stember, C. H. *Education and Attitude Change*. New York: Institute of Human Relations Press, 1961.

Stern, G. G. "Characteristics of the Intellectual Climate in College Environments," *Harvard Educational Review*, 33 (1963), 5–41.

———. "Environments for Learning." In *The American College*, ed. N. Sanford, pp. 690–730. New York: John Wiley & Sons, Inc., 1962.

———. "The Measurement of Psychological Characteristics of Students and Learning Environments." In *Measurement in Personality and Cognition*, eds. J. Messick and R. Ross, pp. 27–68. New York: John Wiley & Sons, Inc., 1962.

———. *Scoring Instructions and College Norms: Activities Index–College Characteristics Index*. Syracuse: Psychological Research Center, Syracuse University, 1963.

Sternberg, B. "Personality Traits of College Students Majoring in Different Fields," *Psychological Monographs*, 69 (1955), 1–21.

Storr, R. J. *The Beginnings of Graduate Education in America*. Chicago: University of Chicago Press, 1953.

Summerskill, J. "Dropouts from College." In *The American College*, ed. N. Sanford, pp. 627–57. New York: John Wiley & Sons, Inc., 1962.

Sutherland, R. L., Holtzman, W. H., Koile, E. A., and Smith, B. K. (eds.). *Personality Factors on the College Campus*. Austin, Texas: Hogg Foundation for Mental Health, 1962.

Swidler, L. "Catholic Colleges: A Modest Proposal," *Commonweal*, 81 (1965), 559–62.

Teevan, P. C. "Personality Correlates of Undergraduate Field of Specialization," *Journal of Consulting Psychology*, 18 (1954), 212–14.

Thistlethwaite, D. L. "College Press and Changes in Study Plans of Talented Students," *Journal of Educational Psychology*, 51 (1960), 222–34.

————. "College Press and Student Achievement," *Journal of Educational Psychology*, 50 (1959), 183–91.

Thistlethwaite, D. L. and Wheeler, N. "Effects of Teacher and Peer Subcultures Upon Student Aspirations," *Journal of Educational Psychology*, 51 (1966), 35–47.

Thomas, J. L., S.J. *The American Catholic Family*. Englewood Cliffs, N.J.: Prentice-Hall, Inc., 1956.

————. "Nationalities and American Catholicism." In *Catholic Church, U.S.A.*, ed. L. Putz, C.S.C., pp. 155–76. Notre Dame, Ind.: Fides Press, 1958.

————. *Religion and the American People*. Westminster, Md.: Newman Press, 1963.

Thomas, R. *The Search for a Common Learning: General Education, 1800–1960*. New York: McGraw-Hill, 1960.

Thoughts of the Young Radicals. New York: The New Republic, 1966.

Tickton, S. G. *Needed: A Ten-Year College Budget*. New York: Fund for the Advancement of Education, 1961.

Trent, J. W. "Progress and Anxiety," *Commonweal*, 81 (1964), 40–42.

University of California, Berkeley, Faculty Senate. *Education at Berkeley*. Berkeley and Los Angeles: University of California Press, 1966.

Vaccaro, L. C. "Three Ways Out for Small Catholic Colleges," *America*, 113 (1965), 580–82.

Van Ackeran, G., S.J. "Current Approaches to Theology." In *Christian Wisdom and Christian Formation*, ed. J. B. McGannon *et al.*, pp. 83–110. New York: Sheed and Ward, 1964.

Veroff, J., Feld, Sheila, and Gurin, G. "Achievement Motivation and Religious Background," *American Sociological Review*, 27 (1962), 205–17.

Veysey, L. C. *The Emergence of the American University*. Chicago: University of Chicago Press, 1965.

Vreeland, Rebecca and Bidwell, C. E. "Classifying University Departments: An Approach to the Analysis of Their Effects Upon Undergraduates' Values and Attitudes," *Sociology of Education*, 39 (1966), 237–54.

————. "Organizational Effects on Student Attitudes: A Study of the Harvard Houses," *Sociology of Education*, 38 (1965), 233–50.

Wagman, M. "Attitude Change and the Authoritarian Personality," *Journal of Psychology*, 40 (1955), 3–24.

Wagner, H. R., Doyle, V., and Doyle, Kathryn. "Religious Background and Higher Education," *American Sociological Review*, 24 (1959), 852–56.

Wakin, E. *The Catholic Campus*. New York: Macmillan, 1963.

————. "How Catholic is the Catholic College?" *Saturday Review*, 49, no. 16 (1965), 92–94, 105.

Wakin, E. and Scheuer, J. F. *The De-Romanization of the American Catholic Church*. New York: Macmillan, 1966.

Wallace, W. L. *Student Culture*. Chicago: Aldine Publishing Co., 1966.

——. "Institutional and Life-Cycle Socialization of College Freshmen," *American Journal of Sociology*, 70 (1964), 303–18.

——. "Peer Influences and Undergraduates' Aspirations for Graduate Study," *Sociology of Education*, 38 (1965), 375–92.

Wallis, W. A. "The Plight of the Small College," *Atlantic*, 216, no. 5 (1965), 124–26.

Walsh, J. E., C.S.C. *Education and Political Power*. New York: Center for Applied Research in Education, Inc., 1964.

Walsh, J. L., C.S.P. "What the Students Want," *Commonweal*, 82 (1965), 206–9.

Walters, E. *Graduate Education Today*. Washington, D.C.: American Council on Education, 1965.

Ward, L. R., C.S.C. *Blueprint for a Catholic University*. St. Louis: B. Herder and Co., 1949.

——. "Is There a Christian Learning?" *Commonweal*, 59 (1953), 605–7.

——. *New Life in Catholic Schools*. St. Louis: B. Herder and Co., 1958.

Warkov, S. and Greeley, A. M. "Parochial School Origins and Educational Achievement," *American Sociological Review*, 31 (1966), 406–14.

Wattenberg, B. J. and Scammon, R. M. *This U.S.A.* New York: Doubleday, 1965.

Webb, S. C. and Crowder, Dolores G. "Analyzing the Psychological Climate of a Single College," *Teachers College Record*, 66 (1965), 425–33.

Webster, H. "Some Quantitative Results," *Journal of Social Issues*, 12 (1956), 29–43.

Webster, H., Freedman, M., and Heist, P. "Personality Changes in College Students." In *The American College*, ed. N. Sanford, pp. 811–46. New York: John Wiley & Sons, Inc., 1962.

Wedge, B. M. (ed.). *Psycho-social Problems of College Men*. New Haven: Yale University Press, 1958.

Weigel, G., S.J. "American Catholic Intellectualism: A Theologian's Reflections," *Review of Politics*, 19 (1957), 275–307.

Weller, W. "The Relationship of Personality and Non-Personality Factors in Prejudice," *Journal of Social Psychology*, 63 (1964), 129–37.

Westoff, C., Potter, R. G., and Sagi, P. C. *The Third Child*. Princeton, N.J.: Princeton University Press, 1963.

Westoff, C., and Potvin, R. H. "Higher Education, Religion and Women's Family-Size Orientations," *American Sociological Review*, 31 (1966), 489–96.

Whitman, E., Keating, B., Trimble, G., and Saxlehner, E. "Doctoral Dissertations in Religious Education," *Religious Education*, 61 (1966), 50–64.

Wicke, M. F. *The Church-Related College.* New York: Center for Applied Research in Education, 1964.

Williamson, E. G. and Cowan, J. L. "The Role of the President in the Desirable Enactment of Academic Freedom for Students," *Educational Record*, 46 (1965), 351–72. An abridged version appears in L. Dennis and J. F. Kauffman (eds.), *The College and the Student*, pp. 252–83. Washington, D.C.: American Council on Education, 1966.

Woodring, P. and Scanlon, J. (eds.). *American Education Today.* New York: McGraw-Hill, 1963.

Wright, J. J. "Catholics and Anti-Intellectualism," *Commonweal*, 63 (1955), 275–78.

Yamsuchi, H. J., S.J. "Theology As An Academic Discipline." In *Christian Wisdom and Christian Formation*, ed. J. B. McGannon *et al.*, pp. 111–28. New York: Sheed and Ward, 1964.

Yinger, M. J. *Religion, Society and the Individual.* New York: Macmillan, 1957.

Zahn, Jane (ed.). *Religion and the Face of America.* Berkeley: University of California Extension, 1959.

INDEX